INVISIBLE
darkness

STEPHEN
williams

Bantam Books NEW YORK TORONTO LONDON
SYDNEY AUCKLAND

INVISIBLE

darkness

THE STRANGE CASE OF PAUL BERNARDO

AND KARLA HOMOLKA

INVISIBLE DARKNESS

A Bantam Book / published by arrangement with Little, Brown and Company (Canada) Limited

PUBLISHING HISTORY

Little, Brown and Company (Canada) Limited edition published 1996
Bantam edition / January 1998

All rights reserved.
Copyright © 1996 by Stephen Williams
Introduction copyright © 1996 by Kirk Makin

BOOK DESIGN BY DANA LEIGH TREGLIA

ISBN 0-553-56854-x

PRINTED IN THE UNITED STATES OF AMERICA

OPM   10 9 8 7 6 5

author's note

I have changed the names of certain individuals in this story. In certain cases this has been done to protect the privacy of the many innocent victims of Karla Homolka and Paul Bernardo (although surely the murder victims were the most innocent of all). In Canada, every survivor of a sexual assault is a "Jane Doe." That means that there are approximately twenty Jane Does in this story. With the exception of one individual, whose circumstances seem to demand she become the only "Jane Doe," I gave all the other Jane Does pseudonyms. Every other detail of their sad tales is all too true.

introduction

Why would anyone want to write a book about one of the most savage sprees of violence in North American history? Probably only one question is asked as frequently of the author of such a book, namely: "What do you think of Karla?" I'll apply myself to the former, leaving the latter to Stephen Williams, whose three years of research has furnished, within these pages, as comprehensive and decisive a response to the Karla enigma as anyone might wish for.

In the summer of 1995, the jarring contents of the Bernardo-Homolka saga spilled out for the first time in a Toronto courtroom. The news media knew a stunning story when it saw one, and the public found itself wallowing in every last morsel of minutiae. People quickly divided into two camps. The clear majority surrendered to the barrage, clinging to each account with horror and amazement. A minority assiduously attempted to shade their eyes from the goings-on.

I am not so foolish as to argue there is anything noble about the fascination most of us feel for tales of murder, any more than there is anything noble about slowing to gawk at an automobile collision. But both compulsions have at their roots the same human well-spring—empathy, horror, identification and the need to witness just how far human beings like ourselves can go in harming other human beings like ourselves.

While those who opted to filter out anything to do with Bernardo and Homolka undoubtedly passed a more carefree summer, evidence is lacking that they were any more virtuous than those who succumbed and anguished through Canada's trial of the generation. To watch, recoil and analyze is human. The day will hopefully not be soon upon us that we are so satiated we lose our capacity to both gape and grapple with the question of how fellow human beings could carry out such acts of depravity.

With the acting out of the final scenes, the names Paul and Karla have become as recognizable in many quarters as Bonnie and Clyde. Yet, even that parallel falls in some ways short of the mark. The acquisitive, morally vacuous, would-be hipsters from Southern Ontario achieved a plateau of notoriety all their own through a trail of torture and savagery so numbing it seems inconceivable it could ever become the stuff of fond folklore. Paul Bernardo and Karla Homolka were like gasoline and fertilizer. While we will never know just how dangerous they might have been had each operated solo, we do know that put together, they packed enough explosive potential to blow up the entire neighborhood.

Beyond feeding our need to know, there is a second reason a project like this is necessary, even laudable. Contrary to many other murder stories, a great deal must be learned from how Bernardo and Homolka became what they were and how they were finally brought to ground. At the moment, the record is splintered and incomplete.

The number of important issues raised by the case is almost endless. It includes the privacy rights of victims in the face of virtually unprecedented intrusion, the largely uncharted art of plea bargaining, whether there is a limit to the public exposure of videotaped torture and the seeming inability of police forces to work together. In addition, Bernardo and Homolka will certainly not be the last stranger-to-stranger serial killers in our midst. Only by grasping what factors give rise to them and their mode of operating can we hope to more swiftly catch those who follow in their footsteps.

Williams is a rather rare bird these days in the world of true crime writing: a writer rather than a journalist. For three critical years, this afforded him an advantageous perch. In not being obliged to file daily news stories, he had few distractions or obligations. It also meant he could largely avoid the compromising loyalties, alliances and enmities that tend to build between daily journalists and the sources upon whom they rely for information. Williams was ultimately privy to a great deal of information, but the results suggest he felt beholden to no one. Neither the insights he was afforded into the inner workings of the investigation nor the strategies of the Bernardo defense camp have dulled his blade.

To be sure, some will not care for his characterization of the authorities who worked agonizing hours only to have their quarry evade capture due to a combination of inexperience, bad luck and ineptitude. But it needs to be said that contrary to the feel-good approach that marks much of the post facto inquiry into the Bernardo-Homolka disaster, it takes more than heroic effort to make a hero. Indeed, few other police investigations can have yo-yoed so dramatically from superhuman effort to unforgivable stupidity.

Some readers may even arch a brow at Williams's treatment of Karla Homolka, the chilly figure who raises this case from a merely sordid tale to one that is compelling in its complexity and enigma. They will be few in number. Apart from her sad fan club of feckless pals and a coterie of mental-health professionals who ought to know better, no one is buying into the vision of Homolka as a misbegotten victim in this Shakespearean tragedy. The vast bulk of the public has loudly expressed its view of Homolka—not that even this consensus about her calculating nature and her barely perceptible soul is likely to penetrate the tightly strung cocoon in which Homolka huddles against the world.

Finally, there may be those who complain that the worst villain, Paul Bernardo, has received less scrutiny than his wife.

It is true, he does. But for good reason. Bernardo belongs to a well-known breed of giggling, garden-variety psychos who are destined to spin out of all control and reveal themselves. Unlike Homolka, he got his just desserts and will never present a danger to us.

Homolka, on the other hand, will walk among us again. And soon. While the nature of Bernardo is clear, Homolka presents an infinitely more complex and challenging puzzle. Indeed, her inscrutability is a central part of why she seems likely to rank as one of the world's most infamous female outlaws. Until now, few, if any, of the many questions that swirl about her have been adequately answered. How was such a person bred? Would Bernardo have killed without her encouragement and cool sense of survivalism? To what extent, in reality, might Homolka have actively participated in the murders of Kristen French and Leslie Mahaffy?

Any serious inquiry must also look into the way Homolka was handled by the authorities once she came to their attention. That they sat down at the negotiating table with her as a tool to entrap Bernardo was quite understandable, even astute. But that they continued to backfill and justify their actions even as the truth about her complicity and duplicity leaked out—plumping all the while for her virtue and victimhood—was a sad and weak-kneed failing. We need to know Homolka thoroughly, if only to better guard against her once she is free. We must also

ensure that we are never again collectively taken in by the hope-
ful notion that a woman can never equal a man in the capacity
to do evil.

Kirk Makin
Toronto, 1996

I SAY THE UNIQUE AND SUPREME
PLEASURE OF LOVE LIES IN THE
CERTAINTY OF DOING EVIL.

—baudelaire

'm psychic."

"What?"

"That's what I do now. I give psychic readings."

Psychic readings? The last time I saw Nikki had to be twelve years ago. She was flat on her back on a leopard-skin rug. My olfactory memory of the stripper was specific. There was about her an intense, musk-based fragrance, this due to an addiction to Opium, a popular perfume of the eighties. The scent lingered even now, though I was under the impression Yves St. Laurent had long since abandoned the product. She had always been Rubenesque. A favorite dancer at a legendary dive called the Silver Dollar, by now she was, shall we say, post-Rubenesque. Still, Nikki looked good.

"You're writing a book about the murders," she said, lighting a cigarette in the dim light of Buddy's Bar. The bar is a proscenium of sorts for all manner of bad actors who enter, strut and exit this incredible play I've come to observe. If I learned anything from my long sojourn here, I learned that if you linger long enough center stage at Buddy's, chances are you'll end up changed—not necessarily for the better.

Buddy's is on the main floor of the Parkway Hotel, Convention Center and Bowling Lanes, one of half a dozen hotels in the small city of St. Catharines, Ontario, twelve miles up the road from Niagara Falls.

The door near the large horseshoe-shaped bar where Nikki and I are sitting leads into the bowling lanes. The sound of flying bowling pins can be deafening. It's a beer, shots and wings joint that is about as "politically correct" as Nikki. In fact, the whole town of St. Catharines is just about as "politically correct" as Nikki. Maybe that's why we all have become, we observers, so comfortable here.

I give psychic readings. But Nikki didn't have to be psychic to know that I was writing a book about "the murders." I'd been living in the hotel since not long after a twenty-six-year-old ex–Price Waterhouse accounting trainee named Paul Bernardo had been arrested on February 17, 1993, and charged with sixty-two counts, including aggravated sexual assault, wounding, sodomy, assault with a deadly weapon, buggery, kidnapping, anal intercourse, confinement, indignity to a human body, as well as the murders of two schoolgirls, fourteen-year-old Leslie Mahaffy of Burlington, Ontario and fifteen-year-old Kristen French from St. Catharines. It quickly became the most highly publicized arrest in Canadian history.

But it was the troubling presence of Paul's strikingly attractive wife, Karla, that made this dark local play turn into a worldly operatic event. Once it was understood that Karla's youngest sister was alone in her parents' basement with Paul and Karla when she suddenly and mysteriously died on Christmas Eve, 1990, the case attracted the attention of the world press.

Newsweek dubbed them "The Ken and Barbie of Murder and Mayhem." Paul and Karla are iconic, *Baywatch*-gorgeous specimens of the young, upwardly mobile, educated middle class. At first sight it was impossible to believe these paradigms of contemporary suburban life could be so deeply depraved. But here I am waiting for a cop named Vince Bevan, when Nikki the stripper-turned-psychic tells me:

"You know, they called me in on this case. Vince Bevan, the cop in charge—I'm sure you know Vince. He called in quite a few of us, you know."

"You mean strippers?"

"No, silly, psychics."

She blew a smoke ring that hung like a halo over her VO-and-ginger. "It's fascinating. Bevan looks a little like Tom Selleck. I'll bet you're done waiting for him, too."

Maybe she is psychic, after all. I haven't seen this woman in a decade. And tonight of all nights she walks in here, of all places, and tells me about Vince Bevan. She was right. I was done waiting. He phoned two hours ago and cancelled.

A wise person once said coincidence is God's way of maintaining His anonymity. This chance meeting with Nikki and her seeming second sight is a small example of what I've otherwise discovered; coincidence forms the nucleus of this story.

I wanted to speak to Inspector Bevan about psychics. Why he was so fascinated with them, especially with regard to the murdered victim Kristen French. I had heard Bevan, a good Catholic, a believer in people such as Nikki, as well as the Father, Son and Holy Ghost, sent a hair clip that belonged to Kristen French to a psychic in Nutley, New Jersey, a few days after Kristen was kidnapped in 1992. Now I wanted to know what makes a guy like Bevan choose a psychic in Nutley, New Jersey, over Nikki in Niagara Falls?

The psychic in Nutley said she saw a leg floating in Burlington Bay. Ten days later, they found the French girl's body in a ditch—with both legs. Two months later, they found a leg in the bay, but it belonged to someone else. I guess we all live and die by the choices we make, except Kristen French or Leslie Mahaffy. I'm unclear how their choices determined how they died.

Somehow, Bevan also mistakenly concluded Kristen had been held captive for thirteen days before she was killed. That, and the fact his task force mistook lividity markings for signs of ritual abuse, precipitated a call to an expert in satanic cults. Bevan did not discover that Kristen was only held for three days until Karla Homolka told him and a pathologist explained how death marks the body.

At the same time, Bevan had a dozen eyewitnesses hypnotized. The results were disastrous. According to his report, all the eyewitnesses said the abductors drove a Camaro. It was cream colored, they said. People all over the region started calling in their neighbors' sons because they drove Camaros. Paul and Karla were driving a gold Nissan when they abducted Kristen. A few weeks later the hypnotist himself fled the country, in a flurry of patients' accusations about his own sexual conduct. It didn't take long before Bevan went around publicly talking about the dead girls as "his ghosts." Possession is, as they say, nine-tenths of the law.

I had all kinds of questions for Inspector Vince Bevan, with whom I was destined to have a half a dozen conversations and ultimately read everything he had to say in hundreds of pages of reports and testimony. In the end it turned out I learned far more from Nikki, who, inexplicably, was never far from the truth.

"They think Bernardo raped and wasted these two schoolgirls, cut one of them up and put her parts in little cement caskets," she said. "But I see two people—neither of them look much like this guy Bernardo. I see two people, both have similar feminine features."

No one, except maybe Nikki, ever took this thing to the next step. "In one of the papers, you know, they called them Ken and Barbie," she said. "In Barbie's world, everything is an accessory—including Ken," and she looked at me with a knowing half smile.

"What brings you to Buddy's?" I asked, unable to resist Nikki, as always.

"My mother's dying. . . . I was born in Niagara Falls, you know."

I had just read in the local paper that the city of Niagara Falls was almost bankrupt. The only thing that was going to save it was a casino and the Maharishi Mahesh Yogi's plan to build an eight hundred and ninety million dollar transcendental-meditation theme park there called Veda Land.

Because it was so low rent, all gimmicks, trinkets and trash, even twelve million tourists a year—a vast majority of whom were Japanese—couldn't save it. It had come a long way since Marilyn Monroe made *Niagara* with Joseph Cotten in 1951 and kissed him tenderly on the *Maid of the Mist*. As if she were reading my thoughts, Nikki laughed and said, "We always called it Nicaragua."

Earlier, before Nikki arrived, a guy named Mark DeMarco had walked into Buddy's with his bowling bag and sat down. DeMarco is a small, sturdily built Italian, forty-three years old, with a certain self-conscious macho edge. DeMarco owns a pawn shop in Niagara Falls. He has the largest collection of Evel Knievel memorabilia in the world. His shop is truly an amazing place. Above all, DeMarco knows what's going down in Niagara Falls and St. Catharines. But I was also warned that he's given to hyperbole.

Mark once told me he knew a beautician from Darte's Funeral Home, where Kristen French was prepared for burial. He said the beautician claimed Kristen's head had been shaved and her tendons cut—a sure sign of ritual satanic abuse. I did not believe this, but as always with DeMarco, I was fascinated by the unorthodox pitch of the man's mind. When he first entered Buddy's, I immediately wondered what was in his bowling bag. This guy was no bowler. Looking around furtively he had unzipped the bowling bag and pulled out the most sinister human skull I have ever seen. "Keep it below the table," he had whispered. Once again I had been stunned by DeMarco.

The skull was small and obviously old—it looked to be the head of a young girl. The jawbone was held in place by a single strand of 12-gauge black wire. It had a kind of yellowish sheen, as though it had been coated with shellac. And it was literally covered with elaborate, precise etchings; a plethora of hand carved signs such as swastikas and a cross made from a series of squares; dates such as 1717 and 1871. The etchings were blackened, so the skull looked as if it had been elaborately tattooed.

There were symbols, such as an eye within an isosceles triangle and words in capital letters, such as BLUE POWER DRUID, incomprehensible phrases such as No CATRO★ or FQ★HAT or KALI—YUGA and others, such as By the Sign I will Conquer . . . No Yellow, No Red, No Black, No Women, Only Pure . . . PURE MEN IN CONTROL—DOGMA . . . Novus ordo sec . . . which meant "New World Order."

"No CATRO" I recognized as a homophobic warning from the Greek catro for "homosexual." The others were obvious messages of "zero tolerance." But what did "BLUE" mean, and why were "DRUID," and "KALI," a Hindu god, cut into a cranium along with "666"—the Mark of the Beast?

In the occult, numbers have significance, which explains why they were all over the skull—"1, 3, 5, 7"—but not what they meant. And words and names such as "Moloch, Vedas, Sumerian, Cabala"; the skull was just covered with stuff such as this, obviously chiseled with a steady, fastidious hand. In and of itself, a human skull is unsettling. This one was very disturbing and definitely some kind of ritual talisman. I couldn't take my eyes off it.

"It's Masonic," DeMarco had said. He told me this old guy came into his shop all the time. He said he was a Masonic historian and he brought in this big, coffee-table–size book with a title something like Hermetic Masonic Rosicrucian Lore and Mysteries. It was violently colored and had all these weird signs and symbols; the guy said it helped him understand the markings on the skull. According to him, the skull was a totem that had belonged to a splinter lodge in the southern United States and it had been carved sometime after 1871.

DeMarco remembered what the old man said about the name Moloch, because it was eerie and apropos: Moloch was the name of the divinity to whom the people of Judah in the last ages of the kingdom had sacrificed their own children. Mark DeMarco wanted me to buy the skull of a sacrificed child for $5000.

In recent memory within a hundred mile radius of Niagara Falls hundreds of children have been sacrificed to something. Since 1980 there had been well over a hundred unsolved sex slayings of young women between the ages of twelve and twenty-four in upper New York State and southwestern Ontario alone. It is a rare individual who knows half a dozen of their names. Unsolved is the catchword. Some criminologists think so many remain unsolved because no one in law enforcement will even consider the idea that women are involved with the sex and death of other women. Nikki told me, as soon as she heard that Kristen French's long, luxurious brunette hair had been crudely cut off that she saw "the hand of a woman."

If Nikki is right, and maybe she is, some part of this incredibly deviant world of sexual sadism, which is all about power, control and humiliation, increasingly belongs to Barbie. And in her world Ken has become an instrument of strange, feminine, violent, pathological yearnings. The woman somehow involved in the crimes with which I am concerned and about which Nikki seems to know a great deal—somehow intuitively—is a diminutive, blond woman-child.

As we sat this Wednesday, April 13, 1993, in Buddy's Bar, at 10 P.M., all that had really happened was that Bernardo had been arrested and was being held without bail. Karla had retained a local lawyer named George Walker, whose offices were, coincidentally, directly across the street from DeMarco's pawnshop in Niagara Falls. The newspapers said Karla was in the psychiatric ward of a Toronto hospital receiving "therapy." One of the nurses on the ward had already told me there was great debate about what kind of person Karla was and how much she really knew about the crimes. The coroner was making plans to exhume Karla's sister's body—suspicion was rampant.

I had a sixth sense there was much more to this story than the official version that Karla Homolka was another victim, an abused sex slave of Paul Bernardo. Vince Bevan had already told press conferences after Bernardo's arrest that they were watching a second and third suspect. Just recently he had revised the earlier statement and become more specific. He had said they were now only watching a second suspect, a person who was no threat to the public safety and a person whose whereabouts he knew exactly every second of the day.

In spite of his good looks, yuppie aspirations and university education there was something callow about Paul Bernardo that suggested the crimes with which he was charged were beyond his scope. The police said he raped fifteen women in the Toronto suburb of Scarborough, where he was born and raised, before he moved to St. Catharines. What they did not say was that he didn't start this dark escapade until after he and Karla met in 1987. As Nikki's second sight suggested, somehow their relationship might very well have created a third separate character—a kind of symbiosis of Dr. Jekyll and Mr. Hyde—a golem with dominant feminine characteristics that came to subsist on sex and death, but otherwise appeared to be the newlyweds next door. Vince should have stuck to his guns in the first instance, when he said they were watching a second and third suspect—he would have been closer to the truth. It made the hair on the back of my neck stand on end.

"DeMarco has had that skull in his store for some time," Nikki said. "You know, the guy's a bit crazy."

It does seem to go with the territory, I thought to myself.

"My sister used to go out with him."

"Small world," I said.

"Especially down here," she said.

Nikki stopped filing her nails. "Can you lend me fifty bucks, Stephen? I've got to go."

I sort of raised my eyebrow.

"Look, what good is a psychic without a phone, and they're going to cut mine off. Be a sweetheart."

Before she left, she asked if there was anything I wanted. "Yeah, explain this whole weird case to me, will you?"

"I'm a psychic, not a shrink. You'll figure it out." And with a stripper's flourish, Nikki turned on her heel, opened the door to a cacophony of bowling balls and walked out of my life once more.

I was down the fifty dollars, three rye-and-gingers, and worst of all on the verge of a truly apocalyptic tale of sedition, violence, sex, death and videotape—unlike anything I was prepared to even imagine.

Because DeMarco knew that Bernardo had joined the Masons just after he moved to St. Catharines—an assertion that turned out to be true—DeMarco had all kinds of Masonic conspiracy theories about which I was very skeptical. And all his talk about ritual satanic cults and human sacrifices, played out in disarmingly normal, familiar, suburban settings, seemed too obvious. In the end, allowing for DeMarco's paranoia and penchant for hyperbole and the distance between appearance and reality, these farfetched observations turned out to be more interesting—and ring truer—than all the elaborate psychiatric and conventional religious rationalizations provided by the case as it unfolded. At least they took deviance and an individual's capacity for evil seriously, without trying to explain it away or forgive it. And Nikki's instincts turned out to be surprisingly prescient. It was Karla who truly had her hand on the skull. I was, not soon but inevitably, to be drawn to understand what Nikki already understood absolutely.

EVIL IS UNSPECTACULAR AND ALWAYS
HUMAN AND SHARES OUR BED
AND EATS AT OUR TABLE.

—w.h. auden

CHAPTER

one

At 7:30 A.M., Monday morning, March 8, 1993, Sister Josephine, a sixty-two-year-old Carmelite nun from Lindsay, Ontario, woke with a start from a tortured dream which inevitably was about her increasingly tenuous relationship with her beloved companion for life—Jesus Christ. The internal struggle between her sense of duty and her waning sense of self-worth seemed hopelessly lost, and her forty-year marriage to the Lord on the rocks. A semiretired teacher, unable to perform even the most menial tasks, she had become totally withdrawn. She had been diagnosed with endogenous depression and hospitalized a week and a half earlier. At least she knew where she was. She was in Room 802 on the psychiatric ward of Northwestern General Hospital in northern Toronto. As Sister Josephine woke up, she realized she was no longer alone.

A pretty young woman (or was she a girl?) with blond, cashmere hair and a provocatively flimsy nightgown was sitting on the bed opposite. She was wearing a set of headphones, rhythmically tapping the fingers of one hand on a fashion magazine to music only she could hear and painting her toenails pink with the other. A perfect angel, Sister Josephine thought, and smiled at her new companion. The nun would soon learn that her name was Karla—with a K. Karla, seeing the nun was awake, held up an enormous stuffed animal that was reclining on her pillow. "This is Bunky," she said, with a friendliness and enthusiasm that the nun found refreshing. Sister Josephine only wished she was her old self and could show some spark of enthusiasm in return.

Dr. Arndt, her psychiatrist, had told her not to worry too much about her present state of dimmed awareness. It was not unusual for people undergoing electro-convulsive therapy—or "buzzing," as he so irreverently called it—to be "out of it" for the first week or two. "Although it works faster than the drugs," he said in his heavy Austrian accent, "it can be a bit discombobulating."

Dr. Hans Arndt was the senior staff psychiatrist at Northwestern. With his accent, he could just as easily have been sent by central casting. At fifty-eight, Dr. Arndt was bald, bearded and bespectacled. A leading exponent of "buzzing," known in lay terms as shock treatment, he was also one of those modern, pharmaceutical alchemists who concocted drug-induced "sleep therapies" that put patients out for at least three days at a stretch. Sister Josephine's angel companion had just been awakened from such a therapy.

Dr. Arndt knew what was wrong with the nun, but he had not come to any conclusion about the mental health of Karla

Homolka-Bernardo. As he had told her lawyer, George Walker, when he agreed to hospitalize her, "I don't know if this girl is mad or just bad."

On February 26, George Walker had first called Dr. Arndt's colleague, psychologist Allan Long, and asked him urgently to organize a psychological and psychiatric evaluation for a new client. And so it came to pass that Dr. Long and his colleague Dr. Arndt arrived at Walker's offices at 4:30 P.M. on March 3, 1993, to be introduced to this bizarre case. Dr. Arndt had no idea who Karla was—but then, again, he had learned not to be surprised by the chemistry of the human soul.

The truth was, Dr. Arndt found Niagara Falls fascinating. Historically speaking, the area wore its psychoses on its sleeve. It represented the best of nature and the worst of mankind—a coincidence of geographic purity pitted against the impurity of human behavior. It was the God-given inexhaustible supply of fresh water from the Great Lakes and the man-made ingenuity of an obscure Croatian engineer that had spawned cheap power at the turn of the century, which had in turn led to massive industrialization. That, in turn, had poisoned the land and the water—the minds would follow.

Like certain psychopathologies, Niagara Falls's symptoms lay dormant, invisible for generations. It appealed to Dr. Arndt's sense of irony that the nearby Love Canal was such a place and had a name that resonated a multiplicity of definitions.

George Walker's law offices in Niagara Falls are in a gray-blue, two-story, aluminum-sided building on the corner of Victoria and Queen Streets directly across from DeMarco's infamous pawnshop. Oddly, Walker had known Karla before the "mad murder publicity." Karla had worked as a veterinary assistant at the Martindale Clinic in nearby St. Catharines, where Walker had taken Kelly, his cancer-riddled Dalmatian, for treatment. He remembered how tender she had been with his beloved pet. After the dog died, he kept its ashes in an urn on the mantel-piece in his living room.

Karla first put a call in for Kelly's daddy in the late evening of February 9. She said she wanted to see Walker about a "domestic dispute." Perhaps it was for the memory of Kelly that Walker agreed to see the "tender" vet's assistant, who was about to become a pariah. An appointment was set for Karla Homolka-Bernardo to come to see him at 3:00 P.M. on Thursday, February 11, 1993.

At first, Walker simply didn't believe Karla's story. It was too incredible. But after she confessed everything, in a relentless, strangely monotonic monologue, his disbelief was quickly replaced by the need for action. First thing to do—her confession in hand—was to start positioning the Attorney-General's office. In return for immunity, Walker told them that Karla would be happy to betray her estranged husband, Paul Bernardo, and testify categorically that he had murdered Leslie Mahaffy and Kristen French.

Walker had a professional responsibility to determine whether or not Karla was sane enough to stand trial. But he wanted more than that; he wanted to turn this determination to his advantage. Walker knew that he needed a psychiatric game plan for Karla's defense argument. Drs. Long and Arndt were meant as a stunning, preemptive strike. With astonishing good fortune, Walker would be able to move a chess piece first—and maybe capture the board.

Considering that Karla's estranged husband, Paul Bernardo, had been arrested two weeks earlier, on February 17, and that police were now ransacking their matrimonial home, Walker knew he had to move quickly. Walker arranged for Karla to secretly meet the doctors who would deliver his psychiatric game plan. They met in the second-floor conference room of his office building at 4:30 P.M. on March 3. At first, when Karla arrived and sat self-consciously in front of the experienced psychiatrists, Walker wondered if they would find her credible.

With the power of a natural actress, Karla showed the doctors her wedding pictures. Dr. Arndt, looking to somehow grab her trust, said the wedding pictures looked more like a funeral.

"I fancy myself as a photographer and perhaps I see something that other people don't," the doctor said, with a forgiving, empathetic voice.

"My God," said Karla with a shock of recognition, "everybody else just oohed and aahed and said how it looked like a storybook wedding." Karla seemed dismayed—but only for a second. "But it really was my funeral. It really was. . . . Yes, that's what it was."

Dr. Arndt now had Karla in his power or—an argument could be offered—was it the other way around? It was Dr. Arndt's opinion that Karla was in a lot of pain and needed to "spill"; an Arndtism for unburdening. Clearly she was able to instruct counsel and fit to stand trial. The opinion was clear. Karla should be hospitalized for a "total workup, comprehensive assessment and therapies." Walker liked that. This scored him some time. And so it was agreed.

Karla's mother, Dorothy, delivered her troubled daughter to Northwestern General Hospital on March 4 at 11:30 A.M. Karla was quickly admitted under her mother's maiden name—Seger. This was a strategy, on the part of the hospital, to try and hide the fact of Karla's admission. It was important that journalists not know about her movements. On the admission form Karla was described as a "twenty-two-year-old female patient with diagnosis of depression."

It was Dr. Arndt's idea to put Karla and the nun in the same room. Perhaps it appealed to his sense of irony. But above all he thought it might give the Good Sister some benefit—a startling jolt of reality. He had warned the hospital that he would be admitting someone who "might be having a high profile," but he thought he would let Sister Josephine find out who Karla was on her own.

Sister Josephine put down her Bible and stared toward her roommate, who was absorbed in her Dog World magazine. The veterinarian's assistant was not one to abandon her passions. But by now the nun had begun to suspect that Karla was more anomaly than angel. By turns, she could be pleasant, stand-offish, taciturn and chatty. Her mood swings always seemed to be in relation to her telephone conversations. She was always on the telephone. Most people who are hospitalized for depression are withdrawn, dysfunctional, wary of the outside world.

Karla had none of these symptoms. In fact, Karla was clearly delighted when she got her own way—unhappy when she didn't. Remarkably outspoken, particularly when she wanted drugs. The more she got, the more she wanted. Some of the nursing staff had qualms about the amount of drugs the infamous patient was ingesting. There was even some talk about substituting placebos.

Wandering the halls in thigh-high baby dolls, wearing push-up bras, clutching Bunky as if it were the Christ child—pleasant when stoned, obstreperous when straight—Karla now presented a far different figure to Sister Josephine.

"Do you want me to have a nervous breakdown?" Karla once yelled. "I feel like I'm going to have a nervous breakdown." Then she had demanded more Demerol. Not only that, she insisted the drug be administered by i.v. push. Up until then, all of her medication had been taken orally. Where did this patient get the idea of the needle? How did she know the medical lingo? The nurses were nervous, to say the least. At one point Karla fixed a night nurse with her strangely ambivalent eyes and demanded, "If I don't get the drugs I want, the way I want them, you and Dr. Arndt will regret it. I'm telling you—you'll all regret it!" The nurse was so angry she called Dr. Arndt in the middle of the night to complain—to no avail. The next day he came in and increased her medication and negotiated a compromise—instead of an i.v. push he would concede to administer certain drugs intermuscularly. "All right," Karla said petulantly. "i.m.—better than nothing."

Sister Josephine's internal debate about Karla's mercurial personality was suddenly interrupted when Karla got up directly in front of her and "put on her Blossom hat." She posed like a model on the runway and sweetly wished the nun happy Easter.

Karla had named the hat after Blossom, a favorite character from a popular TV sitcom. "Paul never liked it when I wore hats," Karla announced coquettishly. "But I am free of him—free! I'm gonna wear whatever damn hat I want to wear."

And with that, with all her hat fascination and Bunky's undying loyalty, Karla left the room in search of God knows what. The incredible thing about Bunky, we would later find out: Karla had given the stuffed bear to Leslie Mahaffy shortly before she was killed. And now the nun was allowed to sit back in the silence of her room and ponder the dilemma of her Lord God.

It was Easter Sunday, 1993, and Sister Josephine was eagerly awaiting her real sister's visit. Of all her spiritual colleagues, of all her family, it was her real sister she trusted most of all.

"Don't you read the papers? Don't you watch the television?" her sister asked, trembling. She knew the reality of the nun's situation.

"That is not Karla Seger, it's Karla Homolka—Bernardo's wife!" she said, with no small amount of alarm. And placing her hand on her sister's Bible, she said, "Don't you understand? For God's sake, Jo!"

So finally the reality of the facade of Karla Seger was explained to Sister Josephine. In the beginning, shock was replaced by denial. In turn, denial was replaced by anger—an anger toward Dr. Arndt, who had put her in this situation in the first place. Here she was, a few yards from the devil incarnate.

Arndt would eventually pose Sister Josephine a challenge: "You need a mission. Maybe Karla is your mission?"

A mission. Yes, the nun needed to minister, to comprehend her ministry; she needed to understand above all the example of another spiritual colleague, Sister Helen Prejean, the New Orlean's nun who had bonded with a killer on Death Row. Sister Josephine was reminded again of Sister Helen's admonishment: "There is no such thing as a disposable human being." There is no such thing, she repeated, waiting for Karla to return with Bunky. There is no such thing as a disposable human being.

But the accursed ambiguity returned to Sister Josephine once more, and challenged her fragile faith. No such thing: "Tell that, oh Lord, to Kristen French and Leslie Mahaffy."

CHAPTER

two

I gave Leslie some of my sleeping pills and Bunky to hold." Karla held up the teddy bear. "I didn't want her to have any pain." It was March 10, 1993, and Karla was "spilling." She and Dr. Arndt were in an interview room on the psychiatric ward of Northwestern General Hospital.

Dr. Arndt is the kind of man who hugs people whom he perceives to be in pain, but even though he perceived Karla to be in pain he found nothing huggable about her. With Karla, he actually thought a hug could be misinterpreted. It was just a feeling he had, to stay away from her; something was not right.

"Holding on to Bunky, Leslie just went to sleep," Karla continued matter-of-factly. "But I knew she'd get killed. I was there when he strangled her. But I didn't watch. I couldn't stand it. I saw so many animals killed at work, but with a person it's different. I saw discoloration, and I had to help him carry her down to the root cellar, because it was Father's Day and my parents were coming over for dinner."

Father's Day? The fifty-year-old father's naiveté had already impressed Dr. Arndt that first afternoon, seven days earlier, in George Walker's office.

Karla pressed on: so then she helped Paul put Leslie's body in the root cellar. The root cellar was a dark closet with a dirt floor and a single exposed light bulb. The room was approximately six by ten feet, off in a corner of the basement. Otherwise the basement was roughly finished, whitewashed with a painted cement floor. Their story-and-a-half pink clapboard corner house at 57 Bayview in Port Dalhousie was fully renovated, with skylights and light beige walls. It was a great house. It had a big cedar deck out back. The root cellar was cooler than any place else and they used it to store Paul's bottled water, tinned goods and things. There were five rough-hewn pine shelves along one side. Leslie's body was wrapped in a blanket and placed on the floor under the first shelf, beside one of those big baskets of potatoes.

Then she called her mother and asked her to bring over some chicken, because with her wedding only two weeks off and everything else that was happening, she had forgotten to thaw something for dinner. It was Father's Day, Sunday, June 17, 1991.

Karla and Paul's parents visited for six or seven hours. Karla said her only moment of panic came when she was preparing dinner and her mother offered to fetch potatoes. "No, no, I'll get them—don't be silly—sit down." But it just "grossed me out," going down and getting the potatoes right beside Leslie's body. The Homolkas left around 9 P.M. and were home ten minutes later. Dorothy Homolka told Dr. Arndt she hadn't seen anything out of the ordinary.

In contrast to the way Dr. Arndt viewed Karla's father, he saw Dorothy Homolka as a nice person—Mother Earth, he called her. Full-bodied at forty-six, she reminded him of a farm girl or "somebody you see rolling up the sleeves, going to the wash-board."

Dorothy Homolka had been born Dorothy Christine Seger in Toronto on September 26, 1946. She told Dr. Arndt that her home life was just like "All in the Family," a popular television show from the late seventies and eighties. She said her mother and father were Edith and Archie Bunker types, which the doctor interpreted to mean they were ignorant, racist and funny. It would fit that Dorothy also saw herself as their bur-bling, miniskirted, blond daughter Gloria, and Karel as the bumpkin, immigrant son-in-law, Meathead.

Dorothy said her parents—who were both still alive and in their eighties—had a very good marriage. Her father had been in the construction business. Her mother had had an extended illness, which meant Dorothy had spent part of her adolescence running the household. She had two brothers and a sister, all living in Ontario. The youngest, Calvin, had been born shortly after Dorothy and Karel got married.

Twenty years is a significant age gap between siblings. Calvin was a "mistake." When Karla was born, Dorothy's youngest brother was barely four. Dorothy said something about how Calvin competed with Karla for the extended family's affection. There was definitely some resentment there.

Dorothy met her future husband in a trailer park on the outskirts of Mississauga, Ontario. It was a rather desolate setting for young love in the early sixties.

The Homolkas, Vaclav and Josefa, immigrated to Canada in 1950, and settled around Woodstock, Ontario. Dorothy's future husband, Karel, who was seven years old at the time, had been born in Stokov, Czechoslovakia, on January 25, 1943.

From the beginning, the Homolkas were farm laborers, first

on their sponsor's farm and then as itinerant workers. The whole area around Woodstock and along Lake Erie down toward Windsor produced tens of thousands of tons of tobacco a year. Then there were the fruit growers in the Niagara Peninsula.

The Niagara Region's prolific orchards and market gardens have become a multibillion-dollar industry. There has always been a lot of work for pickers. The entire Homolka family, which included seven brothers and three sisters, got their first exposure to St. Catharines picking fruit in nearby orchards in the early fifties.

The patriarch of the Homolka family evolved into a self-employed salesman along the way. Vaclav uprooted his entire family and dragged them all over western Canada until he died of cancer in 1957. Always on the move, and given his father's untimely death, Karel Homolka never completed grade six.

When he returned to Ontario, Karel was smart enough to find a girl with an education and a job. At age nineteen, Dorothy had completed grade twelve and secured a secretarial job at the Lakeshore Psychiatric Hospital. Karel and Dorothy said "I do" on December 11, 1965, in Cooksville, Ontario, a quiet village about an hour's drive north of Toronto.

Dr. Arndt could see how Dorothy, at nineteen, would have been very attractive: open, broad face, fine skin, curvaceous. And Karel still possessed a kind of raw animal magnetism. His body was trim and he had good teeth.

The newlyweds moved to Port Credit, a suburb on the west side of Toronto, close to the hospital where Dorothy was working. Karel and his brothers did whatever they could to get by. He struggled, Dorothy persevered.

By the time Karla was born by Caesarean section at Mississauga General Hospital on May 4, 1970, things were going better for Karel. He and his brothers were trading in trinkets and trash—framed Elvises and mulatto girls on black-velvet backgrounds—from sidewalks in shopping malls. After Karla was born, Dorothy became a housewife. She would not return to work for twelve years.

Karla's first sister, Lori Priscilla, was born fourteen months later on June 22, 1971. The Homolka's third and last child, Tammy Lyn, came along two and a half years later on New Year's Day, 1975. Having constantly moved around Ontario since they were married, in March 1975, the Homolkas settled in a St. Catharines trailer park. Although they would move a couple of times again within the small city, they would never leave.

Like his father before him, Karel Homolka became a self-employed traveling salesman, selling lamps and lighting fixtures to furniture stores around the province. While he moved from town to town, Karla gasped for breath.

As a child, her father's namesake was severely asthmatic and frequently hospitalized. The attacks generally occurred around holidays, birthdays and the start of school; whenever Karla became excited or frightened. "Mother," as Dr. Arndt had taken to referring to Dorothy Homolka, said Karla was "cute as a button," and if the snapshots Dr. Arndt saw were any indication, it was true. Blond, wide-eyed, here she is in her little Pioneer Girls' outfit, sweetly smiling, a portrait of innocence. Karla was precocious. She talked early, walked early, and from the time she could walk and talk, she read. When tested in grade school she scored a high intelligence quotient at 131. Karla Leanne Homolka was a very bright little girl.

Throughout grade school, Karla averaged marks in the mid-eighties. Her teachers routinely described her as "eager and enthusiastic, a good student." Early on, Karla established what would become a lifelong academic pattern—poor performance in maths and sciences, against her proclivity for English, languages and related subjects.

In 1978, the Homolkas moved into the house they still occupy today, at 61 Dundonald Street. It was in a new working-class subdivision known as Merritton, directly behind the Victoria Lawn Cemetery. Semidetached, the house seemed much larger than its tiny eight hundred square feet because it was split on four levels.

To a family of five who had lived in trailer parks and tiny apartments it felt like the mansion on the hill. There was a deck and an in-ground pool in the small backyard. Because there was a hydro right-of-way directly behind the house, they could hold on to an illusion of grandeur and more spacious circumstances. The Homolkas set a precedent that year on the fourth of May, when they celebrated Karla's eighth birthday around the pool. The pool became the focal point of their family life.

From Karla and her sister Lori, Dr. Arndt only heard about noncombative "wonderful" parents, who were always supportive and understanding.

Lori, twenty-one, had taken courses to become a medical secretary, but now worked as a full-time checkout clerk at Zehrs. Like her sisters she had blond hair which she often pulled into an austere ponytail. She told Dr. Arndt that she looked a lot like her dead sister, Tammy Lyn, who was by far the most bubbly and attractive of the three sisters. From the pictures the psychiatrist had seen of Tammy Lyn, Lori was deceiving herself. Her tense little face was unfortunately dominated by her father's nose. Although she still lived at home, Lori claimed to be very independent minded. Dr. Arndt noticed that all her nails were bitten down to the quick. She said she had always bitten them.

Both sisters agreed that their mother was the dominant parent, but that their father had a deceptive inner strength. Lori thought her father needed help more than anyone, but he would never talk.

Karla did confess to Dr. Arndt that she had always had it in her mind that she would never marry a man like her father. Personality had nothing to do with it. He was always away and never had a steady paycheck.

Karla was so fixated on her perception of her father's shortcomings that she latched onto Arthur Miller's *Death of a Salesman* for a grade ten English project. With two girlfriends, she made a rather innovative video that focused on the gormless qualities of Willy Loman. Karla's portrayal of Willy was a startling caricature of her father. She played him as if he were a Steve Martin character, a "wild and crazy guy."

From Mother, Dr. Arndt only heard about a Karla that was smart, sweet, active, fun loving, outgoing, a leader, an instigator, always surrounded by friends, academically and socially successful.

She was a daughter who liked her "quiet time"—to read and think—and she loved animals. Karla actually trained their house cat to do tricks. Shadow, their big gray tabby, would sit up and beg or roll over on command. They always had a house full of kids, too. All Karla's friends kept coming around.

"Mind you, something did change when Karla got to high school," Mrs. Homolka told the doctor, thoughtfully. Although the kids still came to the side door in droves, Karla and her friends were no longer quite as open as they had once been.

Dr. Arndt thought ruefully that Mother might be having him on—maybe she had learned a few tricks during that stint at Lakeshore Psychiatric so many years ago. Teenagers are always less open than children—that was hardly a revelation—but also it could be that Mother just wasn't that bright.

Inappropriately, in his view, she was participating in therapy sessions set up for the employees of the Shaver Clinic, a chronic-care hospital where she now worked. These sessions were designed to help her co-workers cope with the trauma that rocked all of St. Catharines in the wake of the crimes. Given Karla's predicament, not to mention her involvement, Dorothy Homolka's participation seemed woefully ill advised, even dim. Or perhaps vainglorious.

Dorothy Homolka went on to tell Dr. Arndt how, as a teenager, Karla and her friends had hung around the pool a lot, listening to music and talking. Karla had also worked part-time as a telephone solicitor for a local photography company— briefly. Otherwise, she was employed in the summers as a nanny for a neighbor with two young boys.

There was another, darker side to Karla that Dr. Arndt did not hear about. About to enter grade seven, with an average of 86 percent, Karla did something she would do over and over again. She inscribed a book and gave it to a friend.

In and of itself, this was innocent enough, except the books were always of a certain type. In this instance it was *Brainchild,* a B.F. Skinner–inspired horror story about behavioral psychologists who program human beings for their own nefarious purposes. The recipient of Karla's largess was an impressionable, portly girl named Amanda Whatling.

Karla graduated from grade eight with an 84 percent average. There is a snapshot of Karla and two girlfriends taken in the school gymnasium just prior to graduation ceremonies. Karla is in the middle and has an arm around each girl's shoulders. One girl looks decidedly unhappy, the other quite radiant. They are all wearing glossy, pastel polyester party dresses. Karla is the only one wearing a corsage.

On the back of the photograph Karla inscribed: "Oh-me & my bestest buddies, Vicky and Lisa. Poor Lisa's been crying over Tom. What am I planning? (There's that devilish glint in my eye!) June 21st, 1984."

When Karla started grade nine, her ongoing struggle with math and science dragged her down a bit. Sir Winston Churchill Secondary School was the largest in St. Catharines, and she was no longer the only pretty blonde in the corridors. Her grades remained average, but her attention began to wander. Not atypically, Karla rebelled and challenged parental authority—such as it was. There were few rules in the Homolka household.

Although her parents allowed Karla to drink, she was not allowed to "car date"—go out with boys in cars. Hardly Czechoslovakia under Alexander Dubček, but it was enough to set off an increasingly independent-minded Karla. Karla's friends remember regular arguments, particularly with her father, whom they perceived to be as strong willed as Karla.

Others, who were closer to the family, such as the Andersons next door, saw a different kind of tyranny, one more in keeping with Dr. Arndt's impression of Mr. Homolka. This version portrays Karel as a man subjugated by the collective will of a household completely dominated by women.

Karla and her sister Lori regularly told their father to "fuck off," and called him a "dumb Czech." When the beleaguered man could not stand the heat, he would flee the kitchen for refuge in the basement.

On the other hand, Karel Homolka had a reputation for a wandering eye. When Lynda Wollis, one of Dorothy's friends and a colleague from the Shaver Clinic, was in the process of a divorce, Karel came on to her. He started hanging around her apartment building. Once, he managed to get past the security system and pounded on her door, all the while professing his affection. When Lynda finally agreed to meet him at a bar to sort things out, Karel announced that he was "in lovink" with her and planned to leave Dorothy and move in with her.

Karel's nickname among the women at the clinic was "the pervert." Lynda said he earned it, because "he always wanted to take you to bed." Dorothy told Lynda that she was relieved when Karel went away on business, because he always wanted sex. Lynda had only tolerated the man for Dorothy's sake; she certainly never encouraged him. It always struck her as odd that the man could hardly speak English after spending more than three decades in Canada. The "I'm in lovink with you" thing put it way over the top.

"I told him, 'Hey, like I'm in the middle of a divorce—the last thing I want is another man in my life, especially my friend's husband,'" Lynda recalled. She sent Karel home and told him to keep his mouth shut.

The next day, Dorothy approached Lynda at work. Karel had told her everything and now she and Lynda had to talk. At Lynda's apartment that evening, Dorothy said she did not think Karel was in love with Lynda, but there was an infatuation. To Dorothy this meant there was trouble in her marriage and her marriage was all-important to her.

"You could save my marriage if you'd sleep with both of us," Dorothy suggested to a startled Lynda, who politely but firmly declined. Lynda's relationship with Dorothy was never the same.

. . .

In the meantime, Karla was developing an interest in the occult. Her friend Amanda remembers that they used to light candles and burn incense all the time. Karla advertised in newspapers for Ouija boards. There was talk about spirits and the "screaming tunnels" that were located somewhere down near the railway tracks outside of town. Karla took to wearing black, dying her hair different colors every other day and changing its style as often. She wore heavy, dark eye makeup.

"When we were in high school she was a little rebel, you know," her close friend Debbie Purdie recalled. "Wore black nail polish, wore the longjohns and boxer shorts. Nobody ever told Karla what to do. She was her own person and her own boss."

Another classmate, Iona Brindle, noticed strange carved marks, like scarification, on Karla's arm. It appeared that circles had been carved into her skin and then filled in with nail polish.

Karla also inscribed a book called *Michelle Remembers* to Iona. Published in 1980, it was one of the first "true" stories about recovered memory, satanism and graphic sexual abuse, co-authored by the "victim-patient" Michelle Smith and her therapist. Karla's inscription simply read: "There is always something more left to say."

Karla admitted to Dr. Arndt that she smoked a little dope and had once popped an upper called a White Cross—probably contraband Ritalin—in grade ten. She told him that it really made her feel good, but then she "crashed" and had to call in sick for work at the Number One Pet Center in the Pen Center Mall, where she was working part-time. Her mother was not aware of any illicit drug use, just drinking at home with friends.

In grade eleven, Karla was accelerated to grade twelve English. But the Pythagorean theorem and the golden mean remained elusive. Even though she liked to dissect frogs, she only got 65 percent in biology. Barely passing in history, she managed high marks in English and scored 80 percent in her law class. Her language skills were such that she acted as a French tutor for her less adept peers.

Tracy Collins, another friend, saw Karla as "a thirty-year-old in a seventeen-year-old's body." One afternoon in the cafeteria Karla whispered in Tracy's ear, "You know what I'd like to do? I'd like to put dots all over somebody's body and take a knife and then play connect the dots and then pour vinegar all over them."

Karla started going with a guy in her typing class. Doug laconically remembered Karla as she was generally perceived—particularly by the boys—as "different." It was hard to say exactly how. The culture of Sir Winston Churchill Secondary School reflected the culture of the town: white, male dominant, working class, heterosexual, jock. Doug appreciated Karla's moodiness and found the fact that she was consumed by the thought of death interesting. She was constantly threatening suicide, but he doubted her sincerity.

Doug wasn't the only one who noticed she was obsessed by death. Karla inscribed Lyn Cretney's yearbook: "Remember: Suicide kicks and fasting is awesome. Bones rule! Death Rules. Death Kicks. I love death. Kill the fucking world." Lyn never figured that one out.

All of Karla's close girlfriends looked the same. The three of them—Kathy Wilson, Debbie Purdie and Lisa Stanton—were around five foot five, 110 pounds with permed blond hair. They dressed a little punk, although pop culture in a town such as St. Catharines was ignorant of Iggy Pop, Lou Reed or even Sid Vicious and the Sex Pistols. Soon, they would form a little clique called the Exclusive Diamond Club. Its charter was simple: recruit rich, slightly older men who were hunks, get a diamond, marry and live happily ever after.

Karla was "the tough one in the bunch," as Kathy Wilson put it. Karla had a pair of real handcuffs, "with keys and everything," ostensibly because she wanted to become a police officer.

Dorothy Homolka told Dr. Arndt her daughter wanted to be a librarian. She told him about Karla's enthusiasm for gymnastics and figure skating, terminated when she fractured her foot at the age of thirteen.

Karla left the gymnasium and the arena behind for the theater. She joined the dance club and took a serious interest in acting, participating in school variety shows and musicals. For three years she studied music, taking voice and singing lessons. Ironically, she categorically refused to sing in front of her class. When it was her turn to perform solo, Karla cajoled the teacher into instructing the entire class to turn its back or—if the assignment was particularly demanding—actually leave the room while she warbled.

On May 4, 1987, Karla celebrated her seventeenth birthday poolside with the members of the Exclusive Diamond Club and Tracy Collins, who had been intrigued by Karla ever since the "connect the dots" incidents. Other friends, including chubby Amanda Whatling, had fallen by the wayside. Amanda liked sports; Karla liked lying perfectly still in the sun listening to the Beastie Boys sing "You Gotta Fight for Your Right to Party."

By July, Tracy Collins's parents had had enough and they forbade her to keep company with Karla. Tracy had failed two courses and the Collinses did not like the way their daughter was changing under the influence of the strange, domineering Homolka girl.

Tracy was not the only one lost to Karla. Her new boyfriend moved to Kansas. They corresponded, but Karla did not see her lost love again until she took matters into her own hands around mid-August. In defiance of her parents, she purchased a plane ticket and surreptitiously flew to Kansas for two weeks. On her first flight beyond her parents' control, Karla told Dr. Arndt that she and her boyfriend did cocaine—"just a little"—and Karla lost her virginity. At least she had called home, Karla told the doctor.

According to what the boy in Kansas later told the police and what Karla told Dr. Arndt, there was nothing unusual about the sex—"it was just sex." But when she got the girl-friends together at the beginning of the semester in September, Karla told tales of sadistic orgies, with bondage and hard spankings.

Karla began grade twelve but quickly became disaffected. She decided to only take two courses and work full-time instead. Karla approached Kristy Maan, the youthful store manager at the Number One Pet Center, and implied that Kristy was something of a role model for her—young, pretty, engaged and employed. Karla's part-time job became full-time. Even better, Karla's fellow Diamond Clubber, Debbie Purdie, took over her old part-time position.

In October 1987, Karla and Debbie were invited to go to a convention in Toronto for people who were involved in the pet industry. It was being held at the Howard Johnson East Hotel in Scarborough, a large suburb on the eastern boundary of Toronto.

The way Karla told it to Dr. Arndt, she went to the convention with her friend Debbie. Then they went out to a club, came back and met Paul and his friend in the coffee shop. They invited the boys up to their room to watch a movie, but Karla ended up having sex with Paul instead. That was it.

"The first time I met him I knew I'd marry him," she told Dr. Arndt. "He puts women under a spell, you know. I fell in love that night."

Then she added: "Of course, that's no excuse."

CHAPTER

three

The sound of the key in Karla Homolka's hotel-room door woke Kristy Maan from a deep sleep. At first she didn't remember exactly where she was. Then she saw Karla and Debbie. They were coming in the door with two more guys. Kristy couldn't believe her eyes. She looked at her watch. She had only been asleep for forty-five minutes. With some difficulty, they had just rid themselves of the first two. Where in God's name did they get these two?

As the pet-store manager, it had been Kristy's choice to bring Karla and Debbie to Toronto for the Hagen show. Every year, for as long as Kristy had managed the store, Hagen sponsored a show of pet supplies and accessories for selected retailers. Normally, they only paid the store manager's way. This was the first time the company had sprung for anybody the managers wanted to bring.

Kristy had decided to to take her assistant manager, Jenny Cable, and Karla Homolka. Kristy liked Karla. She got along with animals, and people. Even Touki the bird liked Karla. When Karla wanted to bring her girlfriend Debbie, who also worked at the store part-time, Kristy figured "why not?" It was pure serendipity.

"Don't be mad," Karla said, to her bewildered boss. "They're nothing like those other two."

A little earlier, Kristy had run next door to the girls' room because she heard a commotion. She found Debbie and Karla with two creepy-looking older guys who were obviously drunk and slightly belligerent about leaving.

After the cocktail party downstairs, when everyone else had gone back up to their rooms, Karla and Debbie had gone to the disco. They must have picked up the creeps there. Dogs Kristy could handle, but not drunks. She went and got her district manager, but he was no match for these men either. They finally had to call security.

"I didn't know where you two were," Kristy scolded Karla. Brunette, petite and attractive, with her stylish eyeglasses, Kristy looked more like an optometrist's model than a cage cleaner from a pet store. "But what you just did, that's crazy. You don't know anyone around here; you shouldn't be bringing people up here. Now, I'm gonna stay right here tonight."

With that, she turned on the television, lay down on the pull-out sofa in front of the window and promptly fell asleep. No sooner was she asleep than Debbie and Karla went out the door and down three floors to the hotel restaurant, a Naugahyde-and-chicken-salad-sandwich joint called Bluffer's Atrium Lounge. It was a little before midnight.

"Oh Kristy, they're really nice guys, honest," Karla cajoled. "They just came up to talk."

Kristy had seen ferrets in heat less flirtatious, less obvious than Karla was now. Kristy considered herself a Christian. She tried to read her Bible every day. But what to do? She wasn't their mother and this wasn't a religious retreat; it was a convention and the girls were over the age of consent.

And Karla was right—they were different. The one guy was goofy looking, but they were both clean-cut, particularly the better-looking one. He was wearing a nice windbreaker, a blue button-down shirt and dark cotton pants. They were older than the girls, but they looked younger than the previous two. And they weren't drunk.

Nevertheless, Kristy was pretty well disgusted. She knew Karla was the instigator—even though everybody called Debbie Purdie "Dirty" Purdie. She had seen no evidence that Debbie was "dirty." Instead, she seemed immature and shy. With Debbie, it was always "Karla this" and "Karla that."

Shrugging her shoulders, Kristy went back to her own room and to bed. She knew the one guy's name was Paul. She would not find out who the other guy was until Paul and Karla were married four years later.

Paul and his future best man, Van, could not believe their good fortune: teenage chicks with a hotel room. The night had otherwise been a bust. The men had thought they would just get something to eat at Howard Johnson's before Van took Paul home and called it a night. Roughly the same age—Paul was twenty-three and Van twenty-two—they had grown up across the street from each other. The Smirnis family had moved away a few years earlier, but Van and Paul kept in touch. When Paul saw the two girls sitting in the well-lit restaurant window, his dour mood changed drastically.

Through the reflection in the glass window, Paul Bernardo saw himself miraculously redeemed in the green-blue eyes of a dirty blonde with a pretty face and a bad perm. By the way she returned his look and smiled, there was little doubt in his mind that he was at least going to get to talk to somebody other than Van that night.

Paul was the kind of guy for whom something always had to be happening. In the past few months, that had been the case. He had graduated with a bachelor of arts degree from the University of Toronto, gone to Walt Disney World with a girlfriend in August, got an entry-level trainee's job at a big accounting firm called Price Waterhouse in September, and flown back and forth to Van's brother's wedding in Fort Worth the weekend before last. He had two girlfriends. One of them was so jealous of the other that she had put her hand through a window at his parents' house a few weeks earlier.

"Sometimes in life you've got to say 'what the fuck' and make your move," Tom Cruise said in the 1983 movie *Risky Business*. Paul had that quote printed out on a wall in his bedroom where he kept a record of clichés that were his mantras. Even though the restaurant had a maître d', Paul ignored him and went directly to the girls' table and boldly asked the one question to which he already had the answer: would the girls mind if he and his friend joined them?

It was apparent right away, to both Van and Debbie, that Paul and Karla had more in common than the fact that they both had swimming pools in their backyards. There was an immediate, inexplicable but very obvious attraction. Karla was ready and Paul was impetuous.

Pleasantries exchanged, they chitchatted. The girls went to the bathroom, giggled and invited the boys up to their room. They were just going to watch a movie. The fortuitousness was part of the buzz.

Kristy Maan shut the door behind her, the lights went out and Paul and Karla went at it. It was a typical HoJo room; small, clean and inexpensively furnished, the pull-out couch only a couple of steps from the bed where Karla and Paul were doing a horizontal mambo.

According to what Van later told newspaper reporters, first Karla was on top, then Paul. But he wasn't really watching, he just saw their silhouette in the dim light. The sheets were moving, a lot.

Debbie was somewhat surprised that the Exclusive Diamond Club President and some totally new six-footer were having sex right in front of them. She also knew that Karla was capable of anything. Karla and Paul kept at it, grunting and groaning and whispering sweet nothings in each other's ear, for about four hours. Once, when they over-heated, Karla poured a glass of ice-water on Paul's back. He was impressed. He liked a girl with attitude.

Ultimately, Debbie fell asleep on the pull-out couch. She did not want to have anything to do with Van.

Sloppy seconds had always been one of Van's fantasies. But when he asked Paul if he could have Karla too, Paul told him to have a go at himself instead.

At eight o'clock the next morning, Paul and Karla took a shower together and exchanged addresses and phone numbers.

"You see, I'm really an old-fashioned kind of girl." Karla explained to Dr. Arndt patiently. "A stay-at-home, Girl Guides, have-a-bunch-of-kids, have-doors-opened-for-me kind of girl."

Dr. Arndt looked around the interview room, found a Northwestern General Hospital Blood/Chemistry work-up form, and took notes on that.

"He treated me like a princess; he swept me off my feet. . . . You have to understand, I liked him back then," she explained, squeezing Bunky. "He was the one guy who was very nice to me; he never bored me like the others. With the other guys I could always do what I wanted and that was boring. In all my previous relationships, I was in total control. I never cared what others thought."

The "one guy" who was always nice to Karla, who never bored her—whom she knew from the moment they met she would marry—was born a bastard on August 27, 1964, at Scarborough General Hospital in the suburbs of Toronto. He had also been very ugly.

There was nothing abnormal about Marilyn Bernardo's thirty-nine-week pregnancy. Paul Kenneth was a twenty-inch-long, eight-pound-ten-ounce bouncing baby boy. But the huge black mark covering the entire left side of his head was grotesque. His mother cried out with horror the first time she saw him.

The hospital records show his parents to be Marilyn Elizabeth Bernardo née Eastman and Kenneth Walter Bernardo. But the records are not entirely accurate. Marilyn Bernardo was not really an Eastman—she was a Hamilton—and Paul was not Ken's son.

Marilyn Bernardo was born Marilyn Joyce Hamilton on May 10, 1940, in Kitchener, Ontario. Kitchener and its twin city, Waterloo, are enclaves of German immigration, approximately an hour's drive west of the Toronto airport. Before the First World War, they were known as Berlin and Little Berlin.

Marilyn's natural parents, Ross and Elizabeth Hamilton, put Marilyn and her two sisters, Claudia and Diane, and her brother, Richard, up for adoption. Marilyn never found out why. Neither did any of her siblings. But Marilyn got real lucky when Gerald and Elizabeth Eastman decided to adopt her.

Gerald Ernest Eastman had become a big fish in a small pond. Born in 1901, he read law at Osgoode Hall in Toronto and was called to the bar in 1928. He joined the Kitchener law office of Clement, Hattin and Company. After World War II he became a full partner. When he retired in 1980, his law firm was known as Clement, Eastman, Dreger, Martin and Meunier.

On July 8, 1931, Gerald married Elizabeth Ruddell. They had one natural child, Marilyn's stepbrother Charles (Dick) Eastman. The senior Eastman soldiered in World War II from 1939 until 1945, when he was honorably discharged a lieutenant colonel.

To hear Ken Bernardo tell it, Marilyn was abused in foster homes and then raped by at least three members of the Eastman family after she was adopted. But he said these things much later, when he was trying desperately to avoid jail and rationalize his own deviate and abusive behavior. Otherwise, there is no evidence to support his allegations.

To her friends, such as Elizabeth Christner, Marilyn was an outgoing and happy teenager who had been raised in quiet, affluent civility by kind, understanding parents. Marilyn attended Westmount and King Edward Public Schools and then Kitchener Collegiate Institute. After she graduated from high school, Marilyn went to work for Ontario Hydro.

An attractive blonde—maybe a bit heavy in the thigh—Marilyn had a broad, open face, rather like the many Mennonite girls who crowded the bustling Kitchener farmers' market on Saturdays.

She met Ken Bernardo in November, 1955. An ignorant, horse-playing, Italian immigrant's son, Kenneth Walter Bernardo had been born on January 29, 1935, to Frank and Mary Bernardo. He was the youngest of three siblings. Ken's brother, Raymond Francis, had been born a decade earlier, and his sister Shirley in 1927.

According to Ken, the Bernardo children endured a kind of minor holocaust of the nuclear family. As the youngest by eight years, he suffered the least abuse but remembered his childhood as troubled and difficult. His father was an old-world authoritarian, who treated the children like stubborn mules. The old man and Ken's brother, Raymond, fought like warring factions in the Italian parliament. Although Ken maintains the family struggled during the Great Depression, that too seems unlikely. By the time Ken was cognizant of his circumstances, it was at least 1940 and his father was prospering and starting to mellow.

Born in northern Italy, Frank Bernardo came to Canada as an orphan at the age of ten. He married a woman of English descent and started what became a very successful marble-and-tile company. Frank retired early, sold the business and played the ponies for the rest of his long life.

Ken's recollection is that his father stopped beating his mother when Ken was around five years old but the relationship between his parents was never tranquil or amicable. By the time the physical abuse and daily turmoil started to abate, Ken's brother and sister were in their mid-teens.

In 1950, the Bernardos made the city papers. Raymond was caught out in some criminal behavior and arrested. The matter was widely reported and humiliated the family. Ken later said his brother was a sadist twice diagnosed as a psychopath. Raymond eventually became a police officer.

In 1957, Ken graduated from Wilfrid Laurier University with a bachelor of arts degree. That fall he went to work at Pearson and Matthews, an accounting firm in Guelph, Ontario. Guelph, another university town, renowned for its veterinary college, was a half-hour drive east of Kitchener.

Although Marilyn was ambivalent about Ken, on May 20, 1960, ten days after her twentieth birthday, she married him. It was a small, unassuming ceremony held at the Eastmans' home on Claremount Avenue, a distinctly white, Anglo-Saxon, Protestant, upper-middle-class address. The groom was twenty-five, but didn't have many friends. Aside from a couple of Marilyn's friends and immediate family, there were few guests.

Marilyn had been unable to make up her mind between Ken and another suitor named Bill, so the Colonel, as her father was affectionately known, decided for her. Colonel Eastman had always been determined Marilyn would marry an "educated man," and that left Bill out.

The newlyweds moved into a tiny apartment at 266 Victoria Street. Following in his father's footsteps, Ken started smacking Marilyn around.

In March, 1961, they moved into a slightly larger apartment on Ahrens Street. He smacked her around some more. On March 25, Marilyn gave birth to their first child, David Bryar. Their daughter, Deborah Gail, was born the following year, on December 14, 1962. Ken was still smacking Marilyn around when he passed his institute exams in 1963. In recognition of the fact that he was now a chartered accountant, the family moved into a little bungalow at 121 Wilfrid Street. Then Ken changed jobs and went to work for Rohm and Haas Canada Limited on the outskirts of Toronto.

Between the way he treated Marilyn and the inordinate amount of time Ken spent commuting, studying and working, it all became too much. Marilyn Bernardo remembers exactly what she was doing on the day Jack Kennedy was shot. She had sought and found refuge in Bill's arms. Thus, Paul Kenneth Bernardo was conceived.

In early January, 1964, the papers were full of stories about the Boston Strangler. His final victim, nineteen-year-old Mary Sullivan, had been found in her apartment, propped up on her bed, naked, with a broomstick stuck in her vagina and a large pink bow tied under her chin. Resting against her left foot was a gaily colored card which read, "Happy New Year."

Right from the time Guy Lombardo and his Royal Canadian Orchestra struck up the band for "Auld Lang Syne" and the big red ball dropped in Times Square, there wasn't much chance 1964 was going to be very happy.

The 8mm Zapruder home movie, which had inadvertently caught the graphic details of Kennedy's assassination, had been replayed over and over again on many hundreds of millions of tiny screens in households all over the world; the grainy image of Kennedy's head snapping forward zapped an entire generation's innocence like zombie dust.

About forty-five days after Kennedy took the bullet and Marilyn lay down with Bill, the ball dropped in the Bernardo household as well. Ken was resigned to his fate, but he would be damned if he would stay in a one-horse town and continue to be cuckolded.

By January 29, Marilyn, Ken and their two young children, Debbie and David, were celebrating his twenty-ninth birthday in their new home on Abbeyville Avenue in Scarborough, a sprawling, strip-malled suburb on the eastern flank of Toronto.

Marilyn was disconsolate. What could she have been thinking? No man in his right mind wanted a woman with two small children, and Bill was no exception. She had never lived anywhere other than Kitchener. Married to a man who ignored and beat her, isolated from her family and friends, with two small children and another man's child in her belly, she was totally alone.

.　　　.　　　.

The mark on baby Paul's head turned out to be exactly what the obstetrician had said it was: a large transient blood clot. It faded from his face six weeks after he was born.

In her diary, Marilyn described Paul as her "easier child, much quieter than the other two." As her friend Elizabeth pointed out, to the detriment of their friendship, compared to the other two, a pack of hyenas would be considered quiet.

Not that their friendship mattered much anymore, anyway. Elizabeth and her husband, David, were very surprised to be asked to be the godparents, when Ken and Marilyn had Paul baptized at St. John's Anglican Church in Kitchener on November 29.

They reluctantly agreed, for old times' sake. They had stopped socializing with the Bernardos long before they moved to Scarborough. The Marilyn Elizabeth knew had become increasingly sullen after her marriage. This Ken Bernardo person was very quiet and temperamental. When he did say something, it was invariably of a negative cast.

Paul was a year old when the Bernardos moved to 21 Sir Raymond Drive in Scarborough's Guildwood Village. For Marilyn this was the next best thing to going home. Another quiet, predominantly white, middle-class neighborhood, it sat on the edge of the bluffs overlooking Lake Ontario. The two-story house had a carport and a big front window. Ken began budgeting for an in-ground backyard swimming pool.

"This one is not the least bit affectionate," Marilyn wrote in her diary. She described her youngest child as "very selfish and stubborn" and listed his allergies—orchard grass, elm, ash, poplar, cotton linters.

Then Marilyn discovered Paul couldn't talk. By two and a half, most children were talking a blue streak. "Stammers a lot," Marilyn dutifully noted.

As it turned out, Paul's tongue was attached to his palate by a strange flange of skin, like the webbing on a duck's foot. He made sounds, but they were unintelligible, more animal-like than human.

Once his parents realized that Paul was literally tongue-tied, he was thoroughly examined. He was sent to a speech therapist named Bonnie Gross at the Scarborough General Hospital. In her report, she noted that Paul had passed all the other childhood milestones; it was natural that his inability to communicate caused him considerable frustration.

All they had to do was snip the duck's webbing. On his grade-four report card his teacher described his academic performance as satisfactory, but said Paul failed to apply himself "because he is of a talkative nature." The Bernardos rejoiced.

Paul had always loved himself. Even as an inarticulate child in primary school, his teacher praised his early penchant for neatness and accuracy. He grew up to be very beautiful and talkative, indeed. And many, many women loved him as he loved himself.

Neat and fastidious and beautiful, he found them at school or summer camp, at work, deliberately or by chance. There were Karen, Nadine, Lisa, Victoria, Kim, Joanne, Anna, Lenore, Laura Lyn and many, many more. They all agreed he was a silver-tongued devil. Basically, he managed to talk the pants off most of them.

Then one day, shortly after he started grade ten, for no reason he ever understood, his mother stormed into his room, threw a photograph of a man on his bed and told Paul he wasn't who he thought he was at all. He was not Ken Bernardo's son, he was really this man's son. She said he was a bastard and he might as well get used to it.

CHAPTER

four

Looking at that picture on his bed was like looking into a mirror. The guy in the photograph looked exactly like him. Paul was both repulsed and fascinated. His mother was a real bitch, just like his father said. Sometimes his father would sit on the couch. It did not matter whether they had company or not. When his mother came lumbering down the stairs, his father would say something like, "Boom, boom, boom, look out, here comes the big, fat cow."

At the time, his mother was living like some giant troll in the basement. She never fed them. She hid food under her bed. There was never any food in the refrigerator. It was an austerity thing. His father did not want to be eaten out of house and home.

His friend Chris Burt didn't really believe him, until he came over one day and saw it with his own eyes. Paul went to Sir Wilfrid Laurier Collegiate Institute. He was in grade ten. So was Chris. To Chris, Paul seemed so together. He was always well dressed. Girls liked him. Paul had even introduced Chris to his girlfriend, Nancy MacEwan. And here he was, living in an incredibly filthy house with no food in the cupboards. And there his mother was, blinking in the dim half-light at the bottom of the stairs. She had big, puffy eyes and her hair stood on end like a Brillo pad.

Paul told Chris about how his father would sneak downstairs in the middle of the night to have sex with "it," then run back upstairs to his own bedroom.

Paul never told Chris or anyone else that his old man was also sneaking out of the house trying to look in the neighbors' daughter's window.

One night in June, Ken sneaked out and got caught. The police came to the door around three in the morning. They asked old Ken what he thought he was doing prowling around in his nightclothes, peeping into other people's windows.

Apparently the twenty-six-year-old woman, in whose basement bedroom window he was trying to peek, had been sitting outside her house in a girlfriend's car at the time. She watched Ken come out of the house, cross the street, go up her driveway and walk right to her window, without any hesitation—meaning he had done it before.

Her blinds were closed, so he gave up and scurried back to 21 Sir Raymond. He was wearing white pajamas with a blue pinstripe. The women freaked and called the cops. There had been rumors in the neighborhood about him, but she had never believed them because he was friendly with her father.

The old man was stressed right out that night. Ken stood at the door, shaking, and his Coke-bottle glasses were all fogged up. The cops took note. They no more believed his lame, cock-amamy story about being woken up by a noise and having to check it out than Paul did. But there wasn't much they could do except warn him and write up a report.

Then there was the business with Paul's sister.

Debbie did not remember exactly when the sex stuff started, but she knew it had been going on long before her mother got sick and her parents started sleeping in separate bedrooms. It just got a lot worse after they moved back from Barrie. Her father had taken a job in Barrie and moved the whole family up there for a year. And then they all came back to their old house on Sir Raymond and everybody was happy. Debbie was ten years old.

Her little brother Paul, who had always been a little different, suddenly became outgoing and talkative. He had started playing soccer when they were in Barrie and he signed up for the Guildwood league when they came back to Scarborough.

He joined the Cub Scouts. He started playing baseball in the community house league. Ken Bernardo even started coaching the team. That lasted about a year. Like Debbie, Paul started to swim seriously and take lessons at the YMCA. In the end, they both got National Lifeguard certificates. On the surface, every-thing appeared normal.

But it was not. Marilyn Bernardo became really mean, and she looked different. Her skin dried out. It felt like the sandpa-per on Ken's workbench in the basement. Debbie's mother was always yelling. Her hands, face and eyelids puffed up. Her nice, shiny hair grew dull and brittle, and her fingernails were a funny color.

And Marilyn Bernardo got really fat. Debbie knew her mother was sick, that it was not really her fault, but she did not understand what a thyroid was. For some reason, areas around the Great Lakes, and particularly Lake Ontario, on whose shore they lived, were the most frequent sites of thyroid disorders in the world. Even if Debbie had understood, it wouldn't have made any difference.

Her mother started staying in her room all the time, with the curtains drawn and the lights off. She stopped cooking and doing chores. Both her mother and father told Debbie she would have to try and do the housework—before and after school. Debbie was not very good at cooking and cleaning. And her mother was always yelling at her and her brothers. Their father would tell them that it was not their mother's fault that she was sick, but then he would make fun of her and call her a "bitch."

Her father started sneaking into Debbie's room at night. He told her not to tell her mother, because it would just make her angry. Because Debbie was a heavy sleeper, she started putting shells and old coins in a metal garbage can and lodging the garbage can in front of her bedroom door. She slept with a flashlight. When her father tried to open the door there would be a hell of a racket, and she would shine the light in his face.

Debbie always made sure her curtains were closed because he used to climb out on the roof and try to watch her undressing at night. He would say he was just checking the eaves trough, even though it was dark.

She remembered it occasionally happened during the week, but the garbage-can thing seemed to help. Then there was Sunday night. Every Sunday, the whole family would settle down in front of the TV to watch "Walt Disney" and her mother would lie down with the boys and her Daddy would call her over.

He would sit there and finger her, while they watched Mickey Mouse. Sometimes it hurt and she would say "ouch."

"What's going on there?" her mother would ask. But she never did anything.

Once, during the day, when Marilyn had taken Paul and David out somewhere, Ken cornered her in the small bedroom upstairs, and laid down on top of her and started going through the motions.

"What are you doing?" Debbie demanded.

"I'm making love to you," he told her.

Squirming out from underneath, she managed to run off. It

would be another eight years before Debbie figured out how to run off for good.

The revelation that Paul was a bastard had a devastating effect on him, but it was relatively invisible. He quickly realized that it gave him a certain cachet, particularly with the girls he selectively told. It created in him a difference that set him apart, eliciting sympathy and interest. But it was a cancerous fact, as much for the way in which he was originally told as for the way in which it was subsequently handled—or rather, not handled.

Neither the man whom he now knew to be his stepfather nor his mother would confront the issue. He managed to find out his real father's name and that he had an insurance business in Kitchener. But that was it. His mother refused to ever discuss the subject. The only real change: whenever she yelled at him, which was often, she now called him the "bastard from hell."

CHAPTER
five

Nancy MacEwan had a vivid memory of Noel Francisca's grade twelve law class on the afternoon of January 24, 1980, not because of the severed head in the pail but because of Paul Bernardo's question.

Nancy liked Paul. He was going out with her friend Anna. And Paul had introduced her to her Chris Burt, the boyfriend Nancy would eventually marry.

Two homicide detectives made a presentation that day.

They showed the class full of teenagers a tray of slides, including one of a naked torso and another of a severed leg. One slide was a blowup of a tentative cut that went through the flesh and partially into the thigh bone. The detectives explained that people who cut up bodies often make one or two tentative cuts before they choose their exact spot. It meant that the killer was probably inexperienced. There was a small piece of metal that had lodged in the bone, and it caught the light of the flashbulb and glistened like a diamond in the sun.

The torso had been wrapped in green garbage bags and tossed in a Dumpster. Identification was difficult without the other pieces, but forensics told them it was the torso of a southeast Asian female who had given birth at least once. Shortly afterward they found the leg, wrapped in an unusual burlap coffee bag.

From soil samples, they determined the bag had been in Kenya and Montreal. They tracked the bag from an importer in Montreal to a repackaging distributor who gave the discarded bags to a woodworking company. Two men who worked for the woodworking company had killed the woman.

But it wasn't the story about how the coffee bags bagged the bad guys—or the gruesome slides of the woman's head with its black eye, which they found in a pail—that stayed with Nancy. It was Paul's question.

"If two people were committing sodomy in their own home," he asked, as if it were the most natural thing in the world, "how would the police be able to charge them? Would they sneak into the house to watch them and then arrest them?"

The class broke into uproarious laughter.

Regardless of the fact that he was a bastard, that his mother was a complete bitch whom he was beginning to wish dead and his father a sexual deviant who molested his half sister and tommed around the neighborhood peeping in the middle of the night, Paul Bernardo was determined to make something of himself.

The anomaly was the fact that Paul became a real chip off the old step-block. Like his stepfather, he was also good with numbers. Throughout high school he maintained average marks, but he almost always scored in the eighties in maths and science.

And like Ken Bernardo, Paul was remarkably consistent. He hardly ever missed a day of school. He wanted to get ahead. He liked money and was not afraid of work. From the time he started high school, Paul worked part-time after school.

He started out delivering newspapers. Occasionally, he found work as a security guard. He waited tables in restaurants—the Crock and Block on Markham Road, Mother's Pizza, the Howard Johnson's out by the airport.

In one of the restaurants, he met a small-town Amway entrepreneur, Byron Breen, who sponsored Paul as a distributor.

He studied judo. He became a Queen's Scout, the highest rank a young knot tier could achieve. He went to camp every summer. He was a counselor-in-training at Camp Wabanaki on Vernon Lake in Muskoka and he trained to be a leader at Camp Ki-Wa-Y, a YMCA camp on the outskirts of Kitchener. He had a few summer romances, friendly affairs mostly. Laura Mason let it go further than that. One night they had intercourse in a cornfield. "It wasn't that memorable," she recalled. "It was Mennonite style, just quick."

When he wasn't working, studying or camping, he was out with a girl. Lisa Williams, whom he met at the Crock and Block, for instance. Lisa drove him nuts because she would always show up for work in her little school uniform—maroon, knee socks, maroon sweater, white blouse and a green, maroon and yellow plaid tartan skirt. She was petite, about five foot three, a hundred pounds, with shoulder-length blond hair. At their peak, Lisa and Paul were going out maybe twice a week. He managed to talk her pants off once in a ravine, after plying her with wine and giving her a T-shirt that read "Hands Off" on the front and "Property of Paul" on the back. People were walking by when they both had their pants off, so they put them on again and left. Lisa did not think he had an erection.

In Nancy MacEwan's opinion, Paul changed dramatically after he started hanging out with the Smirnis brothers. The three brothers, Steve, Alex and Van, lived directly across the street from the Bernardos at 24 Sir Raymond. Their parents owned a restaurant and the brothers were always trying to buy friends with free drinks and souvlaki. They had that real crude macho attitude about them—particularly Van and Steve—and after a while, Paul started to walk the walk and talk the talk. His whole attitude toward women seemed to change.

One day, Paul just dropped Nancy's friend Anna and started going after younger girls, in true Smirnis fashion.

The Smirnises were also known to be petty criminals, trading their father's pizzas for stolen gasoline or night fishing on private property—mostly inane, penny-ante stuff.

In 1982, Paul and his friends began taking a ritual trip to Florida at spring break in March. They met some girls who agreed to see them again. Steve Smirnis drove to Detroit with Paul and the others. At the Knight's Inn in Sterling Heights, Steve played the big man and got himself arrested for trying to pick up the tab with a credit card a customer had left in his parents' restaurant.

That was the other thing; Paul was bright. He wasn't a rocket scientist, but he was bright. The Brothers Smirnis were not. Young Van was the worst. Apparently, he had once fallen from a balcony and hit his head. He had never been right after that. Steve tried two-timing Paul behind his back, with a little blonde named Nadine Brammer, who orchestrated the whole thing so that Paul would find out. All Nancy knew was that it had ended badly.

Then Paul started going out with a young raven-haired girl named Jennifer Galligan, whom he met through Steve Smirnis. Nancy remembered Jennifer for two reasons. First, Jennifer was incredibly submissive. Second, Paul told Chris that he always had anal intercourse with her. It wasn't so much the fact that they "frequented that style," as Chris so delicately put it. It was the fact that Paul and Chris talked about it all the time that really got to Nancy.

When Debbie Bernardo finally told her mother what her father had been doing to her over the years, her mother refused to believe her.

"How could you make such things up?" Marilyn demanded. "Why would you say such awful things?"

A couple of days later Marilyn confronted Ken. She asked him how much he loved Debbie and Ken said, "Too much." At least, that's what Marilyn told Debbie. Debbie moved to Kirkland Lake, a once-thriving mining town a long way up north. But she never completely severed the ties.

Less than a year passed, and Paul was serving as an usher at his sister's wedding. Ken Bernardo gave away his only daughter.

After visiting the Bernardo household, it was not hard for Chris Burt to accept the fact that Paul's brother and sister hated it there and had left as soon as they could. He knew that Paul's brother worked in a factory somewhere and that Paul thought David was a real loser and a dweeb.

As for the sister, all Chris knew was she had moved way up north to some godforsaken place, as far away from Sir Raymond Drive and that woman in the basement as possible.

Chris's understanding was that Paul stayed because it was really the only way he could get his education and get a stake. Chris felt sorry for Paul. He had no idea how the guy could take it. Whenever Chris had been over there, the old man never said a word, he just stared at him. He was pretty strict with Paul, because he seemed to want Paul to do well too. But the mother was always nit-picking. Whenever Chris called, he could hear her caterwauling in the background. No wonder Paul never liked to talk on the telephone.

Paul finished high school in 1982 and his parents separated. Marilyn moved into a bachelor apartment in Kitchener. She didn't bother to furnish it. She just put a mattress on the floor. She told Paul that it was all about trying to understand her roots, getting to know her birth sisters, Claudia and Diane.

In her diary, Marilyn noted that Ken was down most weekends. She maintained the apartment for a year, but neither of her sisters, Claudia and Diane, had any idea about why they'd been put up for adoption.

Jennifer Galligan met Paul Bernardo on a double date. She was with Steve Smirnis and he was with Diane Wiedman. She was fifteen or sixteen at the time and Paul was twenty-two, tall, blond, blue-eyed—Jennifer thought he was really good-looking. After they became "boyfriend/girlfriend" they always celebrated the date of their meeting, on August 15, 1986, as their anniversary.

Jennifer had luxuriant, thick, dark hair. Otherwise, she thought little of herself. Jennifer had been adopted, like Paul's mother. Her parents were devout Catholics. To Paul, she seemed guilt-ridden, obsessed with the Blessed Virgin Mary and neurotic. In other words, perfect for him.

Paul had some unusual characteristics, but Jennifer accepted them. He would twitch and sniff a lot, and he would stare into space for long periods of time for no apparent reason. He would always get sexually aggressive around eleven or midnight and two in the morning. Hunger made him horny; alcohol made him violent. Jennifer felt that Paul really loved and hated her all in one; that he hated himself for being the way he was, but that he was so intrigued by the emotion he felt when he did things to her—when he hurt and humiliated her—that he was addicted to it. He seemed to genuinely like it when she cried out, so she learned how and when to do it.

Like Nancy MacEwan, Jennifer Galligan really wondered about Paul's relationship with the Smirnis brothers. She thought that Paul wanted to be heterosexual, but that he had real homosexual tendencies. Paul and Van and Steve were always joking around, pushing themselves up against one another.

Part of Jennifer's bewilderment came from Paul's strong preference for anal sex. After he took her virginity, he only ever really wanted to do it from behind. That and shove wine bottles into her. She let him do it because she loved him, and because he seemed to get such a thrill out of it.

CHAPTER

six

There was blood on the glass, on the frame that was ripped out and on the two punched-in panels. There was even blood on the kitchen windows. There was blood everywhere. Jennifer could smell it. The smell of blood made Jennifer sick. Whoever it was had just started banging on the door really hard. When that person kept pounding, harder and harder, Paul got weird and Jennifer started to cry.

"Don't fuckin' cry," he hissed. "What the fuck are you crying about?"

They had been down in the family room. It was Monday night, September 28, 1987, the day Paul started his big, new job at the accounting firm of Price Waterhouse. He had just come back from a weekend in Texas, where Steve Smirnis had married some girl named Bev from Fort Worth. Jennifer had stopped by to see Paul because she loved him, but things had not been going very well. She was studying nursing and she had brought along her psychology books. Paul said psychology was a good subject for her. Since she was "so fucked up," she could study herself. Insults were not new to Jennifer. They had been going out for just over three years.

When the pounding on the door first started, Jennifer was studying and Paul was sleeping on the couch. Paul went straight up in the air, as if he had been jabbed with a needle, and then he landed on all fours beside the couch. He scrambled over to the stairs and peered up at the front door.

"Oh fuck, fuck," he exclaimed. "She's seen your fucking shoes . . ." Jennifer's shoes were on the landing just inside the front door.

"Come on, get the fuck upstairs," Paul commanded in a hoarse whisper.

Jennifer had no idea what was going on. Why would her shoes make anyone go crazy?

"Don't ask questions," he said, grabbing her arm and dragging her up the stairs into his bedroom.

"Why can't you just answer the door?" Jennifer blubbered.

"I'm not going to fucking answer the door, man. She's too fucking weird." He fixed her with that crazed look of his. "Just shut the fuck up. Another fucking word out of you man, and I'm going to kill you."

And then the person at the door punched her fist right through the two stained-glass panels that bordered the door and cut her hand and arm really badly.

The neighbors called the police, who came and took Lenore away. Jennifer knew about Lenore. She knew her last name was Marcos. She had found pictures of Lenore under Paul's bed.

Lenore was beautiful; a small Filipino girl with jet black hair who had gone to school with Paul and then got a job at the same company.

As far as Jennifer was concerned, Lenore was the last straw. First, there had been the incident at the Halloween dance the previous October 31. She had dressed up in a harem outfit. Because Jennifer had ample breasts and was just dressed in a skimpy little bra thing with pantaloons that came barely above her pubic hair, she did not want all those geek guys ogling her at the Smirnises' house, where she and Paul had gone; she wanted to keep her coat on.

She told Paul she was cold and kept it on.

"I'll show you cold," he said, pulling her coat off and dousing her with a glass of ice water. When she complained, he hit her.

Then there was the time he had tried to strangle her at her graduation. It was at the Harbour Castle Hilton, overlooking the Toronto harbor. Here she was with this really good-looking older guy at her high-school graduation. He had a video camera and everything. Everything was great. Until later, when they went to some deserted place in his car and he put a rope around her neck and made her arch her back. Then he insisted on anal sex and he pulled on the rope. She could barely breathe. Then he got all apologetic and kissy-kissy and lovey-dovey.

Another time he told her to pull down her pants and arch her back and put her bum way up in the air. So she did and he took Polaroid pictures. He told her if she ever left him he would take the pictures and post them on her church bulletin board.

Then there was the trip they took to Florida in August. She wanted to please him and be mature and have a drink and everything, so when he pulled out this ID and gave it to her she was happy. Then he said some girl had loaned it to him.

"Come on, get real—I'm pretty naive, but I'm not stupid," she told him.

Paul said he had actually bought it at a place downtown where you could buy an ID and all sorts of things. Still, something didn't ring true.

.   .   .

To Sheila Blake, young Paul Bernardo was the cream of the crop. Every year the large accounting firm where Sheila worked, Price Waterhouse, recruited a new lot of trainees. Sheila had been the receptionist at the office on Markham Road for more than twenty years and she had seen all kinds come and go.

Sheila talked to Paul all the time. She knew him well enough to know that his home life was troubled. He told her that even though his parents were there he had no one to talk to, so she knew that something wasn't quite right.

Most of Paul's work was in the Scarborough area, but he did have a few clients in Niagara Falls. Craig Munro was Paul's supervisor. Munro was aware of Paul's relationship with "the Chinese," as he called Lenore Marcos. Paul told Munro he had videotaped himself and "the Chinese" having sex. How could he have done that, Munro had asked? Paul said he had the camera propped up on something and Lenore noticed it and Paul told her not to worry, it wasn't turned on. But it was.

Paul was efficient and got his work done quickly. There were no complaints from clients about Paul Bernardo on any level. He hung around with three or four guys who joined the firm at the same time he had: Joe Falzone, Demetrios Voudouris and Rodney Rego, with whom he had gone to university.

Daniel McVicar was a year behind Paul, but worked with him all the time. He was impressed that Bernardo wore Dack shoes, which were very expensive, and had good suits that appeared well made. Daniel knew for certain that one of his shirts was a Ralph Lauren. They were both earning about $28,000 a year at the time.

Paul always carried a comb and a hairbrush in his audit bag and would give Daniel advice about how he should comb his hair. That was irritating. Daniel viewed Paul and his pals, Falzone and Voudouris, with a slightly jaundiced eye. All three of them had difficulty dealing with the female managers and were known collectively as the MCPs or Male Chauvinist Pigs.

To Sheila, Paul was not only good-looking but also outgoing and friendly; he was definitely the kind of guy on whom all the women did double takes, with the exception of a few of the managers. Maybe he was a bit arrogant and chauvinistic at times, but there were all kinds of men like that and very few of them were as full of life as Paul Bernardo.

One of the things Lenore liked about Paul in those days was the fact that he hardly drank at all. When they went out to dinner he would occasionally order a cocktail, but it was usually a light drink, a lady's drink, like a Silver Cloud.

Lenore was thrilled when he bought her a LaSalle watch for her birthday in 1986. That Christmas she went to Baltimore to spend the holidays with relatives and brought back a picture of a boy she met: Paul went berserk and dumped her garbage all over her apartment floor looking for it. He hit her. And she hit him right back. Then he decked her, knocked her right down. After he calmed down, they made up. He gave her a ring.

Early in March, Paul called Lenore and said he wanted to punish her for not being a virgin. If she let him do it, he would forgive her and never bring the subject up again. It was two o'clock in the morning, but Lenore got in her car and drove to meet him at the deserted parking lot in Fairview Mall. Paul spanked her with his belt while she apologized for having had sex with anyone other than him. Later, she recalled that it had not really hurt, but she knew it was strange and she never told anyone, not even her closest friends.

From May through August, Paul and Lenore took university courses together. She was smarter than he was and that bothered him, but they became very close that summer.

In September, they both graduated with bachelor of arts degrees with majors in economics and commerce, from the Scarborough campus of the University of Toronto.

Following in his father's footsteps, Paul enrolled in the program run by the Institute of Chartered Accountants. He and Lenore both got jobs at Price Waterhouse. The world was their oyster.

That's when it really got ugly between them. On a training course instructors had told everyone to meet and mingle, but Paul refused to leave Lenore's side. She had known he was jealous and possessive, but now it was becoming obsessive. Once they went off into a closet for some privacy and he started hitting himself on the head badly enough to leave bruises on his forehead. Lenore thought it was her fault somehow, because he loved her so much. It was starting to drive her crazy.

She thought about breaking off the relationship. She had suspected that he was cheating on her for a long time, but then again she had always hoped she would find somebody like Paul, who loved her and had ambition. He would be hard to replace. She didn't want to make a mistake, so she was somewhat relieved when she found she had not missed him at all while he was away at the wedding in Texas.

On Monday, she just happened to be in his neighborhood. She had gone to a movie with a girlfriend who lived near Sir Raymond, so she thought she would drop over and say hello.

She knew there was another woman in the house immediately because she saw the shoes in the foyer. Now Lenore wanted Paul to face the music. She had accused him many times before of being with this Jennifer woman, and he would always deny it. This time she caught him red-handed. Lenore started banging on the door. There was stained glass, but she did not realize it and she put her hand right through it and needed stitches. The neighbors called the police and it turned out to be the most horrible night of her life.

Then Paul met the woman he would marry, Karla Homolka, in the Howard Johnson's restaurant late in the evening on October 17. It was love at first sight. It was as though they had known each other all their lives.

The following weekend Paul accepted Karla's invitation to come to St. Catharines for a party at her house. They went to a horror film—John Carpenter's *Prince of Darkness*. Afterward while the others partied on, Karla took Paul to her bedroom in the basement. She locked the door and pulled out a pair of handcuffs—real ones—just like his. Paul had never met a girl, ever, who had her own handcuffs.

And then she told him to put them on her, behind her back. She got down on her knees and she told him to lift up her skirt. It was as though she was reading his mind, like she knew exactly what he wanted, what he had to have.

For Paul, this was the clincher. All summer long, his other relationships had been unraveling. They had become so turbulent and unpredictable that he had actually approached and fondled a number of strangers—women he came across Scarborough late at night in May and July. He had not actually raped any of them, just grabbed them and touched them against their will. He had shown them his knife, and they had been scared.

Karla, handcuffed, on her knees and begging for him, was scratching an itch. Paul asked her what she would think if he was a rapist. She would think it was cool. Their love deepened.

He started raping women in earnest.

CHAPTER

seven

A short evening drive into the sunset, the road to St. Catharines from Scarborough took Paul west along the contours of Lake Ontario to Hamilton, where the Queen Elizabeth highway curved south and then east toward Niagara Falls. Twelve miles from the American border, there are three or four exits for the small city. Thus began the ritual. Many a Wednesday night, and every weekend, Paul would drive to St. Catharines to see Karla.

If Paul left Scarborough around 6:00 P.M., depending on traffic and weather, he would arrive in St. Catharines less than two hours later. For the first couple of weekends, Paul went back and forth three and four times between Friday evening and Sunday night.

Despite the Homolkas' imprecations to call them Dorothy and Karel, Paul would only refer to Karla's parents as Mr. and Mrs. H. This boy was polite. Soon Mrs. Homolka saw the foolishness in all that driving back and forth. Dorothy was as enthralled as her daughter with this polite, slightly older, well-to-do, educated, beautiful young man with a good job.

Paul was older—twenty-three to Karla's seventeen—but he did not act or look it. His round, open face and baby blue eyes gave him a boyish, innocent aura. Very quickly, Paul Bernardo became the Homolkas' "weekend son."

When Paul was not at the Homolka house at 61 Dundonald, Karla was writing him cards and letters. The barrage began with a three-page letter on October 27, ten days after they met, and continued unabated for nearly six years. Even after they moved in together and married, Karla would write him little "pillow notes" almost daily.

On November 6, 1987 she presented him with a card featuring three little pigs, inviting him to "call me any time." It revealed something about the lovers' early banter: "To my prince, Love, from your princess."

Paul responded with flowers. She persisted with more and more cards. One, on November 13, featured two cartoon characters in bed and two other characters peering at them through a window: "Roses are red, violets are blue, There's nothing more fun than a pervert like you."

A week later, on the afternoon of November 19, 1987, Jennifer Galligan accompanied Mr. and Mrs. Bernardo to Paul's graduation at the downtown campus of the University of Toronto. Jennifer wore her purple coat. She was really curious to see Lenore Marcos: even though she had seen her blood, she had never laid eyes on her.

After the ceremony and the cheek-kissing congratulations, she and Paul rendezvoused at the Ramada Renaissance Hotel. They had a few black russians. Paul was testy, accusing her of going with other boys. People were looking at them because he was almost yelling at her about how she wandered around letting other men stick their "salamis" in her. Jennifer was dumbfounded. She tried to ignore it and gave him his graduation present—a Brookdale sweater. She told him that she thought it looked "very professional."

"Is this all you got me?" he exclaimed. "I fucking graduate for you and this is all you got me?" Then he stood up and proclaimed, "This one's a real slut . . ." to the entire lounge.

At closing time, Paul walked off, stranding her. When she went looking for the telephone to call her father, she saw him out in the parking lot wildly driving in circles, "doing doughnuts" in his white Capri. She walked over to the car and he seemed to calm down. He agreed that their relationship was over but insisted he should do the honorable thing and drive her home.

After locking the doors and making sure Jennifer had her seatbelt fastened, Paul started grabbing her hair and hitting her at every stoplight. Days later, she still carried an imprint of his fist on her back.

Instead of driving Jennifer home, Paul went to the deserted factory parking lot where they used to park all the time. By then her head ached and her face was a mess. He pulled out his knife, held it to her throat and told her he was going to kill her. Jennifer bolted, but the black russians caught up with her and she tripped on a curb. She finally got away, but only because he dropped his knife between the seats and could not find it. She ran into the ravine and got lost in the woods.

The following evening Paul was in St. Catharines. When he left, Karla gave him another greeting card—this one featuring a cartoon sex maniac with a woman on her hands and knees. "I like that in a man . . ." it read. "Thanks for making me so happy. Love Karla," wrote Karla.

On November 27, Paul sent Karla a rare card featuring the stylized face of a geisha. It said, "Fantasies can come true, even for you and me." Karla was his shelter from the gathering storm.

Karla sent him pictures of herself at age seven, one with a parrot and another with a puppy. Over the next two weeks, the cards and letters kept coming: "Paul—I love you. Please don't stop loving me . . . Tomorrow . . . and forever, I love you. . . . Don't rip off all my clothes and ravish me like a beast for a solid hour. Do it all night. Now, I love you." And "Take it . . . don't break it. Don't you forget it. I love you (I'm running out of original things to say). . . . Please remember always—I love you. Hugs and kisses."

On December 12, Karla took the train to Toronto and went to the Price Waterhouse Christmas party with Paul. It was held at the same Howard Johnson's where they had met less than two months earlier. For old times' sake, they had sex in a stairwell. There were many pictures taken that evening. Karla and Paul looked like a debutante and her date at the ball. Paul and Karla looked so young that one of the senior partners wondered out loud who had brought their children?

In a letter dated December 8, Karla told him she had bought him some gloves but could not find black leather Isotoners anywhere.

And then, on December 15, Paul received a strange, undecipherable message: "All men are not alike. . . . You are so special you mean so much to me . . . , Amo Nunguamobliviscar," which he interpreted as her wholehearted blessing.

On Wednesday, December 16, around 10:30 P.M., Paul attacked Libby Ketchum after she left a bus a few blocks from Sir Raymond Drive at Guildwood Parkway and Livingston Road. Libby was five feet four and weighed 105 pounds. She had long brown hair. Suddenly, out of nowhere, Paul blitzed her from behind. Putting his gloved hand over her mouth, he pulled her between two houses and showed her his knife.

"Now if you're smart, you'll shut up. Don't say a word. I'm

not gonna hurt ya," he told her. "I just wanna talk. If you want to see Christmas, just shut up. What's your name?"

She lied and told him her name was Libby Tauton.

"How old are you?" Fifteen, she said.

"What grade are you in?" She told him. Paul pulled her pants off and forced his hand between her legs. She tried to resist. He put a coaxial cable around her neck and tightened it.

"Just let me have my fun," he said. Then for an hour and a half he forced vaginal and anal sex on her, all the while asking questions about her boyfriend.

"How old is he?" he wanted to know when he inserted his penis in her anus for the second time. "Do you do this with him? No. Oh, so we're pretty special, then."

He took it out and forced it back in her vagina. "Does this feel good?" She lied and said yes.

"Do you really mean that? You're a sweetie because you're cooperating with me. What's your name?" Paul asked again.

Looking through Libby's wallet, he found her ID, including her birth certificate with her real name. "Oh, oh, you lied. You're a liar—you said your name was Libby Tauton before."

"I guess I have one or two choices, Libby Tauton or Libby Ketchum. Now, close your eyes. Close your eyes and make sure they're closed tight. Well, just keep them closed. Put my dick in your mouth. Hold it in your hands. Don't bite, because I can't live with that pain. . . ."

Then he stopped to take off her coat, putting it on top of the trailer in her neighbors' driveway. Libby could not fathom what was happening to her. She was only a few doors from her own door, and here they were between two of her neighbors' houses. It was early—well before eleven. Everybody in the neighborhood was probably still awake. "We're not stopping until it happens," he said.

He made her tell him she loved him and told her to call herself a "slut." Then he asked for Christmas greetings.

"Now, tell it you love it. Wish it a Merry Christmas." And Paul flashed the knife, so she looked right at it and wished it a Merry Christmas.

Because she was gagging on his penis, he asked her if she was okay. And then he came in her mouth. "Oh, you're such a sweetie. I'm not gonna hurt you because you cooperated so well and you were a sweetie."

"I don't care if you do tell the police," Paul said.

"I don't care, 'cause I'm not gonna get caught. It'll just humiliate and embarrass you, and your boyfriend won't like it too much. Your friends'll all make fun of you." She said she would tell them anyway.

"Now, put it back," he commanded, referring to his penis. She started to put it back in his pants.

"Not in my pants, silly, in your mouth. You're funny, oh, you're really funny. Now lick it!"

Before Paul left, he told her to get under the trailer.

"You should stay there for at least twenty seconds. Okay. Don't start yet. Count slowly."

When Libby looked out from under the trailer he had vanished.

The next day Detective Constable Steve Irwin paid a visit to Inspector Joe Wolfe at 43 Division. There are a dozen Metropolitan Police stations throughout Toronto, and Wolfe was head of 43 Division in Scarborough. Wolfe was a middleweight who resembled Jake LaMotta the way DeNiro played him in *Raging Bull,* in his middle years, after Jake retired from the ring, moved to Miami and opened a nightclub.

Wolfe had known Steve's father. Mike Irwin had been gunned down in 1972. He and his partner had answered a domestic in the Toronto suburb of Don Mills one night in February. When they got there, the guy came out with a shotgun and blasted both of them. Mike held on for a couple of days before he died. Steve was only eleven at the time. The fact that he still carried his father's badge—number 4413—told Wolfe all he needed to know about the kid. He was sentimental and obsessive.

Irwin had been assigned to assist homicide with the Margaret McWilliam murder in Warden Woods on August 15. McWilliam had been jogging in Warden Woods, a park halfway between Guildwood Village and the Scarborough campus of the University of Toronto, when she was pulled into the bushes, raped and killed.

It didn't appear that she had been meant to die, that her murder was part of the sex crime. The investigators had concluded she was probably killed accidentally during the struggle.

The violence and intensity of Libby Ketchum's rape gave Constable Irwin pause. He thought there might be some connection between McWilliam, Libby Ketchum and three assaults that had occurred in May and July in the same general area.

Wolfe agreed there could be a connection between the three in the summer and Libby Ketchum, but not with the McWilliam murder. Serial rapists are rare and usually much more sophisticated than the casual or opportunistic rapist—they are invariably acting out some kind of strange, private fantasy, so the details of their crimes are distinctive.

The earlier assaults—on May 4, May 14 and July 27—were naive but violent. The women had all just left buses, they were accosted from behind, the guy had been rough but he did not really "rape" them. He had fondled them sexually, penetrating the last one with his fingers.

The recent attack on Libby Ketchum was one of the most obsessive and extensive outdoor rapes in Wolfe's long career. Nevertheless, it had a lot in common with the previous three— the descriptions of a well-groomed young man who had good teeth and did not smell bad. The rapist talked all the time he was assaulting his victims, and he wanted to hear certain, specific things. All of the attacks had occurred within a short radius of Scarborough's Guildwood Village.

Location was one of the big differences between the attacks and the murder. The attacks occurred in heavily populated areas, usually on the streets where the women lived. In the esoterica of serial sexual crime, location was everything. It had significance for the rapist, particularly if it increased the chances he would be caught.

Irwin was not persuaded. As the years went by, his skepticism about Wolfe's assessment would deepen. Unfortunately it would not help him solve any of the crimes, only cause him to become more cynical. Steve would have been about twenty-seven when he first went to see Wolfe. It was ironic. The guy they were looking for was probably a guy who looked much like Constable Irwin—clean-cut—and just about the same age.

That same day, Karla sent Paul two cards, because it was their "second anniversary." One said, "Happy 2 month Anniversary, Love Karla," and the other, "It's been the best 2 months ever. You're my prince. I love you. Karla."

Two days before Christmas, Mary Booth got off the bus at Lawrence and Bathgate at 12:50 A.M.

Tall—five foot eight, with long blond hair, Mary gave Wolfe pause because she was considerably larger than the last four victims—she weighed around 150 pounds. The literature said location came first, and then the serial rapist haunted his pre-ferred locations and waited for the right woman. The other victims had all been short and slight, with long, dark hair.

Paul scripted Mary exactly the way he had Libby. The se-quence of events was the same: vaginal penetration, then anal penetration, back and forth a couple of times; then he per-formed cunnilingus and made her fellate him.

She was forced to repeat, over and over again: "I'm a bitch, I'm a cunt, Merry Christmas, I love you, Merry Christmas. This is my present to you. I'm doing this because I hate my boyfriend."

He had a knife and he talked the talk: "If you open your mouth, I'm gonna slit your throat. If you scream, I'll slit your throat. Shut up. Shut up or I'll kill you. Bitch. Slut. If you scream, I'll put a scar on your face. What's your name. What school do you go to?"

"If I read about this in the newspaper or if I hear rumors about it, even if it's in the air, I'm gonna come back and I'm gonna rape you and kill you, cuz I know where you live, cuz I have all your ID."

They were in a backyard, two blocks from Sir Raymond

Drive. Mary Booth gave the police an excellent description—white, six foot, 180 pounds, light brown, blondish, collar-length hair, clean shaven with a small mole under a slightly crooked nose, smelled good, no accent, no scars or tattoos. She even noticed he was circumcised.

He was wearing a gold ring with three diamonds on his right hand and possibly a school ring on his other—it had a red stone. He drove a white Capri, and carried a stiletto knife in a dark leather case.

The composite they developed from Mary's description in early January was a dead ringer for Paul Bernardo.

The powers that be decided not to publish it. Composites published in the newspapers can be more hindrance than help. First of all, they signal the press and the public that their law-enforcement professionals are stumped.

Every mother, sister, wife and girlfriend comes out of the woodwork and proclaims her son, brother, husband or lover a rapist. The police quickly fall into a psychological maelstrom of collective innuendo, vendetta and resentment from whence they begin to spin out in ever-widening circles.

All the police really had at this point were two serious sexual assaults, very close together, in a specific confined area. The perpetrator was distinctive—how many boys next door were serial rapists? There was a little pressure—naturally the press was on them—but Wolfe had seen much worse. The press had not made any connection between the assaults and McWilliam's murder. The guy would make a mistake. They would catch him.

For Christmas, Paul gave Karla a $300 dress, a gold necklace and an expensive Gund teddy bear she called Bunky.

Paul got a hand-printed gift certificate: "Upon presentation of this coupon, Karla Leanne Homolka will perform sick, per-verted acts upon Paul Kenneth Bernardo. These acts may be chosen by the recipient of the coupon. This coupon expires January 2, 1988. Love, Karla."

•   •   •

Once Jennifer Galligan started talking, her words quickly became a torrent. Sergeant Kevin McNiff's daughter had asked him to talk to her friend. McNiff worked on the Toronto Island, out of 52 Division. He was a decade off pension, biding his time with righteous, consistent service to his community. Sergeant McNiff met Jennifer in a McDonald's just after New Year's, 1988.

"I was crying and he said, 'Fuckin' stop cryin, you fuckin' bitch. You're givin' me a headache,' and then he'd hit me again, and then he took me to a place where he used to take me to do it behind this factory building, and I could show you the place . . . I mean, I know exactly where it is. And he took me there and he was going to kill me, and at one point he pushed me back and he tried to rape me. He tried to, like, do it again with me, and I'm saying, 'No, I want to get away, I wanna leave,' and he goes, 'Oh, yeah, I'll make you leave,' and he grabbed me by my hair. He pulled my hair and ripped my pantyhose and he, like, was saying 'I'm going to fuckin' rape you, you fuckin' cunt—now!' And then he was like, hitting me and hitting me again, and he would just hit hit hit and and oh, God, all I remember was he started looking for his knife. 'I'm fuckin' going to kill you,' and he was looking for his knife, and he couldn't find it! . . .'"

Jennifer spewed huge chunks of monologue. Sergeant McNiff could barely look at her. All he had been told was that Jennifer had a problem with her ex-boyfriend. They were sitting in a McDonald's. McNiff was trying to sip his coffee, but the furious pace necessary for taking notes mitigated even a sip. The weirdest thing was that when Jennifer spoke her face contorted and it was as if she were playing two roles—hers and this Paul Bernardo person's.

"I just took off like wild thunder. I never ran so fast in my life and I got away and I ran and I ran and I ran, and . . . he's going, 'You fuckin slut.' I remember him standing outside the car and he's going, 'You fuckin slut.' He goes, 'Fuck, I'm going to come after you and when I do you're dead.' And I ran through the forest, and he obviously didn't wanna run through the forest. And I remember there were burrs in my hair, there were burrs in my pantyhose, there were burrs on my coat. . . .

"I remember running up a hill," she said, stammering at the end. "I went into a trance where I saw myself standing at the top of the hill saying, 'You can do it, c'mon.'" Jennifer knew the person at the hilltop was not herself. She thought it was Mary, and drew enough strength from the Blessed Virgin to keep going until she made it to a girlfriend's house. She fell asleep on the sofa, her head pounding. No one called the police.

Shortly afterward Paul tried to see Jennifer, but her father told him to stay away or face big trouble. Jennifer was afraid. Paul knew her school schedule, knew that she always ran a bit late. He started calling her at home, offering to propose to her and give her a big diamond ring. He had always told her that an accountant and a nurse would make a good pair.

Somewhere between her father's noisy indignation and her own fear, Jennifer slipped away from Paul, but she was always looking over her shoulder.

When she finally stopped talking, the sergeant was speechless. The restaurant seemed to fall silent. Gathering his resources, McNiff asked her what exactly she wanted him to do. His "You will want to press charges . . ." was more a statement of fact than a question.

But she said no. She just wanted her money back. Paul owed her a lot of money; more than two thousand dollars. He had given her part of it back in cash, but then he gave her some checks and they started bouncing. She just wanted the money.

There was not much Sergeant McNiff could do about Jennifer's money, and if she would not file charges, what could he do? What he did do, though, because he was so disturbed by what she had told him, was go back to the station, run a check on this creep, write up a supplementary report and pass it on to the detectives investigating the two bizarre rapes that had happened the previous month right around where Paul Bernardo lived.

He found that Bernardo had been written up three times

before: each time Jennifer had been involved. There had been two assaults—one on March 4 and the other on July 26, 1986. The complainant was Jennifer Galligan. Bernardo was never charged. There was a "mischief under" on September 29, 1987, which involved Jennifer and another woman named Lenore Marcos, but again nothing had come of it. This guy had horseshoes up his ass.

Sergeant McNiff knew there was something wrong. There was too much coincidence. For instance, the girl who had been raped on December 23 said her assailant drove a white Capri. Bernardo drove a white Capri. McNiff made out a five-page report, dated it January 5, 1987, instead of January 5, 1988—an honest mistake—and it got misfiled.

Two days later, Karla sent Paul a three-page letter of apology. She had admitted to him that she was not a virgin when they met, and the news had not sat well. "I'm so sorry for what I've done," she wrote. "Hearing you say 'I don't love you' was one of the worst moments in my life . . . I guess I really screwed things up."

Karla did not understand Paul's obsession with virginity; after all, he had not been one when they met. "If you find your virgin," she added, "there will be something wrong with her."

Forgiveness came quickly. Within the week she was writing him another note and calling him her "fantasy."

"You're the best, you big, bad businessman, you," she printed neatly. They had both been to see the Oliver Stone movie *Wall Street,* and she knew that Paul was enthralled with the ruthless stock-dealing Gordon Gekko character played by Michael Douglas. To Paul, Gekko was godlike, as much for his cliché-ridden pronouncements as for his wealth and cutthroat attitude. Gekkoisms sprouted on his bedroom wall, which was covered with inspirational-type quotations. "In my game, you either do it right or you're eliminated," was the one Karla was aspiring toward.

·   ·   ·

On his way back from St. Catharines one night, Paul encountered Jean Baxter. Jean was five foot eleven, lithe with long brown hair. She was walking along a quiet suburban street in the late evening. Before Paul dragged her into the yard behind a nearby house he asked her if she knew "where Port Dalhousie was?" She was standoffish, ignored him and walked on.

He overwhelmed her. Jean tried to fight. Paul had to use significant force to subdue her, tying her wrists with her own belt. He slapped her hard; she welted up badly afterward. Paul had a script. "Say, 'I'm a little slut. I like this. I love you,' " he demanded, so she finally did, while he raped her vaginally and anally.

Jean gave the Peel Regional Police a resonant description: white, around eighteen years old, between five foot nine and five foot eleven, muscular build, blond, wavy hair, blue eyes, no accent, clean shaven, wearing a black leather jacket, blue and yellow shorts and a white T-shirt.

They quickly developed a composite that looked exactly like Paul Bernardo, and then they arrested a courier. Bloodwork cleared the courier within a few weeks. When the press asked, the police departments said this rape had absolutely nothing to do with the Scarborough rapes. How could it? It had happened in Peel Region, near Johnson's Lane and the Lakeshore in Clarkson, halfway between Scarborough and St. Catharines.

Location had become everything.

Paul and Karla's love deepened. They often had sex in his car at Lake Gibson, just off Beaverdams Road. Karla's style of dress became more sophisticated. Gone were the leotards and boxer shorts. No more perms, her hair became blonder.

On Valentine's Day, Karla gave him a coupon entitling the bearer to "receive one cute, little, blond seventeen-year-old girl to put on her knees between his legs, to pleasure him as he has never been pleasured before."

In the spring, she bought a studded dog collar and wore it for him. She even found a greeting card to go with it, saying: "Sticks and stones may break my bones/but whips and chains excite me/only you know how much." Obviously, certain things were on Karla's mind. She started calling his penis Snuffles, and happily noted: "I love it when you shoot in my mouth."

For her birthday on May 4, Paul gave her a ring. She told the Diamond Club girls she was promised and flashed the evidence.

In Karla's high-school yearbook her FM—favorite memory—was listed as, "Camping, August 1988."

"Camping" was a euphemism for a ten-day trip she and Paul took to see the Mouse at Walt Disney World in Florida. She lied to her parents and told them they were going to Paul's grandparents' cottage on Georgian Bay.

It was on this trip that Paul made his first video featuring Karla. In their hotel room at the Marriott they cavorted, half naked, hamming it up for the camera, wearing those famous mouse-ear hats with their names embossed on the foreheads. They look exactly like what they were—Ken and Barbie on summer vacation at Disney World.

That was the summer ninety-year-old Frank Bernardo passed away. Ironically, Marilyn and Ken decided to take an Italian vacation to honor his memory. Left alone at 21 Sir Raymond, Paul became inspired and took a series of Polaroids. Karla rather liked the idea of defiling Paul's mother's house, especially since Marilyn had called her a "slut" the first time they met.

In one picture, Karla is laid back, arms above her head, spread-eagled, grinning from ear to ear with her nipples and genitalia covered in whipping cream. Sixteen pornographic Polaroids in all, they ran the gamut from genital close-ups to squeeze-the-nipple shots. She raised her arms with handcuffs on and smiled through her gag. In another, she knelt with her rear end raised and her cuffed hands behind her head.

With a timing device, Paul managed to capture both of them in a variety of sex acts, from a rear entry to fellatio. Unlike Jennifer Galligan, Karla did not have to be coerced. She happily inserted the wine bottle wherever Paul told her to.

CHAPTER

eight

The bedside clock said 4:30 A.M. For a cop early morning calls were never good news. There had been another rape. The victim was at Scarborough Grace Hospital. The guy had a knife. He had told her he was the Scarborough Rapist and the description fit. It was Thursday, August 15, 1989.

Wolfe had recently assigned Steve Irwin to a task force he had formed to solve the Scarborough rapes. This was the first occurrence since Irwin had been seconded to the task force.

Irwin called the two uniformed police officers who had been first on the scene. It had happened on Packard Boulevard, another quiet, well-populated suburban street in Scarborough. The victim was just off a bus and was walking home around 1 A.M. Four doors away from her own house, the guy had grabbed her from behind and pulled her up between two houses. It was the same modus operandi. First the vagina, then the anus, then the vagina, then the anus and some fellatio. This maniac was nothing, if not consistent.

When Irwin got there Joe Wolfe was already at the scene, waiting for him. Since he and Wolfe had first met in December, 1987, there had been nine more assaults, bringing the total number of rapes allegedly committed by the same man to eleven.

Detective Irwin had first seen Wolfe on December 17, 1987. Shortly after that meeting—which had more to do with Margaret McWilliam's murder than the Scarborough rapist—Wolfe had been promoted to acting staff superintendent.

In 1988, it had started in April. On April 10, the rapist attacked Norma Keenan. Just off the bus at Clementine Square, Norma had long brown hair. The rapist made her repeat, over and over again, "I love you."

Wolfe supposed that there was some kind of voodoo seasonal force at work—the perpetrator seemed to strike in the early spring and summer, then right around Christmas time. In 1988 there had been an occurrence in May, but Wolfe refused to believe the rape in Clarkson was related to those in Scarborough. Then there was Helen Moore on Dundalk Drive in October and Shannon Ellis on Allanford Road in November, and, just after Christmas, on December 27, Linda Cowan on Weir Crescent.

Then nothing for six months. Long sojourns between attacks confused the police. When a serial rapist stopped it could only mean one of three things: he had died, he had moved away, or perhaps been arrested on another beef.

Alas, the Scarborough rapist came back to life on June 20, 1989, when he raped Lydia Davidson at 15 Sonneck Square in Scarborough. Always in the back of Steve Irwin's mind was the steadfast notion that whoever was committing these horrific rapes had also killed Margaret McWilliam.

Irwin had been very young when he was assigned to what was called the Warden Woods Jogger Case. He had probably been assigned because of his previous work on the Alison Parrott case.

Alison, an athletic, intelligent, green-eyed eleven-year-old had been lured to a busy location in downtown Toronto and abducted in broad daylight. Her body was found on July 27, 1986, in Kings Mill Park, at Toronto's western edge. The killer had carried her body into the park and placed it, in a contorted, grotesque position, in a wooded area close to a well-traveled road.

Irwin identified with eleven-year-old Alison. Irwin's father, Mike, had been killed when he was eleven and Irwin had a vivid memory of that period of his life. Perhaps as a consequence, he had developed an almost familial bond with Alison's mother.

Every year, on the anniversary of Alison's death, Irwin called Lesley Parrott and talked to her. He kept her apprised of things. They had become friends, if you could use such a term for two people brought together by such a tragedy. It might have been this quality that endeared him to his superiors. This was the age of science and the sensitive cop.

Steve Irwin believed, rightly or wrongly, that the more personal he got about his work, the better he performed. As an investigator, he saw himself as a miner for details; details in people's memories that had to be excavated in person, at the source. He firmly believed Einstein's maxim that God lived in the details. There was no detail too small or insignificant not to be important.

Although much curtailed, both the Parrott and McWilliam investigations remained open, in part because Irwin was so tenacious. The mystery of the two violent deaths haunted him, as did the memory of his father. He could hardly think about either of the two young women or about his father without tears welling up in his eyes.

His father had not died the night he was shot—February 27,

1972. The following day eleven-year-old Steve listened to the radio for reports about his father's condition, hoping against hope that he would be all right. His mother and uncle were standing watch at the hospital. The radio kept playing "Bye, bye, Miss American Pie, drove my Chevy to the levy, but the levy was dry . . ." and Neil Young's "A Horse with No Name," over and over again. Then Mike Irwin died.

Steve Irwin felt betrayed and cheated by his father's sudden, violent death. He wanted to know his father much better than he had. He fell into a kind of lockstep with his father's reso-nating footsteps, as if, through his own life, his father would become manifest, and the son would finally see, and know, what his father had seen and known. His father had a thing for birds of prey. Steve Irwin became a falconer. He had two birds—a red-tailed hawk and a peregrine falcon. He also had two small children. His father had certain interests and values. Irwin adopted them. Eventually, he had a third child, just as his father had done before him. Then his marriage fell apart. That was not supposed to happen.

Steve Irwin remembered that he and his brother had gone to the dilapidated apartment building where his father had been shot. Their mother had not wanted them to go, but they went anyway. Where his father had fallen, there was a large blood-stain. Steve just kept staring at it, as if, in the bloodstain he might see something that he would recognize. In a way, he was still staring at that dark stain, trying to see the murderous figure in the carpet.

Lightheartedly, Suzanne Brand said, "I saw you lurking at the bus stop last night, Paul. You must be the Scarborough rapist."

"You should not accuse someone of that," he shot back.

They had both worked at Price Waterhouse since 1987, and it was not really that big an office. Suzanne did not have any-thing against Paul Bernardo, she just did not particularly like his macho type or his condescending attitude toward women. Some women might like it—such as that blond bimbo he'd brought to the Christmas party—but not Ms. Brand.

She had been driving home from her husband's hockey game around midnight when she recognized Paul sitting in his car parked against the curb at the corner of Morningside and Lawrence. She had not really thought about that scene—Paul in his car just sitting at a bus stop—until his image coalesced with a story about the Scarborough rapist in the morning paper. When she had seen him at the bus stop, Paul was staring so intently into the bus shelter that he did not see her when she pulled up right beside him and waved. It was the intensity of his oblivious staring that unsettled her.

The Packard Boulevard assault was particularly brutal. Detective Irwin had arrived at 5:30 A.M. The scene was otherworldly. The emergency task force had lit the area with high-powered spots, which made it look more like the set for a TV movie than a crime scene. The cars were in the driveways, the shrubberies and lawns were dew-laden. They glistened and sparkled in the spotlights. Outside the well-lit areas, dawn was just beginning to break. The radio was calling for thunderstorms.

They had placed yellow ribbon around the victim's house, four doors away from where the rape had actually taken place. Cathy Thompson's ordeal had lasted for an hour and a half. She had been gagged with her own sweater and left tied at the wrists, with twine that looped around her neck so that it would tighten and strangle her if she struggled.

"Such a pretty face. It would be a shame if you have a bunch of scars . . ." he had told her, stroking her face with his knife.

He had been gone for several minutes, when she heard a twig break. Out of the dark, he emerged again. He was dressed in black. Then he forced a piece of wood into her vagina and told her he would be watching her, always.

"He told her what she had been doing the night before," Wolfe said to Irwin. "What she had on, while she was reading in bed. What book she was reading. What time she went to the bathroom."

The rapist had taken Cathy's purse—a black leather Jordache clutch, shaped like an envelope. There were some family photos, a few phone numbers written on a piece of cardboard in a red Jordache wallet containing her bank card, her social insurance card, her Simon Fraser University student card, her British Columbia birth certificate and driver's license and Fitness Well membership card. There was three dollars in cash in the wallet.

There was also a mini flashlight, a ladies' gold-colored ring, a set of keys on a gold-colored band, licorice candy, a cream-colored hair pick, a calculator and a packed makeup bag. Wolfe looked at Irwin.

"Amazing how much stuff women can get in a purse."

Some of the uniformed officers were given the list and told to look in all garbage cans in the immediate vicinity. They started interviewing neighbors around quarter to eight. The guys working the city garbage truck were told about the incident and given the list of stuff from the purse and told to watch for it.

Around 8:15 A.M. Irwin drove to 41 Division. No sooner did he get there than he was called back to the scene. They had found footprints in a neighboring backyard. They called the I-dent unit to take impressions and photographs.

Irwin got talking to one of the neighbors, who told him her daughter Erin, a twenty-four-year-old nurse, had also been stalked and approached. Since the papers had begun reporting on the Scarborough rapist, they got a lot of this type of thing. He was quickly becoming a dark, mythic figure, with a life of his own. Apparently, this man had told Erin he would "get her." Irwin promised Erin's mother he would follow up.

Just after noon there was thunder and lightning. One bolt struck the CN Tower and it rained like hell.

"I live for the weekend. It's like I'm dead during the week," Karla told a friend.

During her final year of high school she had applied for and been accepted at both the University of Toronto and York University, but she decided not to pursue a higher education and continued working at the Number One Pet Center.

According to her school yearbook, Karla's "wildest dream" was "to marry Paul and see him more than twice a week." When asked to provide a one-line philosophy of life, Karla came up with her own Gekkoism: "People who make excuses never make any money."

With a pocketful of little liquor bottles, Paul escorted Karla to the Sir Winston Churchill senior prom at the legion hall in St. Catharines that fall. Karla's ex-boyfriend was back from Kansas. Paul decided that he was paying too much attention to Karla and said so. That did not sit well with the boys from Winston Churchill.

Karla, no shrinking violet, felt compelled to sucker-punch a male classmate. She hit Greg square in the head with her purse. It was Karla, malingering with Doug, her ex-boyfriend, then decking Greg, that really started the melee. Greg was typical of a certain kind of St. Catharines youth—hockey playing, hard drinking, semiliterate with a penchant for pugilism. When Greg decided to hit Karla back, Paul stepped in, which inspired a few others, including the Hill brothers to a mass attack. They beat the living shit out of Paul and his little dark-haired friend, Mike Donald, who had once been Lori Homolka's boyfriend.

The police were called. They broke up the fight and the prom. Although Paul knew that several of his assailants were the sons of Niagara Regional Police officers, he went to the police station and tried to lay charges. He had not started the fight. He felt aggrieved. He took Mike Donald as an eyewitness.

The cop in charge was a guy named Murphy—his son was one of Paul Bernardo's alleged attackers. Murphy suggested that perhaps they should charge Karla for sucker-punching her pugilistically inclined classmate instead.

Months later, when one of the guys who punched out Paul became a paraplegic in a car accident, Bernardo reminded Mike Donald about how he had said he would take his revenge—in ways no one would expect, when they were least expecting it. As Gordon Gekko put it in *Wall Street:* "Life all comes down to moments. This is one of them."

·   ·   ·

By September 1989, Steve Irwin was working full-time on the Scarborough rape cases. Part of the job was going around to various stations briefing other cops on the status of the investigation. Irwin had been going through old files and running down dozens of suspects. Late in the fall, he had been partnered with Sergeant John Munro.

Munro's hair was prematurely gray, making him look considerably older than Irwin, who, at twenty-nine, was actually Munro's senior by two years. The pair reviewed files of previous offenders. The literature on this type of offense told them it was unlikely the Scarborough rapist was a repeat offender, but what else did they have to do?

Karla enclosed an amputated puppy tail with her October 19, 1989, letter to her friend Debbie Purdie.

"Just cut right off with nail scissors—NEAT, EH?" she wrote.

Debbie was up north taking animal husbandry at a community college. Karla told Debbie that she had seen two doctors, Linkenheil and Lang, in Toronto for dysplasia of the cervix and Pap smears. Paul helped arrange the appointments. Karla had to go into the hospital for minor surgery. She had no fear of medical procedures, but she was required to abstain from sex for a month. That really disturbed her.

Karla also told Debbie about her new job at a veterinary clinic not far from St. Catharines, where she cleaned kennels, answered phones and held the animals while they were prepared for surgery. Karla was outraged that her boss, Dr. Ker, practically accused her of stealing Ketamine, a sedative used on cats, which affects humans like Angel Dust.

On Tuesday, November 21, 1989, Detective Constable Irwin got another early morning phone call. It was 3:45 A.M. By the time he got to the location on Sheppard Avenue East, Wolfe was already there.

There were footprints in the snow. At 5:40 A.M., Irwin went

to visit the victim's boyfriend, who lived nearby. There were more footprints between his yard and the neighbor's, and still others leading from the boyfriend's basement window through the backyard. The neighbor had gone to bed around midnight and had neither seen nor heard anything.

Kerry Grey was fifteen years old. The boyfriend, who was considerably older, had known Kerry for about three years. They had started to have sex regularly over the past six months. About twice a month, Kerry would sneak in through his basement window around midnight and they would go at it.

The boyfriend told Munro and Irwin he was a locksmith. He and Kerry had made love twice in less than an hour that night. He told them, with a little too much bravado, that afterward she had tried fellating him, but to no avail—he had shot his bolt. The pun was not lost on the detectives. The way the locksmith figured it, at least Kerry was not maimed or dead, so why sweat the details. Irwin was singularly without a sense of humor about all this. The locksmith looked down at his feet.

He and Kerry were not into rough sex—no biting, spanking, not even hickies. She had scratched his back though, so she might have his skin under her nails. As far as he knew, she was on the pill. They did not use condoms. Or lubricants. Because his mother did not approve of Kerry, that's why she snuck in and out. She had left the same way she came in, about one that morning.

At three o'clock Kerry had called him and told him she had been raped beside the Northern Telecom building. The rapist tied her hands, but the knots were no good, so Kerry got loose about thirty seconds after he left. She wanted a shower real bad, Kerry said. When she first called she was still terrified, but she calmed down during the half hour they talked. Kerry went to Scarborough Grace Hospital on her own in a cab.

They suspected the locksmith, but he was too cooperative and cavalier. After a few tests, they quickly determined it was not him.

Meanwhile, the other cops had been interrogating another suspect. By 2:30 that afternoon, Irwin and Munro were at the forensic center submitting the samples. They had a meeting with the scientists. Up until this point, even though they were now on their twelfth or thirteenth serial rape, it had been catch-as-catch-can. They all agreed they should devise some sort of coordinated procedure for handling all Scarborough rape samples.

It was a Wednesday afternoon in early December when Irwin and Munro sat down with Wolfe to discuss the composite drawing that had been developed from Kerry's detailed description of her assailant. They compared this one with the other two that had been prepared in 1988. The composites were very similar.

Developing a composite is a kind of Mr. Potato Head game. Facial features and head shapes are finite and lend themselves to a classification. In the 1880s, Alphonse Bertillon, widely considered the father of scientific detection, developed an identification system called Portrait Parle. The Portrait Parle was a kind of smorgasbord of distinctive facial features lifted from photographs, with accompanying sets of written captions.

It was the basis for all modern systems. Even with computers, a similar coding to Bertillon's is applied to imaging. It is the combinations that made the number of compositions almost infinite.

Most law-enforcement agencies, including the Metro Toronto Police, use the FBI's facial-identification catalog. Noses are average or concave or hooked, the nostrils flared or not and the eyes—close . . . far apart? Is the face oval, round, triangular, long or rectangular? What is the hair color and style, and what about the chin and the shape of the head? Within the system there are many choices, but they are finite.

A face does not have a semantic meaning, but it may trigger important associations to a friend or celebrity. Victims and witnesses often talk in terms of likeability, honesty, homeliness, openness or attractiveness.

Previous victims of the Scarborough rapist had picked out suspects from photo lineups, and the detectives discussed their resemblance to those of the composites. They decided to circulate a bulletin that would include the latest composite internally—there were approximately eight thousand Metropolitan Toronto Police personnel. Again, the decision was taken not to go public.

In December, Karla left her job at the Thorold Veterinary Clinic in the midst of the Ketamine controversy and immediately got another at the Martindale Animal Clinic—this time as a health technician. The Clinic was in a little strip mall on Welland Avenue in St. Catharines. Her duties included assisting the vets with surgery, preparing animals for surgery, administering medication and controlling the drug registry. The hours were 8:30 A.M. to 5:30 P.M. and her take-home pay was approximately $215 per week.

Paul decided to quit his job at Price Waterhouse and propose to Karla. He had worked there since September, 1987, a little over two years, and he did not feel that he had made enough progress or could fully realize his potential with that particular firm. Within hours of quitting, he was on a cigarette run into the United States. On December 8, he crossed the bridge at Lewiston at 4:11 P.M.

On Saturday, December 9, 1989, Paul proposed marriage to Karla at Victoria Village in Niagara Falls. She had always wanted to be a bride. When a Toronto newspaper columnist encouraged his readers to describe about the most romantic moment in their lives, Karla wrote:

"The most romantic moment of my life occurred on December 9th. . . . My wonderful boyfriend of five years—Paul—took me on a romantic walk to the romance capital of the world, Niagara Falls. We walked hand-in-hand alongside the majestic falls. It was a lover's paradise that evening, with red and green Christmas lights all along the falls. Softly falling snow, and other romantic couples strolling in the soft moonlight.

"As we approached the elf-sized Christmas village, Paul told me he had a gift for me. I turned my back at his request. He pulled out a box containing a glass unicorn music box. Perched across the unicorn's horn was a perfect diamond ring. As we waited for some noisy children to leave, he whispered words of love in my ear and hugged me tightly in an effort to keep us warm—it was very cold and windy. Finally the children left and we were alone outside of the elves' church. . . ." She enclosed a photograph of Paul Bernardo in a camel-hair coat.

Paul also gave her a wedding planner. From that day forward Karla Homolka began making plans in earnest.

In Toronto, the Christmas windows were decorated, and the giant Santa Claus parade down University Avenue had come and gone. Christmas was a very special time for the Scarborough rapist. There had been two rapes right around Christmas in 1987 and two more in 1988. There was no reason to expect this year would be any different.

Detective Irwin could almost "feel" his mounting excitement. The time for a proactive approach was nigh. Why not run a decoy around the areas in Scarborough where the rapist had previously struck, and see if they might not provoke an attack? It was better than sitting on their hands.

On Thursday, December 21, Detective Irwin came back to work around 10 P.M. He went out on patrol with his partner and an attractive female officer named Smith, whom they had enlisted to be the lure.

After about five fruitless hours, Irwin got a call from Staff Sergeant Doug Diplock. A young woman had been attacked in the underground-parking garage of an apartment building at 1580 Sandhurst Circle, about ten miles from Irwin and Munro.

The victim's name was Deneen Chenier. She remembered everything her assailant had said, as if she had a tape-recorder in her head, and she kept repeating it: "Shut up, sit down, undo your pants. Undo them, bitch. Is this your first time? I'm going to teach you a lesson, bitch. Shut the fuck up. Drop the keys. Take it off. I'm gonna be back late in a couple of days. Wait three minutes. I'm gonna watch you, and if you come up by then I'm gonna come back and start stabbing away."

Deneen was sure there was someone else with him, possibly

a woman, with something in her hand like a video camera, but her assertions were discounted because she had been badly beaten. Her left knee was injured, she had lacerations on her face, neck and back, and her rectum and vagina were torn. She was on the verge of hysteria.

There were dozens of cops on the scene by the time Irwin and Munro arrived. They had brought in the dogs. They brought in the I-dent guys. At 9:30 A.M., Irwin went back to the squad room and took a sample from a new suspect to the lab.

In the middle of the night, he was back in Four Division District in Scarborough, because Deneen had picked out a suspect named Sylvester from a photo lineup. She was wrong. It was not Sylvester. On the night of the twenty-third, Irwin went home for Christmas.

Paul and Karla rented the movie *Criminal Law* for Christmas. She just knew Paul would love it. *Criminal Law* was made in 1987 and starred Gary Oldman and Kevin Bacon. It was one of Karla's favorite movies. She had done her big English project on it the previous year.

Criminal Law was about a young, good-looking, wealthy serial rapist and killer named Martin Thiel (pronounced Teale) played by Kevin Bacon. Like Paul, he sexually assaulted young women. Unlike Paul, he then killed them.

The way he does it: first he rapes them and then he stuffs disposable diapers in their mouths. Then he strangles them and lights their genitals on fire to destroy any forensic evidence.

The story is about the interaction between Martin Thiel's young attorney, played by Oldman, and Thiel. The attorney knows his client is guilty, but the two are so wily that Thiel keeps getting off. The attorney is ultimately conscience stricken and betrays solicitor-client privilege.

Like Paul, Martin Thiel came from a "good" family. Like Paul, Thiel hated his mother. Like Paul, he was irrevocably damaged by an incident precipitated by his mother. Like Paul, he was young and good-looking and otherwise functional. Like Paul, he resolved his psychological dissonance by raping women.

For Paul, the killing would come later.

CHAPTER

nine

Goldfarb Shulman Patel and Company, a small, prestigious accounting firm in Toronto, was very impressed by Paul Bernardo. He had had a good track record at Price Waterhouse. He was only one exam away from becoming a chartered accountant. They gave him $34,000 a year to start on January 4, 1990.

Otherwise, Paul's life was chaotic. Things were not going well at home. He could no longer stand the sight of his mother and father. He felt as if the walls in his room, where he had posted all those clichés, had become clichés themselves. He was overextended financially.

On the other hand, things in St. Catharines had never been better. He and Karla had scheduled their wedding for June 29, 1991, organized the church, historic St. Mark's Anglican in Niagara-on-the-Lake, and booked the hall—the very upscale Macleod Room in the Queen's Landing Hotel, an exquisite establishment just a horse-drawn-carriage ride away. They were making plans for a sit-down dinner with over one hundred guests. Thirty-four thousand a year—taxed at source—did not cut it. The wedding alone would cost that much. One day, two months after he started his new job; he stopped. He did not give notice, he just never went back to Goldfarb Shulman.

Paul and his old Price Waterhouse pal Joe Falzone started a worm-picking business. Paul was the brains, Joe was the bank. They bought an old gray, full-sized GMC van from the Auto Trader magazine. It had those big windows on both sides and in the back. Two weeks later, the engine blew and they had to replace it. Already Joe was in for more than two thousand dollars and starting to regret it.

Paul had been very convincing. He told Joe worms were big business. A good worm picker could pick ten thousand worms a night. They wore flashlights on their heads and put the worms in womens' nylon stockings. One stocking held five hundred worms. Working two, three nights a week, a good picker could make a few thousand dollars a month. Crew bosses, like Paul and Joe, running two dozen pickers, stood to make considerably more—for considerably less work.

But that spring it rained almost every night, and you cannot pick worms when it rains. They spent most of their time sitting in McDonald's. One day Paul sold the truck, gave Joe a little of his money back and that was that.

Kerry Grey, the girl who had been raped after she crawled out the locksmith's basement window in November, 1989, called the police after spotting the guy who attacked her; he was in the McDonald's in the Shops on Steeles mall in the Toronto borough of North York. She had seen him on Friday. She knew it was him.

Irwin figured, why not? Why not go on a couple of wild-goose chases? After women were raped, they started seeing their rapists everywhere. Kerry sounded so sure. The police had already submitted over one hundred samples—hair, saliva, even blood in some cases—to the Center for Forensic Science, with no results. They were no further ahead than they had been when Inspector Wolfe had suggested there was a serial rapist at work in Scarborough in 1987.

On Wednesday, April 4, Detective Irwin picked up Kerry Grey at 8:00 A.M. On the way to the mall, she told him she had seen the guy who raped her get into the passenger side of an old gray van. It was full size, with windows all around, and had been parked outside the McDonald's.

The license plate was white with black letters, and one of the letters might have been Z. Irwin wondered why Kerry had not got the number, surely she knew enough to do that, but she hadn't and Irwin kept his own counsel. Kerry was only sixteen. They staked out the mall all day long. Other detectives went back with Kerry, but she never saw the guy or the van again.

After Paul quit Goldfarb Shulman, he applied for unemployment insurance. He had paid in, and now UIC could pay the rent.

Paul had been watching the motivational guru, Tony Robbins. From reading magazines such as *Success,* Paul knew there was more to the motivational-tape business than Tony Robbins. There were thousands of practitioners in the United States. They all said pretty much the same thing—each in his own way. If they could do it, so could he. He would just copy them. He started ordering mail-order motivational tapes.

In the meantime, Paul had been smuggling cigarettes with the Smirnis brothers. Van's parents had moved up north to Sutton—a town on Lake Simcoe about an hour's drive from Toronto. They had a small coffee shop at the corner of Highway 48 and Brown Hill. There, the brothers hooked up with a biker named Patrick Johnnie. Johnnie was a Para-Dice Rider. He could finance and fence whatever Paul and the brothers brought across the border.

Van Smirnis was planning to move to Youngstown, New York, a small town just across the Niagara River overlooking the gorge. Van was going to open a video store with his brother Steve. Smokin' Joe's, the Indians' massive cigarette-and-liquor outlet, was just up the road. The video store would make a good front for their smuggling business.

Paul had Karla and St. Catharines. In fact, it was the Homolkas who had allegedly turned Paul on to smuggling in the first place. Contraband was a way of life in the Niagara region.

The money Paul had been making smuggling cigarettes to supplement his income had rapidly become his income. By the time he quit his day job, Paul was making twice as much counting cigarettes as beans. Everything was starting to fall into place and his world was unfolding as he felt it should.

Karla turned twenty on May 4. She wrote to her friend Debbie Purdie, asking her to be a bridesmaid, and gave her the wedding date. "Paul is great," Karla said. "Our relationship gets better every day. He is going to make the perfect husband."

On the twenty-third Paul filed for personal bankruptcy. Even though he could easily have paid off $25,000 in personal debts he had amassed with proceeds from the smuggled cigarettes, why should he? Because he was behind on his payments, his credit rating had gone to hell.

As an accountant, Paul knew he could go broke with impunity. He would be better off bust. If he paid off his credit cards, his credit rating would stay in the shitter for seven years. The reality was, within six months of being discharged from personal bankruptcy he would have a clean slate and all his credit cards back. In the meantime, he could use Karla's.

He was so happy with the way things were going, he decided to rape Sharon Moon. He saw her get off the bus in Scarborough at two-thirty Saturday morning and walk north on Midland Avenue toward Sheppard Avenue. She was slight, with brown shoulder-length hair. She was perfect. Paul had just come back from visiting the Homolkas in St. Catharines. Irwin had the weekend off.

Paul was wearing a baby blue, hip-length nylon jacket with a zippered pocket, a blue-and-white striped T-shirt, tan-colored walking shorts with a pleated front and white tennis-style running shoes—no socks and no jewelry. He looked casual and cool. He parked the car around the block and walked right up to Sharon and said, "Hello." Then, he pulled out his knife and said, "If you scream, I'll kill you." He slashed her face.

Paul took Sharon to a deserted area at the north end of Agincourt Collegiate. He beat her up a bit, tied her hands and feet with twine and raped her. When Paul finished with her vagina and anus, he forced her to perform fellatio and ejaculated.

During the attack he chatted away: "Oh, I'm just coming home from a party. You notice I have a knife. Shut up, bitch . . . If you try and fuck me up or fuck me over, I'll kill you. Don't you try. Don't you dare even try to fuck me up or fuck me over, bitch. I'll kill you . . . I'm gonna leave and you can do whatever you want. Okay, you can start counting now."

After a few minutes, he came back, something he hadn't done since Detective Irwin's first rape investigation—the one on Packard in 1989. He wanted to fondle Sharon's breasts and squeeze her buttocks.

Then he bit her breasts—something new. "Oh, shit," he said, "I want something to remember you by." And he pulled out a big tuft of her pubic hair—another new thing. He stole her purse and wallet with her identification, a makeup kit and her hair brush.

Like many of the previous victims, Sharon got a good look at him. After hospital staff treated the cut and administered the rape kit at Scarborough Grace, the police took her downtown to the forensic identification unit on College Street. Sharon gave the police artist another good description of Paul Bernardo.

From the task force to which Wolfe had first appointed Irwin the previous year, the police had formed the sexual assault squad, to much hoopla and publicity. There was Robbery, there was Homicide—now there was Sexual Assault. Their offices were on the third floor at 40 College Street.

Irwin's cynicism was deepening. When Wolfe assigned Irwin to the squad, Detective Irwin was told that there would be at least sixteen permanent appointments. But there were only ten. Since the squad had taken on responsibility for all sexual-assault investigations in Toronto, there were not nearly enough bodies.

But Irwin also recognized that the squad's mere formation would have a significant impact on the press and public. Even though the media had not reported half the Scarborough rapes—they had only documented six or seven out of a possible fifteen—the press heralded the squad. One newspaper reporter even called it the "elite" sexual assault squad.

The police strategy was simple. They would tell the press that this victim, Sharon Moon, was the first one to get a good look at her assailant. Before, the guy had always worked from behind and insisted, like the Dennis Hopper character in the movie *Blue Velvet,* that his victims not look at him.

Acknowledging the fact that this composite looked just like the first two or three—and a lot like the one they had made in May, 1988—would be detrimental to the ongoing investigation. It would also cause the many victims needless distress. It would also make the police look incompetent. A computer-generated colored drawing of the Scarborough rapist was published in Toronto newspapers on May 29, 1990, with a telephone number.

A $150,000 reward for information leading to the arrest and conviction of the Scarborough rapist was offered. The phones started ringing.

Gone, but not forgotten, especially by the receptionist at Price Waterhouse. Everyone gathered around Sheila's desk and ooh'd and aah'd as they opened the newspaper. They all said "Who does this look like?" And they all agreed: "Just like Paul Bernardo."

On June 28, 1990, one of the members of the sexual assault squad took a call from an employee at the Royal Bank on the corner of Ellesmere and Neilson Road.

One of the bank's customers was a dead ringer for the picture in the paper. The bank employee had not seen him for a while—at least since the twenty-sixth of May—but when he'd come in the previous day his hair was different than it had been. It was exactly the same as it was in the picture. He looked to be twenty-one, maybe twenty-two years old, but the birthdate he had given the bank said he was born on August 27, 1964. He was a university student, the records said. His name was Paul Kenneth Bernardo and he lived at 21 Sir Raymond Drive.

It was Sunday and Karla's parents were having a pool party. They were running out of booze and their wonderful "weekend son" offered to go across the border and replenish the supply.

Tammy Lyn, Karla's youngest sister, jumped up and down, saying, "I want to go, too. I want to go, too."

The sun had gone down and Paul and Tammy still were not back. Karla was outraged and humiliated. It had been literally hours and hours. She knew what Paul was up to. Karla knew Paul wanted Tammy, because he had told her.

Karla knew Paul was seeing other women, too. She also knew he was raping some of them. Karla could deal with that.

"If you really love me," he had said, "let me do it to Tammy." Karla really loved him. In his request, she saw an opportunity to minimize risk, take control and keep it all in the family.

She helped Paul break the venetian blinds in Tammy's bedroom so he could make videos of Tammy undressing at night. That summer she and Paul had started to have sex in the afternoons on Tammy's waterbed. They found Tammy's dildo in her drawer and Paul used it on Karla while she pretended to be Tammy. She pretended to be Tammy and used it on herself while he masturbated.

One night Karla crushed some Valium tablets and sprinkled

the dust on Tammy's spaghetti. Later that night, after Tammy had fallen into a stupor, Karla watched from the bedroom doorway while Paul masturbated beside Tammy's head and ejaculated on her pillow. When he tried to actually have sex with Tammy, Tammy stirred and he had to stop. Karla knew that had not made him happy. While he fantasized that Tammy had really been awake and watched him while he had masturbated, Karla gave Paul a blow job.

Waiting for Paul and Tammy, Karla was drinking white wine like water, and with every gulp she just got madder. She was pacing back and forth in the driveway at Dundonald. Tammy had become her parents' favorite child, always getting little extras. Karla had heard her asking Paul who was better looking? And Paul always said, "Oh, you are Tammy. You are."

When Paul and Tammy left, it had been the middle of the afternoon. Now it was the middle of the night. All their visitors had left and Karla's parents had gone to bed. Finally, close to midnight, Paul and Tammy pulled into the driveway.

It was certainly not supposed to happen this way. It was humiliating and embarrassing. It was very important that Karla regain control of the situation. Now she had two big things to plan: her wedding and her sister's rape.

CHAPTER

ten

"Wake up, Tammy, wake up. There's someone in the doorway." Tricia was frantic. It was the middle of the night. Patricia Garcia was sleeping over at the Homolkas' one last time before school started. She was in that strange twilight zone between waking and sleeping and was sure there was somebody lurking in Tammy's doorway. The door was only slightly ajar, but it was the moving shadow that scared her. Tricia thought it might be Paul Bernardo.

When Paul was at the Homolkas', he supposedly slept on the couch outside Karla's basement bedroom. Many of Tammy's girlfriends—Patricia Coyle and Norma Tellier, for instance—thought Paul was really great.

They thought, "Oh, my God, Karla's so lucky. She has a rich boyfriend with a great car." At first, Tammy really liked him, too. There was even some talk that Tammy had had sex with him that summer. But Tricia was very suspicious of Paul.

He was too generous. All summer long he was always getting them drinks and food and buying them stuff. One day, Tricia and Tammy noticed there was a film and a few white flecks on the top of their Cokes. They just laughed about it and twittered: "Oh, imagine if they were trying to do something to us." When they noticed it again and again, it became less exciting. The girls started dumping the drinks and getting their own. It became a nagging concern, though, because they had no idea what was going on.

One night Norma slept over, too, and the threesome decided to play detective. Most of the time Karla kept her room locked, but that night they found it open. They sneaked in and went through Karla's hope chest. They found a strange bag of white powder.

Now, even Tammy was scared. She called Tricia the next day. What if her sister and Paul were trying to do something to her? It was Tricia's turn to laugh and reassure her. In daylight, it seemed so improbable. Tammy said, "I'm starting to get really scared. I don't understand this. . . ."

When Tricia first went under the covers and woke Tammy up Tammy just laughed. But then she saw the shadow, too. They pulled the covers over themselves and peeked out. Tammy asked Tricia if Paul had slept over that night, but Tricia did not know. By the streetlight she could see whoever it was had on a striped rugby shirt. When they looked again, whoever it was was gone.

Tammy told Tricia to go downstairs and see if Paul's shoes were there. Tricia said, "No, you go." So they both went. Then they saw Paul standing in the Homolkas' kitchen holding one of their Wiltshire knives, and Tammy and Tricia went, "Oh, my

God!'' and ran back to the bedroom and jumped under the covers. They took the phone with them and agreed that if anyone came up the stairs they would phone 911 right away.

They also planned to keep watch, spelling each other every hour on the hour until dawn, but then they fell asleep. The next morning they went down to the family room, where Paul was sleeping on the floor. He was wearing the striped rugby shirt. Tammy and Tricia asked him point-blank if he had come into their room during the night and he said, "No."

Tricia said, "Well, you did."

And Tammy asked "Were you drunk last night?" and he said that he was drinking, so Tammy and Tricia started laughing and said, "Oh, my God, you were so drunk you didn't even know what you were doing." Neither Tricia nor Tammy ever said anything to anybody. School started. Tammy started hanging around with Norma and a different crowd, and she and Patricia drifted apart.

Detective Irwin had finally managed to instigate a system whereby all samples went through him to Kim Johnston, a scientist in the forensic center's biology section. Ms. Johnston was a short, intense brunette with wire-rimmed glasses. The fact that she was diabetic, and therefore lived a somewhat restricted life, only enhanced her enthusiasm for her work. She saw things no one else could see, and that meant something—particularly when it had to do with crimes involving bodily fluids.

As was true of the coroner's office, the Center for Forensic Science was inextricably linked to policing by function. It was, however, separately funded by the province. It was not a division of any police force, and although its management was cooperative with the chiefs of police around the province, it answered to the Solicitor-General. Politics, funding issues and bureacracy were not performance enhancers.

The center received and analyzed samples of one kind or another—hair, fibers, blood, semen, paint, bullets, glass—from crime scenes all over the province.

On Monday, September 25, 1990, Irwin received an excited

phone call from Kim Johnston. She had found a stain on the back of Sharon Moon's panties—the girl who had been raped in May—and she had been able to get a blood typing. It was not a smoking gun, but it would narrow the field considerably.

Even though genetic fingerprinting, or DNA analysis, had become the beacon of modern forensic biology, conventional serology—blood typing—could be very discriminating. According to Johnston's analysis of the stain on the panties, the suspect had to be either a one plus (+1)—which was 42 percent of the population—a one plus, one minus (+1–1)—which was 15 percent—or a two minus one plus (2–1+)–2+1—which was 7 percent.

They already knew that the rapist was a non-secretor. The term non-secreting refers to a small percentage of the population—less than 20 percent—whose saliva will not yield a blood type.

Forensic analysis is a painstaking science of comparison. Since the stain on her panties did not belong to the victim, it belonged to her attacker.

Johnston could now say, categorically, that the rapist lived somewhere in less than 64 percent of the non-secreting white, male population. Therefore, the person who raped Sharon Moon was one among only 12.8 percent of the general male population—in all likelihood, the general male population under the age of twenty-five in Scarborough, Ontario.

First, Detective Irwin was instructed to review all the suspects' samples and determine which ones now fit the refined criteria. He did—there were twenty non-secretors and another twenty-one from whom they would have to get better samples to determine their status.

"Blood them," Johnston said, and she would narrow that group of twenty-plus suspects with conventional serology—in a sample of forty individuals they might find two or three with the correct PGM blood profile. Then they would do DNA testing on those two or three individuals.

Johnston told Irwin that from here on the police must get blood samples from any non-secretor that they might even vaguely suspect. The sample only needed to be the size of a silver dollar.

Although forensic DNA analysis, or genetic fingerprinting, had become important to all policemen in North America, it was still a very young, rapidly evolving science. It had only been developed six years earlier, in 1984, by an English scientist named Alex Jefferies working at Cambridge. DNA procedures for forensic analysis were not commercially available in the United States until 1988. It took approximately two years for a technician to be trained to perform the necessary procedures to obtain reliable DNA results. Pam Newall had been the first trainee from the forensic center. Johnston was the second.

Previously, DNA testing could be done at the Royal Canadian Mounted Police central forensic laboratory in Ottawa— but most, if not all Canadian police with crimes serious enough to justify DNA testing prior to 1990 sent their samples to the United States. Conventional DNA testing took seventy to ninety days.

It was early fall and the leaves were just starting to change. Detective Steve Irwin was "manning the bird," as it is called in falconry. Manning birds was not about training a bird to do what it did naturally; it was about teaching it to return to "the fist," after it had killed.

The trick was convincing the bird that captivity was a better option than freedom. Once the bird appeared to have accepted that idea—by taking the lure and returning to the falconer's outstretched fist again and again—maintaining a bird in that condition demanded unwavering attention.

Returning to the fist was not natural; a little laxity on the part of the falconer and he forfeited his falcon. Even after years of manning, a single kill could send the most exquisitely well-conditioned bird into paroxysms of wildness.

Detective Irwin thought about sexual predators a bit the way he thought about birds of prey, except he had respect and love for the birds.

Between May and September members of the sexual assault squad had submitted more than one hundred and thirty suspects' samples to the forensic center for sector status and blood typing.

Then Detective Irwin got two reports identifying Paul Bernardo as a possible suspect. One, dated June 28, had been called in by a bank employee. The second report was from a nurse named Tina.

Tina had called on September 12 because her husband's friend Paul Bernardo looked a lot like the picture in the paper. Tina said she knew, secondhand, that Paul Bernardo would date one woman and have one or two other girls on the side. According to Tina, Mr. Bernardo would wait until a girl had had too much to drink and then take advantage of her.

"It must be him, then," Irwin thought to himself sarcastically. But there was something else that caught his attention. Something other than the coincidence of two unrelated people reporting the same person: Tina said Paul Bernardo had been "called in" on a previous rape investigation—one in December, 1987—but he had never been interviewed.

"Tina the Nurse" was Tina Smirnis, married to a lifelong acquaintance of Mr. Bernardo's, Alex Smirnis. Irwin and his partner, Sergeant John Munro, invited the couple to the sexual assault squad room to discuss Tina's report. After the forensic revelation of the day before, Irwin and Munro had become busy going after the blood of the twenty non-secretors. Alex and Tina showed up at 10:00 A.M., Tuesday, September 26.

As it turned out, for some reason Alex had put his wife up to her call. Now, he did all the talking. The son of Greek immigrants, he said he was a Christian and an entrepreneur who had owned a number of businesses, including a car-rental outlet, but at the present time he worked in his parents' restaurant in Brown Hill.

Alex had a video of his wedding, in which Paul Bernardo could be seen. He also had two still pictures of Bernardo, one about four years old and the other from their wedding.

Alex had two brothers—Stephanos, who was older, and Van. Stephanos lived in Youngstown, New York, and owned a video store in which their younger brother, Van, worked.

The Smirnis brothers were large boned, tall, with thick thighs. Alex was dark-haired and swarthy, like his brother, Stephanos, who also had a substantial proboscis. Van was fairer, but equally full in the face. Alex wore a mustache that made him look a bit like a heavyset Snidely Whiplash.

Alex had lived all his life across the street from the Bernardo family, at 24 Sir Raymond Drive. The Smirnises had moved away in 1986 or '87, but Paul kept in touch—more with his brothers than him. Alex described Paul as a "person who has tried but not achieved." For instance, he had tried to become a chartered accountant but had failed.

Paul's mother had psychiatric problems and drank, Alex explained, describing Marilyn Bernardo as outlandish, untidy and loud. Apparently, Ken Bernardo was not Paul's real father and his mother called Paul her "bastard child."

Alex knew Paul had dated a girl named Jennifer and, for all Alex knew, might have "beaten the shit out of her." Paul always had young girlfriends who were petite, small and not too bright.

A girl named Karla Homolka from St. Catharines, with whom Paul had had sex the first night they met, was one example. She was only eighteen years old, then, and still in high school, whereas Paul was in his twenties. Alex told the detectives that Karla had said, "If you want to know anything about girls, just ask Paul."

In Alex's opinion, Paul Bernardo's morals "had gone by the wayside." Paul often had two or more girls on the go at the same time. Paul had been dating another girl named Marie Magritte most of the time he had been seeing Karla.

Marie lived on Lower Raymerville in Markham, Ontario. She was a waitress. She was twenty-two, European and intelligent. The way Alex saw it, Marie had been very badly used by Paul Bernardo. Paul was also planning on relocating to St. Catharines, where Ms. Homolka lived, and getting married. This was all very sudden and out of character for him.

Alex went on to discuss Paul's sex life in detail. Paul was very domineering and liked rough sex. He had talked to Alex about having anal sex a couple of times. Paul had this fantasy about about having sex in his business suit with his briefcase in his hand while his wife was in a housecoat, Alex said breathlessly.

Paul had been out driving with Alex's younger brother and he said something about getting some girl and raping her.

Alex told them that Paul had been in Florida in March the previous year, again with Van. Paul had taken a tipsy girl up to his room and raped her when she passed out.

Alex spoke in non sequiturs: his phrasing was awkward and stilted, but he seemed to know more about Paul Bernardo than Steve Irwin knew about his own brother.

Alex said Paul had been a professional worm picker for the past two or three seasons. He always had a van in the spring for worm picking, but he drove a 1980 or 1981 white Capri, otherwise. Recently, he had leased a 1989 gold Nissan 240SX. Alex thought he had worked in accounting somewhere for the past year and a half.

Alex summed up his longtime neighbor and friend as sly, manipulative, trendy, a preppy dresser, a braggart and an instigator. According to Alex, Paul was an insecure non-smoker, maybe left-handed, who would drink to fit in. He was secretive and did not like people going into his room. At one point, Alex thought Paul had been involved in Christian television broadcasting. Paul wore leather jackets. He had extended credit. Alex knew Paul always carried a knife in his car.

Listening to Alex Smirnis was a contact sport. By the time Alex and Tina left, Detective Irwin and Sergeant Munro felt like they had been whacked in the head a half a dozen times. At least now Irwin knew what a real Christian looked like. They did not know whether or not to take Alex Smirnis seriously.

What they did know was they needed to pull the file on the December 27, 1987, rape of Mary Booth. In that file, they found Sergeant McNiff's incorrectly dated supplementary report about his meeting with Jennifer Galligan and what she had told the sergeant about her violent, tumultuous relationship with Paul Bernardo.

The behavior that Jennifer Galligan described confirmed a great deal that Alex Smirnis had said. More than that, Mary Booth said her assailant was driving a white Capri. And the street she was raped on, Bathgate, was only a couple of blocks from Sir Raymond Drive. The composite drawing that had been developed from Mary's description was surprisingly similar to the one that Irwin had arranged to have published the previous May.

The Scarborough rapes were not the only sexual assaults in the city. With one thing and another, Irwin did not get to Paul Bernardo's door until late in the afternoon on November 19, almost two months after they had talked to the Smirnises and pulled the Mary Booth file.

It was a thirty-minute drive from 40 College Street to 21 Sir Raymond Drive in rush-hour traffic. Paul was not home. A lanky man about six feet with wispy hair and Coke-bottle glasses, who appeared very nervous, answered the door. He said he was Paul Bernardo's father, Kenneth. Irwin and Munro identified themselves and gave Mr. Bernardo their cards. The elder Bernardo assured the detectives that he would have his son call them.

And he did. The detectives invited Paul Bernardo downtown for an interview. He arrived at the sexual assault squad offices at 4:00 P.M. Irwin and Munro interviewed him in 3A, a special room the sexual assault squad had set up on the third floor. An unusual room in a police building, 3A had subdued lighting. The decor was early Holiday Inn, with a couch, chairs and a coffee table. It was wired for sound and could be set up for video equipment. Ironically, 3A was most often used to interview the victims of sexual assaults and had been designed to put them at ease.

At twenty-six, Paul Bernardo was only three years younger than Steve Irwin and barely a year younger than gray-haired

John Munro. He appeared to be slightly nervous, but that was natural.

"Come on, guys," he joked, "this is worse than a job interview." Paul talked freely and openly. He had a degree from the University of Toronto. He was one exam away from chartered accountancy: the exam could be taken as many times as necessary; it was offered twice a year by the Canadian Institute of Chartered Accountants. He had worked for big accounting firms for the past couple of years. He was currently unemployed—by choice. He had other plans.

He was deeply in love and would soon marry a beautiful girl named Karla Homolka and move to St. Catharines, where his fiancée was currently working as a veterinarian's assistant. They were going to start a company together, manufacturing and selling motivational tapes.

He told the detectives he knew he looked like the picture in the paper. These three brothers he knew kidded him about how much he looked like the composite. He did not think it was very funny. He would never do anything like that to any woman. He did not need to rape women; he always had lots of girlfriends.

Detective Irwin talked about the Scarborough rapes and Margaret McWilliam's murder. McWilliam had been murdered on August 27, 1987. Paul remembered his dad telling him about that—it had happened on his twenty-third birthday. Paul had been in Florida with his girlfriend.

Irwin and Munro asked him if he could provide samples, so they could use science to categorically eliminate him from any further suspicion. Sergeant Munro explained his rights. In Canada a suspect was not obliged to provide a blood sample, but Paul Bernardo said he was more than happy to do it.

All the coincidences—the white Capri, the proximity of Bathgate to Sir Raymond Drive, his striking resemblance to the composite, the graphic details of his strange sexual proclivities, which Sergeant McNiff had documented during his interview with Jennifer Galligan, the fact that he really did not know exactly where he had been when Sharon Moon was raped in

May—they all dissolved with the detectives' suspicions in an aftershock of recognition.

Detective Irwin and Sergeant Munro saw themselves in Paul Bernardo, and they could not imagine themselves capable of such heinous, despicable sex crimes. Paul did not appear angry, he seemed happy. He didn't hate women, he loved them. He was not secretive, he was forthcoming. Paul was far more credible than his detractor, Alex Smirnis, who, with his awkward, strange way of speaking, might just be trying to collect the reward.

It just did not seem possible that such a well-educated, well-adjusted, congenial young man like Paul Bernardo could be responsible for such horrible crimes. Without hesitation, Paul pricked his finger with the lance they had given him and left a dollop of blood on a cotton swab. He pulled out a tuft of hair and spit on a blotter. He was polite and soft-spoken. Paul Bernardo was gone by 4:45 P.M.

Science would be the final arbiter. In Steve Irwin's opinion, things were so bad that a cop could not get a prosecutor to court on a sexual assault charge without the science anyway. Once he had handed the samples over to Kim Johnston at the Center for Forensic Science the following day, Paul Bernardo was out of sight and out of mind.

CHAPTER

eleven

It was around 9:00 P.M. on Tuesday, November 20, and Karla was sitting in her bedroom in the basement reading the *Compendium of Pharmaceuticals and Specialties*.

She had been very busy for the past two or three months. It was one thing having to plan a wedding the size of the one she and Paul were going to have; it was quite another to have to plan your sister's rape at the same time.

Thank God she had already picked out her wedding dress in

September—the Ilissa design by Demetrios from Tatter's Lane in Niagara Falls, New York. Paul was such a sweetie. He had helped her pick it out, put down the deposit and everything. And she had most of the bridesmaids' measurements—except Debbie Purdie's—so that was well in hand.

Karla had come to the conclusion that the only way to do Tammy properly was to knock her right out. The Valium Karla had for her cat Shadow's urinary problem, crushed and sprinkled on Tammy's spaghetti, had not worked at all.

When she and Paul experimented, mixing crushed Valium in Tammy and Tricia's drinks during the summer, the taste had been bitter and Karla was sure both of them had noticed it.

Then she went out and got a prescription for some sleeping pills called Elavil, but the *Compendium* had said Elavil had a gradual, cumulative effect, so she had not even bothered to fill it. Finally, she figured out exactly what to do.

Being in charge of the drug registry at work, Karla had a working knowledge of the *Compendium of Pharmaceuticals and Specialties,* the large medical reference work that gave detailed information about every drug on the market. The compendium was updated every couple of years. Karla "borrowed" the outdated twenty-second edition from the clinic and brought it home. In the past, her mother had taken Halcion, a well-known prescription sleeping pill, and it seemed to work very well. Karla read up on Halcion. It sounded ideal.

Halcion had the fewest contraindications of all the sleeping potions, and the compendium said it was safe. It was real easy to get, too. Cats and dogs were often prescribed sedatives, but the clinic seldom stocked the drugs. The vets would ask Karla to order whatever was required from the drugstore in the opposite plaza. Karla would walk across the street, pay for it, and bring the prescription back. She and Paul could easily crush a half a dozen pills and mix them in her sister's drinks at Christmastime. That should do the trick. Tammy would make a great Christmas present for Paul.

Because of the fiasco during the summer and the fuss Paul had made when Tammy started to wake up, Karla knew she had to really put her down this time. At the clinic they used an inhalant anesthetic called halothane to put animals out for surgery. Karla knew all about halothane. It was part of her job to administer the anesthetic to animals during surgery.

She did that by monitoring the regulator on the oxygen tank through which a very small amount of halothane was vaporized with oxygen and delivered to the animal through the mask. Vaporized in a very low ratio—one or two parts per hundred parts oxygen—was the only way halothane was to be used. It could be very dangerous in concentrated form.

Since halothane was not a regulated drug and Karla was in charge of maintaining the drug dispensary, she could easily put a bottle or two in her bag. When she got home, Karla put the plain brown bottles in the cupboard under the sink in her washroom downstairs.

The stealing part bothered Karla, and she still had bad memories about the Ketamine incident with Dr. Ker at her old job. Just to be on the safe side, she advised the vets at Martindale that they had best install a new vaporizing regulator because the one they had was not working properly. It had been mixing far too much halothane with the oxygen.

She had really thought this thing with Tammy through. After all, she did not want to kill her own sister; she just wanted to knock her out and give her to Paul for Christmas. They sedated animals before they put them to sleep for surgery, so it should be all right to do it to her sister. There was some risk without the proper equipment—she would have to put the halothane on a cloth and hold it over Tammy's face—but she would make sure Tammy had plenty of air and check her breathing regularly.

That settled in her mind, Karla focused on her wedding. She was just about to pick up her pen and write "Dirty" Purdie another letter about how wonderful her wedding dress was and ask her—for the third or fourth time—to send her measurements and the money for her bridesmaid's dress, when there was an insistent tapping on her window.

"What are you doing here?" she exclaimed when she saw him. She opened the basement window. Paul sometimes came to see her on Wednesdays, but never on Tuesdays. Her pleasant surprise quickly dissipated. He looked and sounded real upset.

"I need to talk to you," he whispered. "It's really, really important. Don't tell your parents I'm here." Karla was almost frantic—what could possibly be wrong? She ran upstairs and told her mother she was going out for a walk.

Paul was bent right out of shape because he had been called in by the police: he told her about the interview and about giving the samples. He told her he had pricked his finger for the blood. He had had to do it, or else they would have been really suspicious.

Karla had never seen him this upset. He was totally panicked. They were just driving aimlessly around St. Catharines. Karla tried to reassure him. She was sure the police did not really know anything, that it was just routine. After all, Van Smirnis had been going around saying Paul looked just like the picture in the paper.

The bastard had probably called him in. If the police had anything on him, they would have arrested him right there. Hadn't Paul always told her he was careful? Besides, she had been with him that night in May when the girl was raped. Karla knew that for sure, and she would say so.

"What if they decide to arrest me, just because they can't find anybody else, because I look like the composite?" And he kept repeating, over and over, "What if they charge me, what if they charge me?"

Karla was totally resolved. She knew she had to put a stop to this aberrant behavior of his. Karla told him to stop worrying. She said the police would not charge people just to solve a case. Paul said the detective had talked a lot about Margaret McWilliam. If they compared his samples to samples taken from Margaret McWilliam, Paul would be absolved.

Paul said the police told him that it would probably be a month or so before they had the results from his samples. They went to the library. While Karla checked out books on computer programs, Paul went through the newspapers on microfiche. With the detailed eye of an accountant, he noted the dates of all the rapes attributed to the Scarborough rapist, the name of the newspapers that had reported the story, the public description of the attacker and any comments made about the rapist. "Cunning" and "very intelligent" were his favorites.

On the same notepad—a long one that Karla had picked up at a bridal shower—Karla noted the date of each occurrence and the main intersection closest to the site. On the same piece of paper, she also wrote out a shopping list. That particular week she required Sun-In to lighten Paul's hair and Freeze-hair spray for herself and she made herself a reminder to order "confetti" favor cards for her wedding.

Over the following weekend Paul and Karla had more intense discussions about his interview and Tammy Lyn. Karla knew that their love was so powerful that it would conquer all. On Monday, November 26, she sent Paul a note: "Please accept my apology even though actions speak louder than words and my actions haven't been great. I swear things will change. Just remember how much we love each other. Paul, I know we can get through this. . . ." Three days later Paul was formally discharged from bankruptcy. That was a step in the right direction.

On December 5, Karla picked up her confetti cards—one hundred of them. She wrote Debbie Purdie yet another wedding-talk letter. There were two absolutely wonderful events in her immediate future, she said "—marriage and a dog."

To celebrate their wedding anniversary, Karel and Dorothy Homolka always went and stayed in a hotel in Niagara Falls, New York, for a weekend: this year, they chose the weekend of December 8. Paul and Karla had high hopes for a Tammy opportunity on that weekend, but for the first time in months Lori decided to stay at home and not go out over the weekend. Paul threw up his hands. Videotaping all the way, Paul took the three sisters, frolicking like palominos in the riot of Christmas lights, across the border for a brief Saturday evening visit with their parents.

"Take good care of my girls, Mr. Bernardo," Karel said to the camera, as they galloped away into the bright Christmas night.

Karla sent Paul two more cards, one for the anniversary of

their engagement on December 11: "Just for fun I made a list of the top hundred things I like to do with you . . . kiss and hug and stuff: 'you know what stuff!'," signed "W-U-V, Karly Curls." She covered the card with sticky hearts. A week later Karla sent Paul flowers.

By December 23, calm had been restored. Perhaps tonight would be the night, except Tammy was scheduled for a sleep-over at her girlfriend Patricia Coyle's. Paul and Karla despaired. Instead, they went cross-border shopping. They left Karla's house about 2:30 P.M. and crossed into the US at 3:00 P.M.

After they came back across the border at 6:30 P.M., the weather turned and a severe winter storm settled in. Mrs. Coyle called and canceled Tammy's visit. Paul and Karla sat in front of Meatland, a butcher shop in a strip mall near Karla's house for an hour. They finished pulverizing the Halcion. Paul had been pounding the pills into powder with a hammer in the Homolkas' basement earlier in the day, when Karla's mother asked about the noise. They got back to the house laden with Christmas gifts and finely ground Halcion around 7:15 P.M.

As far as Paul was concerned, this was going to be the best Christmas ever. He had a new Sony video camcorder and he would get it all on tape. Before they went shopping he had videotaped Mrs. Homolka in the kitchen, the Christmas tree and all the presents downstairs in the recreation room.

The new toy was fun: everyone was captured in the lens, including a prone, shirtless Mr. Homolka, as he lay on the couch watching "60 Minutes" and Mrs. Homolka, in her bath-robe, as she descended the stairs at eight o'clock to watch "Murder She Wrote." Karla sat cross-legged on the floor, put-ting Shadow the cat through his paces.

Karla and Lori lampooned the "Saturday Night Live" televi-sion skit, Wayne's World, with its extreme close-up antics—Paul laughed as the sisters shoved their faces right in the camera lens and yelled "extreme close-up."

It was the Sunday before Christmas, so everybody was drinking, and it was not hard to lace Tammy's drinks. Tammy was sitting in the big stuffed chair with her legs pulled up under her, drinking a special daiquiri Paul and Karla had prepared just for her. Tammy was getting stoned. She wondered why Paul had two cameras.

Paul asked her what it was she was drinking and she slurred the word ice and that really inspired Paul because "Ice, ice, baby, to go . . ." was a line from a song by the white rapper Vanilla Ice, who was one of his role models. He said "Ice, ice, baby, to go . . ." and Tammy looked right into the camera, laughed coquettishly, and defiantly said, "No."

Then Tammy said, right out of the blue, "These guys are trying to poison me." Everyone was in the room when she said it, but nobody seemed to hear her. Karla almost freaked out. Then Tammy went upstairs to get something to eat. She was just getting over mononucleosis and she had been complaining about feeling a bubble right around her ribs. Paul and Mrs. Homolka felt it in the kitchen and they agreed it felt weird.

Tammy started drinking Paul's rusty nail, a tortured concoction of scotch and Drambuie. She downed the whole drink. Then she went upstairs to her bedroom again and called her friend Norma. While she was upstairs, Paul shot more video footage of Mr. and Mrs. Homolka, Karla and Lori around the Christmas tree. Much later, Karla would bitch at Paul, because ever since they were "little, little, little," the three sisters—Karla, Lori and Tammy—had always had their picture taken in front of the tree together. This was the first time they had not, and look what happened.

Paul and Karla had given Tammy ten or twelve 5mg pills, but they did not seem to be having the desired effect. Tammy just seemed a little drunk. Lori told Paul and Karla to stop feeding Tammy drinks but nobody paid her any attention either, so she just went to her room and never came out again.

Finally, Tammy came back downstairs. When Mr. and Mrs. Homolka went to bed they told Tammy to go to bed as well, but she said, "No, I want to watch the movie with Paul and Kar."

Paul had rented *Lisa and the Devil*, an old horror movie about this woman—Elke Sommer—who discovers a mannequin of herself. There's a warped family with a sadistic husband and a nympho wife, a necro son and a butler, played by Telly Savalas. Robert Alda played a priest and Elke Sommer spewed bile and frog chunks all over him. This was the first time Telly Savalas had ever sucked a lollipop on camera.

Paul and Karla were on the one couch: Tammy was on the other. Finally, Tammy fell asleep. Karla went over and poked her. She was out cold. Karla got the halothane. Paul got the video camera. Karla poured halothane on a cloth and held it over Tammy's mouth and nose.

Paul pulled down her green track pants and Karla pushed her shirt up. Paul started videotaping his fingers lubricating her vagina and then put his penis in her. The camera was zoomed in on his penis going in and out of Tammy's vagina.

Karla told him to hurry up and Paul told her to shut up.

Tammy's right hand was casually relaxed across her belly.

"Please hurry up before somebody comes down. . . ." Karla whispered. He told her to shut up again. It was hard to maintain an erection when somebody was telling you to hurry up all the time.

"Okay," he said. "Keep her down, here we go."

Then Karla told him to put on a condom. They had discussed it—Karla did not want Tammy to get pregnant. But Paul did not have a condom. He never had any intention of using a condom. "Keep her down and keep quiet," he whispered.

Karla said it more forcibly: "Put something on. . . ."

"Don't get all worked up. Shut up . . ." he said.

She told him to put on a condom three or four more times. Finally an exasperated Karla said, "Fucking do it. Just do it." By this time Paul had pushed his penis in and out of Tammy, slowly, a half a dozen times. He was having real trouble holding the camera still.

"Yeah, you love me," he declared out of the blue, because he knew that would get to her and maybe settle her down.

"Quiet," she said. Karla had been holding the halothane-soaked cloth over her sister's mouth and nose. Periodically she poured more halothane on the cloth and checked Tammy's breathing.

"Will you blow me?" Paul asked, just as a joke.

"Yes."

"Suck on her breasts," he said. The multicolored sweater Tammy was wearing had been pulled right up around her neck. Karla started to mouth her breasts. "Now, suck," Paul beseeched. Karla's hair fell over her face and the gold chain Paul had bought her on their first Christmas slipped between her lips.

Paul had pulled his penis out and changed shots. Karla was kneeling between her sister's legs. Paul pushed on her head and Karla started to perform cunnilingus on her sister.

"Put your tongue out," he ordered. "Probe. You're not doing it." Tammy had her period, and Karla was very unhappy.

"I am so," Karla whimpered.

"Do it. Lick her cunt. Lick it up . . . Lick it clean. Lick it clean . . ." he instructed her.

"I am . . ." Karla replied.

"Put your fingers inside . . ." he cajoled.

Karla said no. He told her to do it again. Karla was becoming increasingly unhappy and distraught.

"Do it now, quick, quick, quick. Right now. Right inside . . ."

Karla started to do it, pushing her right index finger in and out of her sister.

"Three fingers. Right inside." Then he told her to do exactly the thing she most deplored. "Taste it." Karla refused.

"Taste it. Put it in. Taste it. Put it inside and taste it."

"I did."

"Taste it. Inside. Inside. Inside and taste it. Quick."

"No," she whined, and continued to finger Tammy.

"Inside. Deep. Deep."

"I did," Karla said. Paul repeated himself. "I did," Karla said again. Karla reluctantly licked her now bloodstained fingers.

"Taste good? Not bad, eh?" he inquired.

She said no. He asked again. "Taste good?"

Karla looked right into the camera, daubed her lips on the cuff of her white turtleneck and said, "Fucking disgusting . . ."

Ignoring her, he asked again, "Does it taste good?" Paul knew what was wrong and thought it was funny.

Karla had been holding the halothane-soaked cloth over her sister's face. Now she went back up to check her breathing and Paul inserted his penis in Tammy's anus.

"Up her cunt, up her ass. How's that?" he said happily.

Suddenly Paul just stopped and pulled out, as though he knew something was not right. Then Tammy vomited. Something was terribly wrong. It must have been the drinks and all the food she had eaten before. Karla knew animals were not fed before they were anesthetized. Karla knew what to do. She grabbed her sister and held her upside down, because that was what you were supposed to do with an animal who aspirated its stomach contents while under.

Paul started trying to clear Tammy's throat. It was not fun anymore and they were both terrified. Karla was hysterical. In a split second they decided to drag her across the floor to Karla's bedroom.

Struggling with her lifeless body, they dropped her. The lighting in the recreation room was on a dimmer switch. They could have just turned it up, but they did not want anybody suddenly coming down and finding Tammy unconscious with her shirt around her head and her pants around her ankles.

Once they got into Karla's bedroom, they dressed Tammy. Karla sent Paul upstairs to get the mirror from the front hallway to see if she was breathing. Paul started mouth-to-mouth. Karla called 911. She dumped the halothane down the drain and hid the pills and the empty halothane bottle behind some shelves in the laundry room.

The sirens and the lights woke up Karla's mother and father. Lori stumbled to the top of the stairs. Paul told Mr. and Mrs. Homolka that Tammy had just stopped breathing. Karla watched while the paramedics worked on Tammy. She was buoyed by the fact that Tammy's color seemed to be coming back and it appeared they had a heartbeat. As they took Tammy out with tubes in her mouth, Karla told her parents that Tammy was looking much better.

The police came. It had been tough to get through the snowstorm that had blanketed the city. The two senior officers on the scene went with Tammy. Mr. and Mrs. Homolka followed the ambulance to the hospital. They left Constable David Weeks, a tall, gangly rookie who had only been on the job seven weeks, with Paul, Karla and Lori. Constable Weeks found the situation suspicious.

He sat Paul, Karla and Lori on the couch. He suggested to them that they might have been free-basing cocaine, even though Paul had told him outright, before Weeks said anything, that there were no drugs involved. What else could have caused that unholy burn on Tammy's face, Constable Weeks wondered?

Then the telephone rang and Constable Weeks answered. He went, "Uh-huh," and hung up. "Your sister's dead," he said. Although Tammy had not been pronounced dead until they got her to the hospital, she had actually died around 1:00 A.M. in the Homolkas' basement. Lori ran upstairs and called Mike Donald, her ex-boyfriend.

When Weeks came back down after checking on her, he found Karla loading the blankets on which her sister had vomited into the washing machine. The water was already running before he stopped her and pulled the wet parts out. When Lori came down again, the two sisters hugged each other and started quietly crying. Paul rocked back and forth madly, whacking his own head, screaming.

The senior detective came back to Dundonald and drove Paul, Karla and Lori to the police station on Church Street. Paul and Karla were left sitting on a bench together for almost an hour, waiting to be interviewed. Finally they were questioned, separately.

The police noted that their stories were remarkably similar. Neither Paul nor Karla said anything about halothane, Halcion, or videotape. They both said the marks on Tammy Lyn's face were caused when they dragged her across the carpet to Karla's room. Although the coroner was sure the marks were not rug burns, the police never questioned Paul and Karla about it again.

They were finished by 6:00 A.M. When they got home, Paul and Karla panicked. They could not find the videotape. Paul had left it in the camera. But someone had moved the camera into Karla's bedroom. One of the cassettes was even sitting out on Karla's night table in plain view. Obviously, nobody had bothered to check either the camera or the cassettes.

Dorothy Homolka called her neighbor, friend and co-worker, Lynn McCann, and asked her to come over to the house. Lynn and Dorothy were approximately the same age, and they both worked as secretaries at the Shaver Clinic. It was early on the morning of December 24. Dorothy said that they had just come back from the hospital and their daughter was dead. At first Lynn thought it must be Lori, the middle girl, because she was the one who had really bad asthma.

But it was Tammy Lyn, the most athletic, the healthiest and the bubbliest of the three blond sisters. Tammy would have turned sixteen on New Year's Day.

Lynn had been at 61 Dundonald for a couple of hours when Karla and Paul came home. They were in a grand funk because they said the police had treated them like criminals, interrogating them all night. Then the bastards had not even driven them home, as they had promised they would.

To Lynn, it was all too weird. Apparently Paul and Karla had been watching television with Tammy in the basement when Tammy suddenly stopped breathing. Dorothy told Lynn that Tammy had choked on her own vomit and that Paul had really worked hard giving her mouth-to-mouth, trying to save her life.

Dorothy said she and Karel had been asleep when Dorothy was awakened by something: she thought it was music or the television. She was on her way downstairs to tell them to turn it down, when she saw the flashing lights. The paramedics were already in the house when Dorothy got to the top of the basement stairs.

At noon Dorothy asked Lynn to go with her and Karel and help them pick out a casket. Karel asked Karla to go, too, but Karla told him to "fuck off."

Lynn had lost an infant child and found the whole casket thing very difficult. It was all the more unsettling that Dorothy and Karel didn't cry or show any emotion at all throughout the three-hour ordeal.

When they were done, Lynn was exhausted and went home for a while. She suggested that Dorothy lie down, too, and try to get some rest. Later, when Lynn came back, Dorothy told her they laid down, but instead of resting she and Karel "screwed."

Lynn was flabbergasted when Dorothy told her that somebody had come by and dropped off a death certificate. Tammy Lyn's body was barely cold and they had already concluded her death was accidental?

Tammy Lyn was buried December 27, 1990.

Karla was acting very strangely at Tammy's funeral. It was an open coffin. She would not leave Tammy's hair alone. She kept straightening the corpse's clothes.

Everyone was suspicious. The paramedics had said the washing machine was going when they arrived at the house—at two o'clock in the morning? It was said that Paul and Karla had washed all of Tammy's clothes. There were rumors about Paul and Karla free-basing cocaine. Everyone believed that Tammy's death was rushed through the emergency room because it was Christmas. Maybe the coroner had been drinking?

And then there was the huge, bright raspberry-colored burn that extended from the left side of Tammy's mouth all the way down her chin onto her neck, for which no one had a plausible explanation.

Dorothy had given Lynn three different explanations, at three different times: first she had said it was because Tammy had bad acne, an allergic reaction to a particular kind of makeup; then she said it was the result of excessive mouth-to-mouth resuscitation; and thirdly, because the paramedics had dragged Tammy across the carpet.

In spite of the heroic efforts of the undertakers and makeup as thick as rhinoceros hide, troweled on the dead teenager's face, the mark was still clearly evident.

CHAPTER

twelve

The day after the funeral Karla went to the doctor and got more Halcion. Tammy Lyn Homolka was buried near the Homolkas' house, in Victoria Lawn Cemetery, where the carillon plays eight-track tapes. For some reason it was always playing the theme from The Sound of Music—"the hills are alive, with the sound of music. . . ." They had put Tammy's school picture on the tombstone, along with an engraved soccer ball at the top and a bronzed pair of soccer shoes at the base. Soccer was Tammy's game.

On the weekend of January 12, Karla's mother and father decided to go to a lighting show in Toronto. Karel and Dorothy went to the same show every year, combining a little business with pleasure. This year, it was different. They really needed to get away. Karla's sister Lori went to visit her grandparents in Mississauga.

Under the circumstances, Paul and Karla decided the best thing to do was for Paul to go out and get another girl and rape her. Since they had the house to themselves, he could bring her back there. And this time they would make sure she lived.

Paul went out and found a girl and brought her back. Karla watched from the doorway while Paul had sex with her on the floor of her bedroom. But it was not like a rape at all—no screaming or anything. Neither Paul or Karla had any idea who she was so, they just called her the January Girl.

Paul took the January Girl out to a deserted road around Lake Gibson and let her go. He was only mildly concerned that she might have seen his license plate as he drove off. They never heard anything more about the January Girl. The encounter had not been much fun for Karla, but Karla was not sure whether or not she could stand any more fun. Now she just wanted to concentrate on the wedding and get back to work.

Karla knew Paul was unhappy about not having Tammy to play with anymore. She knew that he blamed her. She did not mind that Paul had loved Tammy. She had loved her, too. She certainly had not meant to kill her. Tammy's death was a tie that inextricably bound her and Paul together. But it was not exactly the tie she had had in mind. Karla decided to cheer up Paul. She decided to pretend she was Tammy, the way she had the summer before, only better.

This time they would make a movie and in the movie Karla would become her dead sister, Karla told Paul. Karla said she was very good at pretending, and with this performance she would bring Tammy back to life. Paul was very happy. He set up the video camera in the basement. Karla would make a wonderful wife.

.   .   .

The movie opens with an extreme close-up of Karla's vagina. The shot is held so long it looks like a still picture. It was as if Paul were studying it, trying to figure out just what it was.

The camera pans to reveal Karla, stark naked, with her legs spread wide apart, playing with herself. The setting is the same as it had been in the video they made with Tammy Lyn, except in this one there is no Christmas tree. Behind Karla, a fire dances in the fireplace.

"Now watch Karla play with herself," says Karla. She holds up her hand. "Watch. There's the hand, and watch what it does."

Paul Bernardo walks into the frame fully dressed with two drinks. He sits down and Karla helps him unbutton his shirt.

"A bit more to drink and then, ahh . . . I'll sit back and relax," he says, appreciating her. With her long blond hair and impeccable skin, Karla is a naked Barbie doll, whose arms and legs move and bend in specific, deliberate ways.

"Let me suck those titties," Karla says and she does. He takes a sip of his drink and responds, "It's tough to be the king."

She strips him leisurely, as lovers do. When she gets his pants off, Karla puts her nose to his penis and announces, "I love you, Snuffles." There is not even a hint of a giggle in her voice.

"I loved it when you fucked my little sister," Karla says casually. "I loved it when you fucked Tammy. I loved it when you took her virginity." Between statements, Karla sucks him and it seems to work, particularly when she tells him he is the "king."

"It's my mission in life to make you feel good," Karla declares.

Paul looks right into the camera and says: "That's why I'm gonna marry her."

"I'm glad you made me lick her cunt," Karla says, stripping off her flimsy teddy top and continuing her labor.

"Are you a full-fledged dyke?" he asks, referring to her "lesbian act."

"That was different," responds Karla. "It was my little sister."

"Love in the family," Paul says smugly. "Do you believe in that concept?"

"You know I had fun doing it," she says, still busy with his anus. "You know I liked it."

"What did it teach you?"

"Well, we like little girls. We like to fuck them. If you're gonna fuck them, I'm gonna lick them."

When Paul asks her how old the girls should be, Karla suggests "thirteen." Her reasoning is that at that age they should still be virgins.

"You should break their hymens with Snuffles," she offers. "They're our children and I think you should make them even more ours."

"I think you're right. You're absolutely right." Paul is breathing a bit heavily. "Good idea. When did you come up with this idea?"

"Just now," Karla purrs, agreeing with him that these other virgins would be the closest thing they could get to Tammy.

"I think the king should turn over, 'cause the little slave has some more things to do and say," she says, controlling the pacing.

Paul obediently shifts position and Karla pulls out a single red rose. It's as though she has a prop box just off camera and is ready for anything. She strokes his chest and thighs with its petals, telling him that they will place this particular rose on Tammy's grave the next day, because it has touched him in "intimate places."

In the dim light, she gets up and goes behind the sofa and pulls out a paper bag. From the bag she pulls a pair of peach-colored panties.

"I have something special for you," Karla announces. "Tammy's underwear to rub all over your body.

"I never want you to forget the time that you took her virginity. When you popped her hymen."

"Best orgasm ever . . ." he breathlessly proclaims.

"What did it last? Sixty seconds?" she asks, concentrating on rubbing his penis with her dead sister's panties.

"Oh yeah, sooo intense." . . .

"I didn't give you my virginity . . ." Karla explains. "So I gave you Tammy's. I love you enough to do that."

"And what else?" Paul asks, loving it when she talks that talk.

"Well. We did something a few days ago," she says, teasingly. "We raped a little girl. Down here in my room. You went out and you found her, got her, brought her back to the house. Brought her downstairs, I was shocked. You fucked her."

Karla keeps up her handiwork, but looks him straight in the eyes and then hugs him. "I let you do that. Because I love you. Because you're the king."

He can barely speak. He grunts.

"I want you to do it again," she says, capturing his curiosity, bringing him back from the edge of orgasm.

"When?" he asks, sitting back on his haunches while Karla considers her answer and slowly caresses his erect penis.

"This summer. Because the wintertime is too hard," she says, finding this new concept difficult to explain with his penis in her mouth.

"If you want to do it fifty times more. We can do it fifty times," she says, rubbing him with both hands. "We can do it every weekend. We can do it whenever we can."

"So why do you want . . . why do you want to let me do it?" Paul asks.

"Because I love you. Because you're the king. 'Cause you deserve it," she says matter-of-factly, agreeing that she will join him when they get "virgin cunts," and she will be there to help him "go from one cunt to another" and "one ass to another." She says she will go in the car with him, if that's what he wants.

"Or I'll stay here and I'll clean up afterwards, like I did on Sunday," she offers. "I'll do everything I can, 'cause I want you to be happy, 'cause you're the king and I love you."

Paul touches her with an ice cube. It is time to go upstairs.

.   .   .

The screen flickers and then comes back to life. The second part of the movie opens on Paul and Karla in Tammy Lyn's bedroom.

"Put this in focus here . . . focus it right." He is giving himself camera instructions. The camera moves in and out of focus before it settles sharply on the portrait of Tammy Lyn that Karla is holding over her face.

"There is my little virgin there. Tammy Lyn Homolka, fucked only by me. Broke her hymen and everything. I wish I still had it today, Kar . . . I think part of the blood is on that white thing that was there."

"I think so," Karla agrees. Paul is now reclining on the waterbed with his legs spread wide apart. Karla hands him Tammy's portrait and then pulls her long blond hair right over her face to enhance her thespian deception.

"I loved her so much. So nice and warm," Paul ruminates. He looks at the picture lovingly, while Karla climbs on to the bed and bends her head to his crotch and once again begins her work. Her hair cascades over his groin and abdomen. Buying right into the performance, he says, "Hi, Tammy."

"Hi, Paul," Karla says. "You know this is your favorite out-fit." Karla is wearing an outfit that she has culled from Tammy's closet—a very short glen-checked skirt that is hiked over her hips, exposing her bare buttocks. She is also wearing a taut black sweater.

"I am your little virgin. I'm glad Kar doesn't know about us," she begins, introducing the charade. "She knows I'm bad but . . . she doesn't know that I do all these things."

"I didn't know she knew anything," Paul says, right into it now. Karla has successfully become Tammy.

"Does she know I suck you off? Does she know that I'm your virgin?" Karla/Tammy asks.

"Yes."

"That you broke my hymen with Snuffles. That you made me bleed. That you were the first boy to ever enter this body? Does she know that? Mmm?" All the while Karla/Tammy continues to stroke and suck his penis. Their activity causes the water in Tammy's bed to slosh. Through broken blinds, the camera records the fact that it is dark outside. Karla/Tammy provokes him with images of anal and lesbian sex acts, and reminds him of his masturbatory sojourns into the teenager's room.

"Oh, Tammy, you're the best orgasm in the world by far," Paul says as the blond hair in front of him moves, rhythmically, persistently between his legs, rocking the stuffed animals and cartoon characters that sway on the waterbed next to him.

It takes Karla fifteen minutes to get him off and she works really hard at it. When he finally comes, she looks directly into the camera, smiles broadly, obviously tired, and waves. As he walks over to the crotch-high camera, his engorged penis fills the screen before it goes to black.

Their love deepened, immeasurably.

CHAPTER

thirteen

After Dorothy Homolka went back to work in January, she went around telling everyone at the Shaver Clinic that she could never have made it through the funeral without Paul. Then she decided to tell Karla to kick him out of the house.

She also told everyone that she and Karel were nearly broke, so the staff at the hospital took up a collection for her. At the same time she was crying poor, Dorothy told Lynn McCann that she and Karel had $15,000 saved and the funeral had only cost them $5,000. Lynn also believed there was no mortgage on their house.

Dorothy had started telling anyone who would listen that she did not want Paul and Karla's wedding to happen; she could no longer afford it—they were on the verge of losing their house. Under circumstances like hers, how could she possibly think about a wedding, anyway?

Again, Dorothy told Lynn a different story. She said she had had a big talk with Karla and asked Karla to cut back, have a smaller wedding. The wedding she was planning was going to cost over twenty thousand dollars and that was a ridiculous burden, regardless of the emotional and financial strain that her sister's death had caused. Paul seemed to have no relationship with his parents, so they were not going to be any help. Karla flatly refused to cut back at all.

When Dorothy told Karla to boot Paul, she explained that the family needed to be alone with its grief. They needed time to heal. This declaration enraged Karla. "How can you do this to us?" she exclaimed. "You know that we need to be to-gether."

When Karla told Paul, it upset him and he became quiet. He had mentally and physically severed whatever ties he had to his mother and father and Scarborough, but he took the news sto-ically and went back home. If that was the way it was going to be, then so be it. The Homolkas' duplicitous behavior was duly noted. Nobody double-crossed Paul Bernardo and got away with it.

His exile lasted one week. On Friday, January 18, 1991, Sir Winston Churchill Secondary School held a memorial service for Tammy Lyn Homolka in the school auditorium. Paul picked Karla up at the Martindale Animal Clinic and dropped her off. Under the circumstances, Paul refused to attend. Karla chose not to sit with her parents and sister during the service.

Afterward, Paul was waiting for her. Over dinner, at Jack Astor's, a downscale St. Catharines joint along the Ontario Street strip, they resolved to find a place where they could live happily together. They would call a real-estate agent and find a nice house to rent. Dinner for two was $35.99, including a glass of wine. From the restaurant it was an easy half-hour drive back toward Toronto and the Relax Inn in Burlington, where they rented a room for the night.

It was fortuitous that Paul and Karla found their dream home that weekend at 57 Bayview in Port Dalhousie. If the bottom had not fallen out of the real-estate market just after the Delaneys bought the house and spent close to one hundred thousand dollars in renovations, the pink-clapboard, Cape Cod–style bungalow on a corner lot would not have been there to rent.

Paul liked water, and they both liked the illusion of style. Port Dalhousie is a small harbor town built around the natural harbor where Twelve Mile Creek empties into Lake Ontario. It was originally settled after the American War of Independence in 1812 by a small group of disgruntled soldiers called Butler's Regulars and a flank of American settlers called Loyalists. Port Dalhousie was the original site of the Welland Canal. Many years before, the canal entrance had been moved a dozen miles south to Port Weller. Now Port Dalhousie was a suburb of St. Catharines, about ten minutes from the city center. Its history gave the town some distinction, but peace and quiet were the essence of its modern appeal. Now its settlers were well-to-do retirees, lawyers, doctors and even Dr. Wade, Karla's veterinarian boss.

The Delaneys—Rachel and Brian—had made a successful hobby of buying houses, fixing them up, and flipping them. They had been doing it for years, with various partners. But 57 Bayview was by far their most ambitious project, and now they were bleeding like stuck pigs. Brian, a part-time male model in his mid-fifties who also owned and operated an extermination business in St. Catharines, was under pressure—not only financial.

His wife, Rachel, an insurance executive ten or fifteen years his junior, liked to close. She was a stickler for quick resolutions. If they could not sell it at something near their asking price of $269,000, then they had to rent it. Otherwise, it was an open vein and they would lose everything. After trying unsuccessfully to sell it for half a year, they had just put it up for rent.

Paul and Karla fell in love with the house and the Delaneys

fell in love with Paul and Karla, in whom they saw closure and resolution. The Delaneys did not stop to ask who this teenager and her fast-talking, jobless, bankrupt fiancé were or how they could possibly afford such steep rent.

The Delaneys did a perfunctory credit check—only on Karla. Karla was not old enough to have a bad credit rating, but she was a local girl and that meant a great deal to people like the Delaneys.

The rent was set at $1,150 per month. Paul said he was an accountant, so it did not matter much that Karla's monthly take-home pay was less than the rent. When the check for the first and last month cleared, that was all the character reference Paul and Karla's new landlords needed. They walked away, counting their blessings.

Paul and Karla were ecstatic. That Saturday night they checked into the Journey's End motel on the outskirts of Port Dalhousie. They needed to be close to their new home. They went to the movies and saw *The Godfather III* at the Pen Center Cinema. They walked by the Number One Pet Center, where Karla got her start. Their love strengthened.

On Monday, Paul ordered the cable-television service and changed the address on his driver's license to 57 Bayview Drive. On Tuesday night, they celebrated at the Port Mansion, a bar in Port Dalhousie. Their house was three times the size of the Homolkas' tiny tinderbox and very chic. It had a Jacuzzi. It had space. It had French doors. It gave Karla real attitude. Fuck her parents, she thought. This was what they got for their inconstancy: buried their youngest—now say goodbye to their oldest.

In Karla's wedding planner, she noted that "Patience," by Guns N' Roses, was their favorite song, *She's Having a Baby,* their favorite movie, and "Saturday Night Live" and "The David Letterman Show" their favorite television programs. On January 30, 1991, Karla marked, in big block letters: "M O V E!" And they did.

On February 19, Karla wrote her friend Debbie Purdie a long letter. She told her all about her research into Rottweilers and their bloodlines, and how much they cost, and how committed Paul was to getting her a dog. "Deb, I really, really want a dog bad now!"

And then she described the house: "Our whole house is done in very neutral shades (which I love)," she wrote. "All of the rooms are white with light gray baseboards and light gray carpeting (except the living room which has a hardwood floor). It sounds boring, but it looks way better than having every room a different color. It's much classier."

And her opinion of Toronto: "I decided a long time ago that we weren't living in Toronto. A. Too dangerous B. Too expensive C. Too many immigrants D. Too crowded, are the main reasons. St. Catharines is good for now until we go south. (In a few years probably). It's a good distance between Toronto and Buffalo for business."

Then Karla told Debbie that Paul's business was booming—nobody really knew what that business was—and that their mutual friend Kathy had married her marine, and the wedding was great, but he was being shipped off to Desert Storm. Kathy was all upset. More about Debbie's bridesmaid dress, and where was the money, and when was Debbie going to come and try it on?

She gave Debbie some advice about life and men: "Never feel guilty about taking from Dale or anybody else. The world will screw you in every way it can, so take as much as you can while you can."

Karla gave Debbie some beauty tips and then nattered on about the guest list and other wedding stuff . . . "The only thing we really need or want are 1. A Dustbuster 2. China 3. Crystal 4. Money. We really don't need anything. Plus, you know how picky we are! As for wedding gifts, please try to let people know that we want money! If they say things like, 'We don't believe in giving money,' tell them to go take a flying fuck!"

Then Karla told Debbie all about her mom and dad: "My parents are being assholes. They pulled half of the money out of the wedding, saying that they can't afford it. Bullshit.

"Now Paul and I have to pay for $7,000 to $8,000 of this wedding. So money is tight . . . but on Saturday, Paul and I just said 'fuck it,' we're doing everything the way we planned and some things even better! Real flowers for everyone, we're paying for the bar, hors d'oeuvres, a cocktail party, EVERY-THING!

"Fuck my parents. They are being so stupid. Only thinking of themselves. My father doesn't even want us to have a wedding any more. He thinks we should just go to city hall. Screw that. We're having a good time. If he wants to sit at home and be miserable, he's welcome to! He hasn't worked (except for one day!) since Tammy died. He's wallowing in his own misery and fucking me!"

Karla continues: "Tammy always said last year that she wanted a forest green Porsche for her 16th birthday. Now my Dad keeps saying, 'I would have bought it for her, if I'd have only known.' That's bullshit. If he really felt like that, he'd be paying for my wedding because I could die tomorrow or next year or whenever? He's such a liar.

"And for the real reason we moved out. My parents told Paul and I that they wanted him to stay at their house until the wedding. They told us that they didn't want him to go back to Toronto. So he stayed. Then a week before we moved they were driving me to work one day and asked me when he was leaving. They said they needed their privacy (after they told him he was their son) and that they needed me as a 'daughter'?! They wanted him to go home during the week and come back on weekends only.

"AFTER THEY TOLD US HE SHOULD STAY UNTIL THE WEDDING!! 1st they took away ½ the wedding money, then they kicked us out. They knew how much we need, we needed to be together but they didn't care. What assholes. Now they wonder why I don't phone them or come to visit. . . . Love, Karla."

Paul had redoubled his smuggling efforts. He had border crossing down to a fine science. Sometimes he made two and three trips a day. It was as if he had become invisible—the border guards simply did not see him.

. . .

One of Karla and Debbie's best girlfriends, former Exclusive Diamond Club member in good standing—a big, talkative, permanently permed blonde named Kathy Wilson—had just married. Kathy's marine, Alex Ford, also happened to be a Mason, an association that appealed to Karla and Paul. Whatever Kathy had, Karla wanted. She did not care about the military and the marine bit—that was stupid—but the Masons, that was something Karla could easily arrange. Karla's parents' best friend, Don Mitchell, was a Mason. He could get Paul into the Grantham Lodge, no problem. The lodge was just up the street. The Masons were a secret organization. Secrecy appealed to Paul and Karla. He could walk to the meetings if he wanted. At his first or second meeting, Paul took notes. "At conception, the programming phase occurs in which the genetic components gather information from actual experiences of the external environment and the process repeats itself. . . . Seeing into the future is merely viewing the past, which is accessible through the unconscious mind."

Karla was delighted. His Masonic notes read like her books about the occult.

In March, Paul went to Florida for two weeks, to celebrate the arrival of spring with Van Smirnis and another friend, gullible Gus. Karla had encouraged him to go, which really surprised Gus.

Once they got to Florida, they hooked up with a bunch of teenagers from Lindsay, Ontario, who were also down for spring break. Paul and Van were roughly the same age—twenty-five, twenty-six. The rest of these kids—Jason, Mark, Dave, Gus—were sixteen or seventeen. Paul liked being around younger guys. He was starting to think about a career in rap music; about how he could become the next big, white rapper, like Vanilla Ice. He had to keep that youthful perspective.

In Daytona Beach, Paul met a twenty-four-year-old nurse from South Carolina named Alison. The night they met, they had sex—anal sex. Paul had never met a girl who actually wanted anal sex. Not only did Alison want it, she liked it. That showed real attitude, as far as Paul was concerned.

Now Paul was confused. He thought he might be in love with Alison, too. He told Alison his secrets: how devastated he had been when his little sister, Tammy Lyn, mysteriously died in his arms the night before Christmas. Now he lived with his other sister, Karla, in a big house on a quiet street in a little town called Port Dalhousie.

When Paul was days late getting back to St. Catharines— because he had decided to stop in South Carolina and see where Alison lived—Karla became frantic. Paul told Karla all about Alison. She was a nurse; she made lots of money. She drove a Pontiac Grand Am; Paul had video and snapshots of him and Alison kissing. Karla was beside herself. She drank a whole bottle of champagne. On March 29, she went to the doctor and got another prescription for Halcion.

Something was wrong. Karla told Kathy and Alex Ford she thought her new house might be haunted. Just after Paul and Karla had moved into 57 Bayview, they started to bicker and fight. Paul was very sensitive to things in the environment. For instance, he could not stand the smell of cleaning products. That was a problem, because Karla had been taught to scrub everything with the strongest abrasives and cleansers possible. A hospital worker all her adult life, Dorothy Homolka had always been very serious about cleanliness. Things had to be antiseptic. Just as they were in a vet clinic. Then Paul had decided there were strange fumes emanating from the drains in the basement. He plugged all the drains. Things seemed to get better after that. But Karla still wondered about the ghosts.

On April Fool's Day, Paul called his old girlfriend, Marie Magritte and told her all about Tammy Lyn and his inconsolable grief. He bought Karla her Rottweiler puppy. They named the dog Buddy. Paul was such a sweetie. Even with his allergies, he went along with a dog. As far as Karla was concerned, Paul deserved whatever he got.

•   •   •

Corrina Jenkins would never forget Saturday morning, April 6, 1991. She got up at 5:00 A.M., passed on breakfast, and dressed warmly so she could jog over to the island and warm up for practice. Corrina was coxswain for the lighweight team from her school, Governor Simcoe. ·

Rowing was a big deal in Niagara. The Henley Regatta, which was held every year in August on the Martindale Pond in Port Dalhousie, drew as many as two thousand competitors. They ranged from teenage girls like Corrina to world champions such as Silken Laumann.

Athletes from as far away as Argentina and Australia came to compete. The five-day event attracted as many as sixty thousand spectators. For a small city like St. Catharines, with its one hundred and thirty thousand citizens, sixty thousand visitors was a staggering influx.

But it was April, and the port was quiet.

Corrina lived with her parents and sister near the antique carnival carousel on the beach park in front of town. She was a good student and a dedicated rowing fan. An ambitious and disciplined child of fourteen, when she was not training or studying she worked part-time at a gas station just across the highway on Ontario Street.

As she had done a hundred times before, Corrina left her house around 5:30 A.M., walking south on Corbett to Main Street. It was dead quiet and pitch black; an hour before dawn, the streetlights were still on.

She turned right on Main and walked east until she came to Henley Hill. Then she turned left and started to head south toward the bridge that links Henley Island to the mainland. It was no more than a twenty-five-minute walk from her door to the clubhouse on the island.

She sensed there was someone behind her and turned to look. Sure enough, there was a guy only fifty feet away. Even though he did not seem to be in a hurry, Corrina was seized with foreboding. He was not wearing rowing or jogging gear, so he was not a rower or someone just out for a run. What was he doing out here on the way to Henley Island at this hour in the morning? Corrina quickened her pace.

As she turned to look again, there was a car driving past, headed for the bridge, no more than a few hundred yards ahead. It was a station wagon, driven by a lady with blond hair who waved at her. Everything seemed to have slowed down, as if she were underwater or something. She saw the woman so clearly that she noticed her roots were starting to show. Corrina felt incredibly heavy and stifled, unable to breathe properly or move fast enough to avert whatever it was that was about to happen.

Suddenly, he was on her. But this sort of thing never happened in St. Catharines, so she must still be having a nightmare. The taste of her own blood convinced Corrina otherwise.

He had placed one hand so tightly over her mouth that her lip was cut on her front teeth. He had his pelvis pressed into her back. Struggling, she tried to pull his hand away from her face to tell him she could not breathe. His hands were too big and too strong. He pulled her through the ditch to a path that went up the wooded hillside. They had crossed the road in flat seconds, like two dancers staggering through a mad tango, and were now over on the right-hand side just before the bridge.

"This is just a joke," he said. "So shut the fuck up."

She managed to pull his hand away and scream. Immediately, he put it back over her nose and mouth, harder still. It took all her strength and concentration to pull it away again. Gasping for breath, she barely whispered: "Please don't cover my nose. I can't breathe."

Now they were across the road before the bridge and up at the top of the hill where it became bush. They both fell. She begged him again not to cover her nose. He pulled her back up. They were moving further into the wooded area. He still had his hand over her mouth. They came to the area where the field met the bush in the corner, just at the edge by the water.

She could hear the sound and voices of the sculling teams getting ready for the morning practice. Strangely, Corrina and the man started walking, as if they were out for a stroll. She was dazed and exhausted. Corrina stopped trying to remove his hand.

He said, "Everything is going to be okay. Just don't try anything or you'll regret it."

Then he pushed her down into a crouched position. He was behind her. He pulled her pants down to her knees. He took out his penis. She felt it between her legs. He tried to stick it in her. He tried again, and then again. He was pulling her head back by her hair with his right hand. She pleaded: "Please don't. Please don't hurt me."

He was half whispering, half speaking, gutturally repeating over and over again, "Shut the fuck up. Shut the fuck up." Then he forced her face to the ground on top of her hands. The fourth time he tried, his penis went all the way in. He groaned and then pulled it out.

He came around front. He was on his knees, too. He lifted her head with her hair, put his penis in her mouth and said "suck it, bitch." She refused to do anything, so he started moving her head. He came a little bit in her mouth. When she tried to spit it out, he said, "You fucking little bitch."

He stuck it back in her mouth and said, "Put your hand on it and move it with your hand." Then he took it out again. He pushed her head down so that her head was on her hands again.

He demanded that she take off her coat. She did. She had on her red nylon rowing jacket which said SIMCOE CREW in white letters across the back.

Then he told her to take off her shirts. It gets cold on the water at spring thaw; over her white bra she had on her Einstein T-shirt, a grey Nike turtleneck, a mock cotton turtleneck, then a royal blue cotton turtleneck and a hooded shirt that said CANADA in red letters on the front.

Once Corrina had her arms out, he pulled all the shirts over her head. Her bra came off, too. Then he made her take off her Reeboks and pulled off all her pants—she was wearing blue cotton panties, Nike Spandex shorts, longjohns and gray jogging pants. Her three pairs of socks came off with her pants. Corrina was completely naked.

He got behind her again and covered her mouth with his hand. Then he pulled her up. He started walking her downhill toward the water. "Please, don't put me in the water. Please," Corrina said. Her voice sounded so small.

"I'm not going to. Just crouch down here by this tree." She did as he said and he pushed her head toward the base of the tree. He had a pair of black Isotoner gloves and he was carrying a pair of used black pantyhose. Corrina remembered thinking "How odd. Why would he have used pantyhose?".

"Wait here for five minutes, don't move and don't make a sound." He started to walk away, then he stopped and said, "Oh, and do yourself a favor: don't tell anyone or I'll have to kill you." Naked as a forest nymph, she knelt at the tree's base, counting, silently.

For some reason she thought about the old carousel on the beach. It was housed in a gazebo, which they closed up in the wintertime. During the summer, the children flocked around it and the hand-carved horses and majestic tigers with fire in their eyes rose up and down to jingle-jangle carnival music. They only charged the children five cents a ride.

After a couple of minutes she glanced up. Dawn was breaking. There were a few swans on the pond. She was alone. Sobbing, she gathered up her clothes from where he had scattered them on the hillside. She ran back to the road and her friend Marilyn was driving by with her father and they stopped. They called the police.

When Karla woke up on Saturday morning, she discovered Paul was not in the house. Karla was worried. He had gone out the night before with his friends. He often got home very late—with cigarette runs and everything—but he seldom stayed out all night, especially on a Friday. Then again, Karla was a very sound sleeper. Maybe he had come home late and got up early.

She went downstairs and started to make herself something to eat. Suddenly the door to the garage opened and he came in. He had something in his hands. He looked really happy. Karla was relieved.

. . .

Corrina told the police that her attacker was about six feet tall, muscular, with brownish-blond hair, pretty short on the top but it seemed to go down the back of his neck, the way some guys were wearing their hair then. She got a good look at him. He was clean-cut. He did not smell. He was probably in his twenties. He had on a green-and-black sweater and blue jeans. They took her to the hospital and administered a rape kit.

"Where were you?" Karla asked Paul as he came through the door from the garage.

"I just raped a girl," he replied. He was so excited he could hardly hold still. He was just like a little kid. Then Paul showed Karla the rowing shell he had in his hand and explained how he had decided to take it because he thought he had got semen on it and he did not want them to be able to do any forensic testing. He was going to burn it in the fireplace.

His Scarborough rape ordeal had long been forgotten. The police must have been making comparisons to samples they took from Margaret McWilliam, after all. Paul had not even been in the country when that happened. As far as Paul and Karla were concerned, he was free and clear. Even his friends, including that idiot Van Smirnis, had stopped kidding him about it.

Next to her own, Paul's well-being and happiness were Karla's greatest concerns. He treated her like a princess and she treated him like a prince. Dogs with championship lines cost hundreds of dollars, and even though Paul had allergies he had let her pick out the best dog.

And they really had not had any fun since the January Girl and the great movie they made in which she played her sister. There was one lame attempt with Tammy's friend Tricia when they first moved. But all they got was a few seconds of video while Tricia was urinating.

Tricia was very wary of them and Karla knew why. Karla had gone to a great deal of trouble to plug the toilet downstairs so Tricia would have to use the one upstairs. But Paul's idea of removing the wall socket in the upstairs bathroom and filming through the small hole had not worked very well. They did not have much fun with Tricia.

One day, when they were driving around Port Dalhousie, Paul pointed out an attractive, young girl who looked to be about fifteen years old. "There's the girl I raped," he said proudly.

Karla was happy for him—whatever the king wanted, the king should have—but she was not as confident about his impunity as he was. What if he had left something behind when he raped her that Saturday morning on Henley Island and they got forensics on it, and somehow made the connection to Scarborough and compared them to samples he had given the police in Toronto last November?

Or maybe this rower girl could recognize him. Paul was supposed to use her pantyhose—he always had a pair in the car with his knife and a piece of cord, but he would no more pull a stocking over his head than he would put a hat on Snuffles.

In Karla's estimation, he had been very lucky in Scarborough. Obviously the police were not that smart, or maybe, just maybe, he had been as smart and careful as he said he was. Nevertheless, now it was far too close to her home for her comfort.

At this rate, Karla could lose him—forever. And of course, she could go to jail for Tammy. After all, as Paul was fond of telling her when he was mad, she had killed her own sister with her stupid drugs.

On top of everything else, there was this Alison person Paul had met in Florida. Karla did not mind pretending that she was Paul's sister when the girl called—she sounded nice. But the fact that Alison liked anal intercourse, when Karla did not, really bothered her. Once again, Karla felt she was losing control.

On her twenty-first birthday, Karla wrote Paul a letter: "You hate me. You say you want to go out with other girls . . . you say I make you sick. You tell me to pack and leave. (You tell me to eat shit and die, etc., etc., etc.)"

She admitted her innate idiocy, her inability to show love

and respect, but she demonstrated her superior intellect with a simplistic tautology: "I think, if we truly loved each other the way we thought we did, in the past tense, we could have been able to overcome anything . . ."

She went on to admit it was all her fault—sure, he had said things to hurt her, but she had said very hurtful things to him as well and so on, blah, blah: "I want us to be happy like we used to be. I think you hate me too much for that to ever happen . . ." Paul and Karla drove up to Kitchener to celebrate her birthday and Paul's Grandfather Eastman's, which coincidentally fell on the same day. They went to the Charcoal Steakhouse for dinner.

Karla knew she had to do something very special to hold this wild, dangerous man whom she loved so much. On the way to Kitchener, she lifted her skirt, pulled down her panties and mooned a car full of teenage girls. Paul loved it. Then Karla remembered Jane.

CHAPTER

fourteen

It was Paul and Karla's intention to make a lot of money on their wedding. The key was to invite a large number of people to the wedding—whether they knew them or not—and tell them to give money, not gifts. Karla was racking her brain for names, when she remembered Jane. There were some things money could not buy. Jane was one of them.

Karla and Jane first met when Karla was still working at the Number One Pet Center and Jane came in all excited about this little Cairn terrier named Toto in the window. Jane was twelve years old at the time. She started hanging around all the time, offering to do odd jobs in the store.

Karla made sure Jane was invited to one of her showers. She also decided to call Jane up and invite her over to the house. Jane was bouncy and blond. She looked a bit like Karla, except she had larger breasts. She really looked more like Karla's dead sister, Tammy. She would make a perfect wedding gift.

When Jane got the call she couldn't believe it. Jane loved Karla. Karla was beautiful and she loved animals almost as much as Jane did. And Karla had been so nice to her when she went into the pet store and wanted to pet Toto.

She had not heard from or seen Karla in three years. The call came right out of the blue. Jane said that she would just love to come over and see Karla's house and meet her dog.

That first night in June was magical. It was as though Karla was the big sister Jane did not have. Jane was the only child of divorced parents and she lived with her mother in Fonthill, a nearby town.

When Jane got to 57 Bayview, Karla was alone. Karla told her that Paul, her fiancé, also lived there, but he had gone out for the night. It would be just like a pajama party or a sleepover, Karla told Jane. Karla and Jane had a great time. They walked into town and Karla bought Jane dinner. They talked and talked and got caught up on old times.

When they got back to the house they watched a video— *Ghost,* with Demi Moore. It was so romantic, so sad. They put on some great music and had some drinks and played with Buddy. Buddy was Karla's Rottweiler. He was just a puppy—a big puppy. He was so great. Karla had a brand-new video camera. Karla loved videotaping; she had made videos for school projects and she took a lot of pictures of Jane playing with Buddy.

Jane had always wanted to try alcoholic drinks, so Karla happily obliged. Karla made Jane some really good drinks. The next thing Jane knew, it was morning and she felt really sick.

When she came downstairs, she met Paul for the first time. Then she threw up. Paul and Karla drove her home. She was in bed with the flu for the next three days. Her mother kept asking her what a married couple in their twenties could possibly want with a fifteen-year-old girl?

Karla called Paul on his car phone. "I have a surprise for you," she whispered provocatively. "Get home."

When he got home he could not believe his eyes: Karla had brought Tammy back to life again. And she was asleep on the floor in their bedroom. She was wearing his white Oxford Hall sweatshirt—the one Karla had shrunk. It was pushed up around her neck. Her breasts were much larger than Karla's. Karla knew that, but she pointed out—again—that hers were better.

Paul was very glad he had reminded Karla about the Boy Scouts' motto: "Be prepared." They had crushed a bunch of Halcion tablets—just in case—and mixed them in a solution that they kept in a test tube in the bathroom. It was blue, like the water in Lake Ontario, which they could see from the second dormer window in their bedroom. Karla had mixed some of her blue water into Jane's drinks. She had also brought another bottle of halothane home from work—just in case.

After what had happened to Tammy, Paul was very concerned about the drugs, but Karla had reassured him. Tammy probably had died because she had had too much to eat and drink just before she was knocked out. It was common medical and veterinary practice not to allow patients food for at least twelve hours before surgery. Jane would be fine. There would be no problem. This time Karla would get it right.

Paul got the video camera. Karla got the halothane and a cloth. She put some halothane on the cloth and held it near Jane's mouth and nose. This time Karla would make sure the girl got enough air. Paul got started making the video he had wanted to make with Tammy Lyn.

First he had to pull off Jane's white cotton panties. He held the camera steadier this time, while he lubricated Jane's vagina. Then he panned to a long shot of Karla administering the halothane. In the background there was the usual bedroom mess. Jane was spread-eagled on the floor, with her head slightly raised on one of Paul and Karla's new king-size pillows. Karla was intent on her work: holding that halothane-soaked cloth just so close, over Jane's face.

Next, Karla started performing cunnilingus on Jane. She licked Jane and then raised her head, licked her lips, wagged her tongue back and forth and smiled wantonly for the camera. Then she did the extreme close-up thing, just the way she had the previous Christmas. Only this time Karla pretended to plant a big, fat kiss on the camera lens.

Then she sucked Jane's breasts, first the right, then the left. When she sat up, Paul caught her smiling face. Karla could get Paul so hard. It was very hard now, so he pulled it out and put it in Jane. This was just too good to be true. Jane was a virgin. He told Karla to keep her down.

"Shit, I'll have to bust it," he said, referring to Jane's hymen.

He focused the camera on his penis as he moved it in and out. Then he rolled Jane over on her side and discovered she had bled on the blanket. He held the camera on the spots of blood and then focused on her buttocks.

"Pretty nice ass, eh?" he said as he used a tissue to wipe the blood off Jane's thighs.

This was exactly the way it was supposed to have been with Tammy. Karla was truly amazing. Every time things started to get a little tense or he became distracted, Karla would do something that refocused his attention on just how great Karla was. Paul guessed he would have to go through with it and marry her now. Where would he ever find another girl like Karla?

Karla had kept her sleeveless lifeguard tank top on, but she was naked from the waist down. She climbed over Jane's face, held up the tank top and rubbed her clitoris on Jane's nose and mouth.

"Okay, okay," Paul said. "Take her hand and put it in your cunt."

Kneeling beside Jane, with her legs apart, Karla took Jane's lifeless hand and rubbed it against her labia. She rotated her hips lasciviously and then got that incredible look in her eyes—that look of incomparable lust and evil that Paul loved so much.

"Put the fingers inside you," he said, and Karla did just as she was told.

And Karla was right. Jane was just fine. They put her up on their bed and she slept through the night. Reviewing the footage—he had almost fifteen minutes—it was perfect. There were those silly helium balloons from Karla's shower hovering in the background. Karla looked great. Everything was perfect. What a great wedding present.

The next day, after they drove Jane home, Paul punched Karla hard a couple of times on her upper left arm and on the left side of her back. Karla was dumbfounded. What could possibly be wrong?

"Everything went smoothly with Jane," Paul explained angrily. "Why couldn't it have been the same with Tammy?"

It was Thursday, June 14, 1991 and to Leslie Mahaffy nothing seemed quite right with the world. It might have been hormonal, or it might have been because of Chris Evans, or her mother, or her boyfriend, Grant. Maybe it was a combination of things: Chris's sudden death in that awful car accident on Monday, her boyfriend, her mother and her hormones. Leslie's counselor called it "the trouble."

"The trouble" was that nothing she heard or did seemed relevant to her life, except maybe the Doors. Leslie lit a Du-Maurier and leaned against the Rock. She had been arrested for shoplifting a couple of months earlier. She had stolen a cassette copy of The Doors' *Morrison Hotel:*

> "Can't you feel it now that Spring has come,
> that it is time to live in the scattered Sun."

The cops charged her with "theft under" and she pled out to the Alternative Measures program. As punishment, she had to keep a scrapbook about criminals, their crimes and punishments; write a letter of apology to her parents and donate twenty-five dollars to a charity. Now she was seeing a counselor.

But now spring was gone with its scattered sun and Chris Evans was dead; she had just come from the funeral home where they had had a kind of wake that would be extended tonight at the Rock.

There had been a so-called "field party"; it seemed a lifetime ago, but this was Thursday. The accident had happened on Monday night and six kids, including Chris, had got in somebody's car and taken off and lost control over the crest of a hill on Sideroad One and collided with a huge, old maple tree. Now four of them, including Chris, had joined the spirit in that tree. It was not entirely true that Chris was Leslie's best friend, but knowing a dead person was a bit like knowing a rock star.

"The trouble" really started at the end of January when Leslie got her interim report card. Some of her marks were awful: 25 percent in visual arts; 35 percent in English; 54 percent in keyboard but 83 percent in history—she seemed to have an intuitive understanding of events in time and space.

The atmosphere at school had become weird: it seemed to Leslie that her teachers were hiding something, treating her differently, but maybe it was just the accident and Chris's death. Leslie had no way of knowing that a series of memos about her from the guidance office were circulating among her teachers. The latest one was marked Confidential and requested that Leslie's teachers call her mother. The urgency was stressed in capital letters, for them to PLEASE CALL MRS. MAHAFFY TODAY, IF POSSIBLE.

It all had to do with skipping classes and making sure Leslie paid for the consequences. Teachers were told not to let Leslie know that her mother was contacting them. Debbie Mahaffy advised "that Leslie is a student who does respond well to praise and will work to achieve it."

When Leslie did find out, it did not really surprise her. After all, her own mother had gone to a justice of the peace and sworn out a Warrant of Apprehension, so that the cops could arrest her when she ran away from home.

Leslie had been trying to do the right thing. A few Saturday nights earlier, Leslie had even phoned home from her friend Nina's house to ask permission to go to the movies and see *The Silence of the Lambs.* Her mother did not think that was a good idea. Instead of going home, Leslie had gone to one of Eric Drage's parties, got stoned, had sex with Jay Booth and stayed at his place. He was twenty and lived in Room 12 at the Crestwood Motel. It was April 1, 1991—April Fools!

The Crestwood Motel was runaway city. Leslie's friends, Nikki Eisbrenner and Kristen Fee, were in Room 9. Nikki's dad had even given her money for the rent. Dave Scott was in Room 10. He was a friend of Jay's and Grant's, but he really bugged Leslie. Once, he had grabbed her butt.

Jay had been picked up on three "fail to appears" and a weapons charge. Leslie was left alone for what seemed long periods of time over those two weeks she lived in Jay's room. Not that Leslie was necessarily unhappy. The way Jay Booth saw it, Leslie could never bring herself to talk about what was going on inside her.

There were a couple of older guys, friends of Dave's, real pigs, dirty looking, like the little, older guy with the mustache, messy brown hair and the beer belly who was always hanging around the motel. Then there was a guy in Room 11, Randy— he was with a strange woman who had a German Shepherd named Ninja.

Leslie had become blasé, detached, cool; probably for some very good reasons, but not being particularly self-aware, like many kids her age, she could only express it through malfeasance. It washed over her like the endless water on which her father floated. He worked for the Ministry of Natural Resources. They called it hydrographic surveying. Never around in the summer, Dan Mahaffy was always off on some lake somewhere, charting its contours.

·   ·   ·

Leslie was leaning against the Rock smoking, thinking. A lot of the local teenagers—the cops called them mall rats—hung around the Rock, smoking the odd joint, snorting this and that, gossiping, dropping acid. The newspaper reports described these gatherings as field parties, but they were more than that. This little enclave was almost as high-tension as the hydro wires that disappeared through the vanishing point along this hydro-electric right-of-way.

Leslie made sure Grant knew she had slept with Jay. As far as Leslie was concerned, she would do as she pleased. One night at the Crestwood Motel—the same night Grant banged on Jay's door—yelling for Leslie to come out at the top of his lungs at three in the morning, yelling out, "She's a pig," over and over again—Grant had sat all night in David Scott's room, the one right next to Jay's, mixing his feral, jealous rage with booze, getting drunk. Leslie had really crossed his wires.

Some of her friends actually thought Leslie took some perverse pleasure in Grant's jealous rages. For instance, she knew the less she said, the more frantic Grant would become. So whenever she was around him, Leslie would be deadly quiet.

A couple of weeks before, Leslie's good friend Amanda Carpino had stayed over at her house. They had gone to Mac's Milk for Slurpees or whatever, and these guys came reeling out of Carrigan's Bar. One had a T-shirt on that said I Hate Ritchies—whatever that meant. They said they had lots of money and would show Leslie and Amanda a good time. Leslie surprised Amanda and said they did not have enough of anything to show them a good time. Leslie was slowly discovering that "the trouble" could be turned into a profound, irrepressible force. "The trouble" was a source of energy and power, and it did not necessarily have to be self-destructive.

After the police picked her up at the Crestwood, drunk, at 3:30 in the afternoon on Friday, April 12, and took her home, she had run away again. Her mother made her dad take the warrant of apprehension over to the police station again, but Leslie eventually went back home—mostly of her own accord. Nikki convinced her. Nikki, who was sixteen, was like an older sister to Leslie.

Nikki called the police and they picked Leslie up in front of the Miracle Food Mart and took her home. This time Leslie stayed and went back to counseling.

She made a couple of deals and a few concessions: no drinking, no skipping school. Her parents set up a reward system—allowance on a daily rather than weekly basis, another five minutes on curfew for every week endured without an incident, stuff like that.

Leslie knew she probably should not be drinking and screwing around all the time. She made it through May pretty well. Her counseler noted: "Leslie has matured over the past few weeks. She believes the situation at home is much improved, in large part because she is actively challenging the trouble."

Chris and the other three dead kids were going to be buried tomorrow. Leslie ironed the waves out of her long blond hair and pulled on a pair of cutoff jean shorts and her navy kangaroo Georgetown top; she slipped into her leather deck shoes and walked over to the SuperCenter, met Amanda and went to the Rock for a cigarette. At 11:15 A.M., "challenging the trouble," she went to school to write an exam.

CHAPTER

fifteen

Exaggerated when dejected or walking deliberately, the men in the Bernardo clan list back and forth on rather large feet, toes pointed out at cartoon-like angles. If on a mission, their gait becomes more pronounced, their bodies leaning toward the anticipated destination, heads hunkered down—not at all unlike the Gotham City–bound Penguin, as Burgess Meredith played him on the old "Batman" television series.

Paul Bernardo was a walking testament to the idea that people become what they behold. He walked exactly like his step-father, and by the way Paul was walking on this fine summer afternoon it was obvious that he was on a mission.

By June 14, 1991, Paul Bernardo had acheived one of his goals: he had fully affected that "Baywatch" look: six feet tall, athletic, lithe, well muscled, tanned, with the boyish, open face and blond hair buzzed on the sides, a bit longish up top; what was euphemistically called, in hairstyling circles, feathered.

He had parked the gold Nissan 240SX in Market Square, and was headed toward the courthouse to retrieve a marriage license. Since Karla worked and he was now "self-employed"—and forms and figures were his metier, anyway—obtaining the marriage license was the least he could do.

As usual, Market Square, in the heart of beautiful downtown St. Catharines, was a hive of activity. A large area with a few hundred metered parking spots, the square was bound by the municipal buildings and the mayor's office, the library and a burger-and-beer joint called Gord's Place.

Every Tuesday, Thursday and Saturday morning, a few dozen vendors took over fifty or sixty parking spaces and set up booths from which they sold fresh produce, meat and flowers.

Directly behind the library was the Niagara Regional Police headquarters where Paul and Karla had been questioned the night Tammy Lyn died. Paul was parked directly in front of the Blue Mermaid, a velour-upholstered restaurant, which was patronized by lawyers and judges. Paul crossed Church Street and disappeared through the courthouse door.

St. Catharines sits on a level plateau surrounded by what an early pioneer described as "a country which for beauty and fertility cannot be surpassed on the continent." That country, which is known as the Niagara Peninsula, produces some of the finest wines, produce and flowers in the civilized world.

There are dozens of successful vineyards and vintners, market gardeners with massive greenhouses, wealthy farmers and a multimillion-dollar perennial-bulb and cut-flower industry that exports a billion dollars' worth of tulips, geraniums and lilies annually to the United States.

Characteristic of the atmosphere of anomaly that has always defined the Niagara Region, the peninsula is not, in fact, a peninsula but a narrow bridge of land between Canada and the United States bound by Lake Ontario on the north and Lake Erie to the south. All that separates St. Catharines and the Niagara Region from the United States is twelve miles and a devastating waterfall.

The peninsula lies further south than most people imagine and is relatively sheltered from climatic extremes. There is more chance of frost damage in the Georgian peach orchards and the vineyards of the Napa Valley than on the peninsula.

But agriculture alone could not sustain St. Catharines. Not with so much cheap hydroelectric power so nearby. It had become a blue-collar factory town, whose main employer was General Motors. The population of St. Catharines was comprised of hardworking people who had come under siege as the economy forced the closure of hundreds of North American plants and factories. St. Catharines had the second highest rate of unemployment in Canada. There was an atmosphere of dissonance, quiet hysteria and chaos, from which Paul Bernardo derived sustenance. He also liked the small city's proximity and the ease of access to the United States. That and a daughter of the city—his beautiful, blushing bride-to-be, Karla Leanne Homolka, whose name he dutifully printed on the requisite forms.

"When was the bitch born?" Paul often called Karla "the bitch," quietly and in public; Mr. Homolka was always calling Mrs. Homolka "the old bitch." It was really a term of endearment.

"I beg your pardon, sir?" said the clerk. Paul smiled and waved her off. Concentrating on the forms: Karla was born on May 4, 1970. That would make her twenty-one already; perhaps he should call off the wedding; she was getting a bit long in the tooth and did not even act like a virgin anymore.

He and Karla were to be married in two short weeks on Saturday, June 29, at St. Mark's Anglican Church in Niagara-on-the-Lake, Reverend Ian Grieve presiding. Paul dutifully filled in all the blanks.

Their wedding was going to be the best. Mazy Jackson, the big Irish woman at the Queen's Landing who organized weddings for the hotel, told them that their wedding was almost the largest and most lavish she had planned in her twenty years as a professional wedding planner.

The only one larger was one she had done—at Queen's Landing, as well—for a Bronfman sibling. Given the fact that the Bronfmans were among the richest people in the world, Paul and Karla were not doing half bad.

Their wedding was going to be perfect. The historic church in Niagara-on-the-Lake with the white horses and the carriage, champagne, a sit-down dinner for one hundred and fifty guests with veal-stuffed pheasant at Queen's Landing, no expense spared.

He put the marriage license on the car seat and drove out of the parking lot. He must think of some special gift for his betrothed.

At 4:30 P.M., Leslie Mahaffy got on the bus in front of M. M. Robinson High School and went to Harvey's in the SuperCentre. Amanda was there with Angie, Frank Corda and Grant. She sat down and ordered a junior burger. Grant was being a grunt and Leslie's silence was golden. As if Leslie were not even there, Grant kept asking everybody, "Why's she mad at me? Why's she mad at me?" over and over again.

Leslie went home and changed: as she rummaged through her drawer she was troubled by her lack of choices. She put on her white Vogue bra. Leslie had managed to coerce her mother into letting her wear the white long-sleeved silk blouse with the short collar, but it had been a real hassle. She and her mother had to have what her mother called "a chat" about it. Leslie could wear it, but her mother wanted it back—without anything spilled on it.

Leslie finally, reluctantly, selected her beige walking shorts with the pleats and slash pockets; they were knee length, so she rolled them up to shorten them a bit. She chose her flat leather whites—accessorize and coordinate. She noticed that her imitation opal mood ring had turned black. There was certainly nothing she could think about that would turn the ring green or orange on her way to the funeral home.

It was around seven o'clock. They were going to make a cigarette run. Karla always went with Paul whenever she could. The guards never bothered stopping a young, good-looking, well-groomed couple from St. Catharines. As in most things, the key to the sagacious management of contraband was appearance—no beards, no fidgeting with fingers, hands visible on the wheel. Looking the Customs agents in the eye, and willing their complicity, Paul and Karla had yet to be stopped.

It took them about ten minutes to get to the Whirlpool Bridge—of three international bridges in Niagara Falls it was the least technologically sophisticated, the least busy and seemed to have the least stringent staff. Nevertheless, the adrenaline always pumped when Paul made a run.

Paul felt good. He had succeeded in profoundly changing his life. Instead of $35,000 annually, taxed at source, he often made $15,000 a month, tax free. And what was the risk? Customs would confiscate the cigarettes, if they found them. Whether they would lay charges or not was a toss-up. Even if they did, the fines were minimal.

"St. Catharines, sir, just over for dinner," he would say, and Karla smiled demurely as they were waved through. The real rush was coming back. A convenient feature in this model Nissan: many concealed compartments built into the door panels. Paul could stuff up to sixty cartons of cigarettes and six forty-ounce bottles of liquor in the doors and behind the speakers. Karla's used black pantyhose were fitted around the bottoms of the panels—if a Customs agent used mirrors or a flashlight, all he would see was black.

Customs recorded the Bernardos crossing at 7:36 P.M. that night. They made the leisurely drive to Steve Smirnis's garage in a matter of minutes. Passing by Van Smirnis's girlfriend's parents' house on the highway outside Youngstown, Paul could not remember what her father did. There was all this assemble-your-own patio furniture out on their lawn.

What else could one expect from the parents of a girl who would take up with Van? Her name was Fuller—Joann Fuller. She was younger than Karla by at least four years, which made her barely sixteen. Van was ten years older, but on a scale of maturity, he and Joann were about the same age.

Karla disliked Van and Joann intensely. To her, they were both losers and it showed in their poor grammar. But they were convenient accomplices, living in the United States, with the video store and all that.

The oldest Smirnis brother, Steve, who was always trying to hit on Karla, lived with his Texas bride, Bev, and their children, in a house in Youngstown. They stored the cigarettes in their garage. All Paul had to do was pull up into the garage—day or night—load up and drive out. Van told him he had even per-suaded a couple of Indians to bring the cigarettes over to the house for him. Paul never had to touch the product out in the open.

He and Karla were home by ten. Paul would accumulate enough cartons of cigarettes—say four or five hundred car-tons—and then meet Van in Oakville, transfer them to Van's car and he would drive them up to Patrick Johnnie's garage outside Sutton.

At 10:45 P.M., Paul called Van from the house. They agreed to meet at the usual spot.

The fashion magazines all said accessorize. Leslie decided to wear her big gold hoop earrings. Her mother drove Leslie and her friend Angie to Smith's Funeral Home. Leslie and Angie stayed for about an hour. Leslie left the funeral home and went to the SuperCentre, where she met Amanda. They walked over to the Rock with Hank Corda and Jim Mahon. Sometime between the time Leslie left the funeral home and arrived at the Rock her mood ring changed color. She did not know why, but she got happy.

The Rock was like a magnet: by the time they got to it, there must have been two hundred people there. Somebody was playing the Doors, loud:

"Blood speed the brain and chop off the fingers
Blood in the bone in the death of a nation. . . ."

There was cold beer. Leslie liked cold beer. She was "in the zone." Amanda came over to say goodbye around 10:30 P.M. and Leslie hugged her. Leslie had never hugged Amanda before, but that was the kind of mood Leslie was in. Jason Booth was watching her: she was just a little social butterfly all night, flitting from one group to the next; sipping a beer here, a beer there.

With her sisters, Christine and Brenda, Barbara Eady, a thirty-something divorced mother, decided to go to Jake's Roadhouse around 9:30 or 10:00 P.M. Jake's was a popular bar in Burlington. Barbara's children, Brooke and Shea, were at the Rock; there was some kind of wake for those poor kids who were killed on Monday night, so Barbara pretty well had the evening to herself. She was standing at the bar when a guy came up from behind her. "Do you believe in angels?" he asked.

He was tall, good-looking, with feathered hair. He introduced the women to his friend Steve, a big, dark brown-haired guy who talked about golf.

"He appeared nervous, like he didn't want to talk to us," Barbara recalled. "He sort of went back and forth all night, kind of upset or something. They had a couple of other girls in tow."

Sometimes the blond-haired guy did not make sense. "You come from a very powerful family," he said, out of the blue. "Why are you here? Are you police? What are you drinking?"

He was talking about reincarnation, too. "How could you not trust a face like mine?" he asked.

Barbara's sister Christine said she did not trust anybody with dimples. A very smooth talker, the young man had a big dimple on his right cheek. He said he was an accountant from Toronto.

When Christine talked to him about Jesus and repenting, his demeanor changed. Barbara put her hand out to say goodbye and he shook it, and then used his other hand to hold over their clasped hands. She told him that whatever he was involved in, he was in over his head and she would pray for him.

Martin McSweeney had been a good friend of Chris Evans. He pounded back eight or ten beers at the Rock that night in memory. Martin was a big lad and he had been so upset by his friend's untimely death that the beers hardly touched him.

Martin told Leslie Mahaffy he would walk her home. On the way they stopped at the Mac's Milk store, where Leslie always bought candy for her little brother, Ryan. Martin had called his home from the pay phone, but there was no answer.

Walking up Duncaster to Barlow, Leslie and Martin dragged their heels, talking. The way Leslie looked at it, with her mother an inch was a mile. Since she had blown her curfew when she was not home at exactly 11:30 P.M., it did not matter what time she got home.

She and Martin sat down on the bank of the hill behind Leslie's house. They talked some more and kissed a bit. Then they went through the backyards to Leslie's house. Leslie tried the side door of her house; it was locked. So were the windows. She had debated with her mother about curfew—her mother was adamant she should be in by 11:30 P.M. at the latest. Leslie had argued, saying that this was an unusual circumstance, to no avail. But she still could not believe that her mother had locked her out.

She went to the front door. It was locked, too. Martin said he could not wait any longer, he had to get home. After he left, she walked around the back of the house again. Leslie watched Martin go down the hill behind the house and into the ravine. Then he disappeared in the dark.

.   .   .

At two o'clock the phone rang and rang. Even though the
phone was right beside Amanda's bed, the sound came from far
away. Amanda's mother finally answered it, woke Amanda up
and told her it was Leslie. It was a warm night. The window
was open and a light breeze billowed the curtains.

Right away Leslie started telling Amanda that the cops had
come to the Rock. A big spark had exploded out of the fire the
guys had built and one of those huge trees almost became a
burning bush. Leslie said she had left about two hours after
Amanda, around 12:30 A.M. and Martin McSweeney walked her
home. Leslie told Amanda that she was alone, she had no
money. She told Amanda that she had fooled around with Martin when they had been alone; that she really liked him.

Amanda had to break off twice—when a beep comes on the
line it means somebody else is trying to call. It was Amanda's
sister, sick at a sleepover. Halfway through the conversation,
Amanda's mother went to get her sister.

Leslie wanted to know if she could come over, just for the
night?

"I don't think it would be such a good idea," Amanda told
her. The last time Mrs. Carpino had let Leslie stay over, Leslie's
mother had given Amanda's mother proper shit the next day.
Why not just go home and ring the bell? Amanda advised.
Things had been pretty good at home lately, there had not been
much trouble, it was no big deal.

To Amanda, Leslie sounded upset and confused. Maybe it
was the shock of finding herself locked out. She was talking
quickly and kind of loud. She kept saying she did not want to
go home. The last time Leslie had run away she had copped her
grandmother's cash card, dyed her hair and somehow got hold
of some phoney ID.

Leslie's hair was naturally frizzy and a little bit curly but she
liked to wear it straight. She always told Amanda if she really ran
away she would take her hair straightener, her makeup, address
book and clothes. Amanda believed her, but tonight Leslie had
none of that stuff. She said she got the quarter for the phone call

from somebody. She never said who. It was so quiet in the background that Amanda mentioned it. She just assumed that Leslie was at the pay phone in Mac's.

They talked for about a half hour. When she hung up, Amanda never thought the end was near; she just assumed Leslie would go home.

Paul did not notice the name of the bar—it was some country-and-western joint, next to the Keg. He often met the Smirnis boys at the Keg in the plaza off Kerr Street in Oakville, just before Trafalgar Road. The Keg had closed at midnight. Paul had barely sat down when they announced last call. The boys moved next door.

When they came out there were a couple of cops at the doughnut shop in the plaza. So they waited about twenty minutes until the police left. Then the Smirnis brothers left. It was Paul's plan to steal a few more license plates before he called it a night. Stolen plates came in handy. Canada Customs had spotters on the American side who randomly reported people with large quantities of cigarettes in their cars. Sometimes, a tourist would even call Customs. They would call ahead to the border and report license plates.

The experienced smuggler picked up his cigarettes and started toward the border, pulled over and quickly changed the plates, crossed the border with impunity and then changed them back on the other side. Paul headed across the highway into Burlington, where he had scored a couple of sets of plates a few weeks earlier.

A territorial animal, Paul drove directly to the spot where he had parked the car before. He got out and cut through a tall hedge with a short fence around it. He tried to cut behind and then lost his footing and sank backward into the hedge. He felt like an idiot. Regaining his footing, he cut across the backyard.

Suddenly he saw someone walk around the house into the backyard. It was a girl. He watched as she checked the doors at the back of the house. In the dim light cast by the street lamps, she looked good. There were no lights on in the house. Paul thought to himself that when she got in, he might be able to do a little voyeurism. She was hot, he was there—why not? He started toward the other side of the house. She had gone around the front and unexpectedly came back down the side Paul had started to explore. They were both surprised.

"What are you doing here . . . ?" She was not scared—she sounded upbeat, kind of happy.

"What are you doing here?"

"I live here," she said.

"Well, I'm trying to pick a house over there," Paul said. She said, "Cool."

Paul could not believe his good fortune. Maybe he should take her back to St. Catharines and give Karla a special present, too.

The girl said she had been locked out of the house. Paul suggested that she just knock real loud on the door or throw something at the window and wake them up. But she said that her mother was going to be real angry and just yell and scream at her. Paul said that she really should ring the doorbell, but she said she just could not do that.

"I don't know where to stay," she said. "Have you got a cigarette?" And that was when Paul made up his mind—he had a place where she could stay.

"I have some in my car," he said. Going back to the car, the girl was carefree, twirling around, doing pirouettes, circling the friendly stranger, just as if they were boyfriend and girlfriend.

The girl lived on a quiet cul-de-sac called Keller Court. Paul's car was parked around the corner. When they got back to the car, Paul gave her the cigarette she wanted. He asked her what her name was.

"Leslie Mahaffy," she said. "What's yours?"

"Oh," he said, "that doesn't really matter . . ." Bending over, he got his knife from under the seat.

"Okay, Leslie," he said, showing her the knife, "close the door."

She did. Then he threw her his red turtleneck sweater from the backseat.

"Put this over your head. You're coming home with me," he told her. Paul started the car and drove off. "And don't try to figure out where we're going, just keep that turtleneck on your head or else."

CHAPTER
sixteen

Like a rapist, Paul crept into the bedroom and placed his large hand over her mouth. He shook her awake. A heavy sleeper, it took her a few minutes to come around. She blinked, looking at him incomprehensibly. He whispered, "Be quiet, there's somebody in the house," and took his hand off her mouth.

That got Karla's attention. She sat bolt upright, suddenly awake. By the clock radio it was three o'clock in the morning. "Look," he said. "Just stay up here and don't come down for a while and be quiet. I brought someone home." He left the room and Karla heard him go back downstairs. She could tell. Paul was very excited.

Karla was curious. What in God's name was he up to now? With Paul, there was never a dull moment; she had not been bored once since they met. She got up and snuck down to the point in the stairs where she could just see into the living room.

There was a girl, kneeling on the edge of the oriental-style rug in the living room in front of the fireplace. She had Paul's red turtleneck wrapped around her head, so she couldn't see anything. Paul told her to unbutton her blouse. Then he stood back and turned on his video camera. The blindfold, if it could be called that, made finding the buttons on her blouse awkward. When the girl had finished, the silky blouse fell loose at her sides above her khaki shorts and parted to reveal a white bra. That gave Paul another idea and he stopped the camera.

"Tell me your name," he said, sounding more like a security guard in a shopping mall coercing information from a lost child than the sex-crazed rapist and abductor he was.

"Leslie Mahaffy," responded the frightened child, whose bra had now been pulled above her breasts.

Karla knew that Leslie Mahaffy was Paul's way of reciprocating for Jane. But Jane was one thing; Leslie was quite another. Karla wondered where he had found Leslie. If Leslie was taciturn and compliant, like the January Girl, there should be no problem. Paul had watched the movie they'd made in January a dozen times. This was the summer and Karla had told him that she wanted him to do it again, meaning snatch another girl like the January Girl and rape her. When he asked, "When?" Karla had replied, "This summer . . ." Now here they were.

But if this girl was not as easy to handle as the January Girl, then what? Karla was a control freak and a pragmatic woman. And she knew her man. She knew that Paul was getting very excited, and that he was going to have his way with this little girl named Leslie Mahaffy for some time before he decided whether or not to involve her. Karla went back to bed and promptly fell asleep.

· · ·

Her mother's good blouse was still undone when Paul propelled Leslie down the hall to the main floor washroom, instructing her where to turn while the camera wobbled.

"Oh, my God," she said when she realized they were in a bathroom and he wanted her on the toilet. She could hear the camera. Her father had one. Every year at Christmas they made a family video and sent it to her Nana in Florida.

"Be good for me, okay," Paul told her, as he focused on her thighs and pubic hair while she urinated. After congratulating Leslie on a beautiful job, he directed her to the toilet paper on a white roller at her left and filmed her wiping herself before she pulled up her white panties and shorts.

Naked, Leslie was propped on her left elbow at the end of the double bed in the room Paul and Karla called the guest bedroom on the main floor, her legs spread so that her left foot touched the carpet, while her right perched on the edge of the bed against the tousled white bedding. One red arm of the turtleneck blindfold fell between her breasts. The soft light of morning filtered through the closed venetian blinds behind her, but she could not see a thing.

In that room, Paul had intercourse with Leslie. Not on the bed, since the old wooden-framed double that had once been Karla's was a squeaky, unreliable affair. The spindled footboard sometimes pushed away from the frame. Then the whole thing would collapse.

He moved Leslie to the gray-carpeted floor, using the bed comforter and the patchwork quilt he had brought from his childhood bedroom to cushion them. He wanted to have her face on tape, so while she lay there, naked with her head facing the bedroom door, he videotaped the right side of her face without the blindfold. Starting with a close-up of her vagina, the camera's eye roamed up her tanned body, past the white marks left by the bikini she had worn while catching the early summer sun; past the small mole below her left breast.

"Keep your eyes shut," he told her.

And she did.

Karla woke up and found the house quiet. She tiptoed to the vantage point she had taken earlier that morning and scanned the main floor. There was no sign of anyone. She noticed two things: their good champagne flutes were out on the dining-room table and the door to the guest bedroom was shut. Karla was suddenly very angry.

"That asshole," she thought to herself. "Imagine, using my champagne glasses on some bitch he has just picked off the street." The champagne glasses, as Paul and Karla called them, really got to her. Now she was mad and did not much care what he was doing or with whom. She was coming downstairs, taking the dog out for a walk, getting herself something to eat and getting on with the day. She did not care what he was doing to her—what was her name . . . Leslie—Karla was just going to go about her business. She would be quiet, but she was resolved. She pulled on her halter top and Spandex pants. She took Buddy out for a long walk.

Whenever Karla had nothing else to do, she read. So after the dog was walked and Karla had eaten, she decided to take the dog up to the bedroom and read her new book. She got Buddy's food and water dishes and took him with her. She had been looking forward to this book. It was getting a lot of bad publicity. She had clipped a review. They had bought it at WaldenBooks across the border in April. It was called *American Psycho*.

By noon, Leslie's mother was frantic. She had called all of Leslie's friends. Martin McSweeney said that he walked her home. They had found all the doors and windows locked, and it was late so he had to go home. He had left Leslie standing beside Mrs. Mahaffy's house. He just figured she would ring the door-bell and go in. That is what Amanda Carpino told her, as well. Leslie had asked if she could stay at Amanda's house, but

Amanda had said no. As far as Amanda knew, after they had talked for about a half hour, Leslie was going to go home and knock.

The police were blasé. This had happened too many times before with the Mahaffy kid, the one they had picked up drunk and stoned in April at the Crestwood Motel. Her mother had reported her missing a number of times before. On an earlier occurrence, the girl had been gone for two weeks and turned up all right. The police were concerned, but they really thought it was a bit premature to take Leslie's disappearance to heart.

Paul had already given Leslie her instructions. She was to take off all her clothes, so that he could take a good look at her body in the light of day. He positioned her near the closed guestroom door in front of Karla's old dresser, which was stacked with peach and green towels that had not been put away. He reminded himself to give Karla a smack for slacking off.

David Bowie's song "Changes" played on the clock radio. The sound was tinny and cheap. Leslie was dressed, and now she was going to undress. She dropped her mother's blouse with her left hand and proceeded to unzip her shorts, letting them fall to her ankles. Finding the clasp on the back of her bra was no problem, she let it fall to her feet as well and then slipped off her white bikini briefs. Naked, except for the blindfold, Leslie crossed her hands self-consciously over her stomach. She had been in the dark for what seemed an eternity, and there was nowhere to hide.

Her stomach was a little round for Paul's taste. Then, again, she also had to go to the bathroom. All the champagne, vodka and whatever else Paul gave her to drink had taken its toll. Nothing was private anymore, except the darkness. He videotaped her urinating, again. Leslie could hear the camera motor, but she did not speak as he went for a close-up.

Leslie had been so good that Paul decided to reward her and himself by letting her have a shower. Paul knew that for Karla cleanliness was next to godliness. He left the glass shower door open and filmed Leslie as the water streamed over her, soaking the blindfold so much that she had to press it to her face.

"Scrub your bum real well," he instructed.

"What," Leslie asked, unbelievingly, through the haze of a horrendous hangover.

"Scrub your bum really well."

"Okay," she said.

And she did.

He had led her up a flight of stairs and into a room. Leslie's hair was still damp from the shower. The wet blindfold had been replaced by a dry one, Paul's old red-and-blue striped Polo turtleneck. It was wrapped around her head like a thick turban. She was wearing only her shorts and her bra, but the house was warm, even for June, and the champagne was warming too.

The sound on the radio upstairs was better than the one downstairs. Paul tuned it to CFNY—after 10 P.M. they played very cool music. It happened to be Leslie's favorite station. She sat cross-legged and tried to listen to the music, just the music. He videotaped her as she tried to sing along. It was a rap. The turban tilted her head sideways and she tried to move her lips, although they were puffy from his violent kisses and all that burning alcohol. In his close-up shot, Paul captured her tongue waving slightly, "la, la, la," as if she were alone and faraway. On her chin there was the budding sign of a pimple.

She was just sitting there, when she heard him ask her whether she would like to have sex with two people.

Karla, off to the side behind him, watched silently. She could see this scared little girl, who started to whimper and make weak protests, so she whispered to Paul: "Tell her the other person's a woman."

Paul told her she was going to get a big kiss. He turned on the camera and watched as Karla moved in front of Leslie and bent over to give her a kiss, pushing on the younger girl's lips twice, making it squishy and moist. Leslie did not move, but Karla knew full well that sharing this kind of kiss with another woman would excite Paul.

He pulled a straight-back, wooden dining-room chair they had inherited from some relative to a spot about six feet away from the comforter Karla had spread on the floor in front of the closed door. The height was just about right and he angled the camera to frame approximately where they would be positioned: Leslie on the left, Karla on the right. It was setting up a Paul Bernardo sandwich.

Pink Floyd was on the radio—the long, rhythmically simple "Money." Paul gave Leslie a kiss on her left cheek as he settled in, moving the champagne bottle to his side. He pulled up his white T-shirt a bit and Karla immediately headed for his scrotum while Paul trained Leslie on his less-than-erect penis.

"I want you to lick up the shaft and then kiss at the top of my dick," he told Leslie matter-of-factly, as if he were telling a child how to butter bread.

"Where do I lick?" she asked.

Karla was already there, licking up and down like a hungry kitten, when Leslie began following instructions.

"I want you to kiss at the top," he told them. "I want you to do it about three or four times, okay?"

Karla got into a rhythm and Leslie followed her lead, their lips almost touching. While the rest of Leslie's body remained inert, Karla moved sensually from Paul's penis to his testicles, sucking and licking, while he variously watched them or eyed the camera. Karla's hair looked good, just enough mousse in her bangs to give them some life. He patted her head and ruffled his fingers through the bangs approvingly.

"Come over here, so you can lick it all," Paul told Leslie, leaning her on her left side while he kneeled with his buttocks in her face. "You can lick the hole. Okay. Find your way."

While Leslie tried to "find her way," the music changed. For Paul it could not have a better moment. REM was playing their superman song. "I am, I am superman, I can do anything. . . ." whined the refrain, while Karla positioned her head under his chest and began sucking his nipples.

"Come on, lick me, Leslie. Ya, you're in my good books," Paul said as the child in the blindfold awkwardly pressed her face into his anus and Karla moved forward to grapple with his penis, masturbating and sucking him in a continuous bob and thrust.

"Make me feed good, Leslie," he said in a singsong voice. "I'm judging you right now, okay? These next two hours are going to determine what I do to you. Okay, right now you are scoring perfect."

Paul reminded Leslie that there were things she was supposed to be saying to him.

"Oh, ya, okay," she said although she was not in the time or place to really say anything, since she was having trouble just breathing between his flesh and the blindfold.

When he finished, Paul smiled like a happy camper and moved up to cradle Leslie's head, giving her a big smooch, while giving Karla the old thumbs-up. He poured Leslie a full glass of champagne which she drank right down. So he poured another.

Her face was not even in the frame when he asked her to say her full name. After a false start, she said it: "Leslie Erin Mahaffy."

"When were you born?"

"May 26, 1976," came the meek reply.

Karla wanted more, so she whispered a series of questions in Paul's ear for him to ask. What was her favorite pastime?

"I like spending time with my friends," Leslie said, as he panned to her head, which was tilted far to the right.

"You're a good girl," Paul told her, advising that if she needed to go to the washroom all she had to do was say the word.

Karla wanted to get the next scene right. She spread the comforter and one of their electric blankets in front of the hope chest, along with her new king-size pillows. Leslie was lying with her legs spread, with Karla kneeling and kissing her vagina. Paul tried for a close-up of Karla's face. Raising her head, she smiled and wagged her tongue, with that devilish glint in her eye.

"Just to let you know, Leslie, that's not me," he said, as though Leslie would not know from the touch of Karla's lips and the soft brush of long hair on her thighs.

"Now she's going to judge you on how good it is. Put the tongue right up the hole, okay," he directed. Karla was splayed on her back, eyes closed like a happy sunbather while Leslie lay on her stomach with her blindfolded head between Karla's legs.

"Is she making you feel okay?" Paul asked Karla, and he saw her smile.

Whatever Paul got, Karla wanted, too. She moved to a kneeling position, arching her buttocks while Paul told Leslie to "caress and make her feel good."

"Put your tongue right in her asshole, push it right in," he said. Leslie touched Karla's thigh, and did as she was told.

The whole scene lasted a little more than twenty-five minutes.

His knife was in its case just in front of the hope chest. The coiled electrical cord was at his side, part of it stretching underneath the beige electric blanket that Leslie was propped on. Her ankles and wrists were bound with the brown cord Karla kept in the kitchen closet with Buddy's dog stuff. The blouse was pushed above her buttocks and her face pressed into the carpet, covered by her curls and turban.

Karla was operating the camera and everything was going to be well framed. Paul spread his legs astride Leslie and entered her anus, turning to smile at Karla.

"You won't shit for me, so you get it up the ass, okay," he told Leslie, bending both knees and grinding his groin into her.

"Okay, I'll try again," she begged.

But Paul Bernardo was not about to stop anything.

"No way you're going to shit after this, trust me," he grunted, telling her he was "pushing everything deep inside."

Karla's hand was steady. Even when Leslie screamed in pain for her help. No shaky handheld video camera effects, as the helpless teenager cried out in pain.

When no help came from the woman, Leslie used her wits.

"Just let me go, I won't say anything about you," she told Paul. "I'll never tell. I'll never double-cross you." But it was as though he was not listening: instead he told her he was teaching her a lesson.

"I want to see my family and my brother and my friends," she cried, but Paul just continued.

"I want your ass up in the air. Get it up there," he demanded, half pulling her into a more upright position, so that her whole balance centered on her head.

"Fix my mask please," she asked. It was not off, but she told him that it was falling. Paul retied the striped turtleneck and jerked toward Karla and the camera—covering the lens with his hand. That was the end of Leslie Erin Mahaffy.

CHAPTER

seventeen

Bill Grekul and his wife, Linda, struggled to put their canoe in the water. It was around six in the evening on Saturday, June 29, 1991. There was a lot of rock and debris, making the enterprise awkward. Bill noted that the lake was down quite a bit.

Bill worked with stone at the Walker quarry. Lately, things had not been so good at home. He and Linda had not really been out alone for a long time. What better way to try and smooth troubled waters than with a twilight canoe ride on Lake

Gibson. It was a hot, muggy night. He reasoned it would be much cooler out on the lake. Maybe they would talk.

The area around Lake Gibson was steeped in history and it was just remote enough to encourage an imaginary paddle back into the nineteenth century, except Bill Grekul's canoe had a motor, which did not make the launch any easier than trying to imagine that he and Linda were back in a better time.

The irony of a motor-driven canoe was lost on the Grekul's. Stonemasons tend to be pragmatists, not dreamers. To the Grekuls, Laura Secord made chocolates. They did not appreciate that over the crest of the hill just off to their left, the real Laura Secord had once saved Canada from an unruly band of marauding Americans.

American officers had occupied the Queenston Heights home Laura Secord shared with her wounded husband and their five children. On the cusp of the War of 1812, one well-lubricated evening, Laura overheard some of the American officers outlining an attack.

On foot, Laura scrambled an impossible twelve miles to warn the British. She ended up in the camp of Lieutenant James FitzGibbon, at a huge stone house owned by John DeCew, the ramparts of which could just be seen above the crest of the hill overlooking the Grekuls' launch.

A few years earlier the St. Catharines historical society had torn down the dilapidated DeCew house, where an exhausted Secord had altered the course of history. The site was now a large fieldstone patio surrounded on four sides by a substantial waist-high fieldstone wall.

Embedded in the magnificent fireplace there is a commemorative brass plaque, which succinctly tells Laura Secord's story. Until Vietnam, 1812 was the only war the Americans had ever lost. Around six on a summer evening, the sun catches the plaque and creates a startling explosion of light.

Bill Grekul's footing gave way and he almost dropped his end. Looking down, he saw what appeared to be a crude, flat concrete lid. It had separated, under his weight, from a large concrete block. Inside the block there was some kind of peculiar fish unlike anything Bill had ever seen before; moist, it was a purplish flesh color. Showing Linda, he poked it with his paddle.

Transfixed, he had to remind himself why he was there. He held the canoe for Linda. Refusing to accept what he saw for what it was, he reluctantly stepped in after her and pushed off from a small isthmus of rocks. Determined as Bill was to make this evening something special, when he stepped on that cement block the die was cast. Everything would change irrevocably.

Divided from the reservoir and waterworks that supply the city of St. Catharines by historic DeCew, where it intersected with Beaverdams Road, Lake Gibson was a stone's throw from Merritton and Highway 406, east of Lundy's Lane, which ran over the Welland Canal to Niagara Falls.

Brock University and the Shaver Clinic were just east from the two bodies of water, toward the suburb of Port Dalhousie and Lake Ontario.

The area surrounding the lake was still relatively unpopulated, characterized by recreation areas, historic landmarks, agricultural and hydroelectric enclaves, the odd private home, fishermen and, after dusk, lovers in search of seclusion.

Mike Doucette cast a critical eye at the people in the motorized canoe. Doucette, a forty-two-year-old paper-mill technician and lay minister with a ponytail and beard, often went out after dinner to fish Lake Gibson from the shoreline. Well off the beaten path, the lake was only fifteen minutes from his house in Thorold.

The guy in the canoe was hollering something about cement and fish—Doucette was fishing from shore and had just cast out. He thought he felt a slight tug on his line and was intently watching the spot in the water where his hook had dropped, poised to declare "fish on," which is what he always did, mostly for fun, when he went out fishing with his adult son, Michael. He was a little miffed. Fishing was supposed to be a contemplative sport. And here was this guy with his motor, and his mouth, running.

Determined to accomplish what he had set out to do—have some kind of interlude with his wife—Bill Grekul did not point the canoe back to shore until around 8:15 P.M. It had been a bust. The image of whatever it was in that concrete block had followed them, a large misshapen fish swimming just below the lake's surface. Every time he looked in the water he saw it. On his way back he hollered at the fisherman again: "Did you see it?" Mike decided the only way to shut the guy up was to go over and have a look at whatever it was that had him in such a lather.

It looked like his son had hooked a big one so Mike waited until that was resolved and then he reeled in. A couple minutes more and he had navigated the rocky shoreline. The water level was exceptionally low, even for a Friday night.

There it was, just like the guy said. What appeared to be a crudely made cement block had come apart and inside there was something that looked like a human thigh and a foot embedded in the wet cement. The stranger with the motorized canoe said that he thought it could be body parts. Even though he knew the guy was right, Mike heard himself say no.

It looked like the block had been painted black. It resembled a miniature coffin, about two feet long and a foot deep, the kind in which a tiny infant might be buried.

The lid had simply come off. Even though it was the hottest June 29 on record, Mike shivered. It was no fish. It looked like a human thigh, but it could not be. Doucette stood straight up. He looked at Bill Grekul uncomprehendingly. Whoever he was, he was right about one thing: the thing in the concrete was a human body part.

The light had started to go. And there was another block. He moved quickly; it, too, had a lid. Doucette pried it off. On this lid he noticed bloodstains. Inside there was a young girl's calf and a foot.

.   .   .

"We were almost suckin' mud. See, during the weekend we cut our diversion back to get down to the maximum amount of water we can divert . . ." Bob Brickman started to explain, but Sgt. Bob Walkinson did not want to know. He just wanted to know if Brickman could maintain the water level in Lake Gibson where it was.

Brickman worked for the local hydroelectric company in St. Catharines. He was in the process of "zeroing out" for the week when the call came in. Zeroing out is what hydroelectric guys call it when they match the water used by the region to generate hydroelectric power in any given week to the amount taken in from the St. Lawrence Seaway.

On Friday, June 29, 1991, zeroing out caused the water in Lake Gibson to drop to 554 feet above sea level around 5:30 P.M., which was as low as Hydro could go in Lake Gibson before they started getting debris caught in the valves—before they started "sucking mud," as Brickman called it.

It was not particularly difficult, what the sergeant wanted. Bob would have to make some adjustments at Indy Two, an antiquated water-intake valve just off the town of Allanburg on Lake Ontario. It was all done by remote control. Bob did not mind. In the seventeen years he had worked for the utility, he could not remember any similar request.

Lake Gibson was a manmade lake, built specifically to supply water for power generation to the immediate Niagara area; including St. Catharines, Niagara Falls and Welland. Later, the cops would want to know how it worked, so he told them: "Power generation is all a question of balance. We generate as much as we can during the week and of course the lake goes down and then we have to zero out by Sunday night—we have our guidelines, can't break the contract with the Seaway. Our normal elevation is around 557.90—that night we were near the bottom line. We start again at zero clock Sunday night, we start a whole new week again. Efficiency and balance, that's what power's all about—the best water to get the best megawatts."

.   .   .

Every time a flashbulb popped it seemed to temporarily stun Marilyn Bernardo. She was like a giant mole suddenly thrust into the light, blinking uncomprehendingly. She had been chewing a big wad of gum all during the wedding ceremony. An exceedingly large woman, Marilyn was also sporting a large, filthy cast on her right leg.

Jason Mooney regarded Marilyn Bernardo with bemused disdain from across the room where he had just gotten himself a drink. They were in the Queen's Landing, a rather well-appointed hotel in Niagara-on-the-Lake, at her son Paul's wedding reception. There were well over one hundred people for a sit-down dinner—pheasant stuffed with veal, the whole nine yards—overlooking the Niagara River. It was a beautiful warm evening. From here, Canada and the United States were so close an average swimmer could probably cross the mouth of the river and hit the Youngstown Marina in fifteen minutes. A reception line had formed outside the Macleod Room, where the dinner would be served.

Mooney was a dark-haired, good-looking eighteen-year-old kid. He was the kind of youth who wears baseball caps backward—especially when he's on vacation, which was where he'd met Paul Bernardo during spring break in Daytona Beach a couple of years earlier. Ten years the groom's junior, Jason looked up to Paul. Paul was always well dressed. He seemed to be able to pull girls with a glance. The first night they'd been in Daytona last year, they walked into a bar called The Beach Party. An hour later Bernardo walked out with this outrageous biker chick. Nobody saw him again until the next day.

Paul always had a wad of money on him, but Jason could never quite figure out where he got it. Just what he did for a living was not clear. He was always full of schemes, but he was also secretive to an extreme. He said he was an accountant, but Jason never saw him with a sharpened pencil or a ledger. He had no visible means of support, at least not as far as Jason could see, not since the beginning of 1990 when he had quit working for Price Waterhouse. Whatever Paul did, it worked, and Jason's admiration grew.

Jason still went to school and worked part-time in a road-house outside Lindsay, Ontario, where he lived with his parents. His father was an insurance salesman. His mother was a homemaker. They lived a nice small-town life. Even though he was middle-class and came from a well-to-do family, Jason had never seen anything quite like this wedding, or Paul's mother, for that matter.

At the wedding rehearsal the day before, Jason had come in a bit late with Mark Warner, a pal of his from Lindsay who had also met Paul in Florida, and another guy named Andy Douglas, who neither he nor Mark had met before. Earlier, when the three of them got to talking, Andy told them that he too was surprised to be included in the wedding party, because, like them, he did not really know Bernardo that well. No one, except Paul's pal Van, who was also the best man, seemed to know Paul Bernardo very well.

All of a sudden this woman the size of a cement truck in a blue tarpaulin threw a fit. Mrs. Bernardo rolled right up and pushed her sweaty, meaty face in his face, cursed him up and down, yelling and screaming, inches from his nose. Jason had never laid eyes on the woman before in his life, let alone met her. What a head case. Jason just laughed and walked away.

Paul had once told Jason that if he saw his mother in a field he would kill her. Now he understood why. Paul also told him that the guy with the Coke-bottle glasses was not his real father; that his mother had slept around and he was actually the son of a very wealthy member of the Canadian establishment. The guy must have been pretty desperate, Jason thought to himself.

There was a kind of strange atmosphere about all this, but Jason put it down to extremes, such as that woman or Paul's sister with the uncontrollable, screaming Tasmanian devils she called her children. And the guy Debbie Bernardo was with— presumably her husband and the children's father—looked like he was completely stoned. Then there was Karla, with that look in her eye. But Jason was not complaining. The drinks were free, and besides, Karla had a younger sister named Lori, whom he had just met. She was hot.

Jason took a sip of his drink and watched in astonishment as Marilyn Bernardo braced herself against the wall, extended the leg with the cast and slowly slid to the floor.

Irene Votjek, who was the next person to be greeted in the receiving line by Mrs. Bernardo, also looked on, stunned. For Irene, it was a kind of double jeopardy—the invitation had surprised the hell out of her and her recalcitrant Irish husband, Trevor. They barely knew Paul—they had met him once through Steve Smirnis, while they still had their boardinghouse in Niagara-on-the-Lake. They did not know Karla at all. But a party was a party, and how often did one get invited to the Queen's Landing in Niagara-on-the-Lake to party for free? Still, Irene had not anticipated anything like Mrs. Bernardo.

As she extended her hand, the woman collapsed to the floor. Now she was sitting with her back against the wall, looking up expectantly at Irene as if nothing out of the ordinary had happened. Irene immediately bent over.

"Are you all right?"

She knew the woman was Mrs. Bernardo, because she had just been introduced to Kenneth Bernardo. Concerned, Irene glanced back at Mr. Bernardo, but he was oblivious.

The woman must be drunk already, Irene thought to herself.

"Let me get you a chair . . ."

"No, no. I'm just fine," Marilyn Bernardo replied in an unreasonably loud voice. "I'm here now, so I'll just stay."

From a distance the flashbulbs popping along the edge of the lake looked like giant fireflies. "It has to be someone pretty sadistic to do that to a person." Michael Doucette shook his head, looking at the blocks. Long beams of light from the police flashlights crisscrossed in the darkness. Every few minutes a flashbulb exploded unexpectedly, temporarily blinding him. The cop did not look up from his notebook.

"You know, whoever did it, they're not from around here," Doucette said.

"Why do you say that?" the cop asked, perfunctorily.

It was around 11:00 P.M. and the place was swarming with cops and firemen. They had found another three or four blocks. They were all mini–coffin size—around two feet by two feet by one foot. Each one contained body parts. Doucette went through the parts of the body in his head—two arms, two legs, two feet—but obviously the legs had been dismembered above the knees, the head—that should make eight cement blocks. He glanced toward the bridge. There were now five blocks in an ill-defined line about a hundred feet north off the roadway in a little cove along the lake's shore, just east of the bridge. Mike wondered where the torso was.

"He dumped the concrete in only three feet of water. If he had dumped the stuff over the bridge, three hundred feet further down the road, the water there is quite quick and deep. We might never have found her there. That's why I say he's not from around here. He doesn't know the lake."

It was so romantic, the wedding. Everything from the service and 1 Corinthians—"love never fails . . ."—to the horse-drawn carriage and the bride and groom's tour around Niagara-on-the-Lake, sipping champagne from those exquisite flutes, Paul and Karla benevolently waving to all the people on the street, every moment recorded on videotape.

Paul had the Absolute Limousine Service take them along the road, past the vineyards and the lavish private homes, to the miniature church. In the shadow of General Brock's massive four-hundred-foot Queenston Heights monument, the little church was really just a silly tourist attraction. But there was something so romantic about how they stopped, and bending their heads so they could get through the tiny door—the steeple on the miniature church was only a few feet taller than Paul—they both signed their names and put the date below the hundreds of inscrutable Japanese names.

But the best part of all was the party. What a party. And the gossiping; the bridesmaids were all abuzz. They were awash with stories about Paul's bizarre behavior—how he had got so drunk when the boys took him out for beers that he opened the car door and hung his head out only inches from the road as they sped down the Queen Elizabeth Way. Or about how he had picked up these two slutty-looking girls in Niagara Falls and brought them back to 57 Bayview—he said he got them for a couple of the younger single guys.

Or about how he had come into the bedroom at 57 Bayview where Patti Loyala, one of the bridesmaids, was sleeping. He locked the door and then reached into a hole behind the dresser and took something out. He left, only to return with Karla. Paul walked over to the bed, pulled down the bedclothes and lifted Patti's nightgown above her head. Patti did not know what to do, so she pretended to be asleep. She was not sure whether Karla was encouraging him, or whether she was trying to stop him. It must have been around four in the morning.

Kristy Maan was also surprised to be invited to the wedding, because she had lost touch with Karla when Karla left the Number One Pet Center. Then Karla asked Kristy to be a bridesmaid. Kristy was stunned when she discovered she was the stand-in for Karla's dead sister, Tammy. As it turned out, she and Tammy were exactly the same dress size. Tammy's dress fit Kristy like a dream.

It was Debbie Purdie's story about Karla that Kristy thought most strange. Since that night in 1987 when Karla brought Paul back to the hotel room at the Howard Johnson's in Scarborough, Kristy had been fascinated by Karla. There was just something about her. How did a teenage girl from St. Catharines snare this rich, well-fixed, good-looking older man with the great car?

Debbie and Karla had been out shopping before the wedding and they had stopped in a pet store. Karla picked up a big leather studded dog collar and tried it on. Debbie said to her, "That's a bit big for Buddy, don't you think?"

Karla replied, "Well, actually it's for me." Karla bought the dog collar. "Don't tell anyone," she said, "but Paul gets off on this stuff."

CHAPTER

eighteen

The first thing Sergeant Larry Maracle saw when he got to the Faywell Road Bridge early Sunday morning was a man holding a fishing pole. That would not normally be remarkable. A lot of people fish around Lake Gibson and the reservoir. But this guy was not fishing. He was using his fishing pole to prevent a human torso from drifting under the bridge.

"The torso was that of a female," wrote Sergeant Maracle in his notebook. "It was minus the head and appendages. There were no obvious scars or trauma to the torso, other than dismemberment.''

Sergeant Maracle, a full-blooded Mohawk Indian, was a large, able, steady man. The officers on the scene the night before had found everything but the torso. Maracle had just been assigned to the investigation. What he saw—the torso bobbing upright, held by the tip of a fishing rod—he found unsettling.

It was pulled from the water. The police took pictures, numbered the cement blocks, one through seven, put them in plastic bags and shipped everything to the pathologist at Hamilton General Hospital.

Exhausted from the nightlong celebration of their nuptials, the newlywed Bernardos spent a quiet day resting at home on Bayview Drive. They did some last-minute packing. Traveling light, Karla packed a single-burner hot plate.

By the time pathologist Dr. David King and his assistants began to extricate the body parts from the cement blocks the following morning, Paul and Karla were boarding a plane in Buffalo. From there, they would fly to Chicago, then make their connecting flight to Hawaii.

Sergeant Maracle went to Hamilton General Hospital. He was there with Sergeants Walkinson and Briggs, Dr. King's assistant, Paul Swioklo, and the Niagara Regional Police identification unit's Constable Michael Kershaw and a civilian employee named Smith.

They used a sledgehammer and a chisel: Block 1 contained the left upper arm; Block 2, the right upper arm; Block 3, the head; Block 4, the right forearm and hand; Block 5, the left thigh, the lower right leg and foot; Block 6, the right thigh and left lower leg and foot; Block 7 contained the left lower leg and foot and left forearm and hand.

The procedure was partially videotaped and Constable Kershaw took dozens of still photographs. There were no tattoos or scars. There was no jewelry or clothing; no ring lines on any fingers; no nail polish on any nails. Her hair had been reddish brown to blond. It was lighter colored at the ends. The ears were pierced. The eyes were brown. The teeth had braces.

Sergeant Maracle had been working on the Melanie Warner case when he was called to Lake Gibson. Melanie Warner was reported missing on May 14, 1987. Her stepfather had been charged with first-degree murder, but her remains had never been found. Melanie could easily be the person whose remains were in these cement blocks. Sergeant Maracle brought photographs and dental records with him the following day.

The postmortem team now included two particular specialists from Niagara Falls, dentist George Burgman and orthodontist John Thompson. The only way to identify this dead girl would be through dental records. They X-rayed the head and the other body parts. It was determined that whoever this was, she had been about fifteen years old and her name was not Melanie Warner. They collected various samples and then put the body parts in cold storage for the night.

Sergeant Maracle called Child Find. They gave him the names of four missing teenage girls: Leslie Mahaffy, Kim McAndrews, Melanie Warner and an American girl from Minnesota, Shannon Burns. He struck Melanie Warner off the list. Both Mahaffy and Burns had blue eyes, so that left McAndrews.

On Friday, they laid out the body parts in a way that they might have fit together. It looked like a grotesque puppet without strings. They took photographs and measurements. There was a tentative cut in the bone on the right femur of the torso, close to where the bone had ultimately been cut through. That helped Dr. King conclude that she had been dismembered with a power saw.

She had been approximately five feet five or six inches tall. Half of the right humerus bone was missing. The body parts weighed ninety-one pounds. Alive, the girl had weighed between one hundred and ten or twenty pounds. They removed the upper and lower jaws and gave them to the dentists.

Dr. Thompson took twelve periapical X-rays and made a plaster model of the jaw. When Drs. Burgman and Thompson got together later that day and compared information, they knew who it was.

Leslie Mahaffy had a speed bracket–type brace on her upper and lower jaw, a formidable combination of hooks, coils, springs and arch wires that was uncommon in North America. This, along with four missing bicuspids and a filling matched Leslie's profile.

The next day the police drove the jawbones to Bracebridge, where Leslie's dentist was vacationing. He confirmed what the other dentists had concluded. That afternoon, Detective Sergeant Bob Waller began to organize Superintendant Laidlaw and Police Victim Services member Pat Smith for a long, dark drive to Midland, where the Mahaffy's were staying at the Park Villa Motel. It was Wednesday, July 10, Debbie Mahaffy's forty-fifth birthday, when the police arrived and told her it was her daughter.

Because the girl had brown eyes, the police had earlier assured Mrs. Mahaffy that it was not Leslie in Lake Gibson. But Debbie Mahaffy had not believed them. She instinctively knew that death and cement could turn even the bluest eyes dirty brown.

Paul and Karla had a hell of a time on their honeymoon. They made a video record: footage from the airplanes as they island-hopped, combined with some stalking scenes, as well as many, many interludes with Paul and Karla having fun in their hotel rooms.

They caught some crabs by the seashore and brought them back to their room.

"I killed one. Show them the one I killed," Karla demanded, grinning at the hotel sink full of the remaining live crabs.

"I think it went down the drain. Sorry, Kar," Paul said ruefully. Then they boiled the crabs on the hot plate Karla had shrewdly packed.

Karla wore a bikini, and remarked how boring one particular excursion they took had been. In one video segment, framed against a magnificent sunset, Karla delivered a soliloquy to her new husband, who happened to be showering at the time.

"The beauty of this ocean, this beach and everything here

does not come close to equaling the love I feel for you, sweet-heart," she extemporized, as she videotaped the sun sinking into the bay from their hotel-room balcony.

Rain and clouds dogged the honeymoon. They returned home with the requisite trinkets and T-shirts and a section of the Honolulu newspaper dated July 11, 1991, featuring an arti-cle headlined, "Pulled off road and raped, says woman in Maui."

Karla's parents picked them up at the Buffalo airport and told them the police had found body parts in Lake Gibson and identified them as the remains of that little girl from Burlington.

Paul and Karla were seized by fear and astonishment. After all the trouble they had gone to to make sure Leslie would never be found. Karla was frantic. She knew she should have taken the day off work and supervised the cement work.

On Wednesday, Karla got another prescription for Halcion from a new doctor named Lovegrove. She also went back to Dr. Jaeger and refilled her other prescription for Halcion. Karla now felt she was well prepared for any opportunity that might pre-sent itself. They had Jane and her mother over for dinner to allay the mother's concern about Jane's relationship with Paul and Karla.

Jane's mother continued to be perplexed by the couple's inordinate interest in her fifteen-year-old daughter. But Jane loved Karla and her mother could not reason with her. Paul's strange, impassioned rant about his untenable relationship with his mother, and the fact that his father was not his real father, did nothing to assuage her concern. But Jane was turning six-teen and her mother felt powerless.

Paul and Karla began to go out together looking for new "sex slaves." Paul developed a real thing for a waitress from the Red Hot Chili Pepper, a beer-and-wings joint in downtown St. Catharines. He and Karla followed her home a couple of times.

One night they succeeded in videotaping the waitress un-dressing through her bedroom window. She stood in the win-dow, naked and rubbed lotion all over her body. Paul became so excited he could not steady the camera. As soon as he got back to the car, he masturbated furiously. Karla thought it was too funny.

Occasionally, Paul encouraged Karla to go out on the front lawn at three in the morning and strip. He would watch from the window and masturbate while Karla danced around, bumping and grinding, stark naked on the street. If the neighbors saw it, nobody ever complained.

When she saw the car in her rearview mirror, Rachel Ferron could not believe her eyes. It was the same car—a gold late-model Japanese make—that had followed her two nights earlier. This time, she could not shake him. She had been driving all over St. Catharines for the past two hours, trying to get away, wondering what to do. She kept driving by her boyfriend's house, waiting for him to get home and save her. Finally, he got home and she pulled into his driveway. By that time, she had the car's license-plate number and knew the car that was following her was a gold Nissan.

Rachel and her boyfriend looked out the window and saw someone in the bushes two doors down. They raced outside, but whoever it was ran away. The two got in Rachel's boyfriend's car and started to drive around looking for the Nissan. They found it in a tavern parking lot just up the street. Once they had stopped and made sure she had the right number, they went back to the boyfriend's house and called the police. The uniformed officer who took their report determined the car belonged to Paul Kenneth Bernardo. He lived at 57 Bayview Drive in Port Dalhousie. Rachel reported being followed twice again by the same car before the end of the month, but she never heard anything from the police.

On Monday, July 22, 1991, Constable Michael Kershaw, the identification officer for the Niagara Regional Police, took time out from the Mahaffy investigation to interview a handsome newlywed couple named Bernardo about a break-in at their home on Bayview Drive. They had been on their honeymoon and estimated that there had been thirty thousand dollars worth of stuff stolen.

Entry apparently had been gained through the basement window on the east side of the house. Paul Bernardo provided Constable Kershaw with a detailed list: VCR, Pentax 35mm camera, Compaq III computer and printer, Boss DR500 rhythm drum, Foster model x-26 recorder/mixer, Sony T77 camera, ladies' 18K solitaire ring with a 2 ct. diamond valued at $17,538, a 14K ladies' gold ring with .35 ct. diamond valued at $1,955, a men's Citizen quartz watch and an Alexander Julian watch, both valued at $288, and a 14K men's yellow gold ring with .50 ct. diamond worth approximately $1,955, some dishes and cash. The total loss was exactly $30,286, according to Mr. Bernardo's calculations. He had taken out an insurance policy six weeks earlier.

Constable Kershaw was slightly suspicious. They were so specific about what they had lost, and had itemized it and valued it so quickly. But the veracity of their claim was a matter for their insurance company. If they could prove they had the stuff in the first place, even if they had burgled themselves, it would be difficult to reject. "Break and enters," petty thievery was all too common in St. Catharines. Constable Kershaw was far more concerned about the Mahaffy sex killing and wanted to get back to his work with the cement and paint and the exact nature of the bone cuts. He had been in touch with Dr. Steven Symes in Tennessee, the world's only expert in saw cuts made through human bones. That was interesting stuff. Constable Kershaw might even have to fly to Memphis.

The appointment of thirty-four-year-old Staff Sergeant Vince Bevan on Monday, July 15, as head of the Mahaffy investigation was met with incredulity by Superintendent Jim Moody. Big Jim, as he was known among the rank and file, was liked and respected by the rank and file, but not necessarily the brass. Therefore, his voice was not always heard.

Big Jim was staff superintendent, Number 11 Division, which meant he was responsible for policing in Grimsby, St.

Catharines, Beamsville, Thorold, Port Robinson, Niagara-on-the-Lake, Virgil, St. David's and Queenston. Staff Superintendent Moody had extensive experience with major crime investigations. Had it been up to him, Moody would certainly not have chosen Vince Bevan to lead a homicide investigation, let alone one as difficult as the Mahaffy case. Nevertheless, someone did.

The Niagara Regional Police had been formed by the politically motivated amalgamation of a dozen separate police forces forty years earlier. As a consequence, there had been eleven too many chiefs of police; some of them were put back on the streets, walking beats.

Forty years later, the force was still racked by nepotism, vendettas and infighting, to such an extent that the government had just convened a multimillion-dollar commission of inquiry to investigate everyone and everything, including Vince Bevan's late father, Superintendent Frank Bevan.

Big Jim had known Frank Bevan well before Frank retired and died. Frank had been in charge of purchasing. He was an able and dedicated administrator. Big Jim understood and respected paper-clip counting, and old Frank could count with the best. Vince Bevan might share his father's administrative skills—his most recent job before he was appointed to the Mahaffy investigation had been the installation of a computer system—but he sure as hell did not share his father's self-knowledge. Unlike his son, Frank had known he was not an investigator.

A few years earlier, Sergeant Vince Bevan had arrived at a murder scene near the monolithic power station on the Niagara River. The victim was facedown, dead in the grass. Bevan turned the guy over so he could get a look at his face. Big Jim went berserk.

Superintendent Moody and Staff Sergeant Vince Bevan personified the conflicting forces that crippled modern policing.

Big Jim, who was everything that his name suggested—Irish, Catholic, rotund, large, dogmatic, old school—believed in fundamentals such as shoe leather, common sense and intuition.

He did not believe in bureaucracy or computer technology or rhetoric. Big Jim did not have a university education.

On the other hand, Bevan was bright, university educated, heavily papered, through a multitude of special police courses and seminars, and believed that the key to effective policing was computing and community.

Bevan nodded toward the old methods much the way he genuflected in front of the altar on Sunday mornings—he too came from a long line of Irish Catholics—but when push came to shove, Bevan found refuge in a worldview that had cachet and currency: information management and data processing.

Bevan's kind of policing caught a lot of people with parking tickets and traffic violations. While Big Jim fumed and pontificated, Bevan assimilated every bit of information that came his way.

Big Jim had been able to do something about Bevan then. He could do nothing now. The Mahaffy investigation was out of his jurisdiction. Jim Moody was only a couple of years from retirement himself. He had rocked enough boats. He knew who had put Bevan in charge and why. Bevan had the paper and nepotism prevailed, in spite of the Colter Commission. But Big Jim no longer had a stomach for battles he could not win.

Deputy Chief Peter Kelly enthusiastically briefed Staff Sergeant Bevan the following day. Since Leslie Mahaffy had come from Burlington and was well known to the Halton Regional Police, but her body parts had been found in St. Catharines, it was decided that the investigation would be joint. It was agreed that Bevan, perceived as a good administrator and information manager, would be the head honcho, but he would work with Staff Sergeant Bob Waller and other members of the Halton force.

They had interviewed a couple of the Mahaffys' neighbors about a suspicious man they had seen that Saturday morning. They interviewed the clerk who worked in the Mac's Milk store. He said a man had come into the store and asked if he had seen a fourteen-year-old girl. Khalid Haslam described Dan Mahaffy.

The police determined what kind of cement had been used—Kwik-Mix—and that it likely had been purchased at a Beaver Lumber outlet. They were running down credit-card receipts, but that was the proverbial needle in the haystack. Being a man who saw the future of policing almost exclusively in terms of information and database-management terms, haystack needles were Staff Sergeant Bevan's forte.

All they really had to go on at that point was the paint on the cement blocks and the cement itself—crushed and sifted for hair and other debris.

The paint was unusual. It was industrial, generally applied to engines and motors. Bevan motivated the troops to pursue the paint—what exactly it was, who manufactured it. The next step was to interview all those who might have had an opportunity to obtain the paint at the factory level.

Among the hundreds of people they interviewed, they identified a strange thirty-two-year-old factory worker named Jonathan Yeo, who had a history of aggressive, sexually deviate behavior. Yeo worked at Dofasco, a steel mill in Hamilton.

The paint was not inconsistent with the black paint used in the Dofasco plant. Yeo lived with his wife outside the nearby town of Grimbsy, about ten minutes from Lake Gibson.

Bizarrely, Yeo was living next door to another diabolical figure named John Peter Stark. Stark was the object of a massive, ongoing Metropolitan Toronto Police investigation into the disappearance and suspected murder of his teenage daughter's best friend, Julie Stanton. Stark lived with his wife, Alison. Shortly after the police began to investigate him, Stark picked up and moved way up north to Napanee. Bevan was highly suspicious of Stark because whoever killed Leslie Mahaffy had gone to a great deal of trouble to try and conceal her body. Julie Stanton's body had not yet been found, and wasn't until June of 1996.

There was a Canada-wide warrant out for Jonathan Yeo with respect to the murder of a woman in Moncton, New Brunswick. But before the police could move, another Burlington teenager, Nina deVilliers, would vanish on Saturday, August 10. On August 14, Bevan would discover that Yeo had disappeared from his house on August 9. On August 17, the body of Nina deVilliers would be pulled from a creek in Napanee, very close to where John Peter Stark was now living.

Yeo had killed deVilliers, but Bevan was too slow and Yeo too fast. A few days later, Jonathan Yeo blew his brains out after American Customs prevented him from entering the United States at Niagara Falls.

Stark continued to hold the interest of the police, but they had also been very interested in Yeo—because of the black paint—in relation to the Mahaffy case. Unless they got something from the crushed cement that linked Jonathan Yeo to Leslie Mahaffy, they might never resolve the case.

Bevan had some of the cement casings crushed at nearby Brock University. He kept one block intact. A number of items in the debris were not related to either the manufacture of cement or to Leslie Mahaffy. The length and characteristics of some of the hair led Bevan to believe they belonged to the assailant—someone other than Jonathan Yeo.

At 3:30 A.M. on August 10, 1991, Karla called 911.

"Please hurry," she said. "My friend has stopped breathing." She gave the address and hung up. She went over to Jane's lifeless body and slapped her a couple of times, hard. Jane started breathing again.

"Oh, shit," Karla mumbled under her breath. She ran to the phone and canceled her earlier call. They asked her if she was sure. She was quite sure. It was a false alarm. Her friend was fine.

Jane was far from fine. She was comatose. But she was breathing. Karla got Jane up on the bed and told Paul to watch her. When she came back downstairs she heard a loud crash. Jane had fallen off the bed and Paul was sitting in his music room.

"I told you to watch her," Karla screeched.

All summer long, Jane and Paul had been having fun. Jane appeared to like Paul. Paul took Karla and Jane out together. Paul bought Jane things. She was developing nicely into a "sex slave," when a few unexpected things happened. Firstly, she refused to let Paul have intercourse with her. Jane would perform orally—and had half a dozen times—but she would go no further.

Secondly, Jane had told her horseback-riding instructor that Paul had touched her breasts. In turn, the riding instructor had told Jane's mother, who came over to the house in a rage and accused Paul. Although Paul categorically denied it, he was shaken by the experience and their access to Jane was somewhat curtailed.

Jane had not been a lot of fun for Karla. It was difficult to find a willing female participant who would have sex with both of them. Jane was young and naive. If she snitched on Paul, what would Jane do if Karla approached her? It was time to put Jane down again. Then they could both have fun with Jane.

Karla laced her drinks with the ever-ready Halcion. Paul got the video camera ready. Karla got out the bottle of halothane and started to administer it. Just as they started to take off Jane's pants, she stopped breathing and they both panicked. They had no intention of killing Jane. Paul was frantic. He had hit Karla in June because he was confused about why Jane had lived when Tammy had died. This time they sat up all night with Jane to make sure she kept breathing.

After their honeymoon, Karla's parents started coming over for dinner every second Sunday. At work, Karla appeared lovesick. All she talked about was how much she loved Paul and how much she wanted to have his baby.

Paul and Karla's relationship was a little turbulent, as is often the way with spirited young couples. Karla sent Paul a letter on the first of October: "Once we were an unbeatable team, you and me against the world. We are the perfect couple, we've just gotten sidetracked . . . some couples were meant to be and we're one of those . . . Please, honey, let's try and have a fairy-tale marriage like we were meant to . . . I know what happened to us is all my fault and believe me I'm changing. I love you too much to lose you."

They celebrated the fourth anniversary of their meeting on October 17, 1991. Karla sent Paul an anniversary card: On the front there was a cartoon cat and the words I WOKE UP WITH A WONDERFUL THOUGHT TODAY . . . On the inside front cover Karla had printed in little mice type, in a number of cartoon-like balloons she had drawn, the messages: "Break open the champagne [with a little drawing of a champagne bottle]; 4 lovely years ago that we met; I can't wait until 4 more years of marriage has happened; Remember, Your princess . . . Your little fantasy . . . Your little rat . . . Your little Karly Curls . . . Your little cocksucker . . . Your little cunt . . . Your little slut . . . (heh, heh, heh)," "I love you more and more with each day that passes!, 4 wonderful truly happy years of togetherness, I love you".

On the facing page the word US is printed and framed by another message: "Dear Paul, Oh? Happy Anniversary? Happy Anniversary? Happy Anniversary? Happy Anniversary? Oh, Happy 4th Anniversary to my most terrific, wonderful, best friend and husband in the whole wide world. I love you! Karly Curls XOXO"

Karla was writing to all her friends, telling them she was blissfully happy, and to those among them such as Debbie Purdie who were lovelorn, she freely gave advice.

Kim Johnston gave all the samples from the Scarborough rape investigation back to Detective Steve Irwin on November 6. There were approximately 230 exhibits dating back to 1987. The Center for Forensic Science was not a warehouse. All the samples had been tested and the reports were included. Detective Irwin was to sort through them and determine which ones fit the non-secretor status with the proper phosphoglucomutase, or PGM, type. Phosphoglucomutase is a unique enzyme involved in cellular-energy production, found in blood, semen and hair. Irwin would resubmit those whose status was right for DNA testing. There could be no more than fourteen or fifteen individuals who fit that profile. But Detective Irwin was now working on another investigation.

There were still only ten police officers with the "elite" sexual assault squad, which had to handle all of the sexual assaults in Toronto. Since there hadn't been a rape with the Scarborough rapist's modus operandi since the end of May, 1990, the pressure was off that file.

On November 30, 1991, fourteen-year-old St. Catharines teenager Terri Anderson disappeared without a trace. An elfin blonde, she was a cheerleader and honor student at Lakeport Secondary School. She lived on Linwell Road with her father. Her mother lived out west. At first, the police were skeptical about the father. He was rumored to be a big-time drug dealer from an unconventional family. He quickly became the chief suspect in his daughter's disappearance.

The police reconstructed Terri's movements. That night she had drunk some beer and popped a tab of blotter acid with her friends. She started around 7:00 P.M.. At 9:30 P.M. she was noticeably intoxicated. But by the time Terri went home around midnight, her friends said she appeared to be fine. Her father saw her at their townhouse around 1:00 A.M. Terri seemed fine to him. When he woke up the next morning the front door was ajar and she was gone.

Vince Bevan was promoted to the rank of inspector that fall. At thirty-four, Bevan was almost the youngest inspector in Niagara Regional Police history. Big Jim Moody had been made an inspector when he was thirty-two.

In December, Paul's sister, Debbie, formally laid sexual assault charges against her father. She discovered he was doing to her four-year-old daughter what he had once done to her. Only this time it was not while they watched "Walt Disney" on Sunday nights.

Marilyn Bernardo tried to talk some sense into her daughter. Debbie's brother David tried to explain that once the charges were laid, there would be no reprieve; the system would take over. But her daughter, Samantha, was the last straw. Debbie went to the police. They laid the charges.

Jane sat alone, waiting for her mother, wondering what had happened. Paul and Karla had been so much fun. Jane loved going to 57 Bayview. She thought of Karla as her older sister. Jane had no idea about what Paul and Karla had done to her in June and August. Short-term memory loss is a side effect of Halcion. Karla read the contraindications in the *Compendium*. Halothane had been the insurance. When Paul and Karla really had fun with Jane, Jane was unconscious.

Jane remembered the other things they did together over the summer and into the fall. They went shopping at the Eaton's Center in Toronto. Jane wore one of Karla's dresses and Paul bought them both new clothes.

They went to the CNE. They went to the CN Tower for dinner. Karla was on one side of the table and Paul sat beside Jane. She was really cold and Paul was trying to warm her up. Italian people came up to the table and started singing and videotaping Karla, and then Paul said to Jane, "Let's pretend you're my girlfriend," and he started kissing her.

They stayed in a hotel overnight. Karla fell asleep on the couch and Paul got into bed with Jane. He tried to touch her between the legs. She would not let him. Jane said she did not want to have sex with him, because Karla was there. He kissed her and touched her breasts and made her promise that he would be the first one she had sex with.

He took them to see *Phantom of the Opera*. Jane wanted to sit with Karla, but Paul sandwiched himself between them. During the show he kept touching Jane. They went to see the Royal Lipizzanner stallions at Copp's Coliseum in Hamilton. Paul and Karla liked horses. Karla even rode. They all went to one of Jane's horse shows.

They rented and watched all kinds of videos. They listened to great music. Jane played with Buddy. They would go up into Paul's studio. There were posters on the wall—the Budweiser people, cars and pictures of Paul and Karla in Florida; the other wall was covered with piles of tapes. Paul said he was producing a rap album.

Paul was always nice to Karla when Jane was around. Only once, when they were outside in the backyard, Paul told Karla to shut up and go in the house and she was almost in tears and then she said to Jane, "I think Paul needs a hug—why don't you give him a hug and a kiss?"

Paul would tell Karla that he was going to have a talk with Jane and then take her into the guest bedroom, shut the door and persuade her to give him oral sex. When they came out, Karla would say, "Did you guys have a nice talk?"

It was Friday, December 13, 1991. That afternoon they had gone to the Credit Valley dog show. When they got home, Jane helped Paul and Karla wrap Christmas gifts. Jane had bought Paul the Guns N' Roses *Lies* CD, and Karla napkin rings, with little dots in the shape of bows, and candy canes. Karla had a thing for candy canes—the first time Karla had called Jane, they went to Port Dalhousie and had candy canes, even though it was June.

Karla suggested they open their presents right then and there and Paul said that he had searched for Jane's presents far and wide and one of them was even a "boyfriend/girlfriend" present.

Even though Jane had kissed Paul in front of Karla and had fellated him frequently over the summer and been told by Karla that everything was all right, Jane was still disgusted when he did stuff like that in front of his wife. She looked at him and said something like, "Can't you just shut up?"

Then they went into the family room and sat down by the Christmas tree. Jane opened her presents. They had given her a large Gund shaggy dog. Karla had a whole collection of Gund stuffed animals upstairs in the bedroom.

All the time Jane was opening her presents Paul kept telling her that the stuffed toy cost three hundred dollars; it was top of the line, brand-new; it was on the cover of the new Gund magazine. He told her that he just wanted the best for her.

First they gave her the stuffed toy, with a card, signed from Paul and Karla. The gold necklace was just from Paul. He did all the shopping, but Jane had wanted Karla to do it. Karla kept saying to Jane, "You're going to love your presents."

When Jane opened the package containing the Swatch watch, Paul said, "Do you like it? I looked everywhere. You can take it back if you want . . ."

Later, Paul went up to his music room and Jane was left alone with Karla. All summer, Paul had threatened her with Karla. He never forced himself on her, but he would just say things like, "If you want to stay friends with Karla, you will suck my dick." So she would, and then he would want her to swallow it.

The first couple of times she complied, but then she would not.

"There goes your friendship with Karla," he would say. "One minute you say 'yes,' next thing you're saying 'no.' Why do you play these stupid mind games with me?"

One night Karla, Jane and Paul went out for supper and they started talking about Tammy Lyn. Jane felt badly for Karla. Karla did not deserve so much pain. Why did it have to happen to Karla? That was how Jane thought.

Karla told Jane that Tammy had died in her bedroom, that she had mononucleosis. Karla said Tammy had thrown up and inhaled her stomach contents, but Jane's friends at school had told her that nobody dies from mononucleosis, there must be more to it than that. When they got back to the house Paul was outside drinking, and he said she and Tammy had screwed up his life.

Paul was always saying really weird things to Jane. He was always comparing her to Tammy Lyn. There were pictures of Tammy all over Paul and Karla's house, but Jane had never known Tammy Lyn. It made Jane wonder if Paul had done with Tammy the stuff he was doing with her. He would ask her if she was really a virgin. She would say yes, and he would say, "Well, have you seen the light? What it's like, what is death like?"

Jane was finally coming to her senses.

Karla always seemed to be pushing her toward Paul. Jane would sleep in the same room with Paul and Karla. Paul would sleep on the floor and Karla would sleep on the bed, and Paul

would try and fool around with Jane. Jane could not believe it.
Once, she relented in the bedroom and gave him a blow job.
For all Jane knew, Karla had been watching. It was all getting to
be too much. Karla said that she and Paul did not sleep in the
same bed anymore. She told Jane that she was too conservative,
that she should be more liberal.

When Jane told Karla that she did not feel the same feelings
for Paul as he did for her—after all, he was twenty-eight and she
was seventeen—Karla said, "Well, he's the best thing that could
ever happen to you. You don't know what you're missing."

Karla was not going to be the one to tell Paul; Jane would
have to do it herself. Resolved, Jane marched upstairs and told
him.

"The bad thing about you is you said I'd be the first one you
had sex with and now this," Paul told her. Then he went
downstairs, picked Karla up and started to carry her back up the
stairs.

Karla seemed tired that night. She had a headache. Paul
smoked some dope and he was probably drunk. He had certainly been drinking, telling Jane she was worth nothing; that
she had no value in life. Because it looked as if they were going
to ignore her now, Jane asked Karla if she was mad.

"No," said Karla, "but I'm a little bit upset at you."

Paul carried Karla upstairs and neither of them came back
down again. Jane's mother arrived forty-five minutes later, at
eleven o'clock. All that time Jane sat alone, waiting. She realized
that Karla was not her friend at all. Karla had meant the world
to Jane. She had been Jane's best friend. Jane had trusted her.
Now she knew Karla had just been using her. Jane never went
back to 57 Bayview Drive.

When Janine Rothsay got to the Bernardo's house, ten days
after Jane left, everyone was doing bombs—drinking beer out
of straws. Karla was upstairs, so Janine sat down with Joann
Fuller and had a few shots of vodka.

Janine and Joann were friends. They were both seventeen.
Janine worked for Joann's fiancé, Van Smirnis, at his video store

in Youngstown. Janine thought Van was cool. It was December 23, and Paul and Karla Bernardo were having a little impromptu Christmas party. Janine had never met Paul and Karla, but she had talked to Paul many times on the phone when he called the store. Van and Joann brought Janine with them.

Paul was in the living room with Lori Homolka's ex-boyfriend, Mike Donald, and Van. They were making a video, so Joann and Janine just sat there. Janine was wearing a blue sweater and jeans. When Janine had to go to the bathroom, she got up and asked where it was.

She closed the bathroom door, but did not think to lock it. The next thing Janine knew, Paul was in the bathroom with her. She told him to leave because she had to go. Paul said he did not mind.

Janine was sitting on the toilet. Paul got down on his knees and started to kiss her and tried to push her legs apart. Janine told him to stop—she already had a boyfriend, he was married, his wife was upstairs. Paul told Janine that he knew she wanted him. Then Paul locked the bathroom door. Janine yelled for Joann. Later Joann said she had tried to come for her, but Janine never heard anybody. Paul raped Janine on the bathroom floor and then Janine threw up.

Outside the bathroom, Mike Donald heard the commotion. "The fuckin idiot's in the bathroom with Joann's friend," he said to Van. "I should teach him a lesson and go to bed with Karla."

Van and Mike thought Janine's calls for help were expressions of her passion.

After Janine vomited, Paul got mad and let her out. Janine ran out, half dressed, and went into the guest bedroom with Joann and Van. Paul came out and told Mike that he had "licked her all over." It was really erotic, he said.

Joann told Janine everything was going to be okay. But neither Joann nor Van seemed surprised, and they did not do anything. They just kept saying, "It's okay, you're going to be fine." Then Van and Joann cleaned up Janine's mess.

Mike, Van, Joann and Janine all spent the night. In the morning, they sat around the kitchen table and ate Kentucky

Fried Chicken. Karla seemed a little distant, but nobody said anything.

Janine went home to Youngstown with Van and Joann. On the way home Van was oblivious, and Joann asked Janine an odd question. What would Janine do if she was pregnant as a result of the sex she'd had with Paul? Janine never saw Paul Bernardo again. She did not plan to tell anybody else what happened.

On New Year's Eve Paul and Karla went to a bar and dance emporium in Niagara Falls, New York, called the Pleasure Dome. They went with Jason Mooney, Gus Draxis, Van Smirnis and Joann Fuller. During the evening, Paul expressed his extreme hatred for his mother. Everyone except Van and Joann stayed overnight at 57 Bayview.

On January 2, 1992, Inspector Vince Bevan telephoned Detective Steve Irwin to ask about his ongoing investigation into the sexual homicide of Alison Parrott.

Bevan had now focused on Peter John Stark as his prime suspect in the murder of Leslie Mahaffy. He had been told that Irwin knew a good deal about Stark. They had a nice talk, but neither man was of any particular use to the other.

Bevan and Constable Mike Kershaw went to Erie, Pennsylvania, to check out one of Stark's alibis. Stark said he had been at the Colonial Motor Motel in Erie when Leslie Mahaffy was killed. The motel records indicated he had stayed there on May 17 and 18, 1991, not June 17 and 18, as he had told them. Their suspicions of John Peter Stark deepened considerably, but they had nothing concrete.

They interviewed Stark's wife. Then Bevan drove to Oakridges Hospital in Penetanguishene, Ontario, to discuss the Mahaffy case with a psychiatrist and psychologist. Drs. Grant Harris and Marnie Price worked up a profile.

Some things they got right, such as the fact that the offender was bright, careful and organized. He was a white-collar worker and did not work in construction. The dismemberment was done in the basement of a relatively new house. A carefully controlled personality, the murderer looked like a solid citizen and would not do anything to draw attention to himself. If interviewed, he would appear very cooperative. Leslie had been taken on an opportunity. The killer did not live in her neighborhood. He would kill again. He would not return to the dumping spot.

But they got as many things wrong. They said the perpetrator lived alone, acquired pornography, possibly kiddie porn, and according to the doctors, the crime did not involve two people. Whoever he was, they told Inspector Bevan, he was not a classic psychopath.

Bevan instigated a good deal of discussion among the investigators about the possibilities for a dramatic reenactment of the Mahaffy case on television. Bevan saw the media as a way to generate leads—manufacture needles in haystacks. He tried to interest "America's Most Wanted" and "Unsolved Mysteries" in the Mahaffy investigation, to no avail.

On Valentine's Day, Friday, February 14, 1992, Karla bought herself another dog collar. Her valentine card read: "Honey, I love you with all my heart, now and forever. . . . Sweet Dreams."

The next day, Paul reciprocated: "I will always be totally and undenyingly in love with you."

Lori Lazaruk, an attractive twenty-six-year-old woman, and her twenty-three-year-old sister, Tania, thought it odd that the same gold-colored sports car had driven slowly through the parking lot half a dozen times over the past half-hour. It was 12:15 or 12:30 in the morning on Monday, March 30, and the parking lot and the streets were pretty much deserted. The driver seemed to be staring at them. Lori and Tania were sitting in the window of Robin's Donuts at the corner of Lakeport and Lakeshore Roads. There were only one or two other people in the shop.

The corner of Lakeport and Lakeshore was considered the entrance to Port Dalhousie. The town and Lake Ontario were only a few minutes east along Lakeport. Tania had just left work and she and Lori were having coffee and talking.

Then Tania saw the most unusual thing: the lens of a video camera in the lower outside corner of the doughnut-shop window. Because it was light inside and dark outside, she could not quite make out who was operating the camera. It was really weird because it was as if whoever it was operating the camera was trying to point the lens up her skirt. She immediately told her sister. When Lori turned around there was no one there.

The sisters left the doughnut shop at 2:45 A.M. They saw the same gold sports car they had seen drive back and forth earlier. It was parked across the road behind Buffy's Tavern. Lori drove Tania home. As Tania was getting out of the car, the gold sports car drove by very slowly with no lights on. Lori was not particularly scared, but she was starting to become angry and concerned.

Lori drove around the block and saw the car parked a couple of doors down from her parents' house, where she had just dropped Tania. She took the license-plate number and called the police. She said that she and her sister had been stalked by a man with a video camera in a gold sports car. She had two of the six license-plate numbers wrong. She said it was 660 NFM or 660 MFN instead of Paul Bernardo's number—660 HFH. Lori said the car looked like a gold two-door Mazda with tinted windows; it was a GXL or RX7 or something. She told the police that she had followed the car to Port Dalhousie but lost it on Bayview Drive.

The following day, Lori saw the car again in Port Dalhousie. This time she got it right. She called the police again and corrected the license-plate number: it was 660 HFH and the car was not a Mazda, it was a gold Nissan 240 SX. Like Rachel Ferron before her, Lori Lazaruk never heard from the police again.

.   .   .

On April Fools Day, Inspector Bevan sought and received permission to apply for funding to extend the Mahaffy investigation. He got the funding almost as easily as Paul Bernardo got cigarettes across the border.

Paul Kenneth Bernardo was one of five suspects whose samples were resubmitted by Detective Irwin to the Center for Forensic Sciences on Thursday, April 2, 1992. Following scientist Kim Johnston's directions from the previous November, Irwin sorted through the 230 samples she had returned to him, and discovered that only five suspects met the non-secretor and PGM criteria.

Early in April, Paul was notified that his name had been stricken from the record by the Institute of Chartered Accountants for non-payment of his student fees. This meant nothing to Paul. He had never had more money in his pockets or bigger dreams in his head. Since he could be whatever he wanted, he no longer needed their sanction to be an accountant.

The institute records showed him to be unemployed at the time. Technically speaking, that was correct. Except he had never been busier. He was running more and more cigarettes, with greater and greater success. He had started dealing directly with Patrick Johnnie, the biker guy who financed and fenced the smokes from his repair garage on Highway 48 south of Sutton, Ontario. Although Paul had met Johnnie through his pal Van, Patrick Johnnie had become disenchanted with Van.

At the beginning of the year, Paul put Mike Donald to work. He convinced Mike—who was no rocket scientist himself—that smuggling cigarettes was virtually a risk-free way to make money. Paul told Mike that crossing the border with contraband was a trick he could teach him.

Mike Donald was a pleasant, clean-cut kid who otherwise worked as a waiter. Paul told Mike he could become a millionaire if he just followed Paul's advice. Mike was sold. He did what he was told and now he was doing very well. Paul took a piece of Mike's action as well. Paul was far more concerned about how he was going to increase the volume of cigarettes he could get across the border than he was about giving the Institute of Chartered Accountants one hundred and fifty dollars.

Sergeant Maracle had a meeting with FBI Special Agent Chuck Wagner on April 14, 1992. Wagner was stationed in Buffalo. He set up a conference call with Supervising Special Agent Gregg McCrary in Quantico, Virginia, to discuss the Leslie Mahaffy case in detail.

During the conference call, McCrary told Maracle he believed the person who killed and dismembered Leslie Mahaffy either knew her or had seen a light on in the Mahaffy's house. Maracle knew there had been no lights on in the Mahaffy house. He said the crimes were sexually motivated, the murder was secondary. His conclusion was based on the inordinate lengths to which the killer had gone to try and conceal the body. In McCrary's opinion, the killer had fantasized this scenario in the past and he simply acted it out as the opportunity presented itself.

"The killer had tools and experience to carry out dismemberment," McCrary explained. Therefore, he was probably a laborer who was comfortable with the use of tools and materials such as cement.

Consider that the killer took the trouble to drive the body forty miles—it was McCrary's assumption that Leslie Mahaffy had been abducted, raped, murdered, dismembered and cemented in Burlington and that the perpetrator then drove nine hundred pounds of cement to Lake Gibson—because he was comfortable with the disposal site. It was obviously a place where he could readily explain his presence if he was questioned by the police while in the process of dumping the cement blocks in the lake.

McCrary concluded that the perpetrator would now be under a great deal of stress and that would precipitate changes in behavior. He might start abusing alcohol or drugs or suddenly find religion. McCrary was further off the mark than the doctors in Penetanguishene.

He counseled the police to take a proactive approach and use the media. As the anniversary of Leslie's death approached, make use of the press—release selected information about the status of the investigation, about the many interviews with her friends and the fact that they had brought in the FBI.

A substantive media blitz with this kind of information would make the killer even more uneasy. Set up surveillance of grave and dump sites. These kinds of killers often spent a great deal of time in the past—visiting the scenes of their crimes and their victims' graves.

McCrary said the police should encourage the Mahaffy family to hold an elaborate memorial service and enlist them to help the police with the media. There was nothing like a bereaved mother to get the media's attention.

CHAPTER

nineteen

Paul and Karla agreed. What they really needed was another surprise. Karla wanted to play a bigger role this time. On Thursday afternoon, April 16, 1992, prior to the long Easter weekend, they would go out shopping. She would choose their next sex slave, someone with whom they could both really have fun.

They were a long way from the fifty sex slaves and virgins that Karla had said she would help Paul get when they made their movie a year and a half before. That video was one of the best things they had ever done. That and the Jane Doe video. The videos they had made with Leslie Mahaffy were substandard—Leslie's blindfold made the whole thing awkward and unappealing.

There were a lot of virginal teenage schoolgirls to choose from in St. Catharines. Karla suggested they cruise by Holy Cross and that other high school—Lakeport Secondary, near Linwell Road—around three o'clock. Because it was a long weekend, all the classes would be dismissed early. They could take their pick. On Thursday morning before she left for work she wrote a note, cut it out in the shape of an Easter egg and left it on the kitchen counter: "It's Easter soon and do you know what that means? A day off for Karly Curls to spend with her wonderful king. Isn't that great? Miss you. Love you. Karly."

Fifteen-year-old Kristen French had asked her parents about the California Club before they went to Fonthill on Wednesday evening. The long Easter weekend was coming up and Kristen wanted to have some fun. Donna French turned to her husband. Kristen was such a responsible child there was no need for the Frenches to be disciplinarians. Doug said that it would be all right providing Elton went with her. Elton Wade was Kristen's boyfriend. The California Club was a dance club. Everybody went there. The only problem was Elton didn't dance.

Kristen and Elton did a lot of things together. They went to watch his dad play hockey. They went to movies, they watched TV, and they washed Mr. Wade's car. It was a Firebird. Elton played hockey too—for Merritton, and for another team that occasionally traveled out of town. He also played for his high-school team. Kristen often went to watch Elton play hockey and she occasionally went over to his house. They went to Swiss Chalet whenever they could—Kristen loved Swiss—her father brought it home all the time. There was a Swiss Chalet just up the street from their house on Geneva.

Kristen had Elton's ring on the middle finger of her left hand. It had a big E on its face. Elton had dated one of Kristen's best friends, Julie Fitzsimmons, until Julie introduced them on the third of August. Since then, Kristen and Elton had been inseparable.

Except for the two weeks Kristen had spent in Florida during March, when her parents had bought her a Mickey Mouse watch with a real leather strap. That was cool. She had fun, but she spent a lot of time wondering what Elton was doing while she was away.

Then there was the blue couch in Kristen's basement. They had had sex on the blue couch a couple of times, but they always used a condom. Nobody knew.

Before Kristen went to bed around ten that night, she left her parents a list of gift suggestions for her forthcoming birthday. Kristen would be sixteen on May 10.

Kristen was not one to lie in bed. On Thursday morning, April 16, 1992, she was up at seven to face what looked to be a rather cruel spring day. "There are a number of things I want for my birthday," she told her mother. "I really must sit down with Elton today and go over my list."

Kristen wasn't allowed to go out during the week—unless for a very good reason. But her parents let Elton come over pretty much whenever Kristen wanted, so Kristen suggested she would invite him over for dinner.

Kristen was favoring her back that day. The fact that her right leg was shorter than her left meant she had to become an alternate—which was the coach's polite way of relegating her to spectator status—on the Holy Cross rowing team. She also had to curtail her precision figure skating. Rowing and skating were two activities in which Kristen had taken enormous pleasure. Kristen had been skating since she was six, first at the St. Catharines Winter Club and lately with the Merritton Precision Figure Skating Team.

"Good morning and goodbye," was all she said to her father. It was barely 7:30 and Doug French was out the door. He worked for Wegu Rubber in Whitby; they sold tires and other rubber products. He was the salesperson in the Niagara Region, a tall man with black hair that was just beginnning to thin and a square jaw that gave him an affirmative aspect. Both Kristen and her mother felt he worked too hard, but today was going to be a light day for him. Only moments after he left the house he pulled the big red Chrysler up in front of Perkins Restaurant just off Lake Street. His pal Donnie McCallum was in there, waiting for him. His coffee was already on the table when Doug sat down.

Kristen pulled on a pair of maroon bikini panties and put on her black lace bra. She got this bra and a pink one just like it from a box of clothes one of her mother's bosses, Bill Bright, brought to work one day. He brought it for Kristen to look through and she was glad he had.

She put on some blush and a bit of eyeliner. Over a pair of opaque green tights, she pulled on boxer shorts with the Georgetown University bulldog symbol on them. The bulldog was blue, the shorts white. All the girls at Holy Cross wore boxer shorts under their skirts. To get the particular hang that was fashionable the shorts had to be medium/large. At almost five feet five inches tall, Kristen weighed close to 120 pounds.

She latched her gold chain around her neck. There were the Praying Hands her father had given her and the letter-form gold charm, Today, Tomorrow, Forever, she had got from Elton.

At the same place she had bought the green tights—Le Château in the Pen Center—she got her green plaid kilt. She pulled on her white turtleneck with the embossed letters HC—for her school, Holy Cross—over the left breast pocket, along with her green V-necked sweater, which also had the letters HC embroidered in gray over the left breast.

Kristen had amazing, long brunette hair, of which she was justifiably proud. She had just had a perm, which made her hair keep its place. While she lightly brushed it, patting it into shape, the diamond stud in her left ear caught the light and flashed in the mirror. Elton had given her that too. She grabbed her olive green Kettle Creek book bag and went to the phone.

It was 7:45 A.M.—lots of time, since her mother always drove her to school around 8:15 A.M. She dialed Elton's number, fiddling with her knapsack. It was a few years old and starting to fray at the edges. There was a rip at one end of the zipper and the pull loop was torn. Kristen would definitely add a new Kettle Creek bag to her birthday list.

Donna French was making Kristen's lunch: ham-on-white, a maple-filled cookie in the shape of a maple leaf and a box of iced tea. She could see her daughter on the phone from the kitchen. Mrs. French did not need to guess who she was talking to. The Frenches approved of Elton. He was clean-cut, polite, and he seemed responsible. That his parents were divorced, that Elton lived with his father and his girlfriend did not faze them. After all, even though it had been twenty-two years, Donna was Doug's second wife. She was fifteen years his junior.

Doug had been married to Joan Slade for fifteen years—he had a daughter named Pam Radunski who, at forty, was approximately Donna's age; she lived in Capreol, north of Sudbury. Brad, thirty-seven, and Brian, the baby at thirty, both lived nearby in St. Catharines—they were good boys but seemed to be at loose ends. Dwayne, who was thirty-four, had moved to California and was doing quite well. Then there was Darren, Kristen's brother, Donna's son, who, at eighteen had just got a summer job as a press operator at Lindsay Rubber off Cushman Road. They were a close-knit family. It was as though Kristen and Darren had three older brothers and a sister.

Donna had gained some weight over the past decade but she was still a handsome woman and her eyes had a certain sparkle. She had started working in a halfway house seven months earlier. It was a place where convicts were reintegrated into society. Things had not become any easier, the way they were supposed to for good people such as the Frenches. The recession had wreaked havoc on the economy in St. Catharines. In 1991, Doug had had a heart attack.

When Kristen was no more than two years old, Donna had shut the kitchen door on her left baby finger. Donna cried for days after the doctors amputated the tip. Given the length and breadth of God's bounty when it came to Kristen French, nobody in the family, including Kristen, really got too excited.

Kristen had been a Brownie and a Girl Guide. If she applied herself she would get her bronze medallion this summer and become a lifeguard. Some of the kids called her Browner, as

much for her mane as for her academic prowess. It might be a
touch derogatory, but if that was as bad as she ever got she
would be very lucky.

Her brother called her kid. The "kid's" marks were always in
the high eighties. Kristen was on the grade nine honor roll. She
did volunteer work at a nursing home. Her girlfriends called
her Kris; the men in the family still called her Kristie.

Kristen looked at her watch—the background was a profile
of Mickey on red. There was a gold band around the watch
face. It was just after eight. She hung up the phone, drank a
glass of orange juice and put her lunch in her bag along with a
copy of *Introduction to Business in Canada*. She slipped on her
maroon Bass loafers; the right shoe had a lift. The chiropractor
had said it would help ease her back pain. Her back would need
some attention, since she was about to start a part-time job as a
shampooer at a hair place called Al's Locker Room.

She wore her black leather-and-suede jacket with puffy
shoulders and two leather straps on the bottom that tied up—a
derivation of the motorcycle jacket. It was very cool.

The drive to school barely took five minutes. Kristen complained about her leg; it was numb, she said; she thought the
thing in her shoe was supposed to help. It was hard to see an
angel in pain, but Donna could not do anything about the
numbness in Kristen's leg at that very moment. She dropped
her daughter in front of Holy Cross and went on to work.

The morning passed without incident. Kristen's two morning classes, advanced geography and advanced introduction to
business, were over quickly.

Dr. Patti Weir, the vet with whom Karla worked at the Martindale Clinic, was bemused. Karla's strongest point as an employee
was her reliability. She had only missed four or five workdays
over that past few years. But Dr. Weir viewed Karla with a
slightly jaundiced eye. There were things about Karla that she
found disquieting. Every Thursday, for instance, Karla would
go to the library and come back with a bag full of library books,
which she would keep under her desk.

The books always contained graphic descriptions of sex and death. True crime, such as *Stranger Beside Me,* Ann Rule's book about Ted Bundy, or *Dying to Get Married* by Ellen Harris, a sordid story about the bizarre courtship of Julie Miller Bullock, which was characterized by extreme sexual and sadistic violence that ended in murder. It was set in Missouri in the fifties. The most bizarre and gruesome by far was one called *American Psycho.*

Karla would enthusiastically read the most graphic passages out loud to the other girls at the clinic. They were never nice. Karla's tastes in literature were so consistent that Dr. Weir thought it very abnormal.

Karla was also manipulative. For instance, the way she manipulated the receptionist, Sherri Berry, prior to the long Easter weekend. For some reason, it was very important to Karla that she have the extra half day on Thursday off. It was Sherri Berry's turn, but Karla started to work on Sherri the week before. She succeeded. Karla was gone by noon on Thursday, April 16, 1992. Sherri was still there.

Doug French had left the restaurant and gone to pick up his paycheck. From there, he went to John Deere to meet with Norm Lassard and give him quotes on some rubber products. He went home around 1:00 P.M., did some paperwork and paid a few bills.

Kristen ate her lunch in the school cafeteria with her friends, Lori Armstrong and Ana Lara; Ana and Kristen sort of stole Lori's M&Ms and ate them. Kristen and Lori laughed and giggled but Ana, who had only met Kristen three weeks earlier, did not talk much. Ana really wanted to be Kristen's friend. Kristen was effervescent, happy.

Kristen's math class started at two. Her math partner, James Dowling, thought Kristen was really good-looking. He had known her two earlier boyfriends: Ryan Shepard, who had moved to Kitchener the year before; and before Ryan there was Ryan Smith. That was James's problem: his first name was not Ryan.

Kristen had so much self-confidence. James would not mind getting a little closer to Kristen. Maybe at the California Club tonight. "Are you going?" he wondered.

They were friends, but not in that way. Nevertheless, Kristen usually told James what her weekend plans were—since she did not say anything, maybe she would be there. James knew her new boyfriend was big Elton Wade, but Mr. Wade stickhandled pucks—he did not dance. Kristen did seem to be a little stuck up sometimes, just by the way she talked. In James's estimation, she was very intelligent and very pretty.

Doug drove over to the Wayside Center to pick up Donna's car-ownership papers. He then drove over to the registry office to get her new license-plate stickers. He was home by three.

When her last class ended at 2:43 P.M., Kristen did not dawdle. She could not wait to get home. It was Thursday, but it felt like Friday. She always let her dog out of its pen and fed her at 3:00 P.M. This afternoon, she was eager to talk to Elton again. There was something else she wanted to tell him. Kristen almost always walked home; the same route everyday. She waved to Ana Lara in the hall.

"Bye, Kristen," Ana said. Kristen hurried to her locker, then headed for the Lake Street exit.

Kristen always went across Lake Street, east on Prince Charles Drive, south on Royal Road and then east on Linwell, walking on the north sidewalk across the intersection at Howard Avenue to Geneva—they lived on Geneva—and then Kristen was home. She loved the way her dog, Sasha, jumped for joy at the sight of her. It took about fifteen minutes at the most to walk home. It was still raining lightly.

Linwell Road is a main thoroughfare in St. Catharines. At three in the afternoon there was always a steady stream of cars. It was the kind of street a person might have to wait a couple of minutes to cross, in the middle of the day.

At 3:30 P.M., Doug French looked out the window and saw the dog still in its pen. He thought Kristen a bit late and wondered where she was.

The phone rang. It must be her. What time was it now?

"I'll have her call you when she gets in, Elton," he told his daughter's attentive boyfriend.

In retrospect, Doug would probably say at that moment he was seized with such powerful foreboding it was like an angina attack of the mind. It went through his system like the dye they had pumped through his arteries during the angiogram. He suddenly felt excessively warm and faint.

At four o'clock he decided he would go out and get stamps, taking a circuitous route along Linwell Road, right by Holy Cross. Just before he went out, the phone rang again.

"No Elton, she's still not home," Doug said. "I'm starting to get a bit worried."

Looking intently for his daughter, whom he knew was dressed in her Holy Cross school uniform, Doug French did not notice Janet Migata, who at that very moment was walking past the parking lot of Grace Lutheran Church just beyond Howard Avenue. Janet saw a Bass loafer in the middle of the church parking lot and wondered what it was and why it was there.

There were as many churches in St. Catharines as there were doughnut shops. Johnny Carson once told millions of "Tonight Show" viewers that St. Catharines was the doughnut capital of the world. The mayor, Joe McCaffery, still fumed about that one.

Doug bought his stamps and took the mail over to the Grantham post office. Darren had just arrived home from work when Doug pulled up to the house around 4:30 P.M.

Darren immediately sensed his father was off balance. Doug tried to reason with himself—she probably had a commitment after school he did not know about, or she had gone down to the rowing club. Another ten minutes went by. Before he left the house he picked up the phone and called Donna to ask her if she knew where Kristen was. But Donna did not know. She should be home by now, Donna said. She's probably talking to somebody.

After talking to Doug, Donna called the school. They paged

Kristen over the public-address system. Her name echoed in the abandoned corridors and classrooms.

Doug French, who was not born yesterday, suddenly became very suspicious of young Mr. Wade. He picked up the phone. In no uncertain terms he demanded: "Have you seen Kristen, Elton?" Emphatically, Elton replied that he had not.

"I'm going out to look for her," Doug said and put down the phone.

At 4:30 P.M. Donna left work, went to the bank and drove home. It was not until she saw the dog still in her pen that she too was overcome with a sick, hopeless feeling. It took all her inner resources simply to get out of the car and go in the house. Sasha was a blue-eyed rotund ball of white fur. Kristen had bought the Samoyed-Husky cross with her own money. She always came directly home after school, let the dog out of its pen, took it for a walk and played vigorously with Sasha for half an hour or so. Kristen would never leave Sasha unattended.

Donna called Cher Knotley at the unisex hairdresser on Scott. Kristen sometimes baby-sat for Cher. Kristen also baby-sat for Donna's boss and a woman named Judy Pula on Margery Street. She called them.

Then Donna started on the girlfriends. On a long shot, Doug went down to the rowing club on Henley Island to see if Kristen had just happened to stop in.

"Is that a shoe?" Sandy Grabatian, the secretary at Grace Lutheran Church, said to herself as she rushed out to her car on an errand at 4:55 P.M. The Easter weekend was one of the busiest two or three weekends of the year for the church. Grace Lutheran had been built two decades earlier by its parishioners, German immigrants with vivid images of Luther and the manifesto he pinned on his famous water closet's door fixed in their minds. The early morning services were still conducted in German at Grace Lutheran.

"I should pick that up and put it in the lost and found," she thought to herself as she pulled out of the parking lot and maneuvered into the busy long-weekend traffic.

When Elton pulled up in the Frenches' driveway, Kristen's brother, Darren, was standing in the doorway. The dog was still in the pen. Mrs. French was crying. Darren got in with Elton and told him no one had seen Kristen. They went over to Henley Island to look. They ran into Mr. French by Scorecard Harry's, a popular sports bar on the fringe of Port Dalhousie. He had looked all over the island and no one had seen her.

Back at the house, Darren and his girlfriend went over to Holy Cross to look. Elton started to phone around and talked to a bunch of people. Then he joined Darren at the school. They went inside and looked all over, even in the boiler room. Empty schools are strange places. He thought he could hear Kristen's name echoing in the corridors.

Mrs. French thought about Tammy Rovert, her oldest sister Joyce's daughter. Kristen was supposed to be a bridesmaid at her wedding next month; she had already picked up her dress. It was green. She had been a bridesmaid at Tammy's sister's wedding a year and a half earlier. Kristen was so beautiful in those bridesmaids' dresses. At 5:55 Mrs. French, now almost hysterical, called the police. Kristen seemed to have vanished into thin air.

When Sandy Grabatian returned to Grace Lutheran Church a few hours later, she saw the shoe again. A single maroon Bass loafer lying on its side, a lift halfway out. It looked forlorn in the steady rain. She had too much on her mind to read the signs, even when they said the end was near. She walked past the shoe into the church.

CHAPTER

twenty

Unlike almost every other city, town and hamlet in North America—all of which had been planned on gridirons—St. Catharines had the distinction of having been designed on a radius. Its roads follow old Indian trails that converge radially on the city's center, where Twelve Mile meets Dick's Creek. Navigating a radius is a conundrum. Visitors to the small city frequently get lost. Consequently, everyone who lives in St. Catharines is constantly being asked for directions.

When the young, attractive blond woman in the shiny sports car called out to Kristen French for directions, Kristen did not think twice. Kristen blithely walked the fifty yards to where the car had pulled up in the Grace Lutheran Church parking lot. The woman opened her door and stepped out. Her hair was held back in a ponytail. She had a map in her hand.

Kristen French was an intelligent, street-smart girl. In spite of the fact that Linwell was a busy street and it was the middle of the afternoon, if it had been a man alone, or two men in the car, Kristen would never have left the sidewalk.

Paul and Karla had planned it that way. They both knew everybody was always getting lost in St. Catharines. After two years there, Paul still got lost himself. If Karla held a map and pretended she needed directions—to the Pen Center, where she used to work—they would not have any trouble finding another sex slave.

There was a degree of extemporaneousness about it. They had tried the ploy a dozen times already, but the sun, moon and stars would not line up. This time, Karla had pointed Kristen out and Paul thought she looked pretty good. In terms of Paul's personal mythology, Kristen had Jennifer Galligan hair. She was walking alone and coming up to a place where they could get off the road easily. Paul and Karla both appreciated the lethargy of the casual observer. Karla smiled. Kristen leaned over to study the map. It happened so fast that Kristen never had time to realize the map Karla was holding was a map of Scarborough.

Before Kristen could focus, the guy who had been sitting in the driver's seat was behind her with a knife and the girl had jumped into the backseat. Although Kristen tried to put up a fight, the man was too strong, and once he had pushed her down into the bucket seat, the woman grabbed her long hair and pulled hard. Kristen found herself cheek to Naugahyde with the armrest between the seats, unable to move after the driver slammed the passenger door shut.

When she cried out, the man told her to shut up or he would slit her throat. They drove slowly out of the parking lot. They did not seem to be in any hurry whatsoever. The woman continued to hold her hair. Minutes later, they pulled up in a driveway and drove into a garage. The driver got out and shut the garage door. He came back and put a blindfold over Kirsten's eyes. Then his companion jumped out of the car and left them sitting in the car.

Karla ran into the house and disconnected all the phones. She took them upstairs and dumped them in the closet, leaving only the phone with the answering machine connected. While they kept sex slaves, it was best if Karla or Paul returned any calls they might get. Karla closed all the blinds and made sure all the doors were locked. Paul brought the girl in the house and took her upstairs. He told Karla to stay put.

It was just after three in the afternoon when Paul guided Kirsten into the upstairs washroom across the hall from the master bedroom. The blindfold swaddled her forehead like a large, broad bandage. He had tied it at the base of her neck, allowing her long, dark curls to flow freely. Paul focused the lens of the of his video camera on her thighs while Kristen urinated. When she anxiously asked for toilet paper he handed her half a roll. Returning it to him, she politely thanked him.

Finding her maroon bikini briefs in the dark worried Kristen, but she hastily pulled up the beige elastic top and began tugging on her green leotards, straightening them above her knees and pulling them up, along with the navy-and-white Georgetown boxer shorts. Paul noted they were covered in fierce cartoon bulldogs. He liked that. As Paul peered through the viewfinder, a red mark blossoming on Kristen's lower lip was clearly evident, a memento of her belligerent struggle with him when he had tried to get her quietly into the car.

Paul was always pleased when a girl said she had to use the washroom, particularly when circumstances dictated that he should watch. Kristen had to go again.

"Show me something nice," he told her as she sat on the toilet, clutching her kilt around her waist. He reached out to spread her legs further apart.

"There's not much nice to see," said Kristen.

She wiped herself quickly and pulled her panties up with a snap of the elastic.

"Is it past six o'clock?" she asked, disoriented by the blindfold and unable to check her left wrist to see where the Mouse's hands were.

"Ya," said Paul.

"My mom's gonna be worried," said Kristen, expelling a worried sigh of her own. Paul turned off the camera.

Constable First Class Pam Carter had just begun her shift when she received a report about a missing fifteen-year-old girl. Working alone that day, she drove her cruiser over to the Geneva Street address, arriving at 6:37 P.M.

Even though the day was cloudy and dreary, light filtered through the closed blinds in the dormer window. Fully clothed, Kristen was sitting on the gray carpet in the master bedroom. A picture of Tammy Lyn Homolka sat on the television set next to Karla's cherished hope chest. Her parents had given her that on her eighteenth birthday. Now the chest was covered with photo albums and the usual disarray of Karla's clothes. Kristen held the blindfold to her forehead with her left hand, unaware that just behind her shoulder there was a roll of brown cord, the same one that Karla kept in the dog's closet when it wasn't needed to restrain sex slaves. Kristen took a sip from the tumbler of orange juice and vodka Paul had given her.

"Tell my dick you love him," Paul whispered, kneeling beside her and putting her hands on the erect penis which he had released from his blue jeans.

The camera, fixed on the chair across the room, was unmoving as she cried and fumbled with his genitals. Ice-T's Original Gangsta tape blared on the boom box. Every other word sounded like "bitch" or "nigger."

"Tell me you want me to be happy. So maybe you can go home later," he told her.

"I want you to be happy," Kristen said, but she could not see him shaking his head, "no."

"You suck good cock—you sure you never done this before?" he asked, moving away from her, sitting back on his haunches and handing her a drink. Kristen shook her head and took two sips.

Cradling her chin, Paul instructed the sobbing girl to pull down her clothes. She rocked from side to side, pushing the boxer shorts and leotards down to her ankles. Ice-T kept calling himself a "straight-up nigger."

"Please," Kristen cried to him, but he made her lower her underwear as well. Then he told her to bend her knees; he picked up the camera and zoomed in for a close-up.

"Spread your cunt for me," he instructed. "Do it with your fingers."

When he pulled back to take a shot of her face, it was etched with distress.

Downstairs in the kitchen Karla was preparing a chicken dinner, but her heart was not in it. At the best of times, her culinary skills peaked when she was melting processed cheese on nachos and opening a jar of salsa. There was too much excitement upstairs for her to cook. She could hear the pounding music.

Kristen vomited so badly her blindfold came off. Paul called Karla and she cleaned up. They took off Kristen's clothes. There was blood on her white turtleneck. Paul must have accidentally cut her during the struggle in the car. He had not meant to cut Kristen. The knife had only been meant as a symbol to quickly communicate his resolve. Karla dabbed the small wound with peroxide and put a bandage on it. Then she took the laundry down to the basement.

When Karla got back up to the kitchen, Paul had brought Kristen down. While Karla finished cooking, they talked about Kristen's boyfriend, Elton Wade—Karla believed she knew him; and Kristen's dog, Sasha, who was a white Samoyed. Kristen told them she had older brothers and a sister; that she was a child of her father's second marriage.

Karla served the chicken, but Kristen only picked at it. Paul took Kristen back upstairs. There was no more blindfold.

The missing-persons report on Kristen Dawn French was issued at 7:00 P.M. An hour later, a command post was organized at Holy Cross Secondary School and officers began arriving. Some of them knew Kristen French and the family, so they knew something was terribly wrong. By 10:30 officers were making phone calls to Kristen's friends, using an address book that had been found in her bedroom. Checks were made at two teen dances in the area.

Rap music filled the room with images of Los Angeles gangs and funky times. Kristen was naked, half under the sheets of the queen-size bed in the corner of the room. Paul leaned back and placed his groin squarely in her face.

"Okay," said Karla, standing back and holding the camera.

"I'm fifteen years old and I love to suck dick," said Kristen, looking at Karla as she had been told to do and bending her head and mouth over Paul's less-than-erect penis.

"Smile," said Karla, as if she were in a mall somewhere taking baby pictures for Sears. Returning the same half smile she had seen already on the other woman's face, Kristen repeated the words.

"Ya, that's good," Karla assured her.

Paul entered Kristen roughly from behind while Karla focused furiously, even as Kristen cried out in pain.

"Shut up," Paul told her, positioning himself and grabbing a handful of long, brown curls while LL Cool J intoned, "Come on, fool."

Then Paul raised both of his hands and pounded his fists into the base of her back. It was a "thump, thump," done to the

INVISIBLE darkness 231

music. Tersely, he told Kristen to lower her hips and arch her back.

"Smile," called Karla, as Paul bent over Kristen, turning her face to the camera.

Over the next few minutes, Kristen French told Paul Bernardo that she loved him twenty-six times. Each tortured phrasing was different.

"I'm bad," rapped LL Cool J.

Maurice Charbonneau, the principal at Holy Cross, had been sure it was nothing nefarious. There was a momentary flurry at the school when one of the officers found a paper in Kristen's locker with writing about obtaining false identification, sneaking out and going drinking. One of Kristen's schoolmates confirmed that it was just notes from an assignment written for a drama class.

That night Kristen slept on Paul's side of the walk-in closet adjoining the master bedroom. Paul wanted to give her sleeping pills, to be sure that she would not cause a fuss or try to escape. Karla opposed the idea. They had given Leslie Halcion, and even though the police had not said so, Karla knew traces of the drug could have been found in an autopsy.

Kristen was going to die. She had seen them—seen where they lived, heard their dog.

Regardless, Paul gave Kristen one or two pills, and the girl slept.

They rose late the following day.

Officers from the criminal-investigations branch spent most of Good Friday interviewing Kristen's classmates, family and friends. Inspector Vince Bevan was at home on leave, where he was called at 10:20 A.M. Less than an hour later, he was standing in the parking lot of Grace Lutheran Church, securing it as a crime scene. One maroon Bass loafer had been found there. Donna French wept when it was shown to her.

When she finished showering downstairs, Karla filled the silver tray with drinks to take upstairs. Paul was perched on the upstairs bathroom countertop, filming Kristen bathing in the Jacuzzi. Karla stood quietly by the door, watching.

Kristen looked small, kneeling in the big tub with its noisy jets, rubbing herself with a thick black facecloth, while tiny bubbles frothed around her. Her face was serious.

"Smile," he told her. Kristen gave him a half grin. Only the right side of her mouth seemed able to meet his request.

"Is that nice?" he asked.

Kristen looked up at him, her eyes darting back toward Karla. It was difficult to hear anything above the rush of the water, and "nice" did not have anything to do with the humiliation of bathing for her sex-crazed kidnappers.

"Pardon me?" inquired Kristen. Her good manners were automatic.

The story line was about two schoolgirls and the theme was Girls' Night Out. Karla rooted through her clothes for the checkered kilt she had worn when she was in high school. She found a white pullover and her V-necked black sweater. It was as close as she could come to Kristen's authentic schoolgirl uniform.

Kristen tucked her turtleneck neatly into her skirt. After laundering, there was no sign of the blood. Karla's outfit was not nearly as tailored. The pleats in her old kilt were not ironed smoothly, and they would not have lain flat anyway—Karla had gained a few pounds in her first ten months of marriage.

Paul told them to "do the stuff that girls do."

In front of the glass wall of the bathroom counter, Karla had laid out makeup and perfume, everything from tiny sample bottles to her full-size colognes, skin creams and her Clinique cosmetics. Kristen's freshly permed curls billowed around her shoulders as she swept Karla's powder brush over her face.

Karla nattered on about various perfume preferences, Kristen played along. If Karla asked her about Giorgio perfume, Kristen said she also wore it.

"Okay girls, you know what I want you to do," Paul said, "Each one of you pull up your skirt at the same time."

Almost in unison, Kristen and Karla lifted their kilts without so much as a glance over their shoulders. Paul told them to bend over and give him "a nice ass shot." Kristen bent slightly, her buttocks bare. Karla leaned over further, with an arch in her back to lift her less youthful backside.

Through his lens, Paul could see there was no comparison. Karla was wearing white bikini underpants that bunched unattractively between her cheeks.

"Okay girls, back to work," Paul said, and their skirts dropped.

Karla picked through her perfume cache and Kristen spotted Eternity, the only scent that was really familiar to her.

"Sometimes Eternity smells like chipmunks," Kristen offered. Paul was silently confused, but Karla understood what Kristen meant. That faint cedar aroma—it was just like the shavings that they used in pet stores as bedding for hamsters and other rodent pets. Kristen was playing the game. She was being Karla's friend.

Now they could have dinner and watch a movie. This was too special an occasion to eat Karla's day-old chicken. Kristen could have whatever she wanted. McDonald's had just introduced pizza. It would be a first for all of them. And as Kristen was well aware, it would mean she would be left alone with only one captor—Karla.

At the crime scene, police had seized eighteen items as evidence, including three wads of chewing gum, four cigarette butts and one battery-cap terminal. Seventy-four inches from the west curb, they found a torn section of a street map of the Scarborough area. It appeared to have been run over. In the same area, they found a lock of brown hair, partially wet and flattened onto the pavement.

Paul and Karla tied Kristen up because she was bigger than Karla and Karla was concerned that Kristen might be able to overpower her. Paul got the small rubber mallet from the workbench in the basement and gave it to Karla, just in case. He would not be long: McDonald's pizza and the video store—an hour at the most.

Although she was handcuffed and her feet were bound, Kristen could talk to Karla. She could play on their "friendship." She could beg to be set free. Of course, Karla could not let Kristen go. End of discussion. Karla rolled the TV over to the closet doorway. The six o'clock news carried a full report on Kristen's kidnapping.

Paul had rented Karla's favorite movie, *Criminal Law,* and a dark thriller which had something to do with voodoo and ritual sacrifice, called *Angel Heart*. It starred Mickey Rourke. Karla really liked Mickey Rourke. They would have a great time, eating pizza and watching movies. Paul got very angry when he discovered that Karla had let Kristen watch television and that they had seen Kristen's father pleading for his daughter's safe return on the evening news.

Kristen was crying and she had thrown up on the carpet beside the sliding door. Not much, of course, because she had not eaten. Paul told Karla to clean it up while he untied the shaken girl and tried to determine just what had happened.

He could not believe that Karla had allowed Kristen to watch the news. She could be so smart about some things and so dumb about others.

They sat in the bedroom and watched a bit of *Angel Heart* while they ate McDonald's pizza.

The mayor of West Lincoln caught the six o'clock television news flash about a missing girl in St. Catharines and it jogged her memory about something she had seen in a church parking lot there a day earlier. Joan Packham had been driving around doing errands in the rain: picking up her daughter; retrieving her husband's electric razor from the repair shop; dropping off paperwork for her accountants. In the parking lot of the Lutheran church on Linwell Road she had seen what seemed to be a struggle. She put it down to kids fooling around.

Maybe it was nothing, but she called Niagara Regional Police anyway. She was invited to come in to the office and ended up driving her route with two constables and circling the church parking lot. Though she was, admittedly, not good about cars, Joan thought the one she had seen looked like a Camaro or a Trans Am or a Z28. An acquaintance of hers had recently purchased a Z28. To assist her in identifying the vehicle the constables had her look in different parking lots, and they drove her by a Pontiac-Buick car dealership where she spotted five cars resembling the one she had seen. Then she was presented with thirty years' worth of automobile-identification books containing what one of the officers described as "Chevrolets, Fords, Chryslers and many other makes and models."

Inspector Vince Bevan made arrangements for an offline computer search based on 1982 and newer Camaros and Firebirds using the in-house police ORACLE system, which the inspector himself had installed.

"Don't be nervous, it's okay," Karla told Kristen, as they knelt together on the bed in their schoolgirl costumes. Again, Paul wanted girl talk. Kristen asked Karla why her teeth were so straight, and Karla called her "silly."

"Am I shaking?" Kristen asked.

"No, just try to feel at home," advised Karla in her friendliest voice.

"Can I see your dog without it attacking me before I leave?" asked Kristen.

"It's up to him," Karla said, nodding her head toward Paul.

"Before you leave, yes," said Paul, and the "schoolgirls" continued to touch each other.

As she lay back on the bed, Kristen pulled a knot from her

long hair. The overhead fan whirred above her, reminding her of the fan over the black girl's bed in that weird movie, *Angel Heart*.

"If I close my eyes, I'll fall asleep," said Kristen.

"Trust me, you won't," replied Karla.

Karla told Kristen that she was a pretty girl.

"You're pretty, too," said Kristen, responding to the theme and referring back to the first time she saw Karla in the car, telling her that her thought was, "Holy cow is she pretty."

Karla knelt between Kristen's legs and began exploring her vagina with her tongue. Paul had the music up. This rap was all about "go, go and jam." Kristen suggested that Karla was "an expert at this," but Karla said curtly, "Trust me, I'm not."

What Kristen had learned from Karla, Paul now wanted Kristen to do to his wife. While Karla lay back on the bed with both hands behind her head, Paul told Kristen to put her fingers "inside," and he moved in for a close-up.

"Are my nails hurting you?" she inquired with some concern, but Karla told her it felt "real good."

Kristen's face was half buried between Karla's legs when Paul asked her for a smile and told her to say she loved Karla.

Brushing back the mane of hair that was obscuring her face, Kristen put on the biggest grin she could manage.

"I love Karla," she said, and then she asked, "Is that your name?" Paul gave her an affirmative, and decided to try a new angle.

The "schoolgirls" were positioned on the bed, side by side, kissing, with their legs spread apart. Kristen was supposed to masturbate Karla. She turned on her side, raising her knee, trying to find what it was she was supposed to be rubbing.

"I don't want to hurt you," she said, touching Karla lightly. Elton Wade's gold ring shone in Paul's lens. Kristen's left hand moved over Karla's pubic hair. Karla told her it felt good, when Kristen asked her if she was doing "okay for the first time."

"I like little girls," said Karla.

"Thank you," replied Kristen.

"I love you, Christian," said Karla, mispronouncing her name.

"I love you, too. Karla, is it?" replied Kristen with a question in her voice. Karla told her she was right. Now Kristen had a name to go with the face, and everything else she had seen so far. Karla was not a common name. How many of them could there be in a city as small as St. Catharines?

At 11 P.M., a province-wide alert was issued for a 1982 or later model two-door ivory or cream Camaro or Firebird. The description of the car and the missing girl who might have been in it was provided to a feral media. A school picture of Kristen French, holding a bouquet of roses, would hit the news the next day. Speculation mounted. Fourteen-year-old Terri Anderson, who had disappeared without a trace five months earlier, had lived eight blocks from the scene of French's abduction. And police were no further ahead in the investigation of Leslie Mahaffy's murder than they had been when they found her body in cement blocks at Lake Gibson. Hardly anyone ever talked about Krystal Connors, the petite, twenty-eight-year-old dark-haired woman who had been raped, murdered and set on fire just before Christmas in 1990. One newspaper chose to headline its Saturday morning story: "The nightmare's back."

When Paul got into the video at the end of Karla and Kristen's sixteen-minute, forty-eight-second scene, he was wearing a pink T-shirt and white socks. He lay back on the bed, bracing his head upright with his right arm behind him, so he could watch.

"That's beautiful," said Karla, framing her shot from the end of the bed. Kristen was bent over Paul's groin, masturbating him with her right hand. She had rolled her sweater up to her elbow.

"Tell me if I'm pulling hair," Kristen said, not wanting to hurt or anger him, but not really understanding what he wanted either. In less than a minute, she displayed her unfamiliarity with the process by allowing Paul's penis to constantly slip from her grip.

"Kinda play a lot," directed Karla, knowing the clue to maintaining Paul's erections was massaging his testicles.

"Three times and you're out," admonished Paul when Kristen lost her grip, "Three times . . . Give me the knife, I'm gonna kill ya."

A few seconds later, he forgave her.

"Thank you," said Kristen French.

All night long, from 8:30 P.M. until 5 A.M., identification officers were examining the church grounds and sidewalk area with a Luma Lite. They followed a visual grid, using the filters and optics of the portable light source to observe fluorescence in specimens and items that are not normally visible to the naked eye. Luma Lite is only effective in the dark.

By 5:00 A.M., they had gathered four trace-finding exhibits from the grass, the pavement, the road and the church sign.

Paul decided to punish Kristen for not doing it right anyway. He put Kristen on the floor and started to have anal sex with her. Kristen defecated on him. Then she called him a bastard. Without knowing it, she had touched a nerve.

Karla was assigned cleanup duties. Once again, she found herself downstairs in front of the washing machine.

This time there was no water in the Jacuzzi. Just Kristen, naked with her hair pulled back, her head propped against the back of the tub in the peach-colored glow of the heat lamp.

"I'm going to piss on you, okay? Then I'm going to shit on you, okay?" Paul said in a whisper.

The camera was sitting on the toilet tank next to the white-tiled tub. He told the unmoving girl to close her eyes as he knelt in front of her, naked except for a long-sleeved white shirt that bloused around his waist. He took a long pull on a can of beer and set it down on the tub ledge. Faint music came from the other room.

Kristen did not move, even when he slapped her face with his semi-erect penis.

"Don't make me mad. Don't make me hurt you," he said, urging her to smile while he rubbed his groin into her face.

"Don't worry, I won't piss in your face."

Finally, he stood over her and urinated.

Then he moved. Turning his buttocks into her face, he squatted over her face and tried to defecate on her without success.

"You're a fucking piece of shit. But I like you," he told her. "You look good covered in piss."

Kristen's hair was a tousle of weary curls when he photographed her laying full-length in the empty tub. Her eyes were lowered, she had crossed her left hand over her right on her stomach.

While the Jacuzzi filled with water, Kristen perched at the end of the tub, one long ringlet trailing over her right breast. She nervously brushed her hair back from her face, lightly scratching her chest, her legs resting above the water jets.

Opposite her, Paul captured a reflected image in the mirror. Karla smiled, that evil half smile of hers.

It took a lot of time and hot water to fill the Jacuzzi, and the water pressure upstairs had never been as strong with the washing machine running. Kristen bathed in just a few inches of water.

"Pretend like you're in Hollywood. Okay?" Paul said. There was no need to whisper, now that Karla had approved the scene.

Kristen gave him a disingenuous smile while bubbles billowed in the shallow water at her feet.

"Classic smile," noted Paul.

When she gave her hair a final rinse in the tub-side faucet, Kristen bent forward and her face grew very solemn. She looked much older than her fifteen years. Her jaw set as firmly as her father's and the mask of worry that she wore erased her youthful, feminine features.

That night Karla insisted that the three of them sleep together in the bed. With Kristen's promise to be on her best behavior, Karla and Paul agreed not to bind Kristen.

·   ·   ·

On Saturday morning, police were vacuuming the lawn at
Grace Lutheran Church, still looking for clues. They measured
Kristen's usual route to and from school. Total distance: 1.1
kilometers, or half a mile.

At the Center for Forensic Sciences, the flattened lock of
hair was compared to control samples from two of Kristen's hair
brushes. It appeared to have been cut. There were no roots.

Teachers from Holy Cross Secondary volunteered to spend
the day at the school, counseling and comforting concerned
students.

Kristen was lying on the bed dressed in her school uniform
when Paul turned on the camera and jumped on the bed beside
her. It was Saturday afternoon, but Karla was still wearing her
white eyelet-trimmed, spaghetti-strapped nightie.

Paul was naked except for his long-sleeved white shirt. Kristen's hair hung softly. Karla's had been gelled into puffy bangs
and sprayed into stiff strands.

While Kristen bent to suck his nipple and lightly rub his
erect penis, Karla sat at the base of the bed nibbling on his left
foot.

"I want you to guide her through this," Paul instructed.

Karla got up to adjust the camera, checking to make sure
that Paul's head was in the shot and the focus was correct.
While he leaned back into the pillow, Kristen called him "the
best master" and Karla dubbed him "the king." Paul spread his
legs and Karla began fellating him, drawing Kristen to her side
while he instructed them on licking protocol.

"You're not home yet," Paul told Kristen. He wanted to
hear some "love stuff." Karla brought Kristen's hand to her
breast and told her that she was a "good, little sex slave." Kristen thanked Karla.

Then Karla took over the filming, holding the camera steady
and true, framing a close-up shot of Kristen French masturbating and fellating her husband.

"Suck his dick, Kristen," Karla told her. "Move your hand
Kristen. Keep on talking."

When Kristen moved her mouth away to speak to her "master," Paul was suddenly angry.

"Don't fucking look at me, look at my dick and talk to it," he said, slapping her back roughly.

Karla zoomed in and out with her lens.

"Okay," said Karla, cuing Kristen to say a line about how she hated her boyfriend and Paul was her boyfriend and he should "fuck all the girls at Holy Cross," if it would make him happy. The bedsprings were squeaking faster and faster, when Karla interjected with the breathless information that she "got some nice mouth shots."

Suddenly, from the basement, there was a loud whine. The dog was feeling deprived. The sound distracted Paul but Karla urged Kristen on, calling her a "good cocksucker."

"I want to see a mouth full of cum, Kristen," Karla said, over the whirring motor of the camera and the baleful sound of the dog.

But Paul was not hearing the sounds he wanted to hear. Suddenly, he pounded Kristen on the back with his left hand. Kristen did not flinch. Instead, she tried to say the words. Paul hit Kristen five more times. All the while, Karla's hand was steady on the camera.

The camera stopped and Paul took his wedding ring off and moved it to the middle finger of his right hand next to his Masonic ring. It was a cheap wedding ring. He had only paid a couple of hundred bucks for it at D.J. Wholesale Club, and he was afraid it would bend if he had to hit Kristen again. Then it would be a real pain to try and get off.

Back at his office, Inspector Vince Bevan sat down with a report he had received from a Ministry of Transport computer programmer who had dutifully attempted to compile a list of every Camaro registered in the province of Ontario.

There were 124,970 registered vehicles, of which 36,636 were plated or unplated models within the definitive years 1978 through 1981.

"The report was voluminous," Bevan conscientiously recorded in his report.

Officers were assigned to sort the printout by geographic area, and focus on light-colored Camaros in the Niagara Region. When Bevan finally got a chance to sleep on it, he would decide to ask for the information in ASCII, so he could sort it himself on his home computer, postal code by postal code. Inspector Bevan had resolved to locate and examine every single one of those 36,636 Camaros, car by dilapidated car, if necessary.

The fellating of Paul Bernardo left Kristen gasping for air. Once, when she raised herself to her knees to speak at his request, Karla thought she saw him holding a flashlight behind his back. In fact, he was clutching his knife in his left hand.

"All the Holy Cross girls want you," Kristen told him.

"We're running out of tape I think," Karla advised.

Thirty seconds later, Paul was holding Kristen's mouth over his penis while he ejaculated. He told her to "keep it inside." Kristen remained motionless.

At Holy Cross, parents and school officials met behind closed doors for a crisis-intervention session. Friends and relatives congregated at the home of Doug and Donna French, which was being besieged by the press.

Meanwhile, Inspector Bevan discovered that of those 36,636 plated and unplated 1978 to 1981 Camaros registered in the province, only 4,688 were owned by residents of Niagara, Halton and Hamilton-Wentworth. He further brought it down to 2,084 in Niagara, 900 in Halton and 1,698 in Hamilton-Wentworth. Now that was something they could get their minds around.

In the streets, hardly anyone was out walking alone. When anyone saw a Camaro, he called it in.

. . .

Paul pressed the video camera's record button just as the song began. The title track from Ice-T's "Power" boomed over Karla, who smiled as she put the neck of an empty wine bottle all the way up Kristen's vagina. To the rhythm of Ice-T rapping, "Power, power, power," Karla worked it in and out.

"Put it in there hard, Kar," Paul said. Kristen smiled wanly at him. Handcuffed, with her hands behind her back, she was kneeling on another towel where her feet rested, bound by a pair of Karla's black pantyhose. She was still dressed as a schoolgirl and her skirt was raised above her uplifted buttocks.

"Ram her hard. She called me a bastard."

Using both of her hands, Karla forced the glass bottle in and out of Kristen French more than forty times.

Kristen winced, blinking hard, unable to move.

"You can show it hurts if it does, okay," Paul said to Kristen. The girl tilted her head.

"It does a little," she said, adding the smile she knew he wanted.

Paul put the camera on the carpet and took over from Karla, pushing the bottle in hard with his right hand.

"Forgive me, please, I'm very sorry." Kristen apologized. Paul told her to tell it to the camera. He leaned back and called Karla over to him.

"You get me hard," he demanded. "She's not getting me hard." Karla sucked his nipples and his penis. When Paul moved back to Kristen, he had an erection.

"Nasty bitch," Paul said, entering her vagina just as Ice-T was going on about "payback time."

"Who am I?" he asked. "Who wants me?"

"Pardon me?" said Kristen, adjusting her face upward but unable to see his face. Then she started on her scripted lines about him being the "master," him deserving "better," deserving to "fuck every girl" in her school. He raised her skirt higher. Pulling out of her vagina, he then guided his penis to her anus.

Kristen screamed out in pain, a long, anguished howl. She tried to bury her face in the towel but he was still holding her hair. Painfully, she told him she was afraid she was going to defecate. Eight times she cried out that she was sorry, but he continued to grind himself into her buttocks.

"Fuck you," he said, withdrawing. Then he grabbed the top of her thighs and went back to vaginal intercourse, moving in time to the drumbeat, crouching on the balls of his feet.

"Lick my ass, bitch," Paul instructed Karla, and she moved in behind him.

"Touch me," he demanded, bending over Kristen so that she could rub his nipples despite the handcuffs. "Twist right."

Words Kristen had been told to say flowed steadily.

"You have a very beautiful wife. And you really stick together," she noted. "All the girls at my school want to fuck you 'cause you're the most powerful man in the world and you're the sexiest man in the world."

She told him that she deserved to be punished and called him the "king of kings." Paul tweaked his own left nipple.

"Say you want to lick all the little girls' cunts when you get back," Paul demanded.

Kristen did not seem to notice that he was suggesting that she would ever get to go back anywhere, but she told him what he wanted to hear. While a musical rap chorus repeated, "Say it, say it," Paul pushed Kristen further onto her face. "Get your ass up in the air."

Finally, he achieved his orgasm and sat back on his haunches. Kristen's tethered hands reached out to touch his arm.

"You happy?" she asked. "That's what matters, as long as you're happy. You and your wife."

Paul pulled back and slapped her buttocks lightly. Then he slumped against the wall near the blaring boom box. He told Karla to get him a Kleenex.

"What are you, a fucking idiot?" he grumbled when Karla handed him a few tissues. He needed the whole box. He was busy wiping himself and the guitars were picking up Ice-T's pace when Kristen said her last recorded words.

"I don't know how your wife can stand being around you, 'cause . . ." she started.

"Just shut up, okay," Paul said.

Karla's shadow moved across Kristen's face as she walked over to press the stop button. Kristen saw her, but said nothing. Kristen French did not have much time left.

Paul asked Kristen what she wanted for dinner and she said Swiss Chalet, so he went to Swiss and picked up two chicken dinners with extra fries. He paid with a one hundred dollar bill. At Videoflicks he returned *Angel Heart* and *Criminal Law* and rented *Shattered*. He followed Bunting Road to Carlton Street to Geneva, the street Kristen lived on, to Scott, to Secord Drive, to Lake Street, to Lakeport Road, to Lock Street, to Main Street and then to the Swiss Chalet on Ann Street. He got a copy of the *St. Catharines Standard*. Paul was gone about an hour and fifteen minutes.

Lori Lazaruk could not believe her eyes. She was driving across the Martindale bridge out of Port Dalhousie on Saturday evening, April 18, when she passed the jerk in the gold Nissan with the video camera who had stalked her and her sister in March. He was driving back into the Port.

Quickly deciding to follow him again—this time she would make sure she found out exactly where he lived—she swung her car around. Even though she was determined, she lost him again on Bayview Drive. He just seemed to vanish in thin air.

Lori went back to her mother's place and wrote down the license number again, a description of the car that was exactly the same as the one she had given the police the morning after she and her sister had seen him at Robin's Donuts. There was something about this guy and his gold car and his video camera that really disturbed Lori.

When she called, she tried to convey that to the police, again, that there was something about this guy that was not right. This time Lori took down the name of the person with whom she spoke. She was a receptionist. Her name was Judy. Lori told Judy about the previous incident and supplied her current information.

She described the gold Nissan 240SX to a "T" and gave Judy the correct license number—660 HFH—and she told her that the guy must live on Bayview, because she had lost him on that street both times.

Karla's Easter card read, "To the most wonderful man in the entire world, who means everything to me. All my love, Karly Curls."

They drove over to Karla's parents' house early Sunday afternoon for the ritual Easter Sunday family dinner. As usual, Dorothy Homolka had little decorative gifts for her daughters and they had a family dinner together. Nothing was out of the ordinary.

On the television news that night, Doug French told an interviewer that he was convinced his daughter was still alive. "We all are. We just think she's being held captive."

Karel Homolka tuned in to watch "60 Minutes," as was his custom at 7:00 P.M. on Sunday evenings. Then Dorothy watched her favorite program, "Murder She Wrote."

Paul and Karla left shortly after 9:00 P.M. Spring was upon them. After a day of sunshine, the smell of thawing earth permeated the night air.

CHAPTER
twenty-one

It was a beautiful spring day. Lori D'Ascenzo saw Karla from the back window of her flower shop, which was right beside the Martindale Animal Clinic, where Karla worked. Karla was definitely a sun-worshipper. Throughout the summer she often went out behind the clinic on her breaks. That is how Lori had met her. It was only two or three days after Kristen French had been kidnapped, and all of St. Catharines was combing the bushes, the nooks and crannies.

   The Monday after the long Easter weekend was always slow, so Lori went out behind the shop to talk. Karla seemed unusually anxious and agitated. Karla said she was upset about the girls. There was that girl from Hamilton or Burlington or wherever, then the local girl who had disappeared last November—Terri Anderson—and now Kristen French. She said whoever was taking these girls seemed to have an attraction for blond hair and she was afraid she would be next. Strange, Lori thought, since Kristen had long, dark hair and all the girls Karla mentioned were in their early teens, not their twenties.

   Lori and Karla had talked about this before. Karla was always asking Lori what she thought. Karla knew Lori was psychic and had empathic powers. Lori told Karla she was overreacting, she should calm down.

Inspector Vince Bevan was determined they were going to stop every Camaro in the Niagara Region . . . in Ontario . . . in Canada, if need be, until they found the Camaro in which Kristen French had been abducted. He ordered all Niagara Regional Police and any officer associated with the investigation of Kristen French's abduction to stop and check out every Camaro they saw. They were also getting hundreds of calls a day from concerned citizens about Camaros they had seen. Soon, police officers were starting to stop the same Camaro two and three times. That phenomenon generated the inspector's innovative sticker program. Every Camaro they stopped and checked would be given a sticker to indicate that the car had already been stopped. They used the media to get the story about the stickers out. As well, the police invited Camaro owners to voluntarily bring their Camaros into the Niagara Regional Police headquarters and get a sticker.

   Detective Steve Irwin got a call from a Niagara Region constable on Wednesday. The constable wanted Irwin to help him conduct a "discreet" investigation into the background of a suspect named Richard Climie who had been convicted for abducting a young girl in 1984. He said it was in relation to the recent abduction of the young French girl. Detective Irwin said he would do what he could and went about his business. He could not worry about every fallen robin.

At noon on Monday, April 20, at Inspector Bevan's behest, Sergeant Larry Maracle called Nutley, New Jersey, psychic Dorothy Alison and told her about Kristen French. What would Ms. Alison need, to try and help them find her? Sergeant Maracle asked. Dorothy already had a bad feeling, but she held her tongue. She would need a small personal item that belonged to Kristen and a photograph, if possible. Sergeant Maracle got a small barrette that Kristen always wore in her hair from Mrs. French at 1:00 P.M. Two days later, Maracle mailed it to Nutley, along with Kristen's picture.

Linwell Road was a busy street. By midweek the police had interviewed a dozen "eyewitnesses" to Kristen's abduction. A young schoolmate of Kristen's had passed her in his car as she walked east, on the north side of Linwell Road, west of Howard Street, around 2:55 P.M. that afternoon.

Another twenty-year-old woman saw a "creamy yellow Camaro-style car" pulled partway off the road around that time. There were two men in the car and she thought the driver was speaking to a girl in a Holy Cross school uniform, who was walking on the north side of Linwell. The girl had long brown hair—below her shoulders. The woman would never forget the driver's face.

Another woman was cut off by a car speeding out of the church parking lot. She thought it had round headlights. It might have been a Firebird, Camaro or Berlinghetti. Inspector Bevan had her hypnotized and she remembered the car was a yellow-beige color but she still could not pin down the make or model.

By the time half a dozen different police officers finished interviewing a dozen "eyewitnesses," the witnesses were all telling tales of strangely behaved, light-colored Camaro-like cars on Linwell Road that afternoon. They saw the car slow down, they saw it parked in the Grace Lutheran Church lot, they saw the driver, they saw it cut cars off, speed through intersections, run red lights, fishtail and career around corners. They saw it explode into oblivion under a bridge five miles away.

This mythic Camaro blitzed up the canyons and charged over the arroyos in the collective imagination of every cop and civilian in the City of St. Catharines. The word Camaro became as the Bat signal, luminous in the skies, high above Gotham City.

Inspector Bevan narrowed his search terms to Camaros manufactured between 1978 and 1982 that were currently registered in the Niagara region. The color would narrow it down even further.

In St. Catharines, the citizenry got behind the crusade. Mothers turned in sons they suddenly realized drove Camaros, daughters called in their fathers and boyfriends, strangers—seeing a Camaro on the street—immediately recorded license-plate numbers and ran into strange houses in order to report them to the police.

George Angersback, who was responsible for the interior-design instrumentation of the Camaro, had a stock Camaro's four-speed manual gearshift installed on his office chair. He would wile away the afternoons, images of the ultimate Camaro in the cumulus clouds high above the Motor City, shifting the gears on his chair.

Shortly after the Camaro was launched in September, 1966, the fact that *camaro* meant "loose bowels" in Spanish hit the press and the shit hit the fan at General Motors. Heads rolled down the corridors like so many guttered bowling balls. Undaunted, a massive advertising campaign dubbed the car "King Camaro" and "His Majesty," loose bowels and all, and the Camaro began to conquer the marketplace.

"Low and mean. Born to run. Camaro lets you limit your speed without cramping your style," the inaugural ads proclaimed. *Car and Driver* said: "A road machine of the first rank . . . intended for the macho enthusiast . . . a special breed of aspiration car . . . aggressive, quick, agile, dependable."

Inspector Vince Bevan knew that eyewitness reports were

among the most unreliable types of evidence and that the police should always be wary of them. But the imaginations of the inspector and his handpicked team of seasoned investigators were captured by the Camaro. They became as "loose bowels" and voided all other options. From that moment on, everyone—police, media and civilians alike—knew that Kristen French had been abducted by a man or two in a cream-colored 1982 Camaro.

Psychics and Camaros aside, Big Jim Moody wanted to know how Kristen French's shoe got fifty yards into the parking lot, a considerable detour on her otherwise straightforward routine afternoon walk home.

He knew, as did everyone else, that Kristen French was an intelligent, street-proofed, mature, responsible teenager. A young lady like Kristen would never approach a strange man, or two strange men, in a strange car, whether it was a Camaro or not.

Forlornly abandoned, the shoe told Moody that Kristen either knew her abductors or for some reason they did not scare her in the least.

She willingly had walked over to a parked car in which someone then abducted her at knifepoint—the piece of hair the police found had been sliced off by a sharp knife.

As a seasoned investigator, Moody knew that salvation lived within seemingly insignificant details. What about that piece of map from Scarborough? Why Scarborough? What did that mean? By the time Big Jim was able to ask these questions, no one was listening. The task force was engaged in a generously financed frenzy.

Sergeant Maracle began to help compile a photographic inventory of Camaros and Firebirds from 1978 through 1982 and track automotive paint samples used on Camaros through those years on Wednesday afternoon. Instead, they could not get the paint samples from General Motors in Detroit. They got them

that very afternoon from Kim Squires at the local ICI Auto
Color outlet. At 5:20 P.M., Paul and Karla crossed the border at
Lewiston in the gold Nissan. They smuggled some more ciga-
rettes and booze. After all, the rent was due in eleven days and
Karla's birthday was only fifteen days hence.

Inspector Vince Bevan told Sergeant Maracle to fly to Quantico, Virginia, on Wednesday, April 29, 1993, and brief a team
of FBI profilers about Mahaffy, Anderson and Kristen French.
Sergeant Maracle realized he had been working on the Mahaffy
case for almost a year and remembered his lengthy meeting with
FBI Special Agent Wagner and Supervisory Agent McGrary in
the early days of the Mahaffy investigation.

They had told him that whoever killed Leslie probably knew
her and was a laborer, familiar with tools and materials. If the
individual who killed her was so familiar with tools and materials why was there evidence of false starts on her dismembered
body parts? Why were the cement blocks so poorly conceived?
The one containing the torso had separated on the bottom of
the lake and let the torso pop to the surface like a grotesque
cork.

Since there was irrefutable forensic evidence that Mahaffy
had been raped, the FBI's statement that the crime had been
sexually motivated was a no-brainer. That murder was secondary, committed to avoid detection and conceal the crime was
also pretty obvious, although nothing in a murder investigation
should be taken for granted.

That the perpetrator had fantasized the scenario and acted
out only when the opportunity presented itself was neither here
nor there, because it did not give the police a clearer understanding of exactly what had happened the night Leslie disappeared, nor did it point to an individual or explain anything.

When Maracle had talked to McCrary about Mahaffy, it
seemed that McCrary just assumed the killer had made the
forty-mile drive from Burlington to Lake Gibson because he
was comfortable with that particular area and could easily explain his presence at Lake Gibson to police if they happened on

him while he was there. That assumption made little or no sense.

Driving a car with nine hundred pounds of cement-encased body parts forty miles would seem, at first blush, to be far riskier than finding a place to bury the blocks in his own back-yard.

Burlington was a city of appealing disposal sites. Lake Ontario was right there. Why bother with a small, shallow man-made lake such as Lake Gibson? It just did not make any sense.

Those were standard clauses in the pro forma FBI sexual-assault profile, along with post-crime stress, sudden religiosity and possible increased drug and alcohol use. The Niagara Region was a haven for drunks, drug addicts and religious fanatics. How to distinguish between one man's motivation and another's conviction?

Sergeant Maracle developed the profiles of Kristen French and Terri Anderson and caught the next available flight to Quantico. Special Supervising Agent McCrary was waiting for him at the Washington airport on Thursday evening, April 30, 1992.

McCrary turned out to be a bankerly-looking fellow in a good suit. He had been with the FBI for twenty-four years, the last eight of which had been at the feet of profiling guru, John Douglas. Douglas was the inspiration for the Jack Crawford character in *The Silence of the Lambs.* There was a picture in Douglas's office of Douglas with Jonathan Demme, the director of the movie, and the actor who played Douglas, Scott Glenn.

McCrary was being groomed to take over for Douglas, who was near retirement. Sergeant Maracle's briefing about Mahaffy, French and Anderson was scheduled first thing the following morning. Included in the meeting would be McCrary, Agents Steven Mardigian, Jana Munroe, Larry Ankron, Bill Magmaier, and a female student just like the *Silence of the Lambs* heroine, Clarisse Starling.

At 8:20 A.M. Maracle got a call from Staff Sergeant Steve MacLeod, who told him they had just found Kristen French's body in a ditch along Sideroad One, only a few hundred yards from where Leslie Mahaffy had been buried in Burlington. The body was naked but intact; there was some kind of knife wound on the shoulder and her hair had been hacked off.

That day, the group of profilers concluded that the French and Mahaffy killings were not related. The effort to which the perpetrator or perpetrators had seemingly gone to dispose of Mahaffy mitigated any connection. The proximity of the French body to the Mahaffy grave was coincidental.

There was possibly a connection between the Mahaffy and Anderson cases, particularly since Anderson's body had not yet been found. With Mahaffy, the perpetrator had been foiled by the realities of cement. With Anderson, he obviously had found a better way.

As far as Kristen French was concerned, the profilers had been told what no one else knew—there were two offenders. The profilers said their ages likely ranged between twenty and thirty-five. One was dominant, the other docile—this was typical FBI-profile dogma, whenever sex crimes involved more than one perpetrator.

Allegedly, Kristen French had been held for two weeks, which suggested the perpetrators were not living in a multiple-housing unit. They had to be living in a single-family dwelling, probably in a rural area, but possibly in a residential area.

The two offenders were profiled as males with low self-esteem; their behavior was characterized by very poor social and interpersonal skills, especially with women.

Neither was a pedophile, since all of the victims had been over twelve years old. They probably wanted adult females, but were unable to deal with them; victims who had just achieved puberty were less likely to put up resistance.

The low self-esteem bit was derived from the fact that there were two of them and that they had found it necessary to use a knife. They would be longtime friends. The docile one would find reasons to leave the area when the body was recovered, a move which would be totally out-of-character and potentially noticeable. Otherwise, the two were inseparable.

The dominant one would have a record of sexual assaults. This might not have been the first attempt at abduction; there might have been other failed attempts involving adult or elderly females, all motivated by sexual fantasy.

The weaker one was a follower. He had probably bonded with the victim and might have had nothing to do with the homicide. That idea was gleaned from the dressed knife wound. The docile perpetrator might also have had the task of looking after the victim.

There were three possible reasons the hair was cut: one, as a trophy; two, because the smell of a perm was repulsive to the offenders; or thirdly, in an effort to conceal the victim's identity.

The perpetrators would be under a great deal of stress. Again, the profilers strongly recommended manipulating the media—using the anniversaries of the murdered girls' deaths, memorials, victims rights' protests—anything to attract the media's attention and get stories on television or in the newspapers.

On Kristen's upcoming sixteenth birthday, the FBI suggested the police plant human-interest stories with angles such as "Sweet Sixteen but No Prom, No Driver's License, No Graduation, No More Anything Because of Untimely Death." The family should do something at Kristen's grave site on her birthday and her friends should do something at the site where her body was found.

The local police must cover the funeral home, the church and the cemetery, as killers often showed up out of guilt and remorse, or conversely out of curiosity, hunting souvenirs. The press would publicize the fact that many items had been left at the grave site. A hidden video camera at the grave would record any and all comings and goings over the following couple of weeks.

Even though the press had not been told there were two abductors, the FBI recommended that the police use the press to try and drive a wedge between the perpetrators.

The profilers gave Sergeant Maracle an example of what they meant: "The offender is dangerous, as he has killed once already and would not hesitate to kill again; if he has fears of being caught by the authorities, the offender's family and friends could be in grave danger.''

The whole idea was to get as much publicity as possible for the police point-of-view. The Green Ribbon Task Force followed the FBI's advice. There was nothing like a bereaved mother to get the media's attention.

It was a cloudy, overcast day. It had rained during the night. Sideroad One was a paved, unmarked, hilly, country road, bordered by a narrow gravel shoulder and ditches on both sides. It was a walkable distance east from the Guelph Line to the spot where Kristen's body had been found by a scrap-metal picker.

On the north side, there was an open field and an orchard. Mature trees lined the road. Directly across the road from where Kristen's body had been found, there was a very large estate surrounded by several acres of property. A fence bordered the entire property. On the south side of the road was dense forest and brush.

The scrap-metal picker had been out scavenging with his metal detector when he saw the body in the ditch, several feet below road level on the south side, away from the traveled portion. At first he did not know what it was, just that it was not a color anyone would expect to see in the brush.

He was in that area because he knew the place to be a garbage dump. There was garbage several feet from the body. Just to the west there was an elevation of earth that rose even with the roadway, where people pulled in and illegally dumped garbage. A footpath continued in a southerly direction and there were deep tire impressions in the mud. Directly south of the body there was a dense forest and to the east, in the brush, a narrow flowing stream of water, which gurgled through a culvert that drained under the road.

The body was nude, in a three-quarter-prone position, almost parallel to the road. The head was toward the west and the feet toward the east. Beneath the body there were branches and decaying and dried forest vegetation. To the left was a fallen log. Broken tree branches and forest vegetation were placed on top of the body in a halfhearted attempt to conceal it. The scrap-metal picker ran to the nearest house and called the police.

The body was slightly discolored and marked, probably by the vegetation and broken tree branches. There were signs of fly larva in the ears, vagina and anus. Dried blood had drained onto the upper lip from the nose. There was purple discoloration under the fingernails. The right arm of the victim was beneath the body with the forearm and hand extended to the left. The left arm was bent at the elbow, supported by the fallen log.

The scene was extensively videotaped and photographed by the police. The I-dent officers put the feet, hands and head in paper bags before the body was rolled into a body bag. The face appeared to be severely bruised and the lips were a deep purple-black color. Slightly right of the chin, there was a horizontal bruise on the front of the neck.

Legions of police and media arrived. When Inspector Bevan saw that the tip of the baby finger of the left hand was missing, he knew it was Kristen French. He went directly to the Frenches' and told them. The body was removed at 4:20 P.M.

Three and a half hours later a positive identification was made from fingerprints at the Ontario Provincial Police technical services branch building in Toronto. Several hairs and what appeared to be fibers were removed from the body.

The forensic pathologist, Dr. Noel McAuliffe, examined the body. Maggots were present in the vaginal and rectal areas. Having all seen *The Silence of the Lambs,* the police started to debate forensic entomology to establish time of death, but one of the forensic pathologists quickly told them to forget it. Species of flies were unique to specific areas, but there was no database for the Niagara Region. These specimens would start one.

There was controversy about the time of Kristen's death. One pathologist said she had been dead for some time—maybe as long as two weeks. The other, more diabolical scenario, was that she had just been killed—within the past twenty-four hours—meaning she had been held captive, repeatedly raped and tortured for as many as fifteen days. The most diabolical scenarios have the greatest cachet. Inspector Bevan told Mr. and

Mrs. French that their daughter had likely been held captive for two weeks. In spite of a news blackout the inspector had imposed, that was the story the newspapers printed.

Sergeant Maracle phoned Dorothy Alison, the New Jersey psychic, and told her they had found Kristen French's body. Dorothy had known they would.

After returning from Quantico, Maracle briefed the troops. Supervising Special Agent McGrary had added a proviso to the FBI's profile: since Kristen French had been severely beaten and there was deep musculoskeletal bruising around her rib cage, he recommended that the task force concentrate on individuals who had been previously convicted or were suspected of having committed violent sexual assaults.

Kristen French was buried on Karla Homolka's twenty-second birthday. Four thousand mourners turned out for her funeral. Paul Bernardo addressed a birthday card to Karla: "To my lovely, loving wife," and gave her another stuffed toy. Paul and Karla made plans for a summer vacation. Karla wanted to see the Mouse and Paul said he would take her back to Disney World.

The Green Ribbon Task Force was officially formed on Tuesday, May 5, 1992. Task force members began busily videotaping everything, as per the FBI's advice. They set up a hidden video camera at Kristen's grave site. The task force had been amply funded by the provincial government through the Ministries of the Attorney-General and Solicitor-General. They set up hotlines—toll-free numbers for tips—and rented their own offices in Beamsville, Ontario, a small town just up the highway from St. Catharines.

As the head of the Green Ribbon Task Force, Inspector Vince Bevan became autonomous. Although professional courtesy prevailed, he no longer answered to the chief of the Niagara Regional Police. His bosses were bureaucrats at Queen's Park, seat of Ontario's provincial government, and until the money ran out, that was akin to not having any bosses at all.

Now obsessed with the Camaro, Bevan spent days writing

and releasing a voluminous report about the Camaro for the Halton District Body Repair Association, which allegedly reached all twenty-two hundred body and paint shops in the area. He described the car in very specific terms: "Paint code #84 'yellow beige,' manufactured between 1975–79, average condition, paint finish dull, very plain, no chrome or pinstriping."

He was also busy with television. He called Marge Critchford, a producer for "America's Most Wanted" and wondered if they were interested—now that Kristen French had been murdered.

Constable Scott Kenney and Sergeant Brian Nesbitt were assigned to investigate hotline tip 241. The call had been received on May 1. Rob Haney, an Ontario Provincial Police officer in Beaverton, Ontario, called it in.

Constable Haney was a regular at the Smirnises' coffee shop in Brown Hill. Although he said his source wanted to remain anonymous, Constable Haney had been talking to Van Smirnis, who, destitute and unemployed, was serving coffee for his mother and father.

Haney gave particulars of Paul Bernardo, who lived in Port Dalhousie and who had been questioned in Toronto as a suspect in the Scarborough rapes. Haney said Bernardo was aggressive toward women; he had raped a girl in the basement of a house, and could only grow hair on his chin.

Bernardo liked small, petite women; he had short hair and wore similar clothing to the Scarborough rapist. He had a good tan; he had been in Florida once, and a rape had taken place. Whenever a rape took place in Scarborough, he would dissociate himself from his friends and family for a period of time.

The report was long and disjointed. Constable Haney concluded by saying that Bernardo was a very violent and hostile individual who had short hair that was wavy and curly on top and shaved at the back of his head. He appeared to be intelligent and perceptive. He had admitted to beating his wife and had hit other girls on at least three occasions.

Karla wrote and thanked Debbie Purdie for her birthday card.

"I'm getting pregnant. I can't wait," she said, explaining that her pregnancy was contingent on Paul getting a contract to make his rap album.

She also told Debbie that she had got an iguana named Spike from the clinic and that she and Paul were going to change their last name to Teale.

It took ten days for the tip from Constable Haney to get to Sergeant Nesbitt. Following the day Sergeant Nesbitt got the tip, he ran a computer check on Paul Bernardo—through CPIC—Canadian Police Information Center. Anyone in Canada who is charged with or suspected of a major crime by any police organization is supposedly entered in the system. No one had ever entered Paul Bernardo.

According to CPIC, Paul Bernardo had no previous criminal record, nor had he had any police contact concerning criminal activity. Sergeant Nesbitt and Constable Kenney decided to call on Paul anyway, mainly because they had been told to.

At 2:00 p.m. they drove over to 57 Bayview. From an upstairs window, Bernardo watched the plainclothes detectives approach the house. He pondered his limited options.

Nesbitt and Kenney noted that the house and property were well kept and nicely groomed. There was a light gold Nissan 240 SX—license-plate number 660 HFH—in the driveway. The vehicle was clean and in good shape.

The detectives, who were both short—Nesbitt was stockier than Kenney, who looked much younger than his forty years—knocked on the front door. When they did not get an answer, they walked around behind the garage. Nesbitt noted that there was a backyard with a large deck, partially enclosed by a privacy fence. No one was home. They started back to their cruiser.

Upstairs, Paul was resolved—he would have to confront them sooner or later. There was no time like the present. Steeling himself, he opened the front door.

Walking back to the front steps, Nesbitt and Kenney identified themselves and showed Paul their badges. Nesbitt explained that they were investigating the death of Kristen French and that his name had surfaced in their investigation. Paul invited them into the living room. Struggling to get a grip, he sat down and tightly clasped his hands together in his lap.

The detectives noted that the house was clean and well appointed. A wedding picture was prominently displayed. Paul's wife was an attractive, young blonde. There was a Masonic certificate on the mantel. The young man was good-looking, with fine features. He appeared to be well-spoken and in good physical shape. Nesbitt described the look as "preppy" in his notes. His hair was short on the sides, slightly longer on the top, with a bit of a wave.

When Nesbitt asked if he had ever been involved with the police in the past, Paul readily admitted that he had been called in as a suspect in the Scarborough rape investigation because he looked like the composite they had published in the papers. At that point, Paul knew that he had them and he relaxed.

He went on to explain that he had been interviewed by Toronto police officers in November of 1990 and had voluntarily supplied samples for testing.

He told them his wife was a local girl, Karla Homolka, and they had been married in June, 1991. He told them that she was an animal health technician who worked at the Martindale Animal Clinic. She was there now—if they wanted to speak to her. He told them that he was an accountant, but he was currently unemployed.

Sergeant Nesbitt asked him where he had been on Thursday, April 16, 1992, around three in the afternoon. Without hesitation, Paul said that he was probably home, alone, writing lyrics to a rap song that he was composing. He said that he actually spent most of his time at home alone writing lyrics. He said he was going to become a rap singer, like Vanilla Ice.

The detectives asked him about cars. Paul told them that the only vehicle he and his wife had was the car in the driveway.

Had he ever owned a Camaro or had access to one, or had he driven a Camaro? Of course, Paul already knew they were looking for someone who drove a Camaro. If they had anything concrete—from Scarborough or Niagara—they would not be chatting away like this. The visit only lasted fifteen or twenty minutes. As they left, Paul watched them look at the Nissan again. It was amazing. They were clueless.

Nesbitt and Kenney got into their cruiser, circled the block and pulled up a block away so they could look at the Nissan and see if it looked like a Camaro—from a distance. They both agreed it did not look anything like a Camaro.

When Nesbitt got back to the station he ran another computer check on Bernardo. Nothing had changed over the past four hours. The next morning, Sergeant Nesbitt decided to call the Toronto Police about the Scarborough rapes. He talked to a detective on the sexual-assault squad. The Toronto detective told Sergeant Nesbitt that he wanted to speak with either Staff Inspector Joe Wolfe or a Detective Steve Irwin. Detective Irwin was in charge of the Scarborough rape investigation. Nesbitt left a message.

When Karla came home from work, Paul told her he had been "as cool as a cucumber" with the police. She bought it, but it scared her. What if they had come with a search warrant? They would have found all the videotapes in her hope chest. They decided to move them right away. Paul had a hiding place, high in the insulation of the loft in the garage.

They also decided it was time to move on the name change. Karla had suggested Teale after the rapist and serial killer Martin Thiel (pronounced teale) in the movie *Criminal Law*.

Paul chose a new middle name—Jason, after the hockey-masked murderer in the movie *Friday the Thirteenth*. He also had a pal he liked named Jason—anything but Kenneth.

He filed the formal application to have his and Karla's surname officially changed from Bernardo to Teale and his middle name from Kenneth to "Jason" on May 15, three days after Kenney and Nesbitt's visit.

·   ·   ·

Detective Irwin finally called Sergeant Nesbitt—eight days later—on May 20. Nesbitt was busy, helping the Green Ribbon Task Force move to its new headquarters in Beamsville. Inspector Bevan had personally negotiated the rent for the old town hall. He had got an excellent deal.

Nesbitt told Irwin about the tip and the interview he had had with Bernardo. Detective Irwin told Sergeant Nesbitt that Paul Bernardo was one of many suspects from whom they had collected samples. With budget restraints and staffing problems at the forensic center, Bernardo had yet to be cleared.

Irwin and Nesbitt commiserated over the magnitude of their respective cases and how overworked they were. There were so many suspects and so little time. Besides, without science, Irwin observed, nobody in Toronto could get their sexual-assault cases to court anyway. Detective Irwin jocularly referred to his unit by its nickname—the hair-and-spit unit. Irwin agreed to fax Nesbitt some more information.

Nesbitt got three pages and a cover sheet a few hours later. Irwin noted on the cover sheet that he had photos and a video of Bernardo.

The three short pages included a supplementary report about Irwin's interview with Bernardo on November 20, 1990, and a bit of information about the tips they had received, to which their interview had been a response.

Detective Steve Irwin did not send the notes from the interview with Alex Smirnis and his wife, Tina—since both sources were Smirnises the contents of the tips were remarkably similar—nor could he locate the five-page supplementary report Sergeant McNiff had filed after his meeting with Jennifer Galligan in January, 1988.

In Sergeant Nesbitt's opinion, the information he received from Detective Irwin was of no assistance to his investigation.

"There was no information linking our investigation with the Scarborough rape investigation," the sergeant noted.

In the interim, Nesbitt found Rachel Ferron's stalking reports from the summer of 1991, which identified Paul Bernardo as the stalker. He ignored them too.

Even though Paul Bernardo was an uncleared suspect in the

Scarborough rapes, unemployed, with no alibi on the day Kristen French was abducted, and at twenty-eight-years of age had the singular ambition to become a white rapper like Vanilla Ice, he was eliminated as a suspect.

Big Jim Moody just shook his head when he found out about the stalking reports. He had been on vacation in the Caribbean and then he came back and discovered that a task force had been formed and Bevan had been put in charge.

To Big Jim's way of thinking, one of the first things any police investigator would do when investigating a series of sexually motivated homicides would be thoroughly monitor and investigate any stalking reports that involved complete strangers. Particularly when they were marked by unusual behavior—such as the use of a video camera.

At that point Big Jim did not know that Sergeants Nesbitt and Kenney had been tipped and had interviewed the guy both Rachel Ferron and Lori Lazaruk had reported for stalking.

He did not know that Nesbitt and Kenney had actually found and reviewed Rachel Ferron's report after they interviewed Paul Bernardo. Nor did he know that Nesbitt and Kenney knew that the man Ferron's report identified was the very Paul Bernardo who was one of five uncleared suspects in the Scarborough rapes, on whom the Metropolitan Toronto police were doing serious science. He did not know that the rapes had mysteriously stopped after Bernardo moved to St. Catharines. It was not Big Jim's job to know those things, it was Inspector Vince Bevan's.

Not only were Inspector Bevan's investigative skills in question, his administrative and information-management skills were not nearly as accomplished as Big Jim had previously been led to believe. If they had been, Rachel Ferron and Lori Lazaruk's reports would have been red flagged and in front of the inspector in a matter of hours. Instead of being "cleared," Paul Bernardo would have been put under twenty-four-hour surveillance and thoroughly investigated. All Big Jim could do was shake his head.

• • •

At the end of May, Karla went into the flower shop and asked Lori D'Ascenzo to come out back and talk. Behind the clinic, beside the Dumpster, she told Lori that someone was watching her. Karla said that her husband's personality had changed too. She asked if Lori thought there might be a spirit in the house. Lori told her it was not a spirit, it was a ghost—a woman's ghost—and it did not like her husband. The person had died suddenly or violently, Lori said, and she did not know she was dead.

"How would I get it out of the house?" Karla asked.

"You should put ammonia down all the drains in the house," Lori said. "Ghosts don't like the smell of ammonia."

Lori gave Karla an amethyst and told her to keep it in her pocket: the amethyst would absorb all of the bad karma around Karla. At night she was to put the amethyst on the east window and allow the morning sun to soak up all the negative energy it had accumulated while it was in Karla's pocket.

She also told her to put holy water and consecrated ashes in every corner of her house. And a pink carnation in the front window.

"And you should tell the ghost to go with God's love to the white light."

About two weeks later, Karla came in to see Lori. Karla was her old, bubbly self again and happily reported that the ghost seemed to have left and she and her husband were no longer fighting.

CHAPTER

twenty-two

The corpse was wearing a fine black necklace, as well as a beige bra, a once-white T-shirt—which was inexplicably inside out—and a pair of soiled panties. The T-shirt had a blue-and-red circular postage-mark symbol. It said, Via Downtown Montreal.

They pulled it out of the water in broad daylight at the Harbor Game and Fish ramp in Port Dalhousie and put it under one of those yellow emergency blankets. It must have floated up when the flood gates at the north end of Martindale Pond were opened for the first time on May 23, 1992. Even though six months in the water had grotesquely distended the remains, it was obviously the body of a small, slight female. She had been no more than five feet tall and weighed well under a hundred pounds. Her hair had once been long, beautiful and blond.

Inspector Bevan, who was already on the scene when Sergeant Larry Maracle arrived, correctly guessed it was Terri Anderson, the little girl who had gone missing the previous November.

John "Bubba" Matille went to Niagara Regional Police headquarters on Church Street in downtown St. Catharines and described an incident he had witnessed at Paul Bernardo's house. What he had seen made him think that Paul might have murdered Leslie Mahaffy and Kristen French.

John was a university student. He shared a house on Linwell Road with Andy Douglas. Andy was a business-administration student at Brock. Douglas knew Paul Bernardo and had been in Bernardo's wedding party. As his nickname suggested, Bubba was a big, strapping lad, whose claim to fame was his wrestling prowess. Everybody said Bubba had Olympic potential.

One afternoon, he and Andy had met Paul Bernardo for beers on the patio of the Port Mansion, a bar on the main street in Port Dalhousie, overlooking the boat launch and Lake Ontario. Afterward, they had gone back to Paul's house.

Andy noticed a photograph of a pretty, young girl prominently displayed on the top of the television in the living room. One of the guys asked who it was and all of a sudden Paul started getting upset and crying. Not really knowing what was going on, they tried to comfort him, but Paul started hitting himself on the head. He kept saying, "I don't fucking care . . . you don't fucking know. . . . I just don't fucking care," over and over again, and they believed him.

"She fucking died in my arms, right in my fucking arms," he repeated a dozen times, continuing to hit himself with his closed fists in the face and head.

In the midst of this scary performance, Bubba managed to figure out that the photograph was a picture of Paul's dead sister-in-law, Tammy Lyn Homolka. Bubba's roommate, Andy, was aware of the circumstances. The girl had died suddenly at Christmastime in 1990. At one point Andy calmly suggested that Paul should just try and let it go, try to get over it, and Bernardo had attacked him and started whaling on Andy. It had taken some effort on Bubba's part to get Bernardo off Douglas.

Bubba had never seen anything like it. He could not get the incident out of his head. Then he heard some of the other guys saying Bernardo really looked like a composite drawing of the Scarborough rapist in Toronto, and that he had been interviewed by police in Toronto.

Bubba became convinced that Paul Bernardo could have murdered Leslie Mahaffy and Kristen French. He had no proof, just a gut feeling.

Inspector Vincent Bevan took the FBI profile at face value. He did not give it much thought, really, except that he was ambivalent about the assertion that the Mahaffy and French homicides were unrelated. It was the placement of Kristen's body only 546 yards from Leslie's grave at the Halton Memorial Hill Gardens that had really got to him. He believed that Kristen's disposal, in that specific spot, was the deliberate act of a sick mind. There were others who shared his view. He applied for an order to exhume Leslie Mahaffy's remains.

Kristen French had been badly beaten. Inspector Bevan wanted to determine whether or not Leslie had been similarly abused—particularly on her back. As they had determined during the French autopsy, some of the worst damage had not been visible.

Dr. McAuliffe had peeled back the layers of Kristen French's skin and muscle like an onion. A similar examination of Leslie's torso might tell them things they did not yet know. Since she had been in pieces and there were no superficial signs of trauma, Dr. King had not been as thorough during Leslie's autopsy.

It took the authorities three hours to get Leslie Mahaffy's

casket out of the ground. They started at 7:00 A.M. The casket
did not arrive at the forensic-pathology unit in Toronto until
noon. The body parts were in a white body bag. There was a
denim jacket, a terry-cloth robe, a handmade rag doll and a
flower in the casket, which was half full of water.

A dissection of the back area revealed two small, asymmetrical circles of discoloration located on the right and left sides at
chest level; nothing remotely like the extensive bruising Kristen
had sustained. Nonetheless, Bevan remained resolute. In his
mind, the murders were related. After the examination, they
placed Leslie's remains in a new casket. She was back in the
ground by 7:00 P.M.

On their first wedding anniversary, Karla sent Paul a card: "It
just gets better and better and better. . . . Much love from the
girl who wriggled her way into your heart—me."

The best intentions are the fastest road to hell. For the next six
weeks, Inspector Bevan became a television producer and concentrated on making the most significant and extensive crime
reenactment docudrama in the history of North American television.

Inspector Bevan took his creative inspiration from "reality-
based" television. "The Abduction of Kristen French" was
characterized by fast cuts, dramatic sound effects, fade-ins and
fade-outs. The theme music was written and performed by
Kristen's brother, Darren, and there were tolling church bells to
accompany the authoritative voice-over. Gelled lenses captured
sympathetic images of bereaved parents, wearing their inconsolable loss like Spanish moss, backlit against giant-size posters of
their dead daughters, while the opinions of expert consultants
were beamed in by satellite and hypnotists served up the requisite mumbo jumbo. "The Abduction of Kristen French" had all
the production values of an "A Current Affair" segment.

Inspector Bevan managed to achieve an enviable dramatic
tension, inspiring equal measures of horror and sympathy,

which generated tens of thousands of telephone calls to the hotline after the ninety-minute opus aired at 8:00 P.M. on July 21, 1992.

The inspector gave himself and King Camaro starring roles. Wearing his trademark cowboy boots, Bevan stood stiffly beside his cream-colored, aging co-star, with the endearing, slightly rusted fender on the rear driver's side.

"This is almost exactly like the car that was used in the abduction of Kristen French," he said with all seriousness and sincerity.

Watching it at home, Paul Bernardo was beside himself. Paul had told Karla how cool he had been with the two plainclothes detectives who had come to interview him, but he did not tell her exactly why or how he had managed to achieve that cool. Now she knew.

"The Abduction of Kristen French" confirmed all their suppositions, and told Paul and Karla that they would never be caught by the Green Ribbon Task Force. The task force did not have one important, salient fact right, and all their suppositions were wrong.

And now that Inspector Bevan had given the world all the wrong facts, the task force would be so busy dealing with every crackpot within a thousand miles of St. Catharines, it would never find the two of them. Karla was relieved. Neither of them knew exactly why, but it was just as they both suspected—they were just meant to be. It was party time.

The program outraged the media. It revealed, for the first time, that the police considered the Mahaffy and French murders linked, and that there were two people involved. The media had never been told about the FBI profile.

Contrary to the profile Inspector Bevan had obtained from the doctors in Penetanguishene, this profile erroneously stated that one of the perpetrators was a blue-collar worker who was familiar with power tools, understood building materials and had access to a metal shop. This and much else in the program had not been previously released to the media.

The larger media outlets in Toronto saw red. They saw "The Abduction of Kristen French" as indicative of an indefatigable arrogance on the part of Inspector Bevan. It was also an expression of the worst kind of regionally based "favoritism."

By choosing to work exclusively with a small, independent television station in Hamilton, Ontario, Inspector Bevan had managed to alienate all the major broadcast and print media, unnecessarily creating yet another powerful, mysterious enemy.

Bevan did not care. His bosses and other members of the immediate community were very impressed. Modern policing is an impatient bureaucracy. Activity is revered for its own sake. The police received literally thousands of calls to the hotline. The response was so overwhelming that the lines had to be manned for an entire week.

What Paul and Karla had imagined came true and Inspector Bevan spent every minute of his waking and working hours reviewing tips that had already been reviewed by other investigators, to make sure nothing was overlooked. Even so, Paul Bernardo and Karla Homolka were as invisible to him as they were to the many Customs agents who routinely waved them across the border.

Somehow, Rachel Ferron's reports were overlooked. And Lori Larazuk's. Sergeant Nesbitt's interview with Paul Bernardo disappeared in a plethora of irrelevant data. Bubba Matille's gut feeling might as well have stayed in his stomach. The fact that Paul Bernardo was only one of five prime suspects in the massive Scarborough rape investigation in Toronto meant nothing in the land where the Camaro was king.

Spike was an abused iguana. He was scheduled to be euthanized, when Karla rescued him and brought the lizard home. He was in bad shape. Karla brought a handful of syringes along with the reptile. Karla was adept at injecting Spike with vitamin supplements and slowly she nursed him back to health. Spike was about three feet long.

Iguanas are strange reptiles. In *The Night of the Iguana,* a play by Tennessee Williams that Karla had studied in high school, the lizard represented the unknowable, the prehistoric, something troubling, dark and sexual.

One day toward the end of July, just after "The Abduction of Kristen French" had aired, Paul and Karla were feeling especially buoyant. Joann Fuller and Van Smirnis had come to visit for the first time since the New Year's incident, when Paul had punched Van repeatedly in the back of the head while Van was driving Paul and Karla home from the Pleasure Dome early that New Year's Day, 1991. Paul had banned Van. Van was now sucking up, trying to get back into Paul's good graces.

As usual, Buddy, the dog, was chasing Spike all over the house. This rigmarole irritated Spike, and when Joann tried to touch him, he bit her finger and drew a little blood. Spike seemed to sense that Joann was persona non grata. However, Spike needed to learn not to bite people. As punishment, Paul and Karla took him into the guest bedroom and tried to discipline him.

Iguanas use their tails to defend themselves and Spike tried to thrash his tormentors. When Spike inadvertently bit Paul in the melee, Paul grabbed him, took him to the kitchen, put him on the chopping board and cut off his head. He did not get all the way through on the first strike, so he just kept chopping until he did. He left the severed head and the body on the chopping block. Karla threw the head out and started cleaning the body, just like that, as if they had planned to kill the iguana all along.

She skinned and gutted it, cheerfully explaining its innards to Joann.

"Oh," Karla said, "Spike was a boy after all. See . . ." She showed Joann tiny, little gonads that looked like pearls. Karla showed Joann all the various organs, some of which she could not get out of the cavity.

Karla was most concerned about covering up the details of Spike's ignominious end at the clinic where she worked.

"I'm not going to tell them what happened," she announced. "I'm just going to tell them it died and we buried it outside, otherwise they'll want me to bring it in to analyze why it died."

Karla resolved to tell her co-workers that Spike got a cold

and died suddenly, and Paul was so sad that he went and buried him. To Joann, Karla acted like a god or something while she was dissecting Spike. When she was done, Paul threw the carcass on the barbecue. Karla kept the skin.

In Central and South America and the British West Indies, where iguanas are very common, their meat is highly prized.

"It's called bamboo chicken," Van declared. Paul ate most of it, Karla ate some and so did Van. Joann liked Spike. She refused to eat him.

Michelle Banks did not have high hopes. It was a Monday evening in the middle of August. Mondays in Atlantic City were usually slow. She was standing in her spot at the corner of Michigan and Pacific, when this guy pulled up in a late-model sports car and said, "Hi."

He told her that she was pretty. He said he and his wife were newlyweds and wanted to try something different. It wasn't often Michelle got propositioned to do it with a couple. She couldn't even pronounce ménage à trois. Michelle said there was no way she would do it unless he brought his wife back. Ten minutes later he did, but Michelle was still leery.

To Michelle, Paul and Karla were very clean and very well groomed. They looked like they were from a "very, very high-society family." They seemed like a cute little couple. She figured he was around twenty-four—he had a baby face. He was probably about 160 pounds and had blond hair—very preppy looking.

The woman could have been anywhere between twenty and twenty-four. She looked to be cut from the same mold as Farrah Fawcett. The sides of her long blond hair came back a little bit, as if she had put some gel in it. The front had a very light mousse. Hers was a very conservative look, as far as Michelle was concerned.

They kept driving around and around and then coming back and trying to convince Michelle. But Michelle did not go in for any of the weird stuff. The other girls kept telling Michelle that she should go with them, because they were obviously not going to go with anybody else and the money would be lost.

"They don't want nobody else," the girls all said. "Just go, they look all right. What are you worried about?"

Finally, the girl in the car convinced her.

"Come on," she said. "Everything will be okay." Then Michelle and the girl started giggling about price; just making a little fun around the process but the young man did not want to pay what Michelle was asking.

"Oh come on, go ahead, don't be so cheap . . ." the girl told him just as Michelle said, "Oh well, forget it then," and started walking away. The two approached her one more time, and it was agreed.

It was the woman who had talked her into it.

Michelle never got in the backseat of a john's car, so instead she sat on the woman's lap. She noticed that the car seats were not leather. It was a two-door vehicle of some kind. They went straight up Michigan to Atlantic, took a left on Atlantic, through two lights and then a left again, back down to Pacific. The parking garage for the Trump Plaza was between Pacific and Atlantic.

Their room was the second one on the left when they got off the elevator. When they entered the room, the guy paid Michelle and she started getting undressed. Michelle told them she was pregnant. In her experience if a john went crazy and he knew the hooker had a baby inside her, he would think twice about doing physical damage. Paul and Karla told Michelle their names were Paul and Karla.

They had just come back from Florida. Karla loved Mickey Mouse. They had had a good time, so they just thought they would stop off in Atlantic City, do a little gambling and have a little more fun.

Karla was wearing a black skirt with black pantyhose and a black G-string. Michelle remembered because she never wore G-strings. Michelle thought it was a big joke. They all lay down, naked on the bed, and Michelle asked them specifically what they wanted. Paul suggested that Michelle "mess around" with Karla. Michelle knew in a few minutes that Karla knew exactly what she was doing and what she wanted. Michelle thought that she must be like that—sort of a lesbian or bisexual.

Michelle made Paul put on a condom and tried to have sex with him. It was a bust. Michelle tried to start him off with oral sex while Karla rubbed his chest and kissed him. Both of the women tried to get him hard for the longest time, a couple of different ways, but it never worked. Paul was frustrated. He could not maintain an erection and every time he "deflated" the condom fell off. Karla was very sweet and understanding. She was getting her money's worth and seemed very casual and happy to Michelle. When Paul told Karla to come and lie down next to Michelle, she would say, "okey-dokey." To Michelle, that was submissive. Then again, Michelle was a hardened working girl. She ended the session by telling a racist joke. Then Paul got to watch her urinate, so he felt as if he had got his money's worth. Long afterward, Michelle remembered that.

Karla had a little strawberry birthmark on her stomach. Michelle admired it. It was a beautiful mark—a beauty mark. There were no other marks on Karla. Michelle thought Karla was perfect. Michelle Banks was jealous. She had no idea they had videotaped the whole thing with a hidden camera.

Inspector Bevan's guess that the floater in Martindale Pond was Terri Anderson had been confirmed through dental records. The ubiquitous pathologist, Dr. Noel McAuliffe, had ruled out foul play, so Inspector Bevan organized a meeting with the coroner, Dr. Robert Merritt, and Terri's father, Terry Anderson.

The Inspector explained that the coroner had concluded Terri died by drowning and that they did not feel there were any grounds for an inquest.

Toxicology tests indicated that Terri had taken LSD, which is normally untraceable twenty-four hours after ingestion because the body's metabolic processes expel it. That suggested to the coroner that she had fallen into the water and died before her body could expel the traces of LSD.

Mr. Anderson was confused. Terri's friends had told police

that Terri had downed a few beers and done a hit of acid and was obviously stoned around 9:00 P.M. But they also said she had come around later in the evening and seemed perfectly fine. Her father had last seen his daughter shortly after midnight. He had not noticed anything unusual about her behavior.

There was no semen detected. The girl's orifices were not distended or torn, but it was questionable whether or not those sorts of determinations could be made on a body that had been in the water for six months. And where were all her clothes? She had been wearing a leather jacket and tie-up jackboots and tight jeans. These had never been found. Where were they? And why was her T-shirt on inside out?

Inspector Bevan and the coroner were asking Mr. Anderson to accept that his daughter, who had been an excellent student, a cheerleader and a generally well-adjusted child, had, under the influence of a few beers and a hit of blotter acid, gone out and in a stupor neither he nor her friends had perceived, walked into the freezing November waters of Lake Ontario and drowned.

There were so many questions and so few answers. But Mr. Anderson had lived for six months without knowing whether his daughter was dead or alive. Now, after another six months, he really did not know what else to do but reluctantly agree to conclusions that gave him no sense of closure. Demoralized and dejected, Mr. Anderson left the meeting. Finally, Inspector Bevan had a file he could close.

Back in St. Catharines, Paul and Karla got busy. Christmas was coming and the demand for contraband had never been greater. Between October 15 and Christmas, they went back and forth across the border twenty-one times.

With her Medusa-like head of curly auburn hair and her blotter-acid mind, seventeen-year-old Norma Tellier became Paul and Karla's new Jane.

Norma had been a friend of Tammy Lyn's. Karla had com-

Paul and Karla leaving St. Mark's Anglican Church in
Niagara-on-the-Lake, June 29, 1991. (Private collection)

Karla with Buddy the Rottweiler,
June 1991. (Private collection)

SCARBOROUGH RAPIST

On Saturday May 26th, 1990 at approximately 0740 hours, a 19 year old female victim exited the eastbound Sheppard Avenue bus at Midland Avenue. The woman walked north on Midland Avenue to the area of Agincourt Collegiate. The victim was grabbed from the rear by the male suspect and forcibly taken to a secluded area near the north end of the school.

The victim was then sexually assaulted. During the assault the victim was beaten and also suffered injuries consistent with the use of a knife. The suspect fled in an unknown direction.

SUSPECT DESCRIPTION: Male, white, 18 to 22 years old, light coloured eyes – possibly blue, medium to heavy build – muscular, blonde hair – parted and feathered back to the sides, hair to the ears & to collar at back, clean shaven, smooth tanned complexion, no accent, wearing baby blue coloured top and tan knee length shorts, running shoes.

ANY FURTHER INFORMATION, CONTACT THE SEXUAL ASSAULT TASK FORCE AT 324-0543 OR THE SEXUAL ASSAULT SQUAD AT 324-6060

Scarborough Rapist poster
distributed in late May
and June, 1990. (Canapress)

Homolka residence, 61 Dundonald,
St. Catharines, Ontario. (Police photo)

Tammy Lyn Homolka,
Christmas 1989. (Private collection)

Family room in the Homolkas' basement shortly after
paramedics removed Tammy Lyn's body,
December 24, 1990. (Court exhibit #47)

Leslie Erin Mahaffy,
age 14 years. (Canapress)

Concrete blocks containing
Leslie Mahaffy's body parts, on the evening
of June 29, 1991. (Court exhibit #20)

"Project Green Ribbon" props room: "Kristen French" mannequin dressed exactly the way Kristen had been the day she was abducted.
(Court exhibit #145)

Kristen Dawn French, circa 1992. (Canapress)

Number One Sideroad,
where Kristen French's body was found,
April 30, 1992. (Court exhibit #51-2)

Constable Michael Kershaw (left) and Constable
Richard Ciszek enter 57 Bayview for the last time
on April 30, 1993. (Canapress)

Bathroom after the police vacated 57 Bayview
on April 30, 1993. (Police photo)

The Moloch.
Mark DeMarco's Masonic skull,
circa 1873. (Private collection)

Karla in hospital after flashlight
beating, late evening,
January 6, 1993. (Private collection)

Paul in police van just before his trial began
in May, 1995. (Canapress)

pletely forgotten about Norma, even though Norma—or rather, Norma's picture—had made a brief cameo appearance in Karla's epic movie; the one in which Karla had played her dead sister with such aplomb.

As she had done with Jane before, Karla lured Norma to 57 Bayview for Paul. Where Jane was guileless, Norma was cunningly naive. Where Jane was awkward, Norma was assured. Whereas Jane was short, Norma was tall. It did not much matter to Paul.

As she had done with Jane, Karla called Norma out of the blue. Like Jane, Norma came right over. If possible, Norma was more impressed. She could not believe how nice their house was. In Norma's estimation, Paul and Karla had everything. With Norma, Karla was far more open. She told Norma that they were smuggling cigarettes and booze and doing "money scams." Like Karla, Norma was attracted by the dark side and by dangerous men. Norma was the one all Tammy Lyn's friends said was heavily into drugs. Paul and Karla did all the same things and used all the same tricks on Norma. Except Karla did not give Norma a taste of her potions. After Jane and the 911 call in August, 1991, Paul had banned Karla's use of Halcion and halothane.

In late November, they took Norma Christmas shopping at the Eaton's Center in Toronto. Karla insisted that Norma not hurt Paul's feelings and take what he offered her. Paul outfitted Norma at the Jean Machine.

Every Christmas Karla helped her mother, Dorothy, sew stuffed bunny rabbit toys to sell in the gift shop at the Shaver Clinic where Dorothy worked.

They also made Santa Claus dolls. The Homolkas' Santas had long faces and big beards. When the beard was lifted a big penis dropped down. Dorothy's colleagues had always wondered about the propriety of flogging well-endowed Kris Kringles to chronic-care patients.

·   ·   ·

Paul and Karla took Norma to the SkyDome in Toronto for the Credit Valley Kennel Club Christmas Classic on December 13.

They had dinner at the CN Tower. Norma got a strawberry daiquiri straight away. Karla had to show her identification before she got hers. They stayed for two revolutions—each revolution took seventy-two minutes.

Back in the room at the Royal York Hotel, Karla took video footage of an agile Norma doing back flips across the room. Norma was really into gymnastics.

"Do more, do more," urged Karla. She said the same thing when she photographed Paul and Norma kissing.

Then Karla got drunk and fell asleep. After Norma rejected Paul's advances—Norma did not like to be hugged and kissed—she and Paul tried to set fire to the hotel. Paul videotaped the fire trucks and police as they arrived in front of the hotel, from their window.

He and Norma had taken a can of hair spray, and lit a serving cart on fire. The police woke up everyone on the floor and questioned them. When they came to their door, Karla pretended he had been in bed with her. Paul messed up his hair and looked stunned. When they asked, he cheerfully gave police his address and phone number.

Christmas had always been a very difficult time for Paul. The ambivalence of his existence and the duplicity of his family weighed most heavily during the festive season.

The reality of his circumstances—the fact that he was a bastard, that his mother was crazy, that his father had molested his sister and was a peeping tom—was in the starkest contrast at Christmas, when the family always pretended to be happy and normal. Some of his most violent rapes had been committed during yuletide.

Since Karla had helped kill her sister, it had become a bad time for her as well. Karla knew that Paul held her responsible for killing Tammy. He had made that abundantly clear. She had not meant to, but none of those perfectly reasonable rationalizations cut any ice with Paul.

Tammy's death exacerbated Paul's already hopelessly conflicted psyche. The tension between them grew and their resolve floundered. In Tammy Lyn's demise were the seeds of their destruction. When Paul went to war against Karla, he went to war against himself.

The previous Christmas, Jane had abandoned Paul and Karla, never to return. Then there was the incident with Janine Rothsay in the bathroom. Somehow, they got through it.

It was December 23, 1992, the second anniversary of Tammy Lyn's death. Paul and Karla's landlady, Rachel Delaney, had just left. Mrs. Delaney had come over with a Christmas gift for Paul and Karla. Paul thanked her and invited her in for a drink.

With a little dusting of snow outside and carols playing softly in the background, the scene at the Bernardos was a Hallmark card come to life. The house was illuminated, inside and out, with a bevy of Christmas lights. Paul and Karla sat demurely in the living room, chitty chatting with their young friend—Rachel could not remember her name, but she had an incredible mane of auburn hair. Fortune had certainly smiled on the Delaneys when it delivered these perfect tenants. Rachel finished her drink, said, "Merry Christmas," and left.

Norma got a shirt, a stuffed animal, a watch, a necklace and an anklet—it was all expensive—and then they watched an episode of "Sesame Street" that Norma had taped for Karla so she could see a character named Elmo.

When Karla went upstairs and came back down in her pajamas, walked around the corner and went into the spare bedroom, Norma was taken aback. Karla said she just felt like sleeping in the spare bedroom.

Norma ended up beside Paul upstairs in the master bedroom. Where else was she going to sleep? But Norma never liked being cuddled or mauled, and of course that was all Paul wanted to do.

Because Paul was always trying to feel her up and put his penis in her, Norma wore a lot of clothes when she went to 57 Bayview. On that particular night she was wearing a pair of underpants and her usual body stocking. Over the body stocking she had pulled on a pair of Calhoun boxer shorts—they were black with Christmas lights on them. The outline of the bulbs glowed in the dark. She had on a purple T-shirt.

When she moved onto the foam-rubber mattress they had on the floor beside the bed, Paul followed her. He managed to push back the crotch of Norma's body suit and put his penis in her.

Then Norma went to sleep. When she woke up she was up on the bed beside him again. She had no idea how she had got there. Paul was still sleeping, so she went downstairs. Karla was still sleeping too. Norma went back upstairs, got her socks from the foot of the bed and left.

Keith Parker took the last bus at midnight from Toronto and arrived in St. Catharines at 1:30 A.M., Christmas Day. There were no taxis, but Keith did not have any money anyway. He started walking in front of the hospital on Queenston Street. A car drove slowly by and Keith thought the driver was looking at him. Then the car pulled over. Keith bent over and looked in. The driver was looking at him all right, so Keith just kept walking. When he got to the first set of lights on Queenston, he saw a car coming and stuck out his thumb. When he realized it was the same car, he pulled in his thumb and kept walking.

The guy stopped and asked Keith if he wanted a ride. He was dressed in a two-piece suit, with a shirt and tie. The tie was undone. He introduced himself as Paul. It was a nice car. He looked all right, after all, so Keith got in. He had a mobile telephone in the car and the dash was lit up like a Christmas tree.

They talked. Keith told Paul that he had come down to see his girlfriend and kids.

"I don't have any kids," Paul said wearily, emphatically. He said his wife was with her family and that he did not care about Christmas—Christmas was for kids. Paul was acting really strange. He did not look at Keith, he just stared straight ahead. Then he turned the stereo up really loud. Keith asked him to stop and let him out on Hartzell Road by Norma Jean's Restaurant.

But Paul just kept driving. Keith told Paul to stop a second time. Paul turned the stereo down and said, "What?" Keith said that he wanted to get out. They had just passed where he was going. Paul slowed down by a used-car lot and turned the corner and Keith got out. He leaned in, shook his hand and wished him a good Christmas.

Paul told Keith he was not doing anything and he was going to drive around all night. Keith was welcome to join him, but Keith declined. He said no and left. Keith thought Paul might be a homosexual, but he never tried anything. His eyes looked really weird.

Everything had started out all right. The Homolkas got up and opened their presents. Everybody was happy. Later, after dinner, Karla must have been drinking. She was crying and crying, saying she wanted a baby. Paul said, "Oh Kar, it's okay, you know, in a few years . . ." She whined about wanting a baby all the time.

Then Karla went to sleep on Lori's bed. Paul was lying beside Karla. Lori was lying on the floor. They were all staying in Lori's room. Paul and Karla had been there Christmas Eve and Christmas Day. Paul and Lori stayed up talking most of the night. He was saying things like, "I can't understand your sister. She always has to be mothered. . . . She never does anything for me, she always has to do it on command. Like, I always have to tell her to do things, like hug me or kiss me. I'm the one who needs the mothering."

Paul was naked under the blanket. Lori thought he was talking nonsense. He told her if she ever needed someone killed, he knew people who would do it and nobody would be the wiser.

"Yeah, okay, whatever, Paul. I'll let you know," Lori said, but for the first time Paul was scaring her.

Then he told Lori about his "looping" theory. As Lori recalled, it had something to do with dying: people die, but they do not really die, they keep living. He told Lori he was going to write a book. It involved spiders and all sorts of different things.

At 2:30 in the afternoon on Thursday, December 27, Paul and Karla made a cigarette run. Late in the afternoon, they headed up to Sutton to visit Patrick Johnnie and his girlfriend, Linda. Paul had established a friendly relationship with P.J. since he'd ferried him across the border for Patrick's Florida vacation.

P.J. had an interest in a restaurant on the outskirts of Sutton called Happy Daze. They went there for a few drinks and left around midnight.

On the way home, Paul talked about Norma. He told Karla he had had sex with her. What Paul had, Karla wanted. Paul said he was not sure that Norma was "like that," and he was not sure that Norma liked Karla. Karla said it didn't matter.

"I can put her down just like Jane," Karla offered. But Paul had already banned the use of Karla's potion, so he hit her, hard, a couple of times, just to teach her a lesson.

Norma went over to Paul and Karla's on Saturday with her friend Brian. Paul had been drinking. Norma had a glass or two of champagne, just for old times' sake. In Norma's estimation, Karla was sober. She looked fine.

"Why won't you love me, why won't you love me?" Paul kept repeating, and Norma kept saying because she didn't, she just didn't. Besides, she had a boyfriend. Norma said she just wanted to be friends.

Then Karla told her, "Paul's the best thing that could ever happen to you. He could love you. He could give you anything you wanted." And Paul said, "Yeah, you could have the world by the tail."

Norma went out and walked around the block. When she came back they started arguing again. Norma said, "I'm never coming back here," to which Paul replied, "Fine."

"There's eleven years' difference in our age," Norma said. "You're twenty-eight, I'm seventeen. I don't want to have anything to do with you. . . ." After Norma left, Paul whacked Karla several times again. After all, Norma's recalcitrance was probably her fault.

Paul needed to get away. So he went to Montreal with his young friends Gus and Arif Malik on New Year's Day. They had gone across the border to the Pleasure Dome for New Year's Eve. Paul had arranged to have Gus's fire-engine red IROC Camaro stolen so that Gus could collect the insurance money. They took Paul's car to Montreal. The first night they went to the Metropolis and drank their faces off.

As far as Erica Moore was concerned, the bad one in the bunch was Gus. Paul was a sweetie. The other guy, Arif—she never got his last name—he was just an idiot.

She and her two girlfriends, Danielle and Natalie, had gone down to the Peel Pub in downtown Montreal. It was the day after New Year's and they figured a few drinks would do them some good. From the Peel Pub they went to a dance club called L'Esprit. That's where they met Paul, Gus and Arif. From L'Esprit they went to another bar called Ralphies, and then they went back to the boys' hotel.

Erica's girlfriends, Arif and Paul fell asleep. Erica stayed up talking to Gus. They were just sort of being sarcastic, gratuitously insulting one another. At one point, she and Gus were kissing and then he pinned her down—as a joke—but Erica was drunk and confused and didn't like it, so she told him to get off. Gus was a really big guy.

In the morning, when they woke up, Paul told Erica that he did not take kindly to insults. Then he said: "Party's over, bitches," and showed them the door. Erica thought Paul was one of the nicest persons she had ever met.

CHAPTER
twenty-three

Paul came back from Montreal even more conflicted than when he left. In loose psychiatric terminology, he was disassembling. He hit Karla across the back of her head several times with his flashlight. Karla saw the future.

Dorothy Homolka had received two anonymous phone calls advising her to look at her daughter's face. On Tuesday, January 5, Mrs. Homolka went to the Martindale Animal Clinic at lunchtime to see her daughter's face for herself.

The callers were right. Karla's eyes were raccooned and she looked awful. They went to McDonald's, where Karla finally admitted to her mother that Paul had hit her. In spite of her mother's imprecations, Karla insisted on going back to work. She agreed that she would abandon the matrimonial home that night. But when the Homolkas showed up at the appointed hour, there was no one home. Lori called and called. They sent the police and an ambulance, but there was no one home, so they left. Finally, around 9:30 P.M. Paul answered the phone. He said everything was fine and put Karla on the phone. She told Lori to just let it be, everything was all right.

Remarkably, the Homolkas let it be overnight and throughout the following day. With their neighbors, the Andersons, they went to the house the following night and this time found Karla home alone. She was in worse shape than she had been the day before. She told her mother that Paul had made her go on a cigarette run the night before and hit her all the way from St. Catharines to Niagara Falls.

Even so, the Homolkas still had to work at persuading Karla to leave. She kept going on about her things. Climbing the ladder in the garage, Karla started rummaging furiously through all the junk on the upper platform. She said they had plenty of time. Paul had gone across the border with someone named Patrick Johnnie and would not be home until much later. Karla sat on the white loveseat and intimated that Paul had killed Tammy Lyn. Dorothy Homolka suspected it anyway. After they left, Karla's father ran back into the house and grabbed as many of the pictures of his dead daughter as he could carry.

They got Karla to Corrina Hannah's apartment. Corrina was a friend of Lori Homolka's and her husband was a Metropolitan Toronto Police officer, so her place was a good choice for a safe house. Corrina told Karla she had been abused. She knew what to do. They called the Niagara Regional Police, who came and took Karla to the hospital. The doctor in emergency at St. Catharines General said it was the worst case of abuse he had ever seen and gave Karla an injection of Demerol.

.   .   .

In the meantime, the Green Ribbon Task Force discovered a cream-colored Camaro abandoned in the Welland Canal's over-flow channel north of York Road and west of Highway 55. Inspector Bevan was almost sure it was the car they were look-ing for, but he contained his excitement. The wreck in the overflow made all the news reports that night.

When Paul got home, the police were waiting for him. They put him under arrest and took him down to the station on Church Street, where he had been interviewed the night Tammy died. They charged him with assault with a weapon. Released on his own recognizance, Paul finally got home around three in the morning.

After that Paul could not regain his equilibrium. Karla was really gone. He popped pills and drank vodka. He confronted Mrs. Homolka in the parking lot outside the Shaver Clinic. He called the Homolkas on the telephone—Karla's father told him to go to hell.

He got two of his friends to go over to the Martindale Clinic in search of Karla. Paul moaned and cried and orchestrated a sound poem of epic proportions—sitting in his music room long into the lonely night, he proclaimed his undying love for his lost love and continuously exclaimed his commitment to die for it. He howled and howled. So did the dog. He recorded everything. He dubbed "Smoke Gets In Your Eyes" by the Platters over his howling dissertations.

Paul told Patrick Johnnie he needed another car. He said he had inadvertently hit Karla with a flashlight and after she left she had probably called him and the Nissan in to Customs. P.J. fixed Paul up with a lawyer to defend him on the assault charge. And he fixed up an old Mercury Marquis that Paul selected from the cars P.J. happened to have scattered around Brown Hill and Sutton.

The Marquis had a huge trunk and it was relatively easy to install a hidden compartment—like a big false-bottomed suit-case. P.J. drove the Marquis to St. Catharines. He was supposed to meet Bernardo at the Tim Horton doughnut shop on the Queen Elizabeth Way—where the miniature village was—but P.J. seemed to always get lost around St. Catharines. He had to phone Bernardo, and Paul came over and led him back to the house. Over tea, Paul asked P.J. and his girlfriend to intercede with Karla on his behalf. They tried, but could not get past Mrs. Homolka.

On Sunday, February 7, Paul brought a load of cigarettes up to P.J.'s garage. That's when Patrick Johnnie really noticed a difference. Paul was so bent out of shape he told a good-looking woman who came on to him in the Happy Daze restaurant, where they had repaired for a drink, to get lost. That was not at all like the Paul Bernardo Patrick Johnnie knew.

Sergeant Brian Nesbitt introduced himself to Detective Steve Irwin. Sergeant Nesbitt was taking a two-week, major-crime techniques course at the Canadian Police College in Ottawa. Irwin was a keynote speaker. Irwin talked about the intricacies of complex sexual-assault investigations. Afterward, Nesbitt congratulated Detective Irwin on his perspicacity.

While talking about Irwin's ongoing investigation into the Scarborough rapes, Nesbitt brought up Paul Bernardo's name. Irwin told Nesbitt—again—that Bernardo had still not been cleared in Toronto.

Irwin had talked about having fifteen hundred suspects in the Scarborough rape files. Nesbitt asked if they could "borrow" the files, but Irwin discouraged him, saying the files were not sufficiently well organized nor were they in one consistent format.

Irwin made a mental note to call the forensic scientist, Kim Johnston, as soon as he got back to the city. When he did, on January 23, Ms. Johnston told Detective Irwin she still did not have results on any of the five individuals whose samples he had resubmitted in November. They were short-staffed at the center; one of the scientists was on maternity leave, and Ms. Johnston had been away on course. They had so many other cases; homicides always took priority.

Karla euphemistically referred to it as her "diary"; the written memoir of all Paul Bernardo's trespasses Karla began to vigorously document as soon as she left hospital and moved in with her aunt and uncle in Brampton. "Paul was very possessive . . ." she scribbled. "He manipulated my mind . . . I was so afraid he would tell what I did . . . he knew I had trouble hearing him . . . I have an ulcer thanks to him."

Even though Karla liked to portray herself as "hiding out" in Brampton, she kept in touch. And sometimes she made a diary-like entry in her memoir of Paul's abuse. For instance, she noted that Paul's friends, Gus and Mike, had gone to the clinic and tried to find her. She even called Mike Donald and engaged him in a long telephone conversation about Paul and how bad he was and what he had done to her.

As the days went by, she "remembered" more and more things Paul had done to her. On January 12, two days after she had settled into her aunt and uncle's small apartment, she wrote: "He made me sleep in the root cellar; threw knives at me; said he would kill me and make it look like an accident; couldn't go to bed until he said I could . . . I was always terrified when I was with him. Stabbed in November, strangled in December."

When Karla's sister Lori came to visit she watched Karla rewrite the same letter a dozen times, addressing each one to a different friend.

Kristy Maan was one of those friends, and Karla's elaborate but circumspect explanation of her circumstances, an explanation that declared Paul a wife beater under whose spell she had fallen, and from which she had finally, miraculously, broken free, appalled Kristy.

When Kristy got the letter she felt strangely vindicated. She had long suspected something was amiss between Paul and Karla. Shortly after the wedding, she had incurred Karla's wrath when she broached the topic in a post-wedding letter. The way Paul's family had behaved at the wedding put the lie to Kristy's first impression of Paul as a rich, urbane guy with a great car. She also thought Karla looked wan and thin at the wedding, an observation that was met with outraged indignation and then months of silence, during which Kristy was persona non grata.

To Debbie Purdie, Karla embellished her pro forma missive: "Lots—tons has happened. I've left Paul—for good . . . a true wife beater . . . since Tammy died . . . I'm getting a divorce as soon as possible YAY! Write to me. I need to hear from friends."

In her datebook Karla recorded that she went home to St. Catharines to go to the Legal Aid office, see Dr. Plaskos and have her hair done at 3:00 P.M. on January 19. To the doctor, Karla "did not seem depressed or suicidal . . . she seemed quite positive" and appeared to be taking things very well. Dr. Plaskos did some blood work, including an HIV test.

In another letter to Debbie, dated the same day, Karla explained how "he [Paul] took 5 years of my life and I'm not allowing him to take any more . . . I wish I could have turned to you—or anybody—[Buddy] he's my puppy; Paul better not be abusing him or there will be hell to pay . . . I'm really excited about my new life. I can't wait."

Occasionally, she digressed and made what approximated a journal entry on the subject of her immediate needs and aspirations. Her entry for January 21 reads: "So confused about what to do with my life . . . don't know where I should live or what career I should choose; fear that I will go back to him. I wouldn't in a million years. I'd rather go to jail . . . I miss being in the hospital. I should have stayed longer. Dr. Plaskos gave me more Ativan; oh yeah, I just remembered, Paul kicked me in the lower back and there was blood in my urine."

On January 25, it was Karla's father's birthday, so Karla combined a visit home with a visit to "her new lawyer," Virginia Workman.

In another letter to Kathy Ford she described how Paul's

physical abuse did not start until July, 1992. "I got hit every-day—at least once," she revealed.

After Kristy Maan got Karla's "cycle of abuse" letter, she reciprocated with a book about getting out of unhealthy relationships. She sent the book to Karla's mother at the Shaver Clinic. The next thing she knew, Karla called her and told her where she was hiding. Karla invited Kristy to come and visit.

On January 29, Kristy, Karla and Kristy's new baby went shopping at Square One, a big mall in Mississauga. They went to Sears and had lunch at Burger King. Kristy was amazed. Karla appeared more than fine; maybe she needed a little weight—Kristy always thought Karla needed a little weight—but Karla had a real bounce in her step and she seemed inordinately happy. To Kristy, Karla seemed to have completely recovered from whatever hell it was she had been through. Maybe Karla was overcompensating, but she seemed positively bubbly and the incongruity between the details in her letters and Karla's demeanor gave Kristy pause, but little else.

At Paul's father's lawyer's request, Paul wrote a letter on his father's behalf, dated January 29, 1993. It was addressed, To Whom It May Concern.

"I am aware of the charges my sister had brought against my father," he wrote. "It is my opinion that this issue was put to rest years ago.

"I do not understand her actions. She was free to approach any family member, especially my mother, at any time. This issue would have been better resolved out of court.

"A prison term would not only not do my father any good but would cause a great deal of distress amongst the family."

At exactly 8:50 A.M. on Monday, February 1, forensic center scientist Kim Johnston called Detective Irwin. She said Paul Bernardo had raped Cathy Thompson, Deneen Chenier, and Sharon Moon. She had matched Bernardo's DNA to samples taken from each of the three women. She was exhilarated.

Nothing like this had even happened to Ms. Johnston before. There was no doubt that Paul Bernardo was the Scarborough rapist.

Detective Irwin immediately began to mobilize the forces. He organized twenty-four-hour surveillance on Bernardo. He did the necessary paperwork to get a tap on Bernardo's telephone. A computer check on the CPIC terminal told Irwin that Bernardo had been recently charged with assault in Niagara. He sent a request for more, detailed information.

It turned out Bernardo had hit his wife with a big, black steel flashlight and been charged with "assault with a weapon" on January 6. The Niagara Regional Police provided Detective Irwin with a dozen Polaroids of Karla Bernardo taken by the police on the night they laid the charge. Her eyes were raccooned and she had bruises on her arms and legs. She had been kept in hospital for three days.

On February 3, a colleague of Irwin's, Detective Ron Whitefield, called the Homolka household and reached Karla's sister. He told Lori that her brother-in-law had become a suspect in a serious investigation. Within minutes, Karla's mother called Whitefield back. Detective Whitefield said they would like to talk to Karla—as soon as possible, but they would also like to touch base with Dorothy and her husband.

Irwin called Alex and Tina Smirnis and made an appointment to pick up the videotape of their wedding. The Smirnises were already aware of the assault charge in St. Catharines. By the time Irwin got there, Alex was having second thoughts about turning over the videotape. He was inexplicably worried about revenge.

Alex nervously told Detective Irwin that Bernardo loved the video camera and took one with him everywhere he went. Irwin was aware Alex spoke in non sequiturs, but this time he really wondered about Alex's point. He assured Alex that Bernardo's capacity for retaliation would soon be severely limited. Alex reluctantly handed over the videotape.

·   ·   ·

When Detective Whitefield called the Homolkas on Wednesday, February 3, to speak with Karla, Karla was, in fact, there but she was too busy writing a letter to Kathy Ford dated February 3 to take the phone: "I am sitting on Tammy's bedroom floor (my new temporary sometimes bedroom. . . .)." The letter went on to elaborate at great length on the "pattern" of Paul's abuse. And her mother did not feel she could interrupt Karla.

She was in St. Catharines that day for another visit to Dr. Plaskos, who was rechecking Karla's hemoglobin. On Karla's file, Dr. Plaskos noted that Karla told her that she was "frequenting restaurants and bars." Karla explained to the doctor that she was "getting on nicely with her life."

Out of the blue, Joann Fuller called Janine Rothsay. Since Paul Bernardo had raped Janine over the Christmas holidays in 1991, Janine had not had much to do with either Joann or her boyfriend, Van Smirnis. It was one o'clock in the morning. Janine had just come home from work. "Guess who I'm with?" Joann told Janine.

Something had gone wrong and Paul was freaking out because he had to be in court in St. Catharines first thing in the morning. Joann wanted Janine to drive Paul across the border. Janine told Joann that she would not drive Paul Bernardo anywhere and she was amazed that Joann would ask.

The way Joann remembered the incident between Paul and Janine, Janine had had fun. Van said Paul said that Janine said that she loved Paul, and that was good enough for Joann. Joann's thoughts were often shaped like pretzels. In Joann's mind, Janine had never complained and Karla had just said, "Oh well, people make mistakes." Joann could not understand Janine's adverse reaction.

To Janine, it was not worth discussing. Besides, she had been working at the duty-free shop on the Lewiston bridge and wanted nothing to do with smuggling, which she rightly assumed was the reason behind their predicament.

What had happened was Paul had approached Van and said

he needed to make a cigarette run. When they got to Smokin'
Joe's, Bernardo bought forty-five hundred dollars worth of cig-
arettes. They loaded the cigarettes in an old Buick Skylark that
Van had borrowed from a "family friend" for the occasion.

They were planning to take the cigarettes across the border
via the railway tracks that spanned the Niagara River right next
to the Whirlpool Bridge. Paul had constructed a makeshift
dolly that would supposedly run on the railway tracks. They
were just about to load it up when a Customs agent material-
ized out of the dark. Whereupon they ran, abandoning the car
and cigarettes.

Joann called Janine again from the Porter House, a bar at
Church and 5th in Youngstown. Janine told her "no" again,
and Joann said, "Well . . . I think Kristen might do it," and
hung up. Youngstown was a very small town, and as far as
Janine knew, neither she nor Joann knew anyone named Kristen. Janine lay awake wondering who Kristen might be.

Joann finally got another girl named Sue to drive Paul back
to Bayview Drive. Paul said he thought Sue was hot. The agents
seized the car and the cigarettes. The next day they tracked Van
down and charged him under the Customs and Excise Act.

Detective Bruce Smollet and Detective Ron Whitefield traveled to St. Catharines on Thursday evening and interviewed
Mr. and Mrs. Homolka at 61 Dundonald. Dorothy told them
that Karla was staying with her aunt and uncle in Brampton.
They asked Mrs. Homolka to make sure her daughter called
them as soon as possible. In rape investigations, the police always wanted to talk to the women closest to the suspect.

Karla dutifully called Detective Whitefield at 11:15 A.M. on
Friday morning. She said that the earliest she could meet with
the police would be next Tuesday evening. She had to go to a
funeral, and the people with whom she was staying—whom
Karla wanted present during the interview—were expecting
company over the weekend.

Detective Whitefield told Karla that it was a very serious
matter they were investigating. When Karla asked him if anyone

was in immediate danger, Whitefield said he could not answer that. Instead, he thanked her for her courage and willingness to speak with them. She was not, in fact, obliged to speak to the police, he gratuitously told her. Then Detective Whitefield called Karla's mother and assured her that Karla had nothing to fear, she was not under suspicion. He emphasized that it was Paul Bernardo who was being investigated, not Karla.

Upstairs, from his office on the seventh floor at 40 College Street, Staff Superintendent Dave Boothby—one of the most senior police officers on Toronto's eight-thousand-member force—called Inspector Vince Bevan and invited him to a meeting on Monday morning.

Paul drove up north to see Patrick Johnnie; on his way he did a little sightseeing in a few shopping mall parking lots. The police followed Paul everywhere. On February 12, Paul was stopped at the border coming back into Canada. The Customs agents found the hidden compartment and an amount of cash in the Marquis. At 6:00 P.M., Smollet called Bevan and told him they had lost him after he was released. Smollet called for the Ontario Provincial Police helicopter, which was equipped with FLIR [forward-looking infra-red]. While Smollet was pressing the OPP for the helicopter, Paul pulled into his driveway, parked the car and went in the house. Paul's mind was unraveling. Without Karla, nothing made any sense.

Karla had become well known to the bartender at the Sugar Shack, a bar and dance emporium on County Court Boulevard in Brampton, Ontario, where they played oldies from the fifties and sixties. Karla always wore a tight, skimpy, black dress. It was hard not to notice her. She had started coming in toward the end of January.

On Friday night, February 5, Karla was with a woman she called Auntie Patti, and Auntie Patti's friend, Anne. Karla liked to drink green chartreuse with orange juice. A local guy named Jim Hutton came in with two of his buddies. Jim was an appliance salesman in his mid-twenties. He had that "Baywatch" look: six feet tall, fit, sandy, light brown hair.

The boys sat at the table next to the girls. The bartender could see that Jim was Karla's type. They started to talk and then Jim asked Karla to dance. They kept dancing until closing time. Before they left, Karla told Jim she would be back the following night.

By eleven o'clock Saturday night Karla had almost given up, when Jim finally came in. After the Shack closed, Jim and Karla went over to a bar on Main Street called O'Malley's. They got there around 12:30 A.M. Jim said a friend of his owned it. They sat around for a while, drinking and talking. Then they went to Dave Bailey's house. Dave was another one of Jim's friends. His house was only a short walk from O'Malley's. That night, Dave slept on his couch and Karla and Jim went at it in Dave's bed until the small hours of the morning. That was exactly what Karla needed: an orgasm, something just for her. Around 5 A.M., Jim called a cab and took Karla back to her aunt and uncle's apartment on McLaughlin.

Gus Draxis was a tall, dark, heavyset Greek kid. He idolized Paul Bernardo, about whom he was very worried. Since Paul's wife, Karla, had left him at the beginning of January, Paul had not been himself. At Paul's behest, Gus had tried to get in touch with Karla—to no avail.

Gus talked to Karla's dad once and he told him that a lot of stuff had been going on, that Karla was hiding, that Paul had been beating her and stuff. Gus no longer felt on terra firma.

Paul called Gus one afternoon in early February and said he wanted Gus to help with his rap album. The request was unusual. Inordinately secretive about everything, Paul's rap career had been strictly off limits. Paul even told Gus what his rap name was—Young Hype.

Gus went to Port Dalhousie in early February to spend a couple of nights with Paul. Gus thought he was drinking too much and maybe popping pills. Suddenly, Paul declared he had to move out. Gus said Paul would be welcome to move in with him up in Newmarket. So Paul went over to Ontario Street and rented a Chrysler Magic Wagon from Budget. Paul and Gus loaded up the Magic Wagon and drove it up to Gus's house.

Between Port Dalhousie and Newmarket, Paul foresaw that Karla would come back to him after all, and he said to Gus, "I'm not going to start dismembering the place." They turned around, drove back to Port Dalhousie and unloaded the Magic Wagon.

That night Gus fell asleep on Paul's couch. When Gus woke up the next morning, Paul was lying on the floor downstairs, passed out. It was around 9:00 A.M. Gus went to the bathroom and found an open vial of pills. Later, Paul woke up and said that there was obviously somebody who did not want to take him because if there were, they would have done it by then. Gus thought he was talking about God and killing himself. It never occurred to Gus that Paul was talking about the police and his possible arrest.

Karla had to get up first thing Monday morning to get to St. Catharines by 9:00 A.M. In her datebook it was marked "Virginia 10 A.M., Christina 9 A.M., leave early." Karla had been on a first-name basis with Christina since Dr. Plaskos confided that she had been abused. Karla had only recently found similar familiarity with her new divorce lawyer, Virginia Workman. Being abused created some kind of sisterhood and Karla really liked that.

Like bankers gathering to discuss a bad loan, a bevy of senior police officers arrived at the Metropolitan Police Services boardroom on the seventh floor at 40 College Street in downtown Toronto. Inspector Bevan was introduced to Metropolitan Toronto Deputy Chief Chuck Maywood, Staff Superintendent David Boothby, Staff Inspector Steve Marrier, Inspector Bob Strathdee and Detective Sergeant Bruce Smollet.

They reviewed, for Inspector Bevan's benefit, what they had on Paul Bernardo. Inspector Bevan remembered the Henley

Island rape. The Toronto police told Inspector Bevan that Bernardo should probably become his prime suspect in the Mahaffy and French sex slayings.

Although this was the inspector's first introduction to Paul Bernardo, from what he heard he quickly became certain that Bernardo was his man. Still, he left the meeting ambivalent. He had no evidence to link Bernardo with Mahaffy or French. Without some reasonable and probable grounds, the inspector would be hard pressed to get a search warrant, let alone arrest him.

On the very day the police were discussing Paul, Paul's father was convicted of "digital fingering" in a Scarborough court. Somehow Paul's sister had been persuaded to drop the other two more serious sexual-assault charges. Ken Bernardo was remanded for sentencing until 9:00 A.M., Thursday, February 18. He was definitely going to jail. The only questions that remained to be answered were for how long and under what terms?

A lot had gone down while Detective Mary Lee Metcalfe had been on vacation. She had barely hung up her coat on Monday morning, when she and her partner, Ron Whitefield, were swept into a meeting that included a number of prosecutors, the most senior of whom was "Maximum Mary" Hall from Scarborough.

Ms. Hall had earned the nickname Maximum Mary for her determined hard-nosed prosecutorial style and lack of compassion for criminal behavior. She looked the part. A voluptuous woman in her mid-forties, Mary Hall had a decidedly amazonian bearing, accentuated by the helmet-like way she cut her snow-white hair.

There were a number of other detectives, including Steve Irwin, head of the Scarborough rape investigation, and a couple of female officers from the sexual-assault squad, as well as

Detective Metcalfe's immediate superior, Detective Sergeant Smollet.

Detective Metcalfe discovered that she and Whitefield were scheduled to interview a woman named Karla Leanne Bernardo a.k.a. Teale née Homolka at the residence of her aunt and uncle, Patti and Calvin Seger, at 7:30 P.M. the following evening. Karla Homolka's estranged husband, Paul Bernardo, had become the prime suspect in the Scarborough rapes.

In the meeting, they reviewed the DNA evidence and discussed how many "probes" they needed before the prosecutors would feel comfortable in court. Mary Hall said five, Irwin only had two and three probe matches. Pam Newall, Kim Johnston's boss at the center, said she would gladly go to court with one, but later backed away from that position when her opinion was solicited by the director of the ministry's law office, Casey Hill. Irwin was assigned to work with Casey Hill to develop a comprehensive search warrant.

In the meeting, they reviewed video footage of a Greek wedding, in which Paul Bernardo could be seen trying to dance. Its usefulness for a voice-identification lineup was discussed. Since the video was busy and unprofessional, would it be fair to anyone concerned if they used Bernardo's recorded voice for a voice-identification lineup?

An assistant prosecutor was assigned to research "tricks and lies." How far could the police go with a ruse to entrap a suspect who had been identified by science? The meeting broke about noon, with these esoteric questions swirling around like the confetti in the Smirnises' wedding video. Casey Hill gave Detective Irwin a hundred-page search warrant on which he had previously worked, by way of example. It was a formidable document.

When Metcalfe and Whitefield returned to the squad room, they were introduced to Inspector Vince Bevan. He told Metcalfe and Whitefield exactly what he and the Task Force required from their forthcoming interview with Bernardo's estranged wife: firstly, Karla's account of Paul's activities during the time periods June 15 to 29, 1991 (the two weeks between Mahaffy's disappearance and the discovery of her body parts in Lake Gibson), and April 16 to 30, 1992 (the period during which Kristen French was abducted, raped, murdered and dumped in the ditch along Sideroad One).

He also wanted a detailed description of the jewelry Karla and Paul had. The task force knew exactly what accessories the girls were wearing when they disappeared. They had canvassed all the pawnshops in the Niagara Region looking for transactions but found nothing.

Thirdly, Bevan wanted Karla's fingerprints—for elimination purposes. The task force had found a piece of map at the scene where Kristen French had been abducted and there were latent unidentified fingerprints on it.

And one very important last thing: when Karla Homolka had been photographed by Niagara Regional Police at the hospital on January 6, she had been wearing a Mickey Mouse watch very similar to the one worn by Kristen French when she was abducted. Metcalfe and Whitefield were to ask Karla about the Mickey Mouse watch.

When Metcalfe and Whitefield agreed to ask these questions, Bevan accomplished two things. He tipped Karla Homolka's hand and regained control of a suspect that hours earlier he did not know he had.

Karla made a date to go to Cara Taylor's funeral with Norma Tellier on Monday afternoon, February 8. Even though the Taylors were neighbors on Dundonald—Karla thought they lived two doors down on Dundonald—Karla did not know Cara. Cara had been much younger, more Tammy Lyn's age.

Nevertheless, Karla sent Mrs. Taylor a Hallmark "In the Loss of your Loved One" card. Beneath a printed verse, Karla wrote, "Please accept my sincere apologies and sympathy for your loss. Cara was a wonderful girl who will be missed by all. Love Karla Homolka."

Cara's boyfriend, a young man named Caputo, had climbed through her window in the middle of the afternoon. First he had raped Cara, and then he had suffocated her with her pillow. Cara's mother found her dead daughter when she got home from work.

For Karla, the funeral was a catalyst for her reunion with Norma Tellier. Through Norma's aunt, Karla told Norma that she still wanted to be Norma's friend. She told Norma everything that had happened was Paul's fault—she had been under Paul's spell.

Norma had been going over to the Homolkas since Christmas and hanging out with Karla's sister, Lori. Norma told Lori that Paul had raped her twice in December—once at Paul and Karla's house on the anniversary of Tammy Lyn's death and once on Christmas Eve, in Lori's bedroom. Lori was surprised, because everyone had been home at the time.

Norma also told Lori that Paul told Norma that he had had sex with Lori and that Lori had wanted more. That really outraged Lori. Lori wrote down everything that Norma told her. Norma told Lori that Paul had also told her that he had sex with Lori's dead sister, Tammy. Lori said that the family had long suspected Paul and Tammy. They thought he had been buying Tammy's silence with money. When Karla was in the hospital for those three days in January, Lori and Norma had asked her what they should do about the fact that Paul had raped Norma. Karla told them to just forget it; Karla's situation was complicated enough. Lori tossed her notes.

While she was staying in Brampton, Karla discovered that Paul had run up all her credit cards with cash advances. She went ballistic and turned to Dr. David Wade, the vet who owned the Martindale clinic. He was a successful businessman, a Mason and an animal lover; he would know what to do. His perspective was straightforward. If an animal was sick, take it to a vet. If a woman was scorned, get a lawyer. Karla went to Virginia Workman, a well-known divorce lawyer in St. Catharines.

Destitute, Karla easily obtained a Legal Aid certificate. The government would take care of Ms. Workman's fees and Ms. Workman would take care of Karla's marital problems. Karla cancelled all her credit cards and then reported Paul to the Humane Society for abusing the dog. The Humane Society went to Paul's door, prepared to impound the dog, but deferred when they saw Buddy. Buddy was a bit too hardy and happy to have been much abused. Paul explained his predicament, in a cursory way.

Since Karla had got Paul into the Masons, Karla would see to it that he got out. She made sure the Masons knew Paul had been charged with assault, a fact that would ensure his expulsion. Then she called Customs, gave them a description of the Nissan and the license number and reported Paul for smuggling.

Day by day, Karla's voluminous diary grew, but she made no mention of the fact that Paul was the Scarborough rapist, or of the rape on Henley Island, or Leslie Mahaffy or Kristen French. Nor did Karla seek her new lawyer Virginia's professional advice about her imminent interview with the Metropolitan Toronto Police. Karla clearly demonstrated she understood the precarious balance of power between her and Paul when she perceptively recorded in the diary that Paul had "something to lose on one thing" and "everything" on two others.

All Karla really wanted to do now was let bygones be bygones, have fun and get her stuff back. She made a long list in her diary. She wanted her hope chest, her champagne glasses and everything else that was rightfully hers. The best way to sort all this out was a divorce. Karla wanted a divorce. Virginia Workman dutifully prepared the papers.

When Detectives Metcalfe, Whitefield and Smollet introduced themselves to Karla and her aunt and uncle, they told Karla they were investigating her husband for a series of violent sexual assaults and asked her what she thought about that. Karla could tell the detectives were nonplussed when she said that nothing shocked her. As soon as she told them that she knew they were coming, she realized she probably should not have said that either.

The interview—which lasted almost five hours—went along quite smartly for the first little while, until Karla discerned, based on the questions they had started to ask her, that these police from Toronto had somehow put the murders in St. Catharines together with the Scarborough rapes.

They wanted to know if she had a Mickey Mouse watch, but they would not tell her why. She knew why. She suddenly became agitated and visibly nervous.

In response to the detectives' queries about the sudden change in her demeanor, she fumbled. Naturally, the questions would upset her. Her Mickey Mouse watch belonged to her sister, Lori. Lori had lent it to her and now Karla knew they were going to want to take her sister's watch with them. No one asked her how she knew that.

From the look on their faces and the way they responded, Karla thought she had made another mistake when she asked the police how much time someone involved in serious sex crimes could get in jail? They said "a long, long time," and Karla thought they all looked at her very strangely.

Then they asked Karla for her fingerprints! She asked why, but they would not tell that either. Now she was forced to lie about a lot of things and she had not wanted to do that. But Karla was not going to jail for all those things Paul had made her do. It was not her fault. That is what everybody had told her while she was in the hospital—her doctor and the social workers, her friends, everybody. That was what all the books Karla had read said: it was not her fault.

Recrimination is like a prism, bending and reshaping memory. Karla told the detectives, at length, how much Paul had abused her. She was battered. He beat her. Had they seen the pictures the other police officers had taken when Karla was hospitalized? If they had, they could easily see Karla was abused. Anything she did, Paul had made her do it.

Karla had just pretended to like him. She had not really wanted to marry him, but she felt she had to. Since Karla had moved in with her aunt and uncle in Brampton, she was just starting to have fun—for the first time in five years.

Before the police left, Calvin Seger approached Detective Whitefield. Calvin observed that Bernardo had lived in both Scarborough and St. Catharines. It appeared to him as though they were investigating both the Scarborough rapes and the murders in St. Catharines. Whitefield told Calvin that was a reasonable assumption.

Karla became very scared and shaky after the police left. She told Auntie Patti and Uncle Calvin that she knew exactly what the police had been getting at. Even though Karla had told the police that she did not really know, she told Calvin and Patti that Paul was definitely the Scarborough rapist. She also told them Paul had killed Kristen French and Leslie Mahaffy.

Then she called the Niagara Falls residence of criminal lawyer George Walker. She knew Walker's wife, Lori, through the animal clinic. The Walkers took their Dalmatian dogs to Martindale. Lori told Karla to come to Walker's office at 3:00 P.M. on Thursday afternoon.

On Wednesday night, Jim Hutton asked Karla Homolka if she wanted to come over for pizza. He picked her up at the Segers' and took her back to his apartment. They had pizza, they watched hockey on TV and then they made love.

Karla told Jim she was married and that she had left her husband at the beginning of January. It was a terrible marriage, she said. Jim saw a few bruises, but he steered clear of discussing it. Jim Hutton was not looking for a lasting relationship; he just wanted to get laid.

At 10:15 P.M., Jim dropped Karla off at her aunt's and went to play hockey. He thought Karla was a very sweet, young girl. Jim looked a lot like Paul Bernardo and he drove a late model Nissan 240SX. Karla marveled at the coincidence.

Detective Metcalfe felt the interview with Karla had gone very well. Karla was cooperative, even talkative, going on about her Rottweiler dog, Buddy, and her daily work routine at the animal clinic and how she missed everything.

While they were fingerprinting Karla in the kitchen, her Aunt Patti watched with interest. Initially, the fingerprinting seemed to overly concern Karla. Since Karla had never been fingerprinted before, it was not surprising that she was apprehensive and wanted to know why. By the time they were finished, Detective Metcalfe felt that she had gained Karla's confidence.

When Karla called Detective Metcalfe the following morning and told her that she wanted to take Mary Lee up on her offer to drive Karla anywhere she wanted to go, Detective Metcalfe knew she had established a bond. Karla told Mary Lee that she felt very comfortable talking to her, that Mary Lee had made her feel very relaxed during the interview Tuesday night. Karla wanted to talk to her and Detective Whitefield some more, she said.

Karla had an appointment in Niagara Falls at three o'clock in the afternoon on February 11. She told Mary Lee she did not want her parents to know about this appointment and asked her to keep it a secret from them. When Mary Lee asked about the appointment, and Karla admitted it was with a lawyer.

Mary Lee wondered if she and Detective Whitefield should come by a little early and talk for a while, but Karla said no. It took about an hour and fifteen minutes to get there, so they should come by to get her around 1:30 or 1:45.

Karla got in the rear passenger seat. Detective Whitefield drove. Mary Lee leaned against the door and turned partway around so that they could talk. Whitefield was a personable Scot—tall and balding, but it was Metcalfe with whom Karla identified. She had lovely brown hair—"big hair," as they say in St. Catharines—and she smelled as fresh as a bar of soap.

They went south on Highway 10 to the Queen Elizabeth Way and into the Niagara Region. They talked about driving. Karla liked to drive. She had not driven for the longest time, because Paul's car was a standard and he would not teach her how to drive standard.

Karla described her job, how she performed minor surgeries such as clipping swans' wings, amputating puppy dogs' tails and anesthetizing animals. Detective Whitefield told an amusing anecdote about his pet budgie and they all laughed.

Karla went on and on about the different breeds of dogs. She talked about how people should never trust German shepherds. Karla had studied the Rottweiler bloodlines before she got Buddy. The breeder was very important.

"Guess what?" Karla declared. She had met a guy. It felt so good to get back to a normal life. She really enjoyed being with this fellow. They had watched a hockey game and had pizza at his house. He was presently up on an impaired-driving charge, but he was going to fight it in court.

She told the detectives that she was quite ill and was taking antibiotics for an infection. She said that the lawyer they were taking her to see was well known to her before, that she had helped the lawyer's wife get a Dalmatian puppy—for free—from the clinic where she worked. The dog had been born deaf; that's why it was free. She told them how much her dog had cost. They talked about dog toothpaste.

As they passed the exits for St. Catharines, Karla said she detested the city. It was a stupid place with no nightlife. Anyway, she and Paul never went out much after they got married. They just stayed home and watched videos.

Then she talked about their wedding: the horse-drawn carriage, the sit-down dinner, how great it had been and what a great time she had. They had videotaped the whole thing. It was the best day of her life, she said.

The detectives failed to notice the incongruity between the description of her wedding and marriage during the interview on Tuesday night and how she seemed to view it all completely differently as they passed the exits for Niagara-on-the-Lake.

Cross-border shopping was not as economical as it had been, Karla said. Things were getting cheaper on the Canadian side and it was not really worth it anymore. Karla said she really hated the drive between Toronto and St. Catharines.

"You know," she said pensively, "my ultimate downtime would be on a desert island."

About where they were going, however, Karla was secretive and curt. Her directions were barked, like commands. The tone of her voice lost its good-natured camaraderie. When she gave directions, it was as if she were a haughty starlet ordering hired drivers.

The contrast between the way she gave directions and how she otherwise gabbed away as though they had known each other for years and were simply out for a Sunday drive did catch both detectives' attention, but they did not know what to make of it. They really had no idea who or what Karla was. This was Thursday afternoon; they had only just heard her name on Monday. Karla was an enigma.

They turned left onto Victoria Street. Beyond the picture-perfect Falls and sideshow museums on Clifton Hill, Niagara Falls was a one-horse, border town.

Flat, with strip malls and two-story buildings, it had more in common with the industrial boondoggles in Upper New York State than any small Ontario town.

"Right there," Karla snapped as she pointed to a parking lot surrounded by a large wrought-iron fence at the corner of Queen and Victoria. "Pull in there and you can park—for free."

Across the street, there was a big Catholic church called St. Patrick's and a pawnshop. Above the door of the pawnshop, there was a large rhinoceros head that looked as if it had come right through the wall. The rhinoceros always got double takes. Below the rhino head was a big sign that simply said BUY SELL TRADE PAWN—MARK DEMARCO.

Detective Metcalfe politely asked if Karla wished for them to stay in the car and wait for her. Karla pooh-poohed that idea and invited them into George Walker's law offices as though they had just arrived home after a long journey.

Surprised, the detectives sheepishly followed her. Half an hour early—it was barely 2:30—Mary Lee sat beside Karla in the waiting room and read a Maclean's magazine. Walker's office was on the second floor. At three o'clock the receptionist told Karla to go up.

When George Walker emerged from his meeting with Karla, he seemed to have completely lost his tan. His second wife, Lori

Walker, a pert blonde herself, fifteen years Walker's junior, who also worked as his bookkeeper, looked at him with quick concern. The Walkers had just returned from their home on the British West Indian island of Montserrat, where they always spent the month of January.

Walker was a man who wore bespoke suits. He looked a lot like former American president Lyndon B. Johnson. Walker tanned quickly and deeply. At that moment, he looked as though they had never been in the Caribbean. He had become a sickly beige color. Lori really had not been paying much attention. When he mumbled something about Karla, Lori was surprised. She thought Karla had come and gone three-quarters of an hour earlier.

"George, what's wrong?" Lori asked. But Walker waved her off. He was having enough difficulty drawing breath—talking was out of the question. It was Lori who had arranged this meeting. Walker did not handle any family law matters. He had told Lori to tell Karla what he always told women who approached him about domestic disputes and divorce: "Tell her to kill the bastard, then I'll defend her."

Lori had reminded him who Karla was and said that she had just given her fifteen minutes on Thursday. Walker could at least give Karla a little fatherly advice, considering how well Karla had treated Kelly, Walker's beloved Dalmatian.

Karla had told her new lawyer that she and Paul had been involved with the death of her sister, and that she was there when Leslie Mahaffy and Kristen French were killed. She had not killed them, but she was there.

Karla told him there were videotapes of the sex, not the killings—somewhere. She had looked before she left—they were supposed to be on the storage platform in the garage—but Paul must have moved them. Karla wanted immunity. In return, she would be willing to testify against Bernardo. Could Walker get her immunity, she wondered? Walker wondered too.

There was a terrible cruelty in coincidence: because the Walkers took their dogs to this particular vet—Dr. Patti Weir at the Martindale Clinic (there were hundreds of options in the Niagara region, where vets were as ubiquitous as doughnut shops)—Walker became Karla Homolka's father confessor and her defender.

In such disarmingly matter-of-fact terms, she had told him what no one else in the world yet knew: a tale of such nightmarish, unimaginable degradation, sex, death, lies and videotape as to defy the imagination. What Karla readily admitted she had done and witnessed, made young Robin Walker's crime look like a youthful transgression.

In thirty years of criminal practice, Walker had never been dumbfounded. When Karla left his office Thursday afternoon, George Walker could simply not imagine this little "wisp of a girl" anything but a victim of a diabolical Svengali. The mind compensates for behaviors that defy explanation. Disbelieving, Walker went on automatic pilot: he was already thinking about using the battered woman's defense, even though, strictly speaking, it did not apply.

Battered women did not participate in the kidnapping and confinement of teenage girls whom they sexually assaulted themselves. Nor did battered women give their fiancés their younger sisters for Christmas. They did not thoroughly clean house and destroy evidence after they had stood idly by and watched their batterer murder young, helpless schoolgirls. Abused women did not help dispose of the lifeless, dismembered bodies of their batterer's victims.

Occasionally, very rarely, the battered woman would strike out against her abuser and kill him. There were only a few precedents where the fact that a woman was battered was considered to be a sufficiently mitigating factor for acquittal or a lesser charge and much reduced sentence.

Karla had told Walker far more than he had ever wanted to hear but she certainly had not told him everything. The sister, Leslie, Kristen, videotape—she had been there through everything, but had not actually killed anyone. What else did he need to know?

Although he could not imagine Karla as anything but a victim, as he learned more and more and came to know Karla better, a profound ambivalence would replace his initial credulity. But the issue now at hand was to give his new client the best defense possible.

What could he do for Karla? It really all depended on the police and their disposition. He was skeptical about blanket immunity under any circumstances, but it was certainly the place to start. And what was there except the battered-woman thing? Walker was very glad he had made arrangements to go back to Montserrat for a couple of weeks at the end of February. He was going to need another respite.

When Karla came down after only an hour, Mary Lee asked if her lawyer wanted to speak to them. Karla said, "No," the same way she had given them directions. When they asked her where she wanted to go, she just said, "Home."

As they started to retrace their route, Detective Whitefield glanced in the rearview mirror. Karla looked as though she had fallen into a trance. Mary Lee asked if there was anything Karla wanted to discuss.

"Nothing. I don't want to answer any questions," she said, imperviously. "Was that her lawyer's advice?" they inquired. That, too, was a question, Karla replied—hadn't she just said that she would not answer any questions?

Given Karla's newfound recalcitrance, the detectives told Karla that they were now convinced that Karla knew a lot more than she had let on and they were very surprised that Walker had not wanted to talk to them.

"Was he aware we were there?" Mary Lee asked Karla.

"Of course," Karla replied. "And he thought it was very kind of you to provide me with transportation."

On the way back, Detective Metcalfe told Karla that she had extensive experience with child-abuse investigations. She told Karla, at some length, how victims of abuse would disassociate themselves and become "spots on a wall," in order to cope.

Karla came alive. In spite of Walker's admonitions, she talked about how she was so fearful of her estranged husband that every night before he was to pick her up she always had to go into the bathroom and urinate half a dozen times.

Karla had read a lot of books about abused and battered women. In the hospital, the social workers had talked about patterns and cycles of abuse. Her girlfriend, Kathy Ford, who never liked Paul, was working at a women's center in Skaneateles, New York, and had given Karla a sheaf of literature on abuse and battery. Even her new physician, Dr. Christina Plaskos, an attractive, young brunette whom Karla greatly admired, had told Karla she had been abused.

Once in the hospital in January, Karla had been instantly surrounded by empathetic and understanding people. She became the center of attention. Karla took keen notice of how the detectives were now trying to comfort her, bribe her with their empathy and sensitivity.

Totally unaware of the kind of person they were dealing with, the two detectives flew blithely blind. What they did was provide Karla with a model for the kind of behavior and response that she could expect from authority figures. Their counsel was a precious gift. It gave Karla the essential element all grifters must have—the courage of their convictions, even though those convictions are based on absolute fictions.

Metcalfe and Whitefield persisted, indefatigable. They told her that they would understand any situation in which she might find herself; no situation, for an abused woman such as herself, was "beyond hope"; no matter what, Karla was not beyond help. They told her that it had taken a great deal of courage to leave Paul. Having him charged, now that took "real guts," Detective Whitefield said.

Then they got into what the detectives erroneously called the "battered-wife syndrome" and why so many women stayed in abusive situations. As police officers they had a lot of experience with abusive husbands and Karla could rely on them for support and help. Between Niagara Falls and Brampton, by keeping her mouth shut, Karla got a further education.

When they pulled into the Segers' parking lot at 5:30 P.M., it was dark. After they stopped, Karla continued to sit in the backseat, motionless. The detectives were reluctant to break the spell. They thought Karla was scared and did not want to leave their protective company. They thought she was thinking over her options. They continued to talk, Karla continued to listen. They expostulated, Karla said nothing.

Whitefield said that Karla's sister Lori had repeated the phrase that Karla had told Lori that Paul always said to Karla: "Prepare yourself for nightly terror." Mary Lee said that only Karla really knew what that meant and only she could stop the "nightly terror." Detective Metcalfe thought she saw tears well up in Karla's eyes.

Mary Lee Metcalfe and Ron Whitefield would not see Karla again until the middle of May.

That night George Walker had more unexpected visitors; around 11:30 P.M., Sergeant Bob Gillies and Constable Matthews came by his house. They were from the Green Ribbon Task Force. They said they were very eager to talk to Karla. It was as Walker suspected. There had been absolutely no communication between the task force and the Metropolitan Toronto Police.

Gillies told him the Crown might be willing to deal—in exchange for information. To Walker, that meant Inspector Bevan wanted to make a deal. In any plea-bargaining process, the compliance and wholehearted approval of the police for the deal was essential.

Their abiding interest and patter also told Walker that there had been a serious connection made between the suburban rapes in Toronto and the murders of Leslie Mahaffy and Kristen French. The Scarborough rapes were not Walker's problem. His client did not have a penis. With the murders, he was deeply concerned.

Inspector Bevan was waiting outside the police building in Niagara Falls when Gillies and Matthews pulled up around 12:30 P.M., eager to report. Walker had said he would be talking to

Ray Houlahan first thing in the morning. Houlahan was the senior prosecutor in St. Catharines. It was just as Inspector Bevan suspected—and Karla's fingerprints on the map would confirm—Karla was in it right up to her blond bangs.

Bevan wondered what the FBI would have to say about Karla. So much for their theory about two scruffy male laborers. Then again, so much for King Camaro. Whatever, he would soon have all the evidence he would ever need.

CHAPTER
twenty-four

First thing in the morning, George Walker went to regional prosecutor Ray Houlahan's office in the St. Catharines courthouse. Houlahan was an intense, mustached, compact man with a thinning head of gray-streaked, brown wiry hair. As a youthful aspirant to labor organizing, Houlahan had once met Jimmy Hoffa and had become a lifelong fan. Even though Hoffa was now dead and defamed, Houlahan remained steadfast and quick in Hoffa's defense. Houlahan was also a formidable ballroom dancer. Divorced and pushing sixty, Ray Houlahan, like Walker and Homolka, was a dog lover, as well. Although his dog had been dead a decade, its bed was still under his office desk.

The meeting lasted half an hour. George Walker told Houlahan that Paul Bernardo had killed Leslie Mahaffy and Kristen French; that his client, Karla Bernardo, had been there and had been forced to participate. He told Houlahan that Bernardo had apparently videotaped long segments of the sexual assaults but not the actual killings. Karla wanted immunity. She was divorcing Bernardo. In return for immunity, she was offering her damning testimony.

Houlahan said that he would have to put Walker in touch with someone at the head office. Houlahan did not have the authority to negotiate a deal such as this. Walker had expected that. He also knew with whom he would likely be negotiating—the director of the Crown law office, Murray Segal. Segal was a gnomish, stocky jurist with curly black hair, whom Walker knew well. As young lawyers, they had both done a good deal of appellate work in the Toronto Appeals Court. Walker liked Segal. He was looking forward to seeing him again.

Houlahan had Inspector Bevan into his office at 11:00 A.M. He told the inspector what Walker had told him. The inspector said he would gladly get in touch with Murray Segal. It was Houlahan's decision to push up the process, it was Bevan's job to make the call. The police and the prosecutors were two peas in a pod.

"You're asking me to buy a pig in a poke," Murray Segal responded good-naturedly, when George Walker suggested blanket immunity in return for Karla's testimony against her estranged husband. Segal said he simply did not know all the facts yet, so Walker would appreciate that he could not do a deal even if he wanted to.

During their first conversation on the afternoon of February 12, Walker established what he wanted and Segal established his reticence.

"God knows how much she knows about what he did," Walker said sagaciously to Segal. Walker described Karla as a "little wisp of a girl," a phrase he would use many, many times during their negotiations.

Murray Segal was not as ignorant of the situation as his manner suggested. He had been briefly exposed—his peer and cohort Casey Hill was already hard at work on a search warrant for Bernardo's house in Port Dalhousie with Detective Irwin. Segal knew their work had to do with the Scarborough rapes. He was aware they had a good deal of science on Bernardo.

Segal also understood that less than five days before the Green Ribbon Task Force had not had a clue about Karla Homolka or Paul Bernardo, let alone evidence linking them to the murders of Leslie Mahaffy or Kristen French.

Walker quickly sketched out what he knew for Segal. Karla had told him that she had been involved with the deaths of Mahaffy and French—although she did not do the killing herself, she had been there and had watched Bernardo kill the girls. The two of them had also had something to do with her younger sister's death, although Walker had not yet got to the bottom of that malfeasance.

Segal really knew very little about Karla Homolka, and he did not have a fix on who or what Paul Bernardo was. He wondered how many crimes they might be talking about? He wondered if Karla was the genuine article? Maybe the crimes were too serious and plentiful for a plea bargain? Maybe he did not have the authority to conduct the negotiation? But from what Walker had told him, he said his gut feeling was that "the people" might be best served by a twenty-year sentence for Karla in return for her testimony, because Walker knew as well as he did that technically Karla was guilty of first-degree murder.

They talked about lawyers' letters, derivative evidence, even parole issues. Once Segal had a better grasp of the variables and had established that he was the one who should be negotiating with Walker, they should get Karla in as soon as possible.

By the time Segal rang off, Walker knew that all his assumptions were correct. The Niagara police had absolutely nothing on Paul Bernardo in terms of the murders, which was very good as far as his client Karla Homolka was concerned.

On February 12, 1993, the Ontario provincial government officially approved the Bernardos' application to change their name to Teale. It was also the day Inspector Vince Bevan reclaimed Bernardo, or Teale, for the Green Ribbon Task Force.

Bevan convened a meeting at task force headquarters around the same time Walker and Segal were talking. All involved Metropolitan Toronto Police personnel were required to attend. The roster included Staff Inspector Steve Marrier, Detective Sergeant Bruce Smollet, Detective Ron Whitefield, Detective Constable Mary Lee Metcalfe, Detective Constable Janet Neate and Detective Steve Irwin.

The task force was represented by the staff sergeant brothers, Murray and Steve Macleod as well as Detective Sergeant Bob Waller from Halton Region. Waller was the one who had driven up to Midland and informed the Mahaffys that the body pieces the police had found at Lake Gibson were their daughter's.

Inspector Bevan informed those at the meeting that Karla had told her lawyer Paul Bernardo had committed both murders and that she wanted immunity. Bevan said that the victims had been videotaped. Karla admitted she had helped dispose of their bodies. Detective Irwin looked at his shoes.

Copies of all the Metropolitan Toronto Police surveillance reports were handed over to the Green Ribbon Task Force. Surveillance on Karla was immediately initiated. Detective Irwin had been so efficient with the tap on Bernardo's line; perhaps he could do likewise on Karla's phone?

At this meeting Detective Irwin was told that he would handle the post-arrest interview of Paul Bernardo with senior Niagara Regional Police Sergeant Gary Beaulieu. Exactly when that would happen was still being discussed between Irwin's boss, Staff Inspector Marrier, and Inspector Bevan.

From that day forward, all Metropolitan Toronto Police working on the case would work out of the task force headquarters in Beamsville, Ontario. While Detective Irwin made arrangements to check into the Parkway Suites Hotel, over near the Pen Center, Inspector Bevan began to work out the rationalization for his pending deal with Karla Homolka.

As much as fortuity and police incompetence had facilitated Paul and Karla's five and a half years of murder and mayhem, fortune eventually determined Karla's fate. If coincidence really was God's way of maintaining His anonymity, He was singularly absent in St. Catharines when Inspector Bevan and various members of the Green Ribbon Task Force first became aware of an unpublished esoteric article titled "Compliant Victims of the Sexual Sadist."

The article, which would soon be published in the April, 1993 issue of *The Australian Family Physician,* was written by FBI Supervisory Special Agent Roy Hazelwood, Janet Warren, an associate professor in the Department of Behavioral Medicine and Psychiatry at the University of Virginia, and Dr. Park Dietz, an associate professor in the Department of Psychiatry at the University of California and one of the most famous forensic psychiatrists in the United States.

Roy Hazelwood was a clean-cut Texan who kept a Bible prominently displayed on his desk in the Behavioral Science bunker and once proudly told an interviewer that twenty-two of his sexual sadists had killed at least 187 people, mostly women—far more than "your big names, like Bundy and Gacy."

He called sexual sadists the "crème de la crème" of sex criminals and said they were the largest challenge to society and law enforcement yet.

Hazelwood talked matter-of-factly about women who signed slave contracts and sold themselves to sadists for a dollar, about sadistic perverts who collected detective magazines and had a fascination with hanging. He knew of sexual sadists who explained in precise, graphic detail what they were going to do to their victims because the victims' fear heightened the sadists' sexual arousal. After one such litany of horrific deeds, graphically described in minute detail, one apocryphal sadist asked his victim if she "had any questions."

"Compliant Victims of the Sexual Sadist" explained Karla's criminal behavior as that of a victim, not a malingering perpetrator. For Inspector Bevan's purposes it really did not matter whether or not Paul Bernardo was technically a sexual sadist for whom torture and killing were integral elements of his paraphilia or deviation: no one would argue that Paul Bernardo was not sadistic, or with the fact that two schoolgirls were dead. Bernardo's status as a sadist was moot, as was Karla's victimhood.

The sexual sadist, as a singularly defined criminal phenomenon, was a new figure on the law-enforcement landscape. As a unique figure, he had been introduced by the same trio of authors who wrote "Compliant Victims of the Sexual Sadist." Over the previous three years they had also published "The Sexually Sadistic Criminal and His Offences" in *The Bulletin of American Academic Psychiatric Law Journal* (1990), followed by "The Criminal Sadist" in *The FBI Law Enforcement Bulletin* (1992).

The articles explained that the term "sexual sadism" had been coined by Richard von Krafft-Ebing after the Marquis de Sade, a bad fellow in the seventeenth century who had coerced a variety of prostitutes, peasants, his wife and other degenerates into orgies involving bondage, whippings, paddlings and buggery. Krafft-Ebing had published *Psychopathia Sexualis: A Medico-Forensic Study* in the fifties. The book was not available in English until 1965.

Of the thirty alleged sexual sadists Dr. Dietz and Mr. Hazelwood had been able to interview or study, they had identified seven women who had apparently participated in the sadists' diabolical sex crimes. Among those seven, three women actually had been married to their sadist.

Law enforcement frequently stereotypes women. Instead of accessories or partners or accomplices, the authors chose to call their newly discovered female sex criminals "compliant victims."

This theory placed Karla on a par with her dead sister and

the two dead schoolgirls, Kristen French and Leslie Mahaffy. Regardless of what role Karla had played, what her motives had been, or how much enjoyment she had derived from the crimes, Inspector Bevan had the rationalization for Karla's bizarre criminal behavior in these articles. Even before Bevan had the slightest idea about exactly what Karla had done or knew the true extent of her participation, he had her excuse. To the members of the Green Ribbon Task Force Karla Homolka became the perfect "compliant victim."

On Saturday morning, Karla's Auntie Patti drove her to George Walker's office. During their two-hour meeting, Walker outlined the reality of Karla's situation—no matter what, Karla was going to jail. She had to understand and come to grips with the fact that there would be no blanket immunity. The only significant questions were how much time Karla would do and where?

Walker had Karla sign an authorization for him to continue negotiations. The handwritten document names Ray Houlahan, Murray Segal, Casey Hill and Scarborough Crown Attorney Mary Hall as the people with whom Walker was negotiating.

One other thing: if Karla wanted any kind of a deal, she would forget her new boyfriend in Brampton and immediately move back home with her parents.

Things would have been different if Paul had stayed with Marie Magritte. She truly loved Paul. And she was beautiful, too. For Marie, Paul truly was the king.

Paul called Marie for the first time in a long time four days before Valentine's Day. He called about 1:00 A.M. Paul told Marie everything. About how he was working on a rap album; that he and Karla had split up. Marie had not seen Paul since December 21, 1990, when he had rented a hotel room at the Royal York so they could have sex. That was two days before he and Karla raped and killed Tammy Lyn Homolka.

Paul explained to Marie that he and Karla had been arguing a lot. Karla was bisexual, he said. He told her about Michelle Banks, the hooker in Atlantic City and that he had videotaped the whole thing.

"He said that Karla liked brunettes, because they were her opposite," Marie remembered. "It really bothered him that she could get off easier with a girl than she could with him." Their conversation lasted five or six hours.

Paul told Marie he was coming to Toronto on Saturday to see their mutual friend Gus, and he asked if he could see her, maybe take her to St. Catharines to see his house. Marie said she was working at Swiss Chalet from nine to five on Saturday. She could meet him after work for a coffee, if he wanted.

Around 9:30 P.M. on Saturday evening, February 13, 1993, Paul met Marie outside Honey Bee Donuts next to the Swiss Chalet. She agreed to go over to Gus's house. When they got there, Jason Mooney and Gus were planning to go downtown. They went in Jason's car.

It was close to eleven by the time they got down to a club called My Apartment, on Peter Street near the SkyDome and Lake Ontario. There was a lineup, so they went up the street to Club Max instead. Marie and Paul talked. They drank. They danced.

Paul had really changed. To Jason, who now managed Casey's Roadhouse on the outskirts of Lindsay, Paul had once looked like something out of GQ magazine. Now he looked really stupid. He was twenty-eight years old and he had the sides of his head buzzed. He had numerous rings in his heavily pierced ears. On the other hand, Marie was raven haired and very pretty.

By 2:00 A.M. Marie was really drunk. On the way back to St. Catharines, Paul had to pull off to let her out of the car twice. When they got to the house, Buddy was so excited he pissed on the floor. Paul made pizza. They sat on the couch. Paul showed Marie some pictures: Christmastime, Karla and him, his dead sister-in-law.

They did a little typing on the computer:

"Marie loves Paul with all her heart and soul and promises to have wild and violent sex with him tonight and every night. . . . In response, he promises to be a faithful, loyal dog in which sex with any other female is punishable by death by order of her majesty, the Queen Marie, and she will punish him if he is unfaithful."

"Dear Paul you are my first and my only love. I love you." Paul pecked out, "I love you, I love you too always and forever no matter what you think, we should be together, not really together. Love me, hate me, fuck it, let's have sex. Oh, by the way, are you a virgin?"

"No," Marie typed in her reply. "Paul took my virginity. (What did he do with it?) He stored it in his heart forever."

They went upstairs and got into bed. It was 6:15 A.M. on Sunday morning. Around seven they woke up. Marie remembered saying she had to get back and then she feel asleep again.

Inspector Bevan was in his office early Sunday morning when he got the call—Bernardo had gone off to Toronto, picked up a girl and they were both in the house. What should they do, Staff Sergeant Murray Macleod wanted to know? By the time Bevan mobilized the Emergency Task Force and the OPP about that helicopter with the infrared scanner, it was around 10:00 A.M. Marie and Paul Bernardo walked out the front door, got in the Nissan and drove off.

Murray Segal and a tall, leggy, blond assistant prosecutor named Michal Fairburn arrived at George Walker's Niagara Falls office around 10:00 A.M. on Valentine's Day, Sunday, February 14, 1993, to further discuss the issue of Karla's plea bargain, or as Segal preferred to call it, plea resolution.

Walker had a valentine for Segal. He told Segal in much greater detail about Karla's involvement with her sister's death and the fact that a lot of the sex acts with her sister, Leslie Mahaffy and Kristen French had been videotaped.

For his part, Segal was curious about a discrepancy: Walker's client maintained there were ten boxes of cement containing Leslie's body parts; the press had reported seven.

In fact, when the cement casket containing Mahaffy's torso was taken into account, there were eight cement blocks. Why was Karla Homolka adamant that there had been ten? Walker replied that, as Segal knew, the media was not known for accuracy, and his client was simply mistaken. Nevertheless, it still puzzled Segal. By noon, Mr. Segal and Ms. Fairburn were on their way to Beamsville for a meeting with senior members of the task force.

Inspector Bevan and Murray Segal had never met before. Segal outlined the discussions with Walker. He told the police something that Inspector Bevan did not know—that Karla was also involved with her sister's death.

Segal went over information that the task force already had. He brought up the embarrassing fact that Bevan and the entire task force had been chasing a phantom Camaro for almost a year. After the meeting, Murray Segal and Michal Fairburn were fully cognizant of the fact that Inspector Bevan had failed to link Paul Bernardo or Karla Homolka to the murders they had been so vigorously investigating.

After he dropped Marie off in Toronto on Sunday morning, Paul went up to Patrick Johnnie's garage. P.J. knew right away that Paul was under surveillance. The cop just sat across the road in his unmarked car. This guy was not even trying to be inconspicuous.

Patrick Johnnie and the boys who hung around the garage were used to seeing cops conspicuously parked around the area.

One of Johnnie's friends went across the street, and like the smart aleck he was, he sarcastically told the cop that it was Sunday, so he had better hang around because something really big was going to happen.

P.J. never had the slightest inkling that Paul Bernardo was a "skin beefer." Skin beefers were perverts, sexual deviates who hit on children. And that was pretty strange, because Patrick

Johnnie was normally hard to fool. That Sunday was the last time he saw Paul Bernardo.

Jim Hutton picked up Karla at the Segers' on Monday night. He took her back to his apartment on Steeles Avenue. She seemed a bit troubled, but that only made Jim want Karla more. They had sex repeatedly. Karla knew she had broken through at least one barrier. Jim let her stay overnight.

Karla told Jim that some terrible things had happened that she could not talk about. She told him that he would probably hear more about it in the next couple of days—in the news.

Jim was not really listening. To him, Karla was just a very nice, young girl with a flare for the melodramatic, like most girls, and a vivid imagination. He dropped her off in front of the Segers' apartment building on Tuesday morning.

There had been considerable tension between Inspector Bevan and Staff Inspector Steve Marrier over when to arrest Paul Bernardo. Marrier had wanted to pop him right away, in early February. His attitude was understandable. Science said Bernardo was the Scarborough rapist. As such, he was a menace to society.

Inspector Bevan had a different perspective. He had barely had time to assimilate his good fortune—Karla, and what the implications of a close relationship with her implied.

At that particular moment in time, the last thing Bevan wanted to do was arrest the husband before a deal with the wife was done. The longer Bernardo was free and under surveillance, the longer Inspector Bevan had to get his ducks in a row. With Bernardo still on the streets, but under heavy surveillance, who knew what else might turn up? The search warrants were still not completed.

The courage of Inspector Bevan's convictions was among the politicians at Queen's Park and the bureaucrats in the Crown's law office. Countless millions had been wasted on the task force—probably more than ten million dollars. Bernardo's arrest would be Bevan's call. They were going to do the deal with Karla—it had all been sketched out between himself, Segal and Walker—and then they would arrest Bernardo.

Bevan was waiting for that when Sue Sgambati happened. Sue was a big-eyed, petite blonde who worked for Global Television. According to Inspector Bevan, she had confronted him on Wednesday, February 17, and threatened the integrity of his investigation.

This particular blond media personality had a penchant for high, tight miniskirts and cowboy boots, which might partly explain why the inspector deigned to speak with her when he would not speak with anyone else associated with the media.

Bevan was bemused when Sgambati made her demand: either give the media some cogent information about what was going on—something they could use—or she was going to go to air that evening with what she knew.

To the inspector's chagrin, Sue Sgambati knew a lot. She knew they were watching someone and where that someone lived. If Bevan did not give them something to work with, she would report—in detail—that the Metropolitan Toronto Police were closely watching a Port Dalhousie man who was a prime suspect in the Scarborough rapes.

On February 17, Sergeant Mickey Riddle and Gary Beaulieu interviewed Norma Tellier and Jane Doe about their relationships with Paul and Karla.

Around noon hour, the detectives plucked Norma out of school and took her to a hotel room they had set up for interviewing. They wanted details about Karla's version of events.

"We'd like you to tell us in your own words—and with as much detail as possible—what you are aware of that has happened, what Karla may have told you that has happened, and nothing will shock us," Sergeant Riddle told the teenager. "Nothing will surprise us. We have studied greatly compliant victims, as far as people who are abused. Karla is an abused wife."

To comfort an obviously nervous Norma, Sergeant Riddle

earnestly told her that Paul Bernardo was the focus of their investigation.

"That man—I don't know what your feelings of him are at this time—has magical powers of some sort over individuals," he said. "We know that. Karla has lived a living hell for quite some time and we would not be surprised at anything she did under the powers of Paul Bernardo. . . ."

CHAPTER

twenty-five

Inspector Bevan called the arrest team together at 3:00 P.M. and told them the investigation had been compromised by the media and that Bernardo had to be arrested before the evening news. Nobody felt properly prepared. Even though the inspector did not have Karla Homolka's deal in his back pocket, he now saw Bernardo's quick arrest as a way to put it there more quickly.

Detective Irwin had eschewed collaboration with Sergeant

Beaulieu on their interviewing techniques for his voluminous search warrant. He had been working on it night and day since early February and it still was not finished.

The two police officers who arrived at Bernardo's door were definitely pumped. Detective Kelly from the Metropolitan Toronto Police force and Constable Symonds from the Green Ribbon Task Force walked up to Bernardo's front door at 4:00 P.M. The blinds were drawn. Bernardo answered the door. He was dressed in white sweatpants and a black t-shirt.

Kelly cuffed Bernardo and read him his rights on the three Scarborough rapes that carried conclusive DNA evidence. Constable Symonds searched him. The constable placed Bernardo under arrest for the murders of Leslie Mahaffy and Kristen French, as well as for the sexual assault of Cheryl Jenkins on Henley Island. There was as yet no evidence, except Karla's word, to support any of those charges. Constable Symonds also arrested Bernardo for the rape of Norma Tellier, a tenuous charge that would probably have collapsed if it had been tested.

Bernardo asked to call his lawyer. Instead of following his instructions to allow Bernardo to call his lawyer from the house, Kelly demurred and said it would be easier if Bernardo called once they got to the police station. Kelly said he did not feel he could uncuff him and give Bernardo privacy—which was his right.

At 4:42 P.M. Constable Symonds and Detective Kelly escorted Bernardo through the security garage at the Halton Regional Police Headquarters in Oakville and into the prop room.

The prop room was the Major Crimes squad room, redecorated for Paul Bernardo's sake. It was supposed to provide what FBI profiler John Douglas called "the high ass-pucker factor."

All twenty-eight drawers in a black filing cabinet along the left wall were labeled in large, readable black letters with such things as FORENSIC EXHIBITS A, B, C. Above the cabinet there was a map of Scarborough with colored pins marking the location of each rape. Close by, with large, readable letters, was a BERNARDO & HOMOLKA FAMILY TREE poster that had obviously been prepared with great care.

There was also an assignment board:

Team	Assignments	Results
3	B Surveillance	Pending
4	Witness Statement	Synopsis
5	USPolice Liaison	Continuing
2	Scarborough Map	Sent to forensics
	Exhibit	Toronto
1	FBI Profile	On-going
6	Hair & Fibre	Rec'd bk from lab in
		Prop vault
x8x	DNA Match	Moon
		Chenier
		Thompson

Another wall-size chart listed the names of fifteen victims of the Scarborough rapist, the locations of the attacks, the dates, time and DNA results.

On the wall next to that chart there were two blowups of a fingerprint, labelled W and X, then a series of pictures of Bernardo's Nissan 240SX shot from different angles, surrounded by four or five paragraphs of typescript concerning the car, with the heading, BERNARDO'S VEHICLE—1989 NISSAN 660 HFH.

Between the two exhibits there was a washroom. The washroom door had been deliberately left open. The closed door next to the bathroom was labeled Polygraph Room.

On a nearby desk there was Norma Tellier's Tasmanian Devil t-shirt, a poster from the Little Mermaid movie, and the stuffed toy Paul had given her, partially covered by a plastic bag. A gray-beige telephone had a yellow tape label, which read Scarborough Rapist.

There were large bristol-board projects devoted to Bernardo's associates, and Paul Bernardo's family tree, with connecting lines, photographs and captions.

Just outside of Interview Room 2, which was Bernardo's destination, were the Child Find photos of Kristen and Leslie, a picture of Paul, a newspaper clipping and the Scarborough rapist composite drawing. In the corner was the pièce de résistance: a life-size mannequin dressed like Kristen French, complete with a torn Kettle Creek bag.

The mannequin wore a long black wig and was missing one loafer. It was obvious that a great deal of time and effort had gone into the prop room. Detective Irwin had even proposed that they try and get Karla as a live prop, but according to Inspector Bevan, that idea was a bit premature.

The idea was to lead Bernardo through the room—quickly—and weaken his resolve. However, if Bernardo was the classic psychopath and sexual sadist the articles and the psychiatric consultants and American law-enforcement people said he was, the prop room would have the opposite effect. It would flatter and empower a man who had the psychopathological profile that Dr. Peter Collins and Inspector Ron MacKay had described. If Bernardo's interview was any indication, exposure to the prop room did just that.

When Staff Sergeant Murray MacLeod and Constable Richard Ciszek entered the house, Buddy came running, madly wagging his stub of a tail, and did what he always did when he met new people—pissed all over the floor. Constable Ciszek put Buddy on a leash, brought in the Humane Society attendant, who had been waiting outside in a van, and sent Buddy straight to the pound.

Sergeant Beaulieu was so excited he had left all his notes and files back at the task-force headquarters in Beamsville. Detective Irwin seized the moment.

"Do you remember me, Paul?" Irwin asked.

"No," Bernardo said flatly.

"Picked lint off his pants," scribbled Beaulieu on his notepad. Irwin was immediately vexed.

Paul slouched in the chair, his right leg crossed over his left knee. He appeared heavily bored. He was not about to admit to Irwin that he remembered him. Paul wanted to know when he would get something to eat. He wanted to call his lawyer.

Irwin told him to wait until they covered a couple of things—they wanted to go over the charges again, to make sure that he had been properly read his rights and understood his circumstances.

"You got married, June?" Irwin asked.

"You know that. June 29, 1991," Bernardo replied.

They moved on to the honeymoon in Hawaii. Irwin and Beaulieu had been told by the consultants that it would be good to quickly establish they had information they would not otherwise have without Karla's cooperation. "Was there an incident? Something about the camera?"

Bernardo looked at Irwin incredulously. "No comment."

"No comment?"

"No."

"When you gave her a swat for dropping it, was that because you were angry at her or yourself, or just some frustration coming out?" Irwin saw something flash in Bernardo's eyes, so he decided to push it.

"No comment."

"No comment?" Time to segue. "How did you feel when you hit her on the fifth of last month? You said 'no comment' earlier, but we've opened that door up and you've talked . . ."

"I said that I probably would get, you know, convicted of it . . . and that's because, in domestic disputes, the girls usually win," Paul explained, pausing to pick at the ever more elusive pieces of lint on his track pants. "That's just a common thing."

"So what about it, how did you feel when you hit her?" Irwin was encouraged by Bernardo's candor and verbosity.

While he and Beaulieu drove from Beamsville to Halton, they had reviewed what they had learned in a seminar on interviewing techniques. Particularly appealing to the two officers was the "ninety-five/five" interviewing technique.

The idea was to let the suspect to do 95 percent of the

talking, and both Irwin and Beaulieu agreed that was exactly what they would try to achieve with Bernardo. This discussion about the assault charge was the first indication that Bernardo might just accommodate them. Bernardo let out another long sigh and looked at the ceiling.

Irwin pushed: "Isn't there some emotion there, Paul?"

"No comment."

"I would feel pretty shitty if I . . ."

"No comment."

"Hit someone."

"No comment."

"No comment?" Irwin's voice carried his mounting frustration. So much for the ninety-five/five technique.

"Okay, tell me, what's a safe ground to talk to you about? Some things you don't mind talking to us about and other things this 'no comment' phrase comes up. Give us some clues about what you want to talk about. I just wanna hear a little bit about you."

"Well I'm not in a conversational mood right now," Paul said matter-of-factly.

"No?"

"Why would I be?" Bernardo fixed Irwin briefly with his baby blues.

"I don't know. Certainly neither one of us should be, but here we are. It's human nature to talk to people. We're living beings that are able to communicate on such a high level . . ."

Bernardo cut him off. "Except for maybe dolphins and whales. They communicate on a high level."

"Yeah," said Detective Irwin, lost in aspirations about ninety-five/five.

"Monkeys can learn up to five hundred words," Bernardo said.

"But not as many as the thousands and thousands . . ." Irwin retorted. Bernardo cut him off again.

"No. No. Exactly. You're right," he said.

"So, to communicate and talk is a natural thing?" Irwin asked.

"Certainly," Paul noddingly agreed.

Irwin glanced at Beaulieu, but the sergeant was busy scribbling notes. The element of surprise can be very effective in these kinds of interviews, they had been told. Non sequiturs work.

"Certainly, that's why we're here. To communicate and talk," Irwin agreed amicably. "Just out of curiosity. Why did you start having sex with Tammy?"

"No comment."

At quarter to eight there was a knock on the interview room door. Irritated by the interruption, Irwin answered it. Detective Sergeant Waller gestured for him to come out. When he did, the older officer confronted the young detective. He told Detective Irwin that he was off the interview strategy.

Irwin pushed past him and went into the outer offices. He looked to his superior, Staff Inspector Steve Marrier. Marrier gave him a thumbs-up.

Cops and consultants were gathered around two video monitors. Inspector Ron Mackay, the RCMP profiler, was there as were Dr. Peter Collins from the Clarke Institute in Toronto and Special Agent Chuck Wagner from the FBI in Buffalo.

One of the few police officers in Canada trained as a profiler by Behavioral Sciences at Quantico, Inspector MacKay was a tall, white-haired, laconic man.

Dr. Collins was Abbott to Mackay's Costello. A forensic psychiatrist, Dr. Collins was a short, stocky guy with a balding dome, rimmed by thinning dark hair. Dr. Collins's claim to fame was reconstructing and interpreting the fantasy life of psychopathic sex killers. He and Inspector Mackay seemed to go everywhere together. Detective Sergeant Smollet was still there, as was Jim Kelly, one of the arresting officers.

With a quarter of a century behind the badge, Waller was a large man with a rotund face who had a penchant for brown suits. He had been working with Inspector Bevan since the beginning.

Waller had little use for the two Steves—Marrier and Irwin—from Toronto. In the end, it was science, not prescience or police work, that had fingered Bernardo, and now the two Steves were swaggering around as if they had solved the crime of the century.

Another Toronto cop, Ron Whitefield, handed Steve Irwin a bunch of papers on which questions for Bernardo had been scribbled by Inspector Mackay and Dr. Collins.

The fact that Irwin had seized control of this interview was irksome. The real issue was the murders, not a bunch of rapes in the sprawling suburban nightmare of Scarborough. All Detective Irwin's victims were alive. He had had his chance and blew it. Nor had Irwin alerted anybody that a prime suspect in a series of major crimes was on the move and headed in their direction.

Since Bernardo had moved to St. Catharines in February, 1991, for one reason or another the police in Niagara had run him through CPIC seventeen times. How different the response might have been if Irwin had only bothered to enter Paul Bernardo's name in the system.

Irwin made a point of methodically retrieving messages from his pager. He gathered some reports and notes and returned to the interview room. Waller tried to talk to him again, but Irwin was not about to be advised.

As Detective Irwin came in, Bernardo asked to go to the bathroom and was taken out by Beaulieu.

When Inspector Bevan finally entered the Major Crime office, Waller was waiting for him. Waller knew that Bevan had visited the French and Mahaffy families first, but he had not expected it to take as long as it had.

Halton was midway between Toronto and Niagara; they had better audio-visual facilities than the task force or the Niagara Regional Police, and Bevan, always politic, saw it as another good compromise to arrange for Bernardo to be interviewed there.

It was 8:30 P.M. They had been grilling Bernardo since 4:45

P.M. Because Bernardo had not been allowed to call a lawyer, anything they got would be inadmissible.

Inspector Bevan watched the monitor while Waller talked to him. According to Waller, Marrier had said that the Toronto police never stopped interviews just because the suspect asked for a lawyer—he had to refuse to answer questions and demand a lawyer. Marrier said there was "case law" to back them up. If that were the case, why had Marrier not raised it during the many discussions they had had on this very issue over the past ten days?

Then Marrier told Bevan that he actually agreed with Waller—the interview was probably a bust but they might as well let it go, because it would be good for Inspector Mackay and Dr. Collins to get a better read on Bernardo.

Waller recalled Marrier's recalcitrance. The task force had politely asked if he would be prepared to delay Toronto's arrest so the task force could build up evidence. His response had been "less than enthusiastic." And now that Bevan had been forced to pop Bernardo prematurely—earlier than Inspector Bevan had wanted to, before the deal with Karla Homolka was done—nothing would surprise Waller.

Inspector Bevan knew there had been problems with the arrest—he should probably not have instructed his officers to charge Bernardo with the murders. But Bevan agreed with Staff Inspector Marrier about one thing. Even if the interview was totally bungled, it did not really make any difference. Short of a full and complete confession, nothing Bernardo said was going to change the course of history. It was the DNA in Scarborough and the evidence given by his wife in St. Catharines that would put the nails in Mr. Bernardo's coffin.

Bevan had barely said a word during Waller's diatribe. When Waller was through, the inspector simply asked Waller if he could use his office to make a couple of phone calls. That was one of the qualities that inspired loyalty in men such as Detective Sergeant Waller.

Fifteen or twenty minutes later, Waller watched Bevan emerge from his office and approach Inspector Mackay, Dr. Collins and Chuck Wagner. They talked briefly and then Bevan sat down to watch some more of the interview for himself. One minute Irwin was asking Bernardo about what jobs he had as a teenager, the next he was on about rap music. The interview was obviously out of control. The inspector watched Bernardo yawn, pick lint from his pants, cross and recross his legs, yawn again, slouch, sigh. The guy was bored stiff and making a mockery of Detective Irwin—who was indeed dominating the interview—and the whole process.

Bevan heard Sergeant Beaulieu identify singer Cris Cross as "the guy who wore his pants backwards," and smiled.

After five minutes of watching the detective's talk show, the inspector left the building. Over the hour he had been there, Bevan had barely said a word. By ten o'clock he was back at his desk in Beamsville, working on his search warrant.

As Bevan left the building, Detective Irwin came out of the interview room again. Marrier told him he was doing a good job. Irwin asked Marrier about Bernardo's repeated requests for a lawyer. Marrier told him not to worry.

"He's a classic psychopath," Dr. Collins and Inspector Mackay told him. "There's no point in trying to appeal to his conscience," Dr. Collins said, gesticulating to make his point. "He doesn't have one."

Irwin went back to the interview with instructions to emphasize Bernardo's "failures," and a distinct impression that there was no great urgency in arranging a lawyer for Paul Bernardo.

"You used a term 'looping' before," Sergeant Beaulieu observed. "What do you mean by that?" Beaulieu was well aware of Lori Homolka's Christmas story and how strange she had found Bernardo, the way he had talked about birth, death and "looping," which she assumed to be a mystical Masonic theory that devalued the importance of individual life or whatever. Basically, Lori thought, it demonstrated that Paul was crazy and he had put her poor sister under some spell during which Karla was made to commit all those horrible crimes.

"Looping. You take a beat and you repeat that beat—you know, like a computer analyst would."

"What do you mean, a computer analyst would?"

"Oh, if I put a beat on track, say something goes da-da-da-da-da-da . . . What it would do is repeat that point because it's all digital and wavelengths . . ."

"Mm-hmm?"

"To repeat that beat, so go 'da-da-da-da-da-da-da-da,' and then on for as long as your memory would . . ." Bernardo coughed ". . . your computer memory could hold it." Bernardo cleared his throat. "Basically, because you would go on forever . . ." Bernardo suffered from allergies and took antihistamines all the time. He was starting to get congested.

"You would go on forever?" asked Beaulieu incredulously. Neither Irwin nor Beaulieu had a clue what Bernardo was talking about.

"Yes, it's like an error. In one of your computer programs. I don't know if you ever took that in school—it goes around and around and around. It just doesn't exit . . . it's just a term in music."

"How long have you been working on this album of yours?" Beaulieu asked. He was about to follow Dr. Collins's sage advice and emphasize a Bernardo failure.

"I said before, a year, year and a half—part-time, full-time."

"Did you ever enter negotiations with a recording company?"

"No," Bernardo replied. "Not yet."

"Do you expect to?"

"Hope to. Hope to, I mean soon . . ."

"What state of completion are you in, if you had to guess?"

"Oh, see, a lot of it's in my mind, you know, because you have a song and you know what you know—what beat's going to go in that song, like, what the song's about and blah, blah, blah, and then it's a lot of preparation time, you know. If you wanna be a writer you gotta go into love songs and pull out how people feel, you know. And you can't just say, 'There, I love you,' and walk on the beach. You have to be able to put it in an image-type scenario, where you walk on the beach and through the sand, hand in hand. So I've done the research into other people's songs and pulled out their best images and I spend a lot of time doing that. Plus, it's a lot of rhyming and stuff like that, so I spend a lot of time putting words that rhyme together, you know, so I can sit here and say, instead of saying 'rap,' say, rhymes with, say, 'back,' or something like that, you can sit there and have a whole page of what rhymes. I have a rhyme book, too, to back that up. The rhyme book is not as detailed as what I . . ." Beaulieu interrupted him.

"Do you have anything recorded or is it all up here?" Beaulieu pointed to his head. Irwin and Beaulieu looked at each other and stifled a grin.

"It's basically all up here in my head. You know, I've done some speaking over another person's song, you know? I worked hard on it."

"You worked hard on it?"

"Yeah."

"Are you going to take Norma with you when you go on tour?"

"Oh, yeah, but we don't talk to Norma anymore. We don't talk to Norma. I haven't talked to anybody since my wife left me."

As the evening wore on and the detectives were getting no-where, they started to become more specific about the murders. Beaulieu asked Bernardo what he used to mix the cement.

"What cement?"

"For Leslie."

Bernardo cleared his throat. "No comment. I didn't mix any cement for Leslie, so no comment."

"Another one of your failures. Goes back to all these things in life you screwed up but good, because it crumbled and fell apart and up came her body. And that's how we found her. Think a man like you would be a little bit brighter, if you read the instructions."

"If I was to mix cement, I would read the instructions."
"Yeah?"
"Yeah."
"And follow them?"
"I read instructions when I cook spaghetti or rice."

It was almost midnight and no one was any the wiser. Detective Irwin and Sergeant Beaulieu had almost exhausted their resources and the collective resources of their observers and consultants. They had one last trick up their sleeve.

"Do you believe what you're here for?" Detective Irwin asked. "Do you actually know what's going on?"

Bernardo laughed. "Yeah."

"Tomorrow they're going to do a press conference, 10:00 A.M."

"There you go," Bernardo said perfunctorily.

"What do you think they should say about you?"

Snickering, Bernardo said, "Well, I don't know."

"You want to see what they said tonight on the news about you?" When Waller had knocked on the door again just a few minutes earlier, he told them that he had obtained a videotape copy of the evening news and the shrinks thought it might be an interesting experiment to show it to Bernardo.

"It doesn't matter to me," Bernardo said, but the look on his face said differently. Irwin just stared at him. "It doesn't matter to me," Bernardo repeated.

"I've got a TV right outside to show you," Detective Irwin nodded toward the door.

"Doesn't matter to me," Bernardo said again.

"Did you want to see it?"

"No," Paul finally admitted. "Why would I want to see something like that?"

"I do. I want to see it," Sergeant Beaulieu said.

"Because then you'll know that we're not bullshitting," Irwin declared.

"Well, I mean, if you weren't bullshitting, I wouldn't be here." Beaulieu and Irwin stood up.

Waller opened the door. "Let's turn it on," Irwin said.

"Thanks, Bob." Irwin said to Bob Waller. Irwin and Beaulieu got up and stood in the doorway. Irwin motioned to Bernardo to come over to the doorway. He reluctantly got up and shuffled over. They had finally given him a drink of water and ordered some pizza. Bernardo had a cold piece of pizza in his hand. "Do you want to see this, Paul?"

"No . . ." and the television screen flickered to life. While Bernardo's eyes were riveted on the screen, all other eyes were on him.

Over a series of fast cuts, showing Bernardo being led from the house and pictures of Leslie Mahaffy and Kristen French and the recovery sites at Lake Gibson and Sideroad One, a voice came up: "Overwhelmed with relief . . . A twenty-eight-year old man is in custody, charged with the abduction and murder of Kristen French and Leslie Mahaffy. And as our crime specialist, Sue Sgambati, reports, the accused is also suspected in a series of sexual assaults in the Toronto area." Cut to Sue Sgambati, the heavily mascaraed blonde Inspector Bevan said had forced his hand.

"The man in custody is twenty-eight-year-old Paul Bernardo," announced Sgambati. "He was arrested late in the afternoon at the St. Catharines home he rented with a female companion."

She went on to give the particulars of the arrests. Then the scene cut to an old man who looked to be in his late seventies. "This man lives next door to the suspect," said Sgambati.

"I always thought there was something shady there," said old Ernie England. "Which, as I said to my daughter, I don't know what the . . . how the guy pays his rent, a thousand dollars, twelve hundred dollars a month, and he never leaves the house."

Sue Sgambati gave an abbreviated history of the murders and then the camera cut to footage of Doug French sitting in his living room, making the appeal for his daughter's life that Paul and Karla had watched at the Homolkas that Easter Sunday when they went over for dinner: "Kristen, if you are to hear this . . ." said Mr. French, looking directly into the camera, his anguish abundantly apparent. ". . . We'd like you to know that we're thinking of you and everything that can be done is being done, and we'll get you back."

Sgambati concluded by saying, "This investigation has been a roller-coaster ride for the police and it is not over yet. They are still searching for a second suspect. In addition to the murder charges, Bernardo faces sixteen counts of sexual assault in Toronto. Sue Sgambati, Global News. Toronto."

"Reality," Detective Irwin solemnly pronounced. Bernardo had been dramatically affected by seeing himself on television. After eight hours, Inspector Mackay and Dr. Collins were suddenly hyperalert. It had been a stroke of genius to videotape and replay that news broadcast. Seeing himself on television seemed to somehow validate the reality of his predicament and Bernardo was visibly affected. Irwin started to move in for the kill.

"Very real," Irwin repeated. It was difficult for Detective Irwin to contain himself. The past eight hours had been fantasy, a prelude. In spite of himself he repeated it again, "Very real."

"Yeah," came the faint reply. Bernardo was close to tears. Now, for the coup de grace.

"So, your dear old grandmother . . . I hope she didn't see the ten o'clock news." They had already discussed how close he felt to his grandparents, and how his Granny Eastman was still alive and always watched the evening news.

"Nothing I can do if the news put out stuff on me," Bernardo replied, sniveling, petulant, feeling sorry for himself.

"No, no. You're right." Irwin said.

"We didn't do it. They did it . . ." Beaulieu added solicitously. Bernardo was choking back tears and could barely speak.

"All the same . . ."

"This is your chance, Paul—let's go," Irwin's entire effort was about to be vindicated. He had him.

"Huh?"

"Let's deal with it now. It's time. Paul. You can't go on. You can't sit back there and remove yourself," Irwin explained, forgetting why Bernardo was affected, doing that which they had been advised against, trying to appeal to his better nature, his conscience.

"Well . . ." Bernardo blinked a couple of times, rubbed his eyes and sniffed.

"You can't. You have to sit . . ." Watching him closely, Irwin realized he was starting to regroup.

"Oh," Bernardo said, as if he were seeing Beaulieu and Irwin again for the first time.

"And look at everything. In fact, now more than ever."

"No," Bernardo said emphatically. "No comment, and now I want to see a lawyer, and I think I should have a right to do that. . . ."

But Beaulieu just would not give up. "Did you see that poor man on television," he asked, referring to Doug French? "Doesn't that appeal to some sense of decency and honesty inside you? Doesn't it?"

"Well, I have no comment," Bernardo said resolutely.

"Paul. What are you gonna do?" Irwin said quietly. "Are you going to spend your life avoiding everything? You gonna run from everything? Eh? Are you gonna run? There's nowhere more to run."

"Well, that's what you're saying," Bernardo exclaimed.

"That's right." Irwin felt like a surgeon with a dying patient.

"No comment."

"It's time, Paul . . ."

"It's time to say 'no comment.' "

"It's time?" Irwin was stunned. The guy was like a possum-playing boxer.

"No, no comment."

"Who's the second person?" Irwin asked, changed tack.

"No comment."

"Eh? Yeah, we know who it is. We've already talked about it. We know. What do you think's gonna happen to you?"

"Don't know, pal. Don't know what you're going to be putting me through, so . . ."

"I'm not your pal," Irwin said indignantly. Now Bernardo had his goat.

"Well, I just see myself on the news like that. Whew! Sorry, but that's, ah, you know, you just sit there and you look at that, it's like, agh, agh, you know? It's unbelievable but . . ." Bernardo explained. There had been no response to his request for a lawyer. Bernardo well knew they had run out of time a long time earlier and now they were just dancing the night away.

"It's unbelievable that a person can do that?" Beaulieu asked.

"No, it's unbelievable that I'm portrayed as that. But . . ." Bernardo felt compelled to try and clarify his meaning.

"Where's your decency, man? Where's your honesty?" It was very difficult for the average man to accept that another seemingly normal man was capable of such horrendous acts of consummate evil, without any sense of remorse or guilt.

Knowing he had Beaulieu's goat, Bernardo decided to flog it a bit. "Well, I've been telling you honesty and whatever . . . Obviously it's going to go to trial. Well, let's do that because . . ."

"There's no alternative, we're definitely gonna do that," Beaulieu pronounced.

"You know, I'm not going to sit here and admit to something I didn't do, just because you guys arrested me and threw me on the newscast and stuff."

"Are you subhuman?" Beaulieu demanded. He was a decent man, with three young daughters. "What runs in your veins?" he asked.

For more than eight hours, Bernardo had sighed, sniffed, coughed, snickered, whined, picked lint, crossed and uncrossed his legs. Once more he sighed. "No more comment. No more comment."

"And you're doing exactly what we expected, just what the FBI profile told us," Irwin said, sanguinely.

"Whatever," Bernardo shrugged and went back to the lint on his pants.

"And you know what?"

"What?"

"We appreciate it. Because what'll happen is the jury will see it and the parole board, down the road, will see this guy who now suddenly claims to have remorse. But there is none now. And so you'll put the act on down there. They won't believe you . . . you'll end up further and further in deep, dark dungeons. That's where your life is gonna be, Paul."

"Oh." Now Detective Irwin was doing some more of it—talking for the sake of hearing himself talk.

"Somewhere down the road, when you go before the parole board, they'll look back over everything and they'll say there was no remorse. You're just like an animal trapped in a corner. Backed in a corner aren't you? Dead, tight in a corner. There's no way out. We told you we're not happy with Karla. . . ." Irwin declared.

"No?" Now that Irwin mentioned it, Bernardo did not think they had told him that.

"Karla has something to do with this," Irwin declared, stating the obvious.

"Whatever," Bernardo said.

"She's the best rat we've ever had. It just happened to happen because your DNA matched in Scarborough and matched another profile from out here. Karla got found at the right time."

Bernardo stifled a big yawn and then sighed again. Looking at Beaulieu, he asked, "What was your name again?"

"Beaulieu." Then the sergeant spelled it. "B-E-A-U-L-I-E-U."

"French-Canadian, isn't it?" Bernardo asked, with what appeared to be genuine curiosity.

"What about it?" Beaulieu asked belligerently.

Ignoring Beaulieu, Bernardo looked at Irwin and said, "What was your name again?"

Paul Bernardo's departure that night around 12:45 A.M. was the last contact he and Detective Steve Irwin would have. Irwin's bird had refused the wrist once and for all and was gone. Driven to the East Detention Center in Scarborough by two Toronto cops, Bernardo arrived around 1:30 A.M. By the time he got to court the next morning, the lawyer with whom Patrick Johnnie had put in him touch stood beside him. They waived the reading of the charges. Paul was remanded in custody. His appearance lasted approximately sixty seconds. This particular lawyer was destined not to last much longer than the appearance. He would soon be replaced by a lawyer from Aurora, Ontario, named Ken Murray.

Coincidence prevailed. Two Bernardos were before the Scarborough court that day. February 18 was also Ken Bernardo's sentencing date. Prosecutors looked at each other, stunned. The police looked at each other with amazement. The media went wild.

Paul had known what was going down with his father—he had written that letter at the end of January—but nobody else did. Before the judge remanded Ken Bernardo to another date, he sealed Ken Bernardo's file. There was no public good to be served, in the judge's estimation, by learning what infamy had brought the father before him that sad morning. In the judge's opinion, Paul Bernardo's charges were quite sufficient to satiate the prurient tastes of the unwashed hordes.

Jim Hutton was still in a state of shock when he picked up the phone. Karla wanted to know his feelings. He felt betrayed, as if he had been used as a "comforter," but he did not tell her that.

Jim could not imagine that Karla would ever be mixed up in anything such as the Mahaffy and French killings; she was such a sweet girl. But he had no idea what to say to her. He mumbled.

Karla was really concerned that Jim would hate her, but he said he did not hate her—that she was a victim too. Jim tried to offer her some comfort and support.

Karla had really wanted to talk to Jim about the whole thing, but her lawyers told her not to. Karla said she wanted to keep their relationship going, but Jim just said that it was pretty obvious she had her hands full.

Karla was so lonely, she told Jim. She wanted to see people, but it was like she was already in prison, with all the media and everything. Jim tried to reassure her that her lawyers would look out for her and that he would talk to her soon. She sent Jim a Polaroid. In the Polaroid her breasts were exposed and there was that "devilish glint in her eye." Jim wondered who had taken the picture.

. . .

Karla was upset. She showed up at George Walker's office for her appointment at 2:30 P.M. on February 19. The media were onto her—the facts that she wanted immunity and was represented by George Walker had been published. Her parents were beside themselves. Her new boyfriend in Brampton did not want to talk to her.

She and Walker talked about Bernardo's arrest and his arraignment in Scarborough and how bizarre it had been, his father being in the same court at the same time.

What was that all about? Walker wanted to know. Karla told him that Paul's old man was a real nut case, but she really did not know all the details. It probably had to do with Paul's sister, Debbie. The papers had said the charges were twenty years old.

The fact that Paul's old man was a deviant did nothing to hurt their position.

"This is only going to get worse," Walker told Karla.

Later in the day Murray Segal called and advised Walker that the search warrants had been executed. Now that the police were in the house, Segal might not have the authority to stay in communication. Walker was poised. Segal wanted the deal as badly as Walker did. For some reason, they seemed to want it even more after Bernardo's arrest.

Norma Tellier gave Karla a friendship ring and an anklet.

"On Saturday, Cheryl Jenkins's father brought home a Toronto paper. Paul and Karla's wedding pictures were on the front page.

Cheryl had just turned seventeen. She had been in a terrible car accident on her way to a rowing regatta in Georgia the previous year and she still was not right.

The paper had been folded up when her father brought it in. When she opened it, she almost got sick to her stomach. There was the man who had raped her. It was his picture on the front page, beside his blushing bride, Karla Homolka. Cheryl knew

Karla Homolka. Tammy Lyn Homolka had actually been a
friend of Cheryl's. She had attended the memorial for Tammy
Lyn at Sir Winston Churchill Secondary School in early January, 1991, with Norma Tellier, three months before Paul Bernardo raped her.

CHAPTER

twenty-six

"Could you go shopping for me?" Dorothy Homolka pleaded. "I just can't go out this soon after his arrest."

Lynn McCann had seen Dorothy Homolka discommoded before. Only the night before, for instance, just after they had learned that Paul had been arrested. The Homolkas had known his arrest was pending—they had been forewarned—but for people like them, unless they saw it on television it had not really happened.

There was their son-in-law, their beloved "weekend son," handcuffed, hunched over, with the hood of his parka pulled up over his head, stooped between two plainclothes police officers as they led him across the front lawn of that nice pink clapboard house where the Homolkas had spent so many happy hours— every hour on the hour, on every channel.

While Lynn was at the Homolkas' house, a teenage girl— whom Lynn later found out was Norma Tellier—came over with her mother. Norma's mother had a different last name; Lynn did not catch the woman's first name.

Norma, who appeared to be very upset, told Dorothy that Paul had raped her. Lynn could not quite get a fix on Norma or the situation. Norma had been Tammy Lyn's best friend. When Paul raped Norma, Karla was asleep in the guest bedroom. She knew Paul was going to do it, but there was nothing Karla could do, according to Norma. None of it made any sense to Lynn.

Norma told Dorothy that she had already told Lori everything in detail. Then she and Lori had both told Karla, while Karla was still in the hospital. Karla had told them to forget it, so Lori had torn up her notes. If Karla said to forget it, Dorothy decided, then that was what Norma should do.

After Norma and her mother left, Dorothy said Karla was going to make a lot of money on the books that would be written about her.

"Karla will be very wealthy when she gets out," Dorothy declared, sipping her drink.

But Lynn was still surprised to get this latest call. Dorothy never missed work. She had even come back right after her youngest daughter had been buried. Dorothy could easily have taken a week or two of bereavement leave. Instead, she had told everybody at the Shaver that she wanted to get back to work because Paul, who was living with them, was so down about Tammy it was difficult to watch, and Lori was just moping around the house.

Lynn agreed to go shopping for Dorothy. She left work, picked up Lori Homolka and went to the A&P. She bought groceries and took them back to the Homolkas' house. When she got there Dorothy and Karel were sitting at the kitchen table, half drunk, laughing and joking around. They never bothered to thank or reimburse her.

The police finally executed the search warrants and entered the house in Port Dalhousie late in the day on February 19. A crime-scene analysis of this magnitude was like an archaeological dig. The object was much the same as well—knowledge about the past through artifacts.

Like the site of a dig, the house was divided into a grid, whose hundreds of individual sections were all assigned numbers. Using laser lights, metal detectors, high-powered industrial vacuums, jackhammers and plain old magnifying glasses, the I-dent officers began to collect all manner of visible and invisible artifacts such as wall spots, fingerprints, flakes of skin, hairs, fibers and various unidentified dried secretions. Everything that came out of the house had a number and a grid designation. The number of exhibits would eventually exceed a thousand.

Outfitted in sterile white suits that made them look like Ebola fighters, the identification officers felt and acted like the heroes of Raiders of the Lost Ark.

Inspector Bevan toured the site and was shown numerous marks that appeared to be blood spots on the walls; there were newspaper clippings related to the crimes, test tubes with curious contents.

They found a chronological list of all the Scarborough rapes, with Detective Steve Irwin's card attached. It was handwritten on a pad of legal-size paper. There were detailed descriptions of the attacks and the various suspects' descriptions, including eight dates in reverse order from May 4, 1987, through May 26, 1990. Beside each date the main intersection nearest the assault was noted—in a different second script that looked very much like Karla's. The house that Paul and Karla had occupied was no Ark, but it was a forensic treasure trove.

Paul Bernardo was not only a sexual deviate, rapist and murderer; he was also a pack rat. It appeared that he had kept every scrap of paper, every receipt, every note, letter and photograph that had ever come into his possession. He had kept the security guard's uniform he wore when he worked at the Hospital for Sick Children during his university days. In the bedroom closet they found a brown paper bag full of soiled women's panties. Spike the iguana's skin was in the garage.

The cops discovered a cache of what they had been told by the FBI was predictable reading material for a sexual deviant. Books with titles such as *Suffer the Children, Punish the Sinner, Flowers in the Attic, Dark Angel, The Funhouse, The Fury, Fallen Hearts, Perfect Victim, In Broad Daylight, A Deadly Silence, Lisa, Hedda and Joel, In His Garden, The Violent Year of Maggie Mac-Donald, Ritual Abuse, Bitter Blood, A Killing in the Family, Across the Boarder, The I-5 Killer, Who Killed Cindy James?, Masquerade, The Ultimate Evil, Childgrave, Small Sacrifices, Teacher's Pet, The Anarchist's Cookbook, Petals in the Wind, When the Wind Blows, Life with Billy, Poisoned Blood* and *The Confessions of Henry Lee Lucas.*

Henry Lee Lucas was suspected of as many as five hundred murders between 1951 to 1983. He was convicted of nine. After being released from prison for the murder of his mother, he teamed up with another psychopathic killer named Otis Toole, whose mother called him "the devil's child."

The book about Toole, *Devil Child,* was there as well. After Toole introduced Henry Lee to satanism, Lucas became a member of a religious cult and practiced necrophilia. Toole was serving a life sentence in Starke, Florida.

All of these books and many others were about violent sexual crime, criminals and victims, the occult, ritual and wife abuse. From the research done by Special Agents John Douglas, Roy Hazelwood and Robert Resslor and their psychiatric consultant, Dr. Park Dietz, the FBI had determined that 83 percent of the men maintained collections of items related to sexual or violent themes or both.

There were hundreds of books, including a well-marked copy of *The Compendium of Pharmaceuticals and Specialities, 22nd Edition,* with Halcion and halothane marked in highlighter, and a copy of *American Psycho* under Karla's side of the bed.

Two loose items jammed in the copy of *American Psycho* by

American writer Bret Easton Ellis were a thin book review clipped from a Toronto newspaper, entitled "Book a Sad Comment on Our Society: *American Psycho* is Sicko," and a receipt from WaldenBooks in upper New York State, dated April 17, 1991, 8:50 P.M.

Detective Constable Mike Demeester from the Green Ribbon Task Force was sent home to review *American Psycho:* His report read in part, "Patrick Bateman is 26, blond, handsome 'yuppie' who spends more time on facials, workouts, lunch than at work. Bateman is very image-conscious. 'Boy next door' kind of image. Tries to impress his friends with money; feels that most women are attracted to him; drinks scotch and uses cocaine. Uses Halcion to help him sleep; has a beautiful girlfriend; he treats her and other women as objects . . . enjoys the grief he causes victims' families and friends; sexually degrades women by having them perform oral sex after anal intercourse; ideal woman—good-looking, satisfies sexual desires and keeps her mouth shut; videos his girlfriend making love to another female; collects pornographic books and videos such as *Lesbian Vibrator Bitches, Inside Lydia's Ass, Cunt on Cunt,* and his favorite movie, *Body Double.* Scene where power drill used on woman; makes obscene phone calls; knowledgeable about Son of Sam, Ted Bundy, Hillside Strangler and Ed Gein.

"Some of the scenes in the book depict the forcing of a can of hair spray into one victim's vagina; torturing victims with fire, coat hangers, power-nail gun, inserts a rat into a living victim's vagina, dismembering a victim prior to death . . .

"Uses mace, gloves, knives, electric chainsaw, scissors, silencers, power drills, and eats parts of some victims, raw or cooked. Kills both men and women, homeless, prostitutes, friends, and ex-girlfriend. . . . Has sex with severed heads of female victims . . ."

Demeester listed the similarities between Bateman and Bernardo: "Age, hair, image, moody, explosive, pretty wife, degrading sex (wine bottle in vagina?, anal sex), videotapes, stalks victims, sex before death, Halcion."

They also found a slew of how-to-succeed books and business tomes, as well as Nancy Drew books and a copy of *Crime and Punishment* by Dostoyevski. The police seized *Crime and Punishment* until one of the better-read prosecutors finally told the police that *Crime and Punishment* was a classic and probably did not fall into the FBI's category of suspicious reading material.

There were audiotapes on which Paul was heard decrying his hopeless state and talking about his intention to commit suicide because Karla had left him, and tapes with pulsating beats over which he talked and rambled about his "deadly innocence," and it all sounded relevant and incriminating.

There were hundreds of videotapes. Most of them were taped or purchased movies or taped television shows. For instance, it appeared that they had taped every episode of "The Simpsons" over the previous two years. It would take half a dozen police officers a number of months to fully review all the video material, but they had great expectations.

Then they found a short, one-minute-and-fifty-eight-second video in a briefcase at five in the afternoon on Sunday, February 21. The tape confirmed what they had been told by Karla Bernardo's lawyers—that Paul and Karla made homemade sex tapes. Except that all this one showed was Karla Bernardo willingly, lasciviously participating in explicit lesbian sex acts with two unidentified females.

The identification officers first viewed this tape on Bernardo's videotape equipment in the living room. After about ten seconds they knew they had something relevant and got very excited. This "artifact" was duly marked and then removed from the house and taken to the mobile command post, a big trailer that resembled a movie star's Winnebago, parked outside the house.

It was parked on the far curb and had replaced the doughnut shop as the meeting place of choice for all police involved in the investigation. Inspector Bevan viewed the tape first thing Monday morning, February 22. Karla's ex-chauffeur, Detective Mary Lee Metcalfe, happened to be there at the same time. She did not know what to make of her battered charge after she saw what came to be known in policing circles as "Karla's Sex Video."

In the first segment Karla is prone and naked on a king-size bed in what appears to be a hotel room. She is with another woman who could have been her body double.

To the left, only partially in frame, Paul Bernardo is seated by the bedside, leaning forward, with a drink in his hand, intently watching while the woman sucks Karla's right breast and fondles her genitalia. The segment is obviously filmed by a stationary camera, which the police rightly assumed was hidden.

On the tape, Karla can be heard expressing her pleasure with what the woman is doing to her and tells her—as she spreads her legs wide for the camera and the woman's probing hand— that she does not mind that the woman's lipstick has left a ring around her nipple. They all giggle. This segment is approximately forty-five to fifty seconds long.

The scene suddenly changes. In the second segment, Karla is performing cunnilingus on a different woman in a different setting. Naked from the waist down, with legs splayed open, the mystery woman could not be identified; neither upper torso nor face was visible. The camera was obviously hand held by a third party as it zoomed in for a close-up.

Karla worked away on the girl's pubis, then she lifted her head and pantomimed—licking her lips, smiling and kissing the camera. Her eyes were half closed; it was the unmistakable look of a woman who was enjoying her work.

In the third very short scene, Karla was raised up on her knees. Taking the girl's lifeless right hand, Karla slowly lifted her tank top, proudly displaying her own very blond pubic region, and inserted the girl's middle finger in her vagina, all the while coyly smiling and licking her lips.

In these last two short segments there was only ambient sound, no dialogue. Because the young woman was obviously comatose and had dark pubic hair and because the scene plainly had been shot in the Bernardos' master bedroom at 57 Bayview, Bevan assumed it was Kristen French. Leslie Mahaffy was a natural blonde.

Bevan had a meeting with the prosecutors that afternoon at Ray Houlahan's office. Murray Segal, Casey Hill and the regional director for Niagara, Jim Treleavan, who worked out of Hamilton, were also present.

Bevan told them about the videotape, and advised them he believed the comatose girl was Kristen French. He had arranged to have the tape taken to the Ontario Provincial Police lab in Toronto to be analyzed.

Bevan knew only too well that Kristen French was missing the top part of the baby finger on her left hand. With the elaborate equipment in the police lab, they might be able to isolate a frame that would show the girl's left hand and thereby conclusively identify Kristen.

Whoever the two women with Karla were—the first one was adult, awake and appeared to be a willing participant—the problem this tape presented for Bevan was Karla's demeanor. She certainly did not look like anybody's victim. Nevertheless, Inspector Bevan now needed Karla Homolka more than ever.

That Saturday, Bevan announced a news blackout. In the midst of Bevan's blackout, the Ontario Provincial Police issued a press release that declared Bernardo a suspect in the unsolved sexual homicide of Cindy Halliday. Her nude and partially burned body had been found along a highway a hundred miles north of St. Catharines on April 20, 1992, the day after Karla and Paul killed and disposed of Kristen French's body.

Halliday's was only one of a hundred unsolved sex slayings of young women between the ages of eleven and twenty-eight in southwestern Ontario since the early eighties.

George Walker looked at the news reports and shook his head. True to form, it looked like the cops were going to try and pin most of those unsolved sex slayings on Bernardo. Everything they did was bad for Bernardo, which was good for his client, Karla Homolka.

On Monday, February 22, Walker went over sources for bail money with the Homolkas. The deal was close to being done. The Homolkas were going to have to come up with at least a

hundred thousand dollars to keep Karla at home while she ful-
filled her part of the forthcoming plea bargaining. Mrs.
Homolka was obviously distressed by this exercise.

Dorothy's sister Carol, and her husband, Robert, who lived
in Sarnia, had a house worth approximately $220,000. They
were apparently willing to help. Dorothy's brother Allan in
Mississauga could get a letter of credit for ten thousand dollars.
And Don Mitchell, the Homolkas' good friend who had got
Paul into the Masons for Karla, said he would be willing to put
up five thousand dollars. Walker advised the Homolkas to get it
organized right away.

"They've got the search warrant and Karla's going to be
charged with murder." It was mid-afternoon on February 23,
when Dorothy Homolka called Lynn McCann again. Lynn
could not tell whether Dorothy was in her cups or not.

"Where am I going to get the money from?" Lynn knew it
was a rhetorical question and said nothing. "Maybe from my
brother." It was as if Dorothy were talking to herself. "We
might have to mortgage the house." This immediately suggested to Lynn that the Homolkas' house was paid for, making
them better off than almost everybody Lynn knew.

Lynn was not quite sure what Dorothy needed money for—
she assumed it was for legal fees or bail, or something like that,
but it was not the first time that Dorothy had obsessed about
money on the cusp of a tragedy.

There had been a lot of inappropriate wailing and gnashing
of teeth about money when Tammy Lyn had died. Then, a
couple of months after the funeral, after Paul and Karla had
moved out, Dorothy and Karel seemed to have all kinds of
money. Karel got a new van. Dorothy got a new car.

Dorothy revised her original story about being broke and
told Lynn that she had forgotten that they had between twenty
and thirty thousand saved.

In spite of the fact that she had gone around disavowing
Karla's forthcoming nuptials, thereby angering Karla and pre-
cipitating the move to Bayview Drive, less than six months later

the Homolkas put on the most lavish wedding anyone had ever seen. At the most swank hotel in Niagara-on-the-Lake. Even the drinks were free.

The fact that Karla was going to go to jail had not been reported. But the fact that Dorothy said Karla was going to jail suggested to Lynn that Karla was far more deeply involved in the actual murders than anyone in St. Catharines had imagined. Still, Dorothy did not seem the slightest bit fazed. She just kept asking the rhetorical question, over and over again—"Where am I going to get the money?"

Walker and Segal met again between 4:00 and 6:30 P.M. on February 25 at Walker's offices in Niagara Falls. They had been at it for two weeks and they were down to the short strokes.

Segal came prepared to do the deal on the following basis: manslaughter—one for Mahaffy, plus something, and one for French, plus something. He and Walker had agreed, in principle, that Karla's sentence would be ten years for each victim, but that the two terms would be served concurrently.

That would make Karla eligible for full parole in three years and four months from the date she went to prison. Segal agreed that the province would not ask for increased parole eligibility—if she behaved herself in prison, she would be out in three years, four months.

Further, Segal agreed the Crown would write a letter to the parole board supporting early parole for Karla, on behalf of both the Attorney-General and the police. The parole board would be officially advised that Karla had been helpful and that her testimony had been essential for the conviction of her ex-husband.

Both sides would go before a judge in chambers to establish judicial approval a priori. This was very rarely done, but Walker did not want to take chances. Therefore, there would be a court reporter present at this closed-door meeting.

Segal and Walker agreed that the police would formally arrest and charge Karla. Karla would then be released to her parents, on their surety. Karla would waive her right to a preliminary hearing.

They would then all wait on a presentencing report—the appropriate psychiatry and so forth. Her actual trial should take no more than a day, providing they could proceed unencumbered, without interference from any third parties, such as the media.

Between her arrest and her trial, Karla would remain at liberty and make herself available for police interviews and counseling. Segal would make every effort to get the Attorney-General to agree to transfer Karla to a provincial psychiatric institution where she would serve her sentence.

This deal would be contingent on Karla's absolute truthfulness. She would disclose the full extent of all her participation and impart all her knowledge. Any perjury—any lie—would scuttle the agreement.

After Segal left, Karla came in with her parents. From 7:00 until 8:30 P.M. he talked to his client alone, about his discussion with Segal. He told her how much material was coming out of the house—not that any meaningful forensic analysis had yet been done—and that they had found a videotape which he described to her. As far as Walker could determine, they had not found anything else of substance—yet.

Walker told Karla unequivocally that her options were very limited. They could easily charge her with first- or second-degree murder. The deal he had worked out with Segal for two ten-year manslaughter terms to be served concurrently was, even if he did say so himself, nothing short of genius.

Whatever abuse or beatings she had sustained would only go so far with a jury. Given the crimes, and the fact that she could have saved the dead girls' lives—that Kristen French would probably have never been kidnapped but for Karla's participation—a jury would invariably ignore the abuse, of which there had been only one provable incident.

There was also the distinct possibility that witnesses would come forward and give testimony that she was into kinky sex, that she herself was sadistic.

In Walker's opinion, the police had taken great care with the search warrants. It was unlikely they would have any room to maneuver there. The crime-scene people had only been in the house for five days. In all probability, they would stay in there for weeks if not months.

God only knew how they would interpret whatever else they might find in the house. The longer they obfuscated, the greater the danger. It had been Walker's experience with criminal behavior that victory most often belonged to the expedient.

Karla unequivocally accepted the terms of the plea bargain— but she was very afraid of prison. Walker told her that there was a good chance they would be able to get her transferred to a provincial psychiatric hospital. There was even one nearby, in St. Thomas. She would get therapy. It would be easy time.

Walker had retained well-known Toronto lawyer Robert Bigelow to advise him about the red tape and subtleties involved in getting an individual convicted of a capital offense moved from a federal penitentiary to a provincial psychiatric hospital.

Bigelow was also advising him about parole issues and possible psychiatric consultants to examine Karla. While Walker and Bigelow were talking first thing Friday morning, February 26, Inspector Bevan had gone to the OPP lab in Toronto.

The video-lab technician enthusiastically pointed out what he had believed to be many similarities between the girl in the video and still photographs of Kristen French. That was what Inspector Bevan wanted to hear. The technician had not, however, been able to isolate any frame that showed the fingertips of the girl's left hand. He could not conclusively say it was Kristen French.

Karla was already drunk when Wendy Lutczyn got to 61 Dundonald around 1:30 P.M. on Friday, February 26. Dr. Patti Weir, the vet from Martindale, had been there since around noon. Karla had stopped by the clinic on Wednesday, on her way to the Humane Society to pick up Buddy.

The dog had been in the pound since Paul Bernardo had

been arrested the previous Wednesday afternoon. Karla said she was very lonely. She invited Wendy and Dr. Weir over to visit.

Dr. Weir brought over some books from her church. Patti and Karla had been talking about God and faith when Wendy arrived.

Wendy was happy to see that. Wendy's maternalism bordered on neurosis and she felt responsible for Karla. After all, she was the one who had made the anonymous calls to Karla's mother when Karla came back to work after New Year's.

Karla was on medication to help calm her down and she was drinking white wine like it was water. By the time Wendy got there, Karla was flying. But she was very sad too. She kept saying she had no one to talk to. Sure, she had been able to talk to her lawyer, but he was not a psychiatrist. Karla really felt that she needed to have somebody—a friend or a psychiatrist, or both—to talk to or she was going to explode.

They started talking about the dog—the Homolkas' house was so small and Buddy was so big, what were they going to do? Karla said it was okay, her dad was tolerating him, but she was going to have to make other arrangements for Buddy when she went to prison.

Dr. Weir and Wendy were aghast. "What makes you think you're going to prison?" they stammered in unison. She was going to be charged with two counts of manslaughter, Karla told them, so where did they think she was going?

Patti and Wendy wondered whether Karla should be telling them that and Karla said probably not, but she really needed somebody to talk to. Then she told them not to tell anybody. Karla said she was meeting with her lawyer later in the day. She and her lawyer were planning on going to the police station the next day—on Saturday—for her to make a statement.

If she went on Saturday and confessed, then she would only serve three out of ten years at Kingston Penitentiary. Karla said that was how parole worked. She would be eligible for parole in three and one-third years.

If she did not do that she would probably be charged with two counts of first-degree murder, and then she would go to prison for life and never get out.

"She was pretty near drunk when I left," Dr. Weir recalled. "She was on sedatives, and then she'd been drinking a lot of wine. She'd probably had about three glasses of wine while I was there. I left about 1:30 and then Wendy didn't come back to work. Karla finally let her go late in the afternoon and Wendy said by the time she left, Karla had had an awful lot to drink."

Late that same afternoon, Inspector Bevan spoke to Murray Segal and told him that the video-lab technician had pointed out many similarities between the comatose girl in the video and Kristen French.

Segal told the inspector that he and George Walker were arranging to bring Karla Bernardo to the Green Ribbon offices to give an "induced" statement.

That was all Inspector Bevan needed to hear. He went directly to the French and Mahaffy families. He told them about the exact terms and conditions of Karla's deal.

He was candid about circumstances, as far as he and the police were concerned. The question was whether the families wanted to take a chance and hope they found hard evidence in the house or do the deal.

He told the Frenches and the Mahaffys that the police had learned a great deal about the nature of the relationship between compliant victims such as Karla and sexual sadists such as Paul Bernardo. Inspector Bevan elaborated on what they had learned—from friends of Paul and Karla's whom they had been furiously interviewing, as well as from George Walker and Karla—about the bizarre nature of the relationship between Paul and Karla Bernardo.

In the final analysis, Inspector Bevan said taciturnly, it was really up to them. They could wait or take the deal. The families told him they were prepared to accept the Crown attorney's best advice.

. . .

Karla was in bad shape when she arrived at Walker's office at 5:30 P.M. She looked wan and thin. She was volubly agitated and seemed heavily depressed. Over the two hours she was in his office, Walker lost confidence in the current plan.

Defense consultant Robert Bigelow had congratulated Walker on the fact that Walker had managed to avoid any sexual-assault charges against Karla. Those would have made her life much more difficult than a couple of manslaughters. He and Bigelow had also discussed the efficacy of having control of the client's psychiatric and psychological assessments.

Bigelow had suggested Dr. Graham Glancy, an expert in battered-woman's syndrome and post-traumatic stress disorder, to do a workup on Karla. For some reason which was not perfectly clear to Walker, Dr. Glancy had declined.

Walker had then called the psychologist, Dr. Allan Long. Dr. Long was prepared to step in. Walker knew Dr. Long. Everybody knew Dr. Allan Long. Dr. Long was a tall, lean drink of water, who was always at the ready. He was a very accommodating man, who, at seventy, had been around the block a dozen times. Dr. Long suggested his colleague, Dr. Hans Arndt, for the psychiatric assessment. If Karla needed to be hospitalized, Dr. Arndt could arrange it. Walker said he would get back to Dr. Long.

Karla was acting so strangely that night that Walker thought she might actually need psychiatric help. He called Murray Segal later that evening and called off Karla's meeting with the police and further negotiations. He might even have suggested that she was suicidal. For a man so concerned about his client's state of mind, it took Walker an inordinately long five days to have her examined by the doctors.

Karla and her parents were in Walker's offices until 7:00 P.M. They dutifully signed the formal authorization, which Walker then had legally witnessed. In precise terms, the document recorded the details of the plea resolution that had been reached between Murray Segal and Mr. Walker.

.   .   .

George Walker filed the authorization with the court in St. Catharines first thing the following Monday morning.

On Monday, Karla kept her appointment with her general practitioner, Dr. Christina Plaskos. Christina did not mind if Karla called her by her first name. In fact, she had encouraged Karla to do so.

Dr. Plaskos noted that Karla appeared to be "under a tremendous amount of stress and [was] quite emotional," while she was in her office. But Karla was "not suicidal," or even "depressed." Karla knew that she was in deep trouble, and in Dr. Plaskos's opinion that had caused her to become quite emotional.

CHAPTER

twenty-seven

For the son of a railroad worker, George Walker had done well. He had put himself through university and law school on hockey scholarships. As a big defenseman, he had been positively graceful on the ice. However, by the time he was drafted by the Toronto Maple Leafs of the National Hockey League, he had decided Clarence Darrow spoke more eloquently to him than Gordie Howe.

Walker learned his legal lessons well. He had one of the most successful criminal law practices in southwestern Ontario. He drove an immaculate, pearl-gray Jag, enjoyed homes on both sides of the Canada–U.S. border, had a beautiful, blond wife and spent every January at his villa—which they called Journey's End—on the island of Montserrat.

Montserrat was a verdant enclave for the rich and famous, with tap water more potable than Evian. Although Walker was neither rich nor famous, he happened on the property at exactly the right time in 1981. The only other Canadian on the island was Québécois chanteur Gilles Vigneault, whose villa was just up the road from Journey's End.

From the patio overlooking Walker's in-ground pool, the ramparts of Air Studio, owned by former Beatles manager George Martin, are readily visible across the valley. Until Hurricane Hugo destroyed the studio in 1989, the biggest rockers in the world flocked to Montserrat to record their albums.

Walker recounted with relish an afternoon drinking beer with Mick Jagger and Keith Richards. They had often seen Sting in the half dozen restaurants that served indigenous giant frog—listed on the menus as "mountain chicken." Another time the Walkers swore they saw vegetarian Paul McCartney eating aguoudi, a mountain-dwelling beast that looked like a cross between a gopher and a pig.

With Karla secure in the psychiatric ward of Northwestern General Hospital, George Walker gratefully climbed on a plane bound for the island first thing Sunday morning, March 7. When he and Lori had returned from Montserrat two months before, on a whim, he had booked the last excursion fare for the season so he could return during the first week in March and spend seven days by himself. What Karla had told him had taken its toll. He had recently spent too many sleepless nights sitting in his La-Z-Boy, downing Classic Coke, eating junk food and watching CNN. Now he needed the break.

After his plane reached cruising altitude Walker put Karla out of his mind, pushed back his chair and ordered a scotch. "Damned iguanas," he thought to himself, "they've probably eaten all my hibiscus by now."

. . . .

Dr. Arndt truly did not know whether Karla was mad or just bad. Always clutching the teddy bear, half dressed in baby dolls, she sat across from him, quietly answering his every question.

"You are having dreams?" inquired Dr. Arndt.

"Nightmares, just like the Guns N' Roses video "November Rain"—you know, the one where the bride dies." Karla replied. In her dreams, Paul killed the bride. Plagiarized rock videos hardly qualified as legitimate nightmares; then again, the subconscious was a strange country.

In another one of Karla's dreams, Tammy, Kristen, Leslie and Paul were coming to get her. And the previous night, in her dream, Paul had come into the hospital with a scalpel and started cutting her up with no nurses around to stop him. That's why Karla had gone running to the nursing station—"to make sure that the nurses were there and to get more Valium."

When Karla was first admitted to the hospital on March 4, she had not realized that her roommate was a nun. When she did, she did not get the joke. Karla was not subtle. She never bothered to mention Sister Josephine to Dr. Arndt.

Karla stayed in hospital for seven weeks, talking to doctors, taking tests, talking on the telephone, visiting with her family, talking to Sister Josephine, reading and sleeping.

Dr. Arndt gave her a lot of drugs. Karla liked drugs. But they never seemed to work as well as she would have liked. She always wanted more. Karla took so many drugs she had a mild seizure, but now the first week was over.

Karla talked to Dr. Arndt a lot. Talking to psychiatrists was called therapy. She understood these things from her extensive reading, including *Michelle Remembers,* which was a kind of textbook study about the therapeutic relationship between a deeply troubled young girl and her handsome, understanding psychiatrist.

In *Michelle Remembers,* Michelle wore black all the time. A teddy bear like Bunky figured prominently in Michelle's life. In the book Michelle told her psychiatrist, "I loved the bear so much I wanted to become the bear."

Michelle also told her therapist that she was afraid when she started talking, because talking would start her remembering things. "I know that some of the things that happened weren't normal, weren't things that normal people do . . ." Michelle had said. That was just the way it was for Karla.

During their therapy session on March 10, Karla told Dr. Arndt she felt her mother suspected Paul had had something to do with Tammy's death. "I don't think my parents will hate me," she told Dr. Arndt. "They could never stand losing another daughter." That was why Karla could never commit suicide. She couldn't do it to the parents for whom she cared so deeply.

As far as Leslie Mahaffy and Kristen French were concerned, Karla did not feel any remorse.

"There was nothing I could do for either of them," she candidly told the doctor.

Karla told Dr. Arndt about Jim Hutton. "Guess what?" she said, and then told him that while she was staying with her aunt and uncle in Bramptom she had met this guy named Jim and he drove a car exactly like Paul's. He looked a bit like Paul too.

"Wasn't that strange?" Karla asked Dr. Arndt.

Karla had "trusted him enough" to have sex with him. Jim was, for her, someone "to help me erase Paul from my mind." Her parents knew about Jim, but they didn't know Karla was still in contact with him. Karla called Jim from the hospital on March 15.

Paul had taped many of the sex scenes with the dead girls, including the one with her sister, Tammy Lyn. Karla told Dr. Arndt that she had watched them all at one time or another.

Karla had not been able to find the videos when she went back to the house, but she was sure the police had them by now. Dr. Arndt felt as if he were being pumped for information.

The video "with the hand," as Karla called the videotape the police had found on February 21 . . . She could not remember exactly whose hand it was, but she told Dr. Arndt that she knew the girl was alive.

.   .   .

Dr. Allan Long interviewed Karla for the first time on March 13, and outlined the tests he wanted to give her. The battery would include the Halstead Reitan neuropsychological test, the Halstead category test, a tactile finger recognition test, fingertip number writing, Reitan Indiana aphasia screening test, the Reitan Klove sensory perceptual examination, a seashore rhythm test, and seashore speech sounds perception test, a tactual performance test, Trail Making Test Forms A and B, the hand dynamometer, the Wechsler adult intelligence scale—revised (WAISR), the Wechsler memory scale—revised (WAISR), the Forer sentence completion test, an adjective checklist, the thematic apperception test (TAT)—Parts A and B, the Cattell 16 P F test, the California psychological inventory and Jackson's personality research form—E, the Rorschach psychodiagnostic instrument, or ink-blot, test and the Minnesota multiphasic personality inventory, or MMPI.

The Minnesota multiphasic personality inventory was the most important. It established the benchmark against which all other results would be measured. The MMPI required Karla to answer 550 statements about behavior, feelings, social attitudes and psychopathological symptoms—T for "true," F for "false," or ? for "cannot say." The answers would then be scored according to scales established by the test's authors, psychiatrist J.C. McKinley and psychologist Starke Hathaway.

Karla's MMPI profile was characteristic of severely disturbed people. MMPI scores resembled the strange markings on Mark DeMarco's Masonic skull: Karla's score was "814362*"79'0-/5#.L#F"K/".

These kinds of people, Karla's kind of people—people who score "814362*"79'0-/5#.L#F"K/"—harbor feelings of hostility and aggression but are unable to express them.

"They feel socially inadequate, especially around members of the opposite sex," Dr. Long wrote. "They lack trust in other people, keeping them at a distance and feeling generally isolated and alienated."

People with Karla's MMPI score are most often diagnosed as

schizophrenic. They get headaches and cannot sleep. They are easily confused and distracted. They are people who respond as Karla did, tending to be unhappy and depressed, and they "have a flattened affect."

Neither Dr. Long nor Dr. Arndt thought Karla was schizophrenic. In their view, she was hardly "socially inadequate." She did harbor "feelings of hostility and aggression," but she was more than able to express them. Karla seemed to be nothing like her MMPI profile.

During the Rorschach test, Karla was shown a bunch of ink blots. By interpreting the responses, Dr. Long created a portrait of her personality, which was an appropriate description for test results that were always subjective to the psychologist who gave the test.

The thematic apperception test, or TAT, was comprised of a series of postcards with themes on them. It was a similar exercise to the Rorschach test—in both cases the psychologist subjectively interpreted what the patient said in response to visual stimuli—except that the Rorschach ink blots were abstract and the TAT postcards were literal, like cartoons. The patient was shown a postcard and asked to tell the psychologist a story about what he or she saw.

One TAT card had a little sad-faced boy forlornly clasping a violin. There was another with a woman whose substantial breasts were exposed, draped across a bed, and there was a man standing there with his hands over his eyes. The patient was asked what they thought when they saw the postcards? Had the man just raped the woman or had they just had sex? What was the postcard's story? However the individual responded, it meant something in context with everything else.

There was one card that showed a vagina, and another which everyone saw as a penis. If the patient saw a beautiful flower, then the doctor knew that the person was not being forthright or forthcoming.

Dr. Long saw Karla's responses to the TAT postcards as unusual and unique. Her responses suggested that Karla was extremely shallow; that there was "poor integration at deeper levels."

"The patient's stories contained themes suggesting feelings of being trapped," he wrote. "That is, an inability to extricate herself. The themes also frequently involved victimization and violence."

During Karla's entire stay at Northwestern General Hospital she was completely stoned. Dr. Arndt preferred the term "disinhibited." Over the nine days and almost thirty hours of testing and interviewing Dr. Long conducted, Karla ingested thousands of milligrams of tranquilizers, sedatives and antidepressants.

For example, the day before Dr. Long came to see Karla for the first time, she took 300mg of Sinequan, a mindbending antidepressant used to sedate psychotics. A reasonable daily dosage of Sinequan for someone diagnosed as psychotic was 50mg. The Sinequan had been combined with 10mg of Valium, and 75mg of Nozinan, another powerful antidepressant, which also had a sedative effect. Nonetheless, Karla was wide-awake and eager to take her tests.

Dr. Long observed that Karla "enjoyed her work as a veterinary's assistant and this was evident in my discussions with her, as well when she alluded to some knowledge she had about French Poodles which she related to me in an extremely enthusiastic manner." She had obviously discovered Dr. Long preferred French poodles.

At the beginning of April, it became very clear to George Walker and Hans Arndt that they needed to find another psychiatrist who had credibility with the prosecution. Dr. Arndt tried to interest Dr. Glancy again. Again, Dr. Glancy deferred.

Drs. Long and Arndt were viewed with some skepticism in the prosecutor's office. Dr. Long was getting a bit long in the tooth. Both he and Dr. Arndt most often testified as expert witnesses for the defense. Dr. Arndt's reputation as a proponent of "sleep therapy" did nothing to instill confidence with the Crown law office, either.

With a case this high-profile, and under these unusual circumstances, it would be prudent if they could deliver a diagnosis that gave the prosecution a higher comfort level.

Dr. Andrew Malcolm, a dour psychiatrist who was highly regarded by prosecutors, would be ideal. Dr. Malcolm had frequently been called to testify on behalf of the prosecution over the past thirty years. Dr. Arndt called Dr. Malcolm on April 2.

On Monday, April 12, Karla got a letter from her sister Lori, lamenting the fact that she and Karla could not have a "sleep-over."

"Sometimes I feel that you are slipping away and I don't know you any more," Lori wrote. She confided to Karla that she was not happy, or as strong as people assumed her to be. "It really sucks when you have to act like your life is fine."

In a P.S., Lori told Karla that she had heard about Karla's EEG test, the one that would prove Karla's skull had been fractured by Paul.

"It's good . . . in a sick sort of way, because you'll have proof that he really physically hurt you. We all know that he did, but other people may choose not to believe you."

Lori went on to tell Karla that she had never felt so close to Karla as she did then; that she kept all of Karla's letters and reread them all the time and pretended Karla was talking to her.

"I think I'm going insane," Lori reported.

In neurologist Dr. Morgenthau's April 13 report to Dr. Arndt, he stated that Karla had told him she had discomfort in the "left frontoprietal region" of her skull. Karla said that she had sustained a depressed skull fracture when her estranged husband had beaten her. "However," Dr. Morgenthau wrote, "this was not proven by X-ray. Basal skull fractures were suspected, and these again were not proven by X-ray and CT scanning."

From Dr. Morgenthau's perspective, there was nothing wrong with Karla. It was his conclusion that the massive amounts of medications she had been ingesting had caused her seizure and whatever tremors she had allegedly experienced. Karla's EEG was perfectly normal.

. . .

Dr. Arndt had been encouraging Karla to write a letter to her parents telling them about Tammy Lyn. Right after Easter, during one of their therapy sessions, Dr. Arndt perceived her emotional anguish to be so severe that day that he prescribed 30mg Valium by mouth, 40mg intravenously and another intramuscular needle with 10mg of Valium at 10:30 P.M. Since Valium administered i.v. and i.m. can be considered double the potency, her total intake of Valium that day was the equivalent of 130mg, in addition to large amounts of the other drugs that she took. As Dr. Arndt noted in a letter to George Walker, "These are heroic doses and indicative of Karla's requirements."

Karla told Dr. Arndt that Paul Bernardo had made Kristen and Leslie drunk before killing them. He would make them do "shooters," she said. Karla drank, too. Kristen was killed on a Sunday morning. Karla had only had one drink with Kristen.

With Leslie, Karla said she was drunk. Karla had served her sister Tammy Lyn eggnog with rum. When Paul was having sex with Karla's comatose sister, he was drunk. Then Karla said: "I've been here in the hospital for twenty-five days and haven't had any alcohol, and it doesn't bother me."

In spite of the "heroic doses" of serious sedatives, Karla sat down and wrote the letter about Tammy Lyn to her parents in one sitting, on lined paper, in her neat, loopy script. It was a perfectly composed, grammatically correct, unblemished missive; no corrections, false starts or crossed-out words.

Dear Mom, Dad and Lori,

This is the hardest letter I've ever had to write and you'll probably all hate me once you've read it. I've kept this inside myself for so long and I just can't lie to you any more. Both Paul and I are responsible for Tammy's death. Paul was "in love" with her and wanted to have sex with her. He wanted me to help him. He wanted me to get sleeping pills from work to drug her with. He threatened me and physically and emotionally abused me when I refused. No words I can say can make you understand what he put me through. So stupidly I agreed to do as he said. But something—maybe the combination of drugs and the food she ate that night—caused her to vomit. I tried so hard to save her. I am so sorry. But no words I can say can bring her back. I have thought many times of killing myself, but I couldn't put you through the pain of losing another daughter and sister again. I don't blame you all if you hate me. I hate myself. I live with the pain of knowing I unintentionally killed my baby sister every day. I think that's the real reason I put up with Paul's abusive behavior—I felt I deserved it for allowing him to drug and rape my beautiful baby sister. I loved her so much and never wanted to do anything to hurt my "Tamsikins," please believe me. I would gladly give my life for hers. Nothing I can do or say can bring her back. I don't expect you to ever forgive me, for I will never forgive myself.

Karla   -XOXO-

She gave the letter to Dr. Arndt for safekeeping. April 13 was a busy day for Karla. Dr. Malcolm visited for the third time and conducted another hour-long interview.

From Karla's chart, which she dutifully read the following day, she had been portrayed as suitably distressed: "20:45—up to nursing station—states she cannot sleep; is not tired at all, requesting *i.v.* push—call put through to Dr. A."

Fifteen minutes later, Dr. Arndt arrived. He recorded that he found his "patient quite depressed . . . too moved by all that happened today for the medication to properly settle her down. Nozinan does not seem to touch her; the Valium has been given already in rather large quantity, therefore I will try and switch her to Tegretol and see whether it will control her; memory for recent events and concentration are quite bad.

"Interestingly, she wants meds to be given *i.v.*, not even *i.m.* [intramuscular]," Dr. Arndt noted, quoting Karla saying, "I have a high tolerance for pain, I have a high tolerance for medications." Dr. Arndt decided to put his depressed, upset patient "on forty-eight-hour sleep therapy."

At 12:01 A.M. on April 14, Lori Homolka wrote her sister another letter. She told Karla that they were all "really worried" about her.

"We all seem to think that you feel we are going to abandon you and not love you any more because of what has happened. Please don't ever think that way. We're your family, Kar, and we love you unconditionally. What has happened to you is in no way your fault, you did what you had to do to survive and we are so glad for that. You are such an incredibly strong person which I have always admired."

She went on to reassure Karla that she knows who Karla is: "The gentle, kind and loving person that you've always been." The letter is signed, "Your pissy little sissy, Lori," and the Homolka sisters' trademark "XOXO."

Karla tried to explain to Dr. Arndt that her high tolerance for drugs was based on the fact that she had drunk at least sixteen ounces of alcohol a day while married to Paul Bernardo.

Dr. Arndt had a few nagging doubts. Karla had led him to believe that she was "heavily sauced" much of the time she was married to Paul. She also told him she hardly ever missed a day of work. If she was sauced all the time, how would she have been able to function at work every day?

There were other things that did not fit with his final diagnosis of post-traumatic stress disorder and a reactive depression. Her relationship with the man from Brampton, for instance. The fact that she continued to correspond with Jim and sent him nude Polaroids of herself was inconsistent with a diagnosis of post-traumatic stress disorder.

If Karla woke up at 4:00 A.M. she would make sure the nurses recorded the fact that she was awake at 4:00 A.M. on her chart. This vigilance was atypical of heavily depressed persons with PTSD.

Dr. Arndt never satisfactorily reconciled these dichotomies, nor did he resolve all his other doubts. In his role as Karla's therapist, he viewed such resolutions as irrelevant. In Dr. Arndt's mind—the way he had rationalized it—he had become Karla's treating physician and therapist.

In Dr. Arndt's mind, that was also why they needed Dr. Andrew Malcolm. Since Dr. Arndt had become her treating physician, Walker needed another psychiatrist to do the forensic assessment for the court. Dr. Arndt's real responsibility had become Karla's well-being.

Karla was discharged from the psychiatric ward of Northwestern General Hospital on April 24, 1993. By 11 A.M., Karla was in George Walker's Niagara Falls office.

On April 29, 1993 Dr. Christina Plaskos perceived Karla to be "rather flat . . ." She noted that she "has gained 15 lb. . . . she is on a number of meds . . . I'm not really sure why she was put on these meds . . . I found her not to be depressed but basically lacking emotion . . ." Karla told Dr. Plaskos she was going to be charged with manslaughter.

On April 30, Karla made a specific note in her datebook that the search warrants for 57 Bayview had expired, on the anniversary of the police discovery of Kristen French's body.

Twice extended, the warrants had facilitated an exhaustive ten-week exploration of every nook and cranny in the Bernardo household. Sixteen top crime-scene specialists from all over the province had crawled over every inch of the small house at 57 Bayview.

They had jackhammered the cement in the basement and the garage, dug up the lawn, punched holes in the walls and ceilings, stripped the carpets and the contents of the house, seized books and videotapes, pulled out pot lights, taken paint chips and generally decimated the house.

The people who owned the house, Rachel and Brian Delaney, were diligently portraying themselves as victims, too. They wanted the government to buy the house. In the meantime, through Inspector Vince Bevan, the people of Ontario rented the house at the same rate Paul and Karla had paid. Inspector Bevan personally delivered a rent check drawn on the Green Ribbon Task Force account, every month like clockwork.

Drs. Long, Malcolm and Arndt had long discussions about Karla's motivations in Dr. Arndt's basement. "In these discussions finally arose the idea that once Tammy was done, the rest became automatic—the rest is not really much of a problem," Dr. Arndt explained. "You see, once she was an accomplice, it didn't make any difference what happened afterwards. You see, she had to go on—so that is the one thing I was looking for— the hook. Where is the hook?

"The hook? It was Tammy. Prior to that, you know, it was the son the mother and father didn't have and stuff like that. I think it was Tammy that just sealed it for her, because at that point she was an accomplice, she was a participant in the killing of a daughter, and so she didn't want to have the 'son' killed or the other daughter and so on it goes.

"That's the argument that I proposed—and that's what got our Dr. Malcolm on line—because he was looking for how come that all of these various things happened—where is this lady coming off? What is this woman? But once we had this crucial event, which was Tammy . . . If she would have squealed, well, she was under a threat that—one, it would be shown to them that she was involved with Tammy, and secondly, she was constantly under threat that he would harm the others. Whether this was truly the only thing that happened I don't know, but this is what she explained and it certainly makes some sense."

The doctors agreed that Karla was suffering from post-traumatic stress disorder, Dysthymia or "reactive" depression and alexithymia, which literally means "no words for mood." The condition is "typified by difficulty recognizing and verbalizing feelings, a paucity of fantasy life and speech and thought that are concrete and closely tied to external events."

·   ·   ·

Inspector Bevan told a news conference that police were watching a second suspect, someone, he said, who was "not a threat to the public."

The press, acting as publicity agents for the owners of 57 Bayview, dutifully reported that a house in which such horrors had been perpetrated could no longer have any value as real estate.

On April 30, Murray Segal and George Walker had a big chat on the telephone. They arranged to meet and conclude their deal.

Walker left the Falls and met with Segal in his office at 720 Bay Street in Toronto between ten o'clock and noon. Segal told Walker he felt there needed to be additional charges for Karla's role in her sister's death. Walker did not see that at all. Tammy might have been the hook for Dr. Arndt, but briefly she became Karla's stumbling block.

Intuitively and through scuttlebutt he had picked up around courthouses in the Niagara Region, Walker knew that the police had found scant hard evidence in the house.

They were probably in no position to either inculpate or exculpate his client as an accomplice. Karla was still as crucial to Inspector Bevan's case as she had been when she went on her "soma" holiday. Unknown to Walker, Bevan had already discussed the matter with the victims' families and secured their complicity.

By the time Walker got back to the Falls at 1:30 P.M., Tammy Lyn had been reduced from a stumbling block to a small bone of contention. On May 2, Segal and Walker had almost reached a compromise. Walker had agreed that they would accept something for Tammy, as long as it did not entail new charges. He talked to Dr. Arndt about his forthcoming session with the Homolkas and Karla's "Tammy" letter—a meeting which proved to be a non-event. Mother read the letter in front of everyone and shrugged. Karel Homolka slumped in his chair.

The fact was Dorothy Homolka already knew or strongly suspected what had happened to her youngest daughter. Paul had made Karla help him rape her sister, and then Tammy had accidentally died. As far as Dorothy was concerned, Paul had really killed Tammy Lyn and Karla had been an unwitting weapon. Walker had a talk with the Homolkas.

Karla noted in her datebook that Paul had yet another bail hearing on May 3. By the time Walker and Segal met on May 5 in Walker's Niagara Falls office between 8:00 A.M. and noon the deal was done.

Karla would "take two" for Tammy—instead of two ten-year terms for manslaughter, she would get two concurrent twelve-year terms. That would add an extra year to the mandatory time she would have to spend in jail. Instead of three and a third years before she was paroled, it would be four years and four months. Two for Tammy, but no new charges. Effectively, Karla had been completely exonerated in the death of her sister and had escaped any sexual-assault charges whatsoever.

CHAPTER

twenty-eight

The medication is not working anymore," Karla stated matter-of-factly. When Dr. Arndt asked whether or not the family had talked about their previous session, the one in his basement where Karla's mother had read the letter about Tammy Lyn, Karla replied distractedly, "No, not much."

Karla said she did not even remember writing the letter. She must have "blocked it." Her tone was fractious. "Everyone else is just fine now," she declared, "except me. . . ."

Karla was still having dreams about running away with Leslie and Kristen and Paul going after her other sister, Lori. Then she would wake up. There were many times, Karla said, when she did not know whether what happened really happened or whether it had been something she had dreamt. The jacket copy on *Michelle Remembers* was prescient: "Michelle remembers what you'll never forget." Karla never forgot it.

Karla had been discharged from hospital on the following medication: Surmontil 50mg twice a day, plus 200mg at bedtime. Surmontil was another potent antidepressant with a sedative effect. She was also prescribed 200 mg of Tegretol twice a day. Tegretol was a medication used with psychiatric patients to facilitate and speed up sedation. She had been given a prescription for Valium—5mg, twice a day, and 10mg at bedtime—and Chlorpromazine, a major antipsychotic. Karla was taking 50mg of that every hour.

"The medication is not working," Karla repeated. Hans Arndt was amazed. Karla was clearly outstripping even his prodigious prescriptions.

That evening, Drs. Long, Malcolm and Arndt met with George Walker in Dr. Arndt's basement. Walker arrived at 7:30 P.M. He explained that Karla would be in court the following Tuesday and then released on bail.

They discussed the doctors' diagnoses: dysthymia or "reactive depression," as well as post-traumatic stress disorder. PTSD was not considered curable; proper management required years of intensive therapy. Walker did not think that the doctors would ever be required to testify, but he needed their reports.

Before he left to meet Murray Segal at L'Auberge Pommier, a smart bistro just north of Dr. Arndt's house in the exclusive neighborhood of Hogg's Hollow, Dr. Arndt agreed to contact whoever was in charge at the regional psychiatric facility in St. Thomas.

Walker got to the restaurant around 9:15 P.M. It was a modest celebratory dinner, since the deal was done. Walker told Segal what the doctors had said about dysthymia and post-traumatic stress disorder, alexithymia and battered-woman's syndrome.

The doctors had all underscored the fact that Karla was not violent, or a danger to the community. That conclusion would allow Segal to release Karla into her parents' custody with impunity. The dinner went past midnight. Walker did not get home until 1:30 A.M.

Although Mr. Bernardo was destitute, the police had found more than three thousand dollars in Canadian and American currency in the house. The money was not relevant to the crime, nor was cash itemized in the search warrants, so junior defense counsel Carolyn MacDonald recovered it. She used it to pay the landlords Paul Bernardo's arrears. That done, the defense could retrieve anything left behind by the police after the last search warrant expired. MacDonald took pride in this maneuver because she had figured it out on her own.

Ken Murray, Paul Bernardo's lawyer, looked a bit like a malevolent librarian. He was long, lean and lanky. His face had the angularity of Wyndham Lewis's Ezra Pound. He conveyed the color brown, even when he wore black.

A droopy mustache gave him a walrus-like appearance, which was complemented by the round wire glasses he always wore. Murray had spent much of the last decade up in Newmarket, Ontario pleading out Legal Aid certificates. Prior to that, he had been a prosecutor in North York, one of those large cities—like Scarborough—within the city of Metropolitan Toronto.

Murray arrived at 57 Bayview Drive on May 6 with an entourage that included Carolyn MacDonald, and their law clerk, a petite, demure, bespectacled woman named Kimberly Doyle, and with instructions from his client to look in a specific place for a specific package.

Murray had also asked John Lefurgey, a young St. Catharines lawyer who had gone to law school with MacDonald, to come along. Lefurgey had been retained to file motions in St. Catharines and Murray decided Lefurgey at least deserved the grand tour.

The landlord, Brian Delaney, was there as well. When Murray's portable phone rang, he did not seem surprised that it was Paul Bernardo calling collect from jail. He listened and responded with inaudible grunts. When the call was terminated Murray mumbled something about an electric train set, and he and MacDonald charged upstairs. They came down a few minutes later with a package. That accomplished, Murray let the cadre of nameless well-muscled men he had assembled to remove the remaining contents get to work.

Shortly afterward Murray left with his package.

Six hours later, the house was empty. There were some books left, strewn around upstairs. Brian Delaney saw a Honolulu newspaper, dated July 11, 1991. The headline read, "Pulled Off Road and Raped Says Woman in Maui." In the middle of the empty living room, there was a dressmaker's dummy wearing Karla's wedding dress.

Dr. Hans Arndt contacted Dr. R.S. Swaminath, the psychiatrist in charge of the psychiatric facility in St. Thomas.

After Dr. Swaminath saw Karla, he appeared to be ambivalent about her qualifications for St. Thomas. He agreed with Dr. Arndt that she appeared to be under a great deal of stress and that stress might be affecting her psychological functioning, but given her circumstances that was probably to be expected. In conclusion, Dr. Swaminath wrote, "I am not quite convinced at the present time that she would require intensive in-hospital treatment in a secure setting at St. Thomas Psychiatric Hospital. I would suggest that we wait until we know the outcome of her present legal charges, and if it becomes necessary in the future for her to receive in-hospital treatment I would be willing to consider it."

.   .   .

On May 14, George Walker again left Niagara Falls for a Journey's End—this time the motel in Whitby, Ontario. Karla, her mother, Murray Segal and about twenty police officers were waiting for him when he arrived at 1700 Champlain Avenue in the middle of the morning.

Ministry officials and the police had rented two floors of the motel. Karla and her mother were registered in Room 242. Karla's "induced" and "cautioned" statements were to be given down the hall in Room 238. Murray Segal had the final official copy of the "resolution agreement," which he ceremoniously handed over to Walker.

Walker had explained the difference between "induced" and "cautioned" statements to Karla. He pointed out a clause in the resolution agreement: "If the authorities learn through any means that your client had caused the death of any person, in the sense of her stopping life, any proposed resolution will be terminated at the suit of the Crown, regardless of the state the process is at."

And . . . "The statement and any subsequent statement will be a full, complete, and truthful account regarding her knowledge and/or involvement or anyone else's involvement in the investigations into the deaths of Leslie Mahaffy; Kristen French; alleged rapes in Scarborough; alleged rape on Henley Island; the death of Tammy Homolka; and any other criminal activity she has participated in or has knowledge of. An 'induced' statement cannot be used against her in any criminal proceedings."

An "induced" statement was just what it said—an "inducement" for the prosecution to make the deal. Since they were already sufficiently "induced," the day devoted to inducement was a formality.

The "cautioned" statements were given under oath and would be considered evidence. Karla agreed to be audio- and videotaped throughout. The clause in the resolution agreement that Walker considered to be the most important:

"They (the authorities) will provide no protection for a prosecution if it is discovered that she lied, including a prosecution for obstructing justice, public mischief, fabricating evidence, perjury, inconsistent statements and/or false affidavits."

Walker and Karla would give the prosecution "an opportunity to inspect a copy of any psychiatric, psychological or other medical reports."

And finally the last two paragraphs:

1./ She will not give an account directly or indirectly to the press, media, or for the purpose of any book, movie or like endeavor.

2./ She will not seek or receive, directly or indirectly, any compensation relating to the above, including any and all events and occurrences arising from the police investigations, criminal proceedings, or any statements given by her to the police.

Walker spent a couple of hours discussing the forthcoming interviews with Inspector Bevan and various other police officers. Karla would have two interviewers who would act as facilitators rather than interrogators, Detective Mary Lee Metcalfe and Sergeant Robert Gillies. Although they could ask questions, their tone could not be challenging or abrasive. Karla was the storyteller, and every good storyteller needs an inquisitive and interested audience.

At 3:30 P.M., Karla greeted Detective Metcalfe as though she were one of Karla's former bridesmaids.

Karla sat straight up and very still as they adjusted the video camera and checked the audio-recording equipment. Metcalfe sat on Karla's right hand, Gillies on her left.

Karla said she would prefer it if Detective Metcalfe asked the questions. The detectives readily agreed. Mary Lee started by asking Karla about her doctors and her medication. Karla recited the list. Karla had enough drugs in her to stun a horse.

"Do you feel that this medication that you described would affect, in any way, your participation in this interview?" Detective Metcalfe asked politely.

"Absolutely not."

"Okay. Thank you, Karla."

"You're welcome."

"What is the current status of your marriage?"

"Zero. Zilch. It's over."

"Do you see any prospect of any reconciliation with Paul Bernardo?"

"No. I have already spoken to a divorce lawyer and divorce proceedings will be put under way very shortly. . . . The fact that he assaulted me made it absolutely certain that I would not reconcile with him. There is no hope. Absolutely none. I hate him, I don't want anything to do with him. I wish—like, I want him to be totally out of my life."

"You are aware that your husband is a suspect in several crimes, including the Leslie Mahaffy and Kristen French matters. What effect has his alleged involvement in these crimes had upon your marriage?"

"We really didn't talk very much because our marriage was falling apart. . . ." Conservatively dressed, with nothing moving except her mouth and eyes—occasionally Karla would brush her hair back like a movie star—she began her sordid tale with a carefully thought-out understatement. "He liked tall brunette girls because they were opposite to me. He liked them to be virgins—I know that's what you're looking for."

"What was videotaped, Karla?" Detective Metcalfe inquired. Karla had made an offhand remark about something she and Paul had done with one of the girls, which had been videotaped. From the question and her tone, it was obvious Metcalfe did not know about the alleged existence of multiple videotapes.

"The sex."

"What sex?" Metcalfe inquired. Since the return trip to Brampton from George Walker's office on February 11, Metcalfe had not seen Karla, except when she had watched her perform on "Karla's Sex Video."

"What was done with those videotapes?" she asked.

Karla realized conclusively, for the first time, that the police did not have the videotapes. Paul had often played them while they were still together; Karla knew where he had originally hidden them and had been convinced the police had found them.

"I've heard that Paul has edited them." Watching this interview, afterward, it was obvious that Metcalfe was taken aback by Karla's matter-of-fact description of the extent of the videotaping, so much so that she did not ask the obvious following question . . . about where Karla heard that Paul had edited the videotapes. Sergeant Gillies said nothing. Up to this point, the police had no awareness of the extent of Paul and Karla's videography.

"The videotapes were put up in the garage," Karla continued. "There was a platform up there for storage. If you stand up, the roof slopes and there is insulation up there, and the last time I saw them they were up there in the insulation."

"When was the last time that you saw those tapes up there in the insulation?" Metcalfe asked. She knew the house had been literally pulled apart, no strand of insulation left unexplored after Paul's hunting knife was found concealed there. The only other thing in the insulation had been Spike the iguana's skin.

"Well," said Karla, with schoolgirl candor in contradiction of her previous statement, "I have never seen them in the insulation, I was told they were in the insulation."

"Who told you that?" Detective Metcalfe asked.

"Paul. He told me that if anything ever happened to him, that's where they were and I should take them and destroy them. Or if I knew of any police that were coming around, I should take them and destroy them."

"You referred to them, in your words, as videotapes."

"No, I'm sorry, videotape. I believe it was just a singular one."

"Let me take you back briefly for a moment." Metcalfe was very solicitous, even gentle. But she also realized that a good deal of information had been kept from Metro—or from her, at least. "You said that certain parts of Leslie Mahaffy's death and captivity . . ."

"No death was videotaped," Karla snapped. For someone who claimed not to have seen most of the six or seven hours of videotape, she was very specific about what had and had not been taped.

"Okay. Correct me," instructed Detective Metcalfe. "What was videotaped with Leslie Mahaffy?"

"The same thing: the sex and the part of her sitting on the living-room floor saying her name."

"Okay. And what happened to that . . ."

"Videotape? Well, I think you have it—or they have it," she nodded toward Gillies. Karla understood the separation between the two police forces very well.

"And where was that kept?"

"It was kept in the insulation. It was all on one videotape as far as I know."

"Okay. Sorry, I'm just a little bit confused," Metcalfe confessed, but she pursued it, trying to establish exactly what it was they should have been looking for. Even the Green Ribbon Task Force and Inspector Bevan did not know—for sure—that there were videotapes or the extent of Paul and Karla's trophy-taking. "Is there one separate tape for Mahaffy and one separate tape for French?"

"No. They're both on the same tape, as far as I know. As far as I know there is only one videotape, as far as I know. I never watched it. So, well, I was forced to watch it a couple of times, but I never took it out and watched it. So I don't know if it is all on one or if there is parts or whatever."

"Okay. Is there anything else that you can tell me? About Kristen?"

"Yes."

"She was very nice. She was a really nice girl. And she wasn't given any sleeping pills. The way she was killed, she was tied up, she was on her knees with her head curled down like that, kind of in a fetal position on her knees."

"Just a minute, Karla," Metcalfe interrupted, apparently more concerned about whether or not the video camera in the room was capturing all of Karla's gestures than she was about the content of the dialogue. "Just because I know the tape can't see your hands there."

"You know how I like to describe things that I am seeing,"

Karla said, continuing to bond with the female detective. Of course Detective Metcalfe knew; she remembered their nice drive to George Walker's office as if it were yesterday.

"I didn't pay attention to a lot of stuff that he did," Karla continued unabashedly. "Like, I didn't want to see those video-tapes. I didn't want to know about anything. . . ."

"I understand that he left some kind of a note with the videotape saying 'This is what I wanted' or 'This is what I was looking for' or something?" Detective Metcalfe asked.

Karla was not given a chance to answer. All of a sudden, Sergeant Gillies decided to interject. "Okay. Karla," he said, "you're doing very well. What we would like to do is go back to the beginning one more time, when you first meet Paul, and run through it again in chronological order. Can we do that?"

They had been talking about Tammy Lyn, videotape, who heard what, which instructions Paul had given to Karla, in what form, and now Sergeant Gillies wanted to go back to the begin-ning? Even Karla was slightly taken aback.

"Mm-hmm. You want to go back when I first met him, or you want to go back to when everything started happening?"

"That is up to you to decide," said Sergeant Gillies, not necessarily the most gifted manager of "induced" statements. When he made such comments he would either lower his chin, looking pointedly at his subject, or turn his head sideways, look away and wiggle his eyes.

Karla, at her most conciliatory and cooperative, said, "Well, it's whatever you want to hear. Well, I already told you. Well, I guess what I told you before, you may as well toss that whole thing out, because I didn't tell you the truth on everything, as you know. Whatever you want to hear."

Karla did another run-through of the events and demise of the two schoolgirls before they paused for a late-afternoon break.

"I remembered a couple of things while you were gone," Karla told Detective Metcalfe at 4:50 P.M., just after they re-sumed. "Nothing of real significance, but I think I should tell you."

Karla proceeded to tell the detectives that Kristen French

had resisted Paul. "And she said things, you know: 'Some things are worth dying for.' And then he showed her the videotape of Leslie—the part where she says her name, and . . . in order to scare her. And Kristen was very strong, and she didn't even act scared. And I just wanted you to know that, because I think it is something her parents would like to know, and she was very, very strong, and didn't show a lot of emotion throughout the whole thing."

"We appreciate you telling us that," said Detective Metcalfe gratefully.

"Like, I just want to help," Karla said definitively.

There was a power failure at Journey's End at 5:58 P.M. on the second day—Karla's first day of "cautioned" statements. Everyone agreed that was a sign they should stop.

The day had been devoted to a detailed discussion about what had happened to Tammy Lyn Homolka. They had just started on Leslie Mahaffy when the lights went out. Karla's "induced" and "cautioned" statements were characterized by abundant, precise detail.

Karla was anything but "flat" when she and her mother went shopping at a nearby mall that evening. She was effervescent. They went to Miracle Mart, a dress shop—Karla would need new clothes for court—and a pet store; Karla always checked out the pet stores.

She kibitzed with their police escort about dogs, pets, favorite movies and the fact that she wanted Buddy to have a career as a breeding stud. She and her mother dined at the Keg. Karla told the police that she had really wanted to become an Ontario Provincial Police officer.

Then mother and daughter went to the movies. *Indecent Proposal* was playing at a nearby theatre. *Indecent Proposal* was a movie about money and sex. Demi Moore's husband—played by Woody Harrelson—lost all the couple's money in Vegas, and a wealthy older man, played by Robert Redford, offered them a million dollars if the wife would spend one night with him. After their girls' night out Dorothy and Karla had a police escort back to their hotel. Karla asked the police if they carried guns and explained how she and George Walker had met and all about how Karla had arranged for him to get his Dalmatian. The Walkers called the dog Spencer. She would like to go to the movies again the following night, she said.

"During the search of your residence, a videotape was found," Sergeant Gillies continued. He described the segment with the hand and the comatose girl cryptically, as if the details were a closely guarded secret. Although Karla had stopped talking directly to Mary Lee Metcalfe, and Gillies regularly asked questions or interjected, Karla played to the antipathy they imagined Karla felt toward Gillies because of his sex.

At this point, Karla was aware that this 1:58 minute video was the only "porno" they had found. How would Karla have explained Jane? The last thing Karla wanted anyone to know was that she had done exactly the same thing she did to her sister to another, young teenage girl, whom she had befriended and personally lured into the house, a week before Paul brought Leslie Mahaffy home—three weeks before their wedding and six months after she killed her sister.

"Can you tell me the circumstances surrounding the making of that tape?" Sergeant Gillies asked. Karla could not. Gillies talked on about the possibility that there was yet another young woman.

"With another woman . . . what do you mean by 'another woman?' " Karla retorted.

"Not Kristen or Leslie," Sergeant Gillies said.

Karla replied with a question. "Was it Tammy?" Her interviewers did not know that Karla had already told Dr. Arndt a month earlier that whoever it was, the girl was still alive, and Karla chose not to enlighten them.

Gillies could not say.

"Well, I am sure it would be Tammy," Karla stated categorically, advising the officers that the only girls she had ever had oral sex with were the dead trio.

Over the four days and thirty hours of videotaped legal statements Karla covered the same ground time and again. She repeated the same stories, sometimes adding a new wrinkle, sometimes omitting a previously told detail. Because her "affect" remained flat, the only sign that a question was daunting or that she was floundering was her syntax. The interviewers were totally insensitive to Karla's state of mind. The truth, or the consequences, of her "cautioned" statements, was between Karla, her god and the Ministry of the Attorney-General.

"Karla, can I stop you for a minute?" Detective Metcalfe interjected. "Were there any other occasions where you had oral sex with another female, other than Tammy, Kristen or Leslie? Perhaps while you were on vacation . . ."

"On vacation? No, no, definitely not. There is no other incident that I recall."

Detective Metcalfe tried another approach. "Was there ever any other time that you were videotaped . . ."

"Well . . . I was videotaped with my friends, I was videotaped with my dog." Karla played dumb. "Do you mean like videotaped in a sexual way?"

That was what she meant.

"Yes, there was another time. There was a video that Paul and I made. It was—I think, it was after Tammy's death. Yeah, it was, it was while my parents were away at a furniture show, so it would have been in January. January or February, after Tammy's death. We made a tape of us having sex together, basically of us having sex together in front of the fireplace."

Sergeant Gillies handed Karla another still picture taken from the one-minute, fifty-eight-second video. Karla looked at it closely. "That's me, I'm sure. And I don't know whose hand that is. I don't know who that is." The hand in Karla's vagina had become, by now, an infamous, indelible image in the minds of approximately one hundred detectives and prosecutors.

"Whose hand might that be?" Gillies asked.

Studying the photograph intently, Karla digressed. "That's in our house, because I can recognize it from that thing there—that's the pull-out handle on the drawer of Paul's dresser. It's definitely not my parents' house, so it's our house . . . on Bayview. So that would have either been Kristen or Leslie," Karla said, even though she had already told Dr. Arndt it was neither.

"Were there other incidents of digital intercourse?" Whenever possible, the police preferred euphemisms.

"Oh, probably," Karla replied cavalierly. "With both girls, I'm sure. I can't remember specifically, but with both, I'm sure."

"In this picture, what does it show the other girl wearing?"

"It is a sweatshirt. It looks like a sweatshirt, and I don't know if that's underwear or—I don't know if it is underwear or just the bottom of the sweatshirt. . . . It looks like a sweatshirt to me, anyway."

"The fact that the girl would appear to be wearing a sweatshirt, does that help you identify who that party is?" Gillies's voice had a hint of frustration.

"Well, I don't think . . ." Karla started backpedaling syntactically. "Like I said, I am pretty sure that I didn't lend anything to Kristen or Leslie, but I guess I was—I am sure I am incorrect, because it obviously appears that this person is wearing a sweatshirt. But I can't tell from the body."

"The picture I showed you earlier today is from the same video."

Karla absorbed Gillies's statement but did not acknowledge it. "It looks like my sister Tammy. It just gives me an impression. But that's definitely not Tammy. Do you have any other pictures?" Again, Karla responded to a question with a question, which brought Gillies to a standstill.

"Not with me right now, but I will get some others."

"Like, are these clips right after one another or something?" Karla asked.

"Yes."

"Okay, then based on that, this is the bed." That was a revelation. "It's not a pillow, it's probably the bed, because if that's the door, then the bed was right here." Karla pointed at a small spot on the photograph. "I don't know. I am going to have to think about them."

Gillies, starting to give up: "The top picture depicts a hand which appears to have an article of clothing or a rag or something in it." That was a vague image of Karla's halothane-soaked rag.

"Okay," Karla obfuscated. "Possibly—I don't know, I really don't know." Then something struck Karla as odd. "How come this one is so good, and this one is so blurry?"

"I don't know the answer to that question," Gillies replied. He might not have known the single frame in question had been laboriously plucked from the edited tape worked on by enhancement experts.

"Oh, okay. But you can get a clearer one of this, you think?"

"I hope to, yes."

And that was that. The police and the prosecutors just dropped the topic. They had so much information—too much information—and what they realized about the extent of Karla's involvement was, in and of itself, disturbing enough. It was unimaginable that Karla's involvement could be any more nefarious or complex.

After what she had told them about Tammy Lyn, Leslie Mahaffy and Kristen French and what had happened to them, how could there be anything else more seditious that she had avoided telling them?

Toward the end of the third day—Sunday, May 17, 1993, at 8:30 P.M.—Karla said to the detectives: "I don't know if you are doing it because you feel I need it, but I don't need as many breaks as we are taking . . . so you guys break for whatever you want to break for, don't worry about me."

Karla had a unique quality. The more difficult and trying her circumstances, the stronger she became. She consumed other people's emotional distress the way she consumed drugs. She was a sponge for attention; the closer and more intently she was scrutinized, the more she opened up. She fed on her facilitators' astonishment and abhorrence. On the morning of the third day, it got to be too much for Detective Metcalfe; she became ill and had to be excused from the interview. Karla solicitously said that she hoped the detective would soon feel better. Detective Metcalfe was replaced by her partner, Ron Whitefield.

Gillies, Metcalfe, Whitefield and other observers—everyone had who reviewed the thirty-plus hours of taped interviews— were left with two indelible images: one verbal, the other visual.

The visual image was of Leslie Mahaffy's head being dropped, "plop," by Paul Bernardo into the wet cement. Karla had told them, "Well, he kind of joked. Like, I guess he had to joke—I don't know if he was sickened by it or not. But he was kind of joking about it and saying, that, you know, when he—I don't even like saying it—you know, when he cut her head off, he just held it up to him and looked at it and just plopped it in the cement."

The verbal image was Kristen fiercely declaring, "Some things are worth dying for."

Paul Jason Teale a.k.a. Paul Kenneth Bernardo was formally charged on May 18, 1993, with two counts of first-degree murder in the deaths of Leslie Mahaffy and Kristen French, as well as two counts of kidnapping, two counts of unlawful confinement, two counts of aggravated sexual assault and one count of causing an indignity to a human body. He made a brief but sensational court appearance on the nineteenth.

The police told a frustrated press corps that they might well be laying more charges against Mr. Bernardo in the near future.

At noon Karla was escorted back to St. Catharines General

Hospital to provide blood, hair and saliva samples as agreed in the resolution.

It took four officers to ferry Karla and her mother around town: Staff Sergeant Murray MacLeod, Sergeants Osler and Whiteway and Constable Ciszek. From the hospital they went to police headquarters, where MacLeod continued to interview Karla in Room 221—about the problem he was having with his pet Schnauzer. The dog was suffering from something the vet had called separation anxiety. Karla was understanding—Buddy had suffered from separation anxiety, as well. She explained the treatment and prognosis in detail. Staff Sergeant MacLeod was relieved.

At 3:45 P.M. Karla was "transported"—as it was recorded in MacLeod's notebook—across the street to the courthouse. Karla made a brief appearance wherein she waived her right to a preliminary trial and elected for trial by judge alone. She did not enter a plea. Bail was set at $110,000. She was remanded to June 7, 1993. At 5:20 P.M., MacLeod and Ciszek took the Homolka women—Karla, Lori and Dorothy—home.

Inspector Vince Bevan and the Niagara Regional Police held a formal press conference the following day to announce what had already been widely reported—Bernardo had been charged with nine counts of murder and mayhem.

They had also charged his estranged wife, Karla Bernardo née Homolka, of St. Catharines, Ontario, with two counts of manslaughter. According to police, Ms. Homolka's parents had put up their house to make the $110,000 bail and Karla had been released to their custody.

Inspector Bevan made a point of telling the press that there were twenty-two stipulations to Karla's bail, including that she phone him every day, not leave the house without advising police an hour in advance, never leave the house without a family member and abstain from nonprescription drugs and alcohol.

·   ·   ·

Steve Irwin's immediate superior had been talking to an officer who acted as a liaison between the Toronto police and the Green Ribbon Task Force.

The prosecutors had made it known to the Green Ribbon Task Force and Inspector Bevan that they had the impression the interview with Bernardo—the one Irwin had conducted at Halton on February 17—had been audiotaped. Inspector Bevan had been assured that they were videotaping the interview but apparently the technician had forgotten to put a blank tape in the videocassette recorder. Now, the prosecutors were wondering where the audiotapes were?

Detective Irwin did not know what to say to his boss. It appeared he had lost them.

Karla and her mother kept an appointment to see Dr. Arndt. Karla was feeling very badly. "Compared to what," Dr. Arndt jotted in the margin of his notepad.

"The phone rings every five minutes," she whined. "Everyone is fine, except for me."

She told Dr. Arndt that she had talked to the police for three full days in Whitby.

"They videotaped everything," she said.

Karla was surprised to find Sister Josephine in Dr. Arndt's waiting room. Dr. Arndt was talking to Karla's mother, so Karla went into the waiting room to read a magazine.

After she and the nun exchanged pleasantries, Sister Josephine said she had something for Karla. Sister Josephine gave Karla a small wooden crucifix.

Karla was delighted. It was just the way it had happened in *Michelle Remembers,* when Michelle was given a cross wrapped in tissue paper by Father Leo. Just as Father Leo had told Michelle, Sister Josephine told Karla, "If you're feeling frightened, you can hold on to this. . . ."

                    •   •   •

After the Homolkas left Dr. Arndt's office, Sister Josephine gently accused Dr. Arndt of a connivance: he had planned the whole thing, from putting the sister in the same room at the hospital to this coincidence of appointments. The sister had decided to take the doctor's advice. She had given Karla the crucifix, after all. The timing seemed right. Although it might not do any good, it could not do any harm. But whether it was God's will or Dr. Arndt's was another question.

"But the way I organized this," Dr. Arndt later said, a glint in his eye and a "who, me?" look of self-effacement, "it was purely coincidental—a very coincidental meeting. But everybody knows these things don't happen by accident or for no reason." Dr. Arndt suggested it did not matter whether it was his doing or the Almighty's; in the end the fleeting relationship between Karla and the sister seemed to have been good for both of them.

Kim Doyle, Ken Murray's office administrator, law clerk and the liaison between Murray and his client, Paul Bernardo, was bemused. Shortly after they had returned from the excursion to 57 Bayview, Murray had rented videotape equipment capable of copying 8mm video cassettes onto the larger, VHS format.

It was the fact that Murray had paid cash that caught Doyle's attention. Since Bernardo's defense was being paid by Legal Aid, any expenses—computers, telephones, videocassette players and recorders—would have been covered under the certificate. It was not very hard for Kim or Murray's junior, Carolyn MacDonald, to imagine what Murray had taken out of the house that night or why he had surreptitiously rented the taping equipment.

By May 28, there was little question in Kim Doyle's mind that Ken Murray had watched the videotapes and made copies.

Now that Karla was out of the hospital, Dr. Arndt's sessions with her took place in his office, which was in a modest two-story house just north of the hospital.

On his bookshelf, beside DMS-III, the psychiatrist's diagnostic bible, was a piece of the Berlin Wall and a picture of Dr. Arndt inside the Roman catacombs—he was kneeling down inside one of the catacombs, surrounded by thousands of human skulls. Hanging next to the picture was an Ojibway dream catcher.

The dream catcher was a wooden hoop with a woven leather web that spoked outward to the hoop's edge from a large central bead. As Dr. Arndt explained it to Karla, Indian lore had it that dreams float in the night air like moths. The web of the dream catcher allowed the good dreams to pass through; bad dreams became entangled in the dream catcher until they could be sorted out in the light of day.

Clutching the crucifix Sister Josephine had given her, Karla told Dr. Arndt she was sick to death of having to hide all the time. She could not talk to anybody. She started to cry.

"These are the first tears I'm seeing from her," Dr. Arndt scribbled on a scrap of paper.

Karla wanted all her friends to know what was going on with her—but she could not tell anybody. "I do need help, I do need medication," she said, sobbing.

She had gone through all her pills again. Dr. Arndt suggested he put her back in the hospital for a few days of sleep therapy.

"Perhaps we will catch some bad dreams," Dr. Arndt suggested. Karla readily agreed.

After a weekend in dreamland, Karla woke up refreshed. Back in St. Catharines she wrote her friend Kathy about the bottle of beaujolais she had taken to a party and drunk all by herself. Karla said her tolerance was "ridiculously high," but she had had a really good time. "It's nice to get out of the house once in a while. . . ."

Karla explained that the media kept coming around all the time because "they don't have a really good current photo . . . yet. It's kind of like a game now, trying not to let them get a picture."

She ended her chatty letter with a lament about the hatred

people in St. Catharines unjustly harbored toward her. "I really need single girlfriends," she added, "to go out and meet men with."

On June 7, Steve Irwin found the lost audiotapes of Paul Bernardo's arrest interview. Right after that interview, Detective Irwin had gone on vacation. The tapes had been thrown in with his luggage and forgotten.

Furthermore, the police discovered the entire interview had not been taped in the first place. The technician had forgotten to turn on the tape recorder for the first couple of hours. That same day Detective Irwin was reassigned to Intelligence Services. A decade of chasing pedophiles and serial rapists was over—now he would spend his days chasing hate mongers, neo-Nazis, skinheads and the like.

George Walker picked up the Homolka women early on the morning on June 10. They had an appointment to meet the warden and tour the Kingston Prison for Women. It was a good four-and-a-half-hour drive. Lori Homolka went on about how she had met a boy who was "just amazing." Lori said she planned to marry him the following summer. Karla turned to Walker and said, "I'll be able to get a pass for that, won't I?"

Between 2:15 and 3:45 P.M. they met with the deputy warden and the prison coordinator to discuss Karla's medical and psychiatric records. They made arrangements to transfer Karla directly from court—on July 6—without remand for assessment or an appeal period, directly into the prison medical center.

On June 10, Karla wrote to Kristy Maan again: "Tomorrow the police want to speak to me again to 'tie up loose ends,' so to speak. I've heard that they also want to take me back to the house. Why, exactly, I don't know . . . Can a person like me ever be forgiven?

"We had such a beautiful life together in the beginning," she recalled, of her early days with Paul.

. . .

"Oh, my God, I forgot all about this. This makes me feel disgusting." Karla took a long pause after Sergeant Gillies showed her two photographs "taken from a video camera." After all, it was such a beautiful day outside, and she had thought all she would have to do was clarify a few minor details and drive around with the police in their van and show them where she and Paul had dumped "stuff"—stuff like Leslie Mahaffy's torso and Kristen French's crushed Mickey Mouse watch.

Karla felt ridiculous holding those photographs of herself, naked with a prostitute. She had not dressed for such a down-and dirty confrontation. In her crisp white blouse, with a pleated checked miniskirt and long, fitted navy vest, she looked more like a schoolgirl than a whoremonger. Her hair was in a long French braid down her back and she wore white tights to complement her blouse and offset her shiny new Bass loafers.

Sergeant Gillies had called George Walker and said that there were a few things the police wanted to clear up. Could they possibly take Karla out to Lake Gibson and back to the house? Walker agreed. They would make a videotape record of their excursion on June 17, 1993.

When the police arrived to pick her up, Karla offered Sergeant Gillies a gift: a blue hairbrush she said Kristen French had used while she was being held captive.

After the bridges and Lake Gibson, where Karla revealed that Paul had also dumped his grandfather's power saw, they started to drive around in a vain attempt to find Kristen French's discarded jewelry—specifically, the pieces of her Mickey Mouse watch that Karla said Paul had made her discard.

Empty-handed, they went on to police headquarters to identify and initial the photographs Gillies had shown Karla. Then they took Karla to the house on Bayview, so she could show them things there, like places where they might still find fingerprints, maybe even blood.

Karla was looking forward to the house tour. She wanted to see what was left of her personal belongings; rumor had it that her estranged husband's defense team had scooped up all the valuables and that enraged her. Sure enough, her hope chest, the silver tray and her beloved champagne glasses were gone. When Sergeant Gillies was not looking, Karla plucked a tag from an empty hanger in a closet full of empty hangers. It was the tag from Tammy Lyn's bridesmaid dress, the one Kristy Maan had worn. Karla was not going to leave the house without a trophy.

When the police took Karla home, she gave them some more memorabilia: a gray and white skirt and a small bottle of perfume she believed Kristen had worn and used.

The St. Catharines Standard ran an extensive report the following day, describing the phalanx of police divers who had descended on Lake Gibson. Apparently, they were searching for a power saw at the bottom of the lake.

Later in the day Walker met with Karla and her father to review the doctors' reports, which would be filed in support of her guilty pleas.

Karla noted another Bernardo bail hearing in her datebook. "Paul bail hearing/SR, Alex's [Ford] 25th birthday."

At this bail hearing in Scarborough, Bernardo was charged with three more counts of sexual assault and buggery in relation to two new victims. In an unusual move, "Maximum Mary," the hard-nosed prosecutor in Scarborough, adopted the Henley Island rape, as well as other charges from outside her jurisdiction. There were so many charges and victims that every newspaper and news broadcast quoted different statistics.

"There is strength in numbers," Hall told the media when they asked why she had agreed to this unusual move. Vociferous when prosecuting violent sex offenders, Hall told the press that this amalgamation of charges would make it easier for victims to come forward. But there was more to it than that. In her estimation, the more the merrier, because it strengthened her prosecutorial position.

Mary Hall was starting to become a large thorn in her ministry bosses' backsides. She believed that the Crown law office's deal with Karla Homolka was unconscionable. Hall thought that Karla Homolka was at least as guilty as Paul Bernardo. Her understanding of the nature of the relationship between Paul and Karla differed dramatically from Inspector Bevan's.

Hall had Bernardo on the Scarborough rapes. She did not need Karla Homolka. She wanted the maximum the law allowed for both offenders. On the Scarborough rapes alone, Mary Hall was confident she could put Mr. Bernardo away for many lifetimes. While she prosecuted Paul Bernardo for those rapes, the police in St. Catharines could take all the time they needed to develop their case.

Paul was quickly losing his "Baywatch" looks. His dark roots were starting to show. Ken Murray knew that bail for Bernardo was out of the question. The charges were too serious. After umpteen appearances, Murray finally waived Bernardo's right to a bail hearing. Paul returned to his tiny cell in the Metro East Detention Center. The cell was about the same size as Tammy Lyn Homolka's bedroom, without the closet space.

Karla wrote Kristy Maan another letter, in which she told Kristy she could not answer all her questions until after she was in jail. She told Kristy that Kathy and Alex had come to visit and that it was weird "seeing all of my friends 'one last time.' "

"Yes, I can read in jail," Karla noted. "I have *The Road Less Travelled* and a Bible to read. I'm also going to go to Queen's University and study, probably to be a social worker."

She thanked Kristy for all her help and said that she had asked God to help her when she left Paul and "look what had happened since:

1. he's being punished for what he did
2. I got out safely
3. I'm being punished very fairly—they could've charged me with 2 counts of first degree murder instead of manslaughter.

4. I'm getting my university education and
5. I'm much closer to my friends and telling no more lies.

Anyway, got to go!" She instructed Kristy to write her soon, at her "new address."

Karla's trial began in St. Catharines on the morning of June 28, 1993. The first three days were devoted to legal arguments made on behalf of the media—the Canadian Broadcasting Corporation, the national wire press, three of the country's major newspapers—and Stephen Williams, author. The arguments were in opposition to a motion for a publication ban brought by the prosecution. Although Paul and Karla were not co-accused, for the purposes of Karla's trial the pair were portrayed as such by the authorities.

Outside the courthouse, George Walker postured for the media and declared his client's goodwill toward the victims' families and the community in general. Her trial would be expeditious, he assured the press, but it was unlikely the media would be allowed in the courtroom.

In every other case in Canadian judicial history where co-accused defendants were separately tried, publication bans had been requested by a defense lawyer for one of the co-accused.

These requests by defense lawyers made some sense. If two people committed a crime together yet were tried separately—at different times—then, theoretically, evidence made public during the trial of the first person prosecuted would impinge upon the second person's ability to receive a fair trial.

By now, Ken Murray had reviewed all the evidence, including the videotapes, and he had unequivocally concluded that Karla Homolka was as guilty as her estranged husband.

What Murray had seen helped him to rationalize what was arguably an untenable position. The politicalization of this case and what Murray perceived as the Crown's duplicity and arrogance had made it almost impossible for him to function effectively or rationally.

Mr. Murray and his equally deluded client came to the reasonable conclusion that a publication ban was meant to protect Karla and the prosecution, not Paul Bernardo's right to a fair trial. Murray called the Crown's resolution agreement with Karla Homolka a "deal with the devil." Repeating and re-printing the phrase, ad nauseam, the media made of that simple phrase a mantra.

The broadcast and print media had a legion of lawyers lined up to argue rightly, and righteously, that court proceedings should be a matter of public record.

The legal arguments against a publication ban were occasionally impassioned and articulate, but for the most part they were exceedingly tedious and dry.

The most interesting aspect of each day's proceedings was Karla's remarkable stillness. She sat behind the bulletproof glass in the prisoner's dock every day, for seven hours a day, without moving a muscle. It was as if she were a mannequin. Everyone remarked upon Karla's stillness. Finally, the press began to speculate among themselves that she must be stoned.

At breaks, Lori Homolka would take Karla's arm and they would leave the courtroom, arm in arm. Otherwise, Karla remained still.

Her chair moved, though. Almost imperceptibly, magically, day by day, Karla's chair moved until Karla was sitting flush with the right side of the dock. The families of Karla's victims were sitting up front to her left, while her parents and her sister sat up front on her right with Sergeant Bob Gillies, who had become the Homolka family handler, driver and personalized "bulletproof shield." His peers nicknamed him Bob "Homolka" Gillies.

After Murray Segal and Michal Fairburn made the prosecution's precedent-setting argument to suppress the details of Karla Homolka's trial, Tim Breen argued against the motion on Bernardo's behalf.

Ken Murray had subcontracted Breen, a young, articulate, appellate lawyer who lived with Carolyn MacDonald and worked in the downtown law offices of Rosen, Fleming, to contest the publication ban.

Such a ban would ensure that his client, Paul Bernardo,

would not get a fair trial, Breen contended. The best way to guarantee his client the inalienable right to a fair trial would be if the prosecution's "deal with the devil" received full public scrutiny and everything Karla Homolka had to say in evidence of these crimes was immediately known to everyone in Canada. Breen was the only one who rightly pointed out that the police had manipulated the whole scenario, both in the Crown's law office and with the media.

Then George Walker had his say. He drew himself up to his full Lyndon B. Johnson height and strode across the courtroom, his gown flowing behind him. Suffused with the spirit of Clarence Darrow, he spoke about his concern for the community: Walker did not give a damn about anyone outside of St. Catharines—this was strictly a regional matter, and no one else's business.

The modern courtroom tends to be a prosaic place. Today, lawyers stand their ground and ask questions of witnesses or address juries from lecterns.

The flourish, the gowned histronics of the old-style fire-and-brimstone orator, took the lawyers from the big city aback. To see Walker in full flight, doing an Elmer Gantry and proselytizing about family values, the integrity of community and victims' rights, particularly in light of who he was representing and given the circumstances, was both tragic and comical.

And it was not only how he said it, it was what he said. He said that the Homolkas were victims, too; they had already lost one daughter, and in a very real sense, they were now losing another. They, too, were deserving of compassion.

As far as Walker was concerned, the freedom of the press could be damned as well, because the demand for that so-called freedom was driven by greed. When the kettle calls the pot black, so loudly and unabashedly, it generally takes everyone's breath away, and Walker's rhetorical flourishes were no exception. Looking Justice Francis Kovacs right in the eye—another native son—Walker said it: our community. As Justice Kovacs acknowledged the point, Walker, with a swish of his robe, sat down.

.   .   .

The judge adjourned Homolka's trial on Friday, July 2, for the long Canada Day weekend. Court was scheduled to convene again on the following Tuesday morning, when Kovacs would render his decision on the publication ban.

It was hotter than Hades in St. Catharines; a record-breaking summer. The temperature pushed a hundred degrees every day. There was a guy in a Spiderman costume on the street outside the courthouse handing out pamphlets about the government's unholy "deal with the devil." At least Karla was seen for what she was by Spiderman.

Described in the tabloids as ailing, Kenneth Bernardo was paroled. He had done two months of his nine-month sentence. His daughter, Debbie, wrote a letter to the parole board on her father's behalf.

Debbie had already forgiven him for what he had done to her all those years before and now she had found it in her heart to also forgive him for what he had done to her daughter—after all, her father had paid his debt to society.

As soon as Mr. Bernardo hit the streets, he started to try and sell his story about having raised the most notorious sex killer in Canadian history. Since he had barely been on speaking terms with his son since Paul had found out Ken was not his real father and since he had not seen or heard from Paul since Paul got married, over two years earlier, Ken did not know the half of it—a fact that was soon found out.

Over the weekend, Dorothy Homolka went to MultiTech, a retail store in St. Catharines, and bought a color TV for Karla's prison cell. "My daughter's going to need this," she told the clerk. "She's going away for a while."

That weekend the Homolkas had a pool party: it started in the late afternoon and went long into the warm summer night. It was a strange, hapless sight, this raucous going-away party for Karla.

The guests were all drinking. Reporters planted themselves on the hill behind the house. The Beastie Boys' "You Gotta

Fight for Your Right to Party" blared from the boom box. They played some of Karla's favorite Guns N' Roses' songs.

With their long lenses poised, like seafarers searching for the first sight of land, the press corps camped on the hill until someone called the cops, who dutifully ran them off.

Behind city desks, editors poured over the day's takes, trying to determine whether or not Karla's breasts were visible in any of the shots. One of the photographers had caught her earlier, topless, sunning herself.

Karla sat stoically, stoned, under her Blossom hat. Mrs. Homolka talked too loudly, laughing, sipping her drink, saying things such as, "I hope Karla's trial doesn't last much longer; I'm running out of money to buy the girls' clothes."

The next-door neighbor, Lynn Clarke, and Karla's many friends, shielded her from the day of the long lenses with a large sheet of cardboard. One of the guests said, in the true spirit of Karla's Beastie Boys song, "Oh what the heck, the girls are dead, you can't bring them back, why not party?"

"You don't have to talk to them." Dorothy Homolka told Lynn McCann about Paul's defense lawyer's private investigators. "And you'd have nothing to say in his defense, anyway."

To her co-workers at the Shaver Clinic, Dorothy appeared to be basking in the spotlight. She was overheard on the telephone talking to a dog trainer about Buddy the Rottweiler, who by that time had wreaked havoc on the tiny Homolka household. Dorothy loudly exclaimed her astonishment at the fact that the person she was speaking with did not know who she was. Lynn ignored Dorothy. Lynn said Dorothy Homolka was a very strong-willed person, like her daughter. According to Lynn, Dorothy "can put on a big act, if she wants to."

The fix was in and all the solicitors' eloquent words were as dust in the wind. There was a distinct Alice-through-the-Looking-Glass atmosphere in the courtroom that Tuesday morning—everything seemed to be reversed; nothing made sense.

Judges in Canada have been very quick to seal their courtrooms or issue sweeping publication bans that make a mockery of the idea of an open, democratic society. Unlike Americans, who have been reared on the notion that happiness is to be pursued and life and liberty are God-given rights, Canadians have idealized law, order and another outrageous oxymoron: good government. There is no tradition of civil disobedience in Canada.

Kovacs ruled that the American media and the general public were to be excluded from the courtroom. Even though the courtroom in St. Catharines only held 160 people in total—between the press, the police, the families and the lawyers, there were only seventy-five seats left—the public could not be trusted to keep its mouth shut. Kovac's order was less enforceable in the United States than it was in Canada, so the American media were out.

The Canadian media could remain. Although they could not publish what they heard, they could listen to what was said. They were being allowed to bear witness, Justice Kovacs said. The ban was so broad that even Karla's plea was a prohibited bit of information. Her sentence could be published, but not the fact that she had pled guilty.

Murray Segal read into evidence a cursory, bare bones rendition of what Paul and Karla had done to her sister, Leslie Mahaffy and Kristen French. The press was both breathless and speechless.

Previously, the press had no details about this case. Now that they had them, they could not publish. It was probably the two for Tammy, with impunity, that was the real breath-taker. That, and the fact that it was immediately evident to everyone that Karla could have saved all three girls' lives, and that Kristen French would never have been kidnapped if not for Karla. The sister was the astonishing kicker. Still the Canadian media unanimously respected the ban.

Sergeant Bob Gillies and another officer drove Karla to prison that evening. In the van they had her Mickey Mouse posters and her new color TV. They arrived in Kingston at

10:00 P.M. The next day, Dorothy and Karel Homolka granted formal permission to exhume Tammy Lyn's body.

Karla wrote to Kristy Maan: "I'm eligible for full parole in 4 years. Not bad . . . Court on Tuesday was absolute hell . . . That judge really hated me big time . . . Please write soon, it's lonely in here."

CHAPTER

twenty-nine

St. Catharines' Victoria Lawn Cemetery is in Ripley's Believe It or Not. A highway runs through it, and that makes it unique. The cemetery was designed by Fredrick L. Olmsted. Olmsted had designed Central Park in New York. There are more than sixty thousand graves on either side of the highway. A double plot goes for about sixteen hundred dollars.

With Karla in the Kingston Prison for Women and Paul Bernardo held indefinitely without bail in the Metropolitan

East Detention Center, the tent finally went up around Tammy Lyn's grave on the morning of July 20.

At first there were only four workers from Alexander Awnings, a couple of uniform cops, Sergeant Ivan Madronic and Sergeant Brian Nesbitt. No way the media, who had been camping out at the cemetery every day for weeks anticipating the disinterment, were going to get any pictures of Tammy's waterproof, airtight cement vault being lifted out of the grave, not as long as Inspector Vince Bevan was in charge.

They started using the hydraulic lifters to get the vault out around eight; it was a rather delicate operation, the straps had to be just right or the thing would fall and split open and there would be hell to pay.

Eventually there were dozens of uniforms and plainclothes, as well as five coroners and other attendant officials around the grave. There was the funeral director George Darte and a priest, even though the Homolkas were not Catholic.

By 9:00 A.M., there were so many upright bodies that Sergeant Riddle was assigned to make a list. With the tent and the media and Riddle diligently scribbling in his notebook, an observer might easily have thought it was a mob funeral. It took more than four hours to get Tammy Lyn's casket out of the ground. It was placed in a hearse marked MacKinnon & Bowes Limited Removal Service and driven to the coroner's building in Toronto.

The forensic pathology unit at the morgue in Toronto had a full complement of interested bystanders, as well. The chief coroner, Dr. Jim Young, was there, as was the deputy chief, Dr. Jim Cairns. Inspector Bevan and Sergeant Brian Nesbitt were there. Constable Michael Kershaw was taking pictures. Two or three other officers, waving the task force flag, stood around shuffling their feet.

There were two pathologists—Dr. David King from Hamilton and Dr. Noel McAuliffe. Dr. McAuliffe would do the actual work. There were half a dozen assistants, six other doctors, a few more cops and various people from the facility, including an X-ray technician. They all took notice of how well-preserved Tammy was.

Tammy's casket was a repository of curious items—a small brown teddy bear with a yellow ribbon around its neck; a photo of Mr. and Mrs. Homolka in a restaurant; a close-up of Paul and Karla with "Show 1988" written on the back; another picture of Paul and Karla at the site of their engagement; a Sir Winston Churchill '88–89 student-card picture of Lori; an envelope from Paul and Karla's wedding, containing a book of Paul and Karla matches, the invitation, reception card and a napkin for June 29, 1991; a blue and white nylon soccer jacket with a Cobra emblem on the back; a silver-colored neck chain with a peace emblem; a small soccer ball, a rope cord with a CGIT (Canadian Girls in Training) '87 pin; a candy-cane wrapper; a letter from both Paul and Karla dated Dec. 27, 1990; a little picture of Jesus Christ; a plastic heart with three small flowers arranged around it; and a letter from Tammy's friend Tricia Garcia.

The corpse was wearing red-and-white socks. The socks were decorated with bunnies dressed in Santa Claus outfits. The gray track pants had the bottoms rolled up and Tammy's white-and-black sweater was patterned with little Scottish terriers.

Around the left wrist there was a silver chain; on the right-hand ring finger, a small ring; gold-colored earrings in the pierced ears; that flat gold-colored chain Karla had been wearing the night Tammy died—the same one that had become caught in her mouth like a horse's bit while she and Paul were making their Christmas video was clasped around the corpse's neck. The ring on the chain was a man's, gold with a diamond setting.

The doctors took scalp hair, vaginal packing, a couple of vaginal swabs, some skin from the left side of the face, an oral swab, muscle tissue from the left arm, a kidney, breast tissue, pubic hair, a segment of the small bowel, rectal packing, muscle tissue from the left thigh, a segment of the large bowel, some fat from the right thigh, a lung and the liver. Dr. McAuliffe had never had such a large audience and he was very thorough. It was possible that something significant could be discovered in a body that had been embalmed and buried for two and a half years.

Why they were looking for traces of Halcion and halothane was anybody's guess. Given the unstable chemical nature of halothane, it was almost untraceable in the recently deceased. All that would be proven by the presence of these drugs in Tammy Lyn's remains was what Karla had already admitted—that she had killed her sister by administering a lethal combination of Halcion and halothane. The authorities were also trying to determine the cause of that massive burn on the left side of Tammy Lyn's face—which was still quite evident even though decomposition had taken its deliberate toll.

On the swabs and packing they would look for semen and compare the pubic hair to other hairs that had been found in a folded paper towel in a brown paper bag containing six hairs and a fingernail, which the police had recovered from the north closet in the master bedroom at 57 Bayview.

Around 4:00 P.M., Inspector Bevan took Sergeant Nesbitt's notebook and left the room. When he returned he declared that the Homolkas had instructed him to remove the pictures of Paul and Karla, the ring on the necklace and the letter from Paul and Karla and all the pre-printed wedding paraphernalia from the casket. They left the gold necklace.

Tammy Lyn's body was back in its grave by nine that night. Constable Kershaw retrieved samples of Eckels arterial dynotone, and Eckels fumeless dyno, the embalming fluids they had used on Tammy Lyn at the George Darte Funeral Home, and delivered them to the Keith Kelder, a scientist at the forensic center.

There was another spot of blood on a blanket the Identification officers had found in the house, and the decision taken was to test it at a lab in Helsinki, Finland. If the results placed Leslie or Kristen in contact with that blanket, then it bolstered the case against Paul Bernardo.

The sample had to be hand delivered. Chain of possession was important in evidential matters. The question of who would go to Helsinki was easy: the only available senior officer with a passport, Inspector Vince Bevan.

Bevan took his wife. One evening while they were waiting for the lab results, the Bevans took a dinner cruise. On their way in to port, Inspector Bevan was taken aback when a German tourist tapped him on the shoulder and inquired if he was not Inspector Vince Bevan, the chief investigator in that Bernardo case?

On the third of August, Karla spent her first night in her jail cell. Although she had been in prison since July 8, she had been resident in the hospital unit for assessment. She had her first official therapy session as a prisoner with the prison psychiatrist, Dr. Roy Brown.

Dr. Brown was the proverbial old soldier. Born in Kilmarnock, Scotland, on July 29, 1926, he was sixty-eight years old. He joined the Royal Navy in 1943, trained as a pilot and exited the service as a sub-lieutenant (A) after serving in the Pacific.

His medical degree was in emergency medicine, dermatology and venerology from the Aberdeen Royal Infirmary. He joined the Royal Canadian Air Force in 1952 and then completed one year in internal medicine with an emphasis on psychosomatic disorders, followed by a two-year course in psychiatry from which he graduated in 1958. He practiced psychiatry in the Canadian military until 1976.

Then he retired and moved to Kingston, where he embarked—part-time—on a second career as a practicing psychiatrist working on government contracts. At the point when Dr. Brown met Karla, he had almost fully retired. The women's prison was his last contract.

For profile, in Dr. Brown's long prison experience, Karla was without peer. Dr. Brown noted that Karla was "undergoing some increased stress"—undoubtedly related to the fact that she had finally been put in a closet with bars.

K4W, as the Kingston Prison for Women was known throughout Canada, was well over a century old, and had more in common with one of those nightmarish Piranesi gothic visions of hell than a modern correctional facility. Karla's cell was no more than six by ten feet. K4W was a turbulent place.

Karla was allegedly having bad dreams, and Dr. Brown offered to refer her to a psychologist, but "she declined, saying, "I don't want to discuss my life with anyone else." Karla was sufficiently alert to record that Paul was back in court about the "murders and my assault" in her datebook on August 5.

On August 31, Karla's datebook said "Bob + Ivan visiting." "Bob + Ivan" were Sergeants Bob Gillies and Ivan Madronic, both of whom had been assigned by Inspector Vince Bevan to handle Karla in prison. The task force had now shifted its focus to the prosecution of Paul Bernardo. The delicate care and feeding of its star witness was tantamount.

Karla told the two sergeants that prison conditions were far better than she had expected. They reviewed the injuries she said she had received at Paul's hand and a recent letter to Kathy Ford in which she said Paul had kicked her in the ribs sometime in the summer of 1992. No, she had not gone to the doctor, Karla told them, but did they know that in grade twelve, after she met Paul, her grades went down? Also, she had not confided in the prison psychiatrist; she wanted her own psychiatrist, but the prison had said no. Could anything be done?

Karla had immediately enrolled in a non–degree entry-level university program, with a concentration on sociology and psychology. The correspondence course would begin on September 13, 1993, and Karla could hardly wait. Dorothy was going around telling anyone who would listen that Karla was a victim, just like the dead girls. Karla had unlimited access to the telephone and called her mother every day at work.

Dorothy and Karel were just thankful that Karla was away from Paul and safe. Many of the staff at the Shaver Clinic were deeply troubled by the fact that Dorothy had never shown any remorse for anything Karla had done, but they had been officially instructed to indulge Mrs. Homolka, so they did.

On September 5, Karla wrote to Kristy Maan. "I'm really sorry to hear that you feel the way you do. I can't and won't try to justify anything to you. I was under the impression that friends were friends, no matter what. 'A friend is one who knows all about you and loves you just the same.' Thank God almost all of the people I call my friends truly are my friends. I'm very disappointed, Kristy, but I'm not about to try and change your mind. Thanks for everything you've done for me in the past and good luck in the future.

"P.S. By the way I think about everyone involved, every fucking day. It kills me inside to know all of the hurt inside everyone's heart, least of all my own. I just can't deal with it or I'll die inside.

"And don't bother trying to defend my actions. It's not your place to do that. That's my family's position and people who really care about me. Kristy, your letter hurt me deeply, I just want you to know that.

"And also, if you can't accept things now, wait until Paul goes to trial and the publication ban is lifted. Then you will really hate me. So I guess it's better for the both of us that things happened now instead of later. You will never understand what he did to me and no amount of explanation will make you understand.

"And you know what else really amazes me? I get letters everyday from strangers telling me that they understand that I was dragged into this and that I am a victim, too. The police think I'm a victim. One person even told me he thought I was more of a victim than Kristen and Leslie are! And one of my friends turns against me?"

Adjusting to life behind bars was a bit like adjusting to summer camp for Karla, even though it meant living in a cell the size of her old clothes closet. At the insistence of the Crown, she had been placed in segregation. In general population Karla would be dead, cons being less forgiving than police and prosecutors.

"It's not so bad up here," Karla wrote to Dr. Arndt on September 9, explaining that she planned to stay in segregation for her entire sentence because "people do get stabbed in here, and people do get killed." She had personalized her cell with Mickey Mouse posters and all her other "stuff." She told Dr. Arndt she was settling in nicely.

"Four other girls live here with me and they're all nice," her letter continued. "We're usually let out of our cells at night from 6:00 to 9:00 P.M. to socialize. We usually watch TV, play cards and Trivial Pursuit and talk." All in all, Karla and her happy coterie of fellow segregation inmates were trying "to concentrate on having fun, rather than being in prison."

Karla had a few problems. "The health care sucks," she wrote, and she could not get Valium because it was considered a "commodity among inmates." Still, in her lengthy diatribe to Dr. Arndt, written on notepaper decorated with cartoon teddy bears nuzzling noses on a park bench, she managed to give a precise list of the drugs she was still allowed—Tegetrol for the one seizure she had had, the antidepressant Surmontil, and a combination of Nozinan and Benadryl to help her sleep.

With the descriptive precision of a physician, she listed her concerns about the effect of certain drug combinations on her red blood cells and asked Dr. Arndt for his professional opinion. She had scant use for the resident psychiatrist, whom she said she was seeing twice a week. "I really don't like him," she explained in her loopy handwriting. "He's nice enough and all, but I just don't feel comfortable talking to him, nor do I trust him. Someone in here (another inmate) told me that what you say to any doctor in here can be told to the parole board. That really makes me distrust him."

In the Correctional Services Canada psychological services clinical progress files, Karla was called Carla Teale. Her federal prison service number was 287308D. She wrote to friends explaining that although breakfast came at 7:30 in the morning, she did not get up until 9:30, because she did not eat breakfast.

Karla helped clear the meal trays, and "boy, we waste tons of food in here," she observed. Karla sometimes ate the lunch that arrived at 11:00 A.M., and then settled into an afternoon of studying, letter writing or watching TV. Dinner came at 4:00 P.M. and the nurse brought her medication an hour later. Her most strenuous exercise was carrying the garbage down four flights of stairs. "I'm locked up twenty-two and a half hours a day. Unbelievable."

Not that Karla endured social isolation. She reluctantly saw seventy-year-old Dr. Brown in his second-floor office, every Tuesday and Thursday, for about an hour. She was constantly in contact with Sergeant Bob Gillies, who, since his assignment as the blond princess's chief server in her correctional tower, had inescapably become an honorary Homolka.

However, when George Walker visited her, in spite of her avowed disrespect and suspicion of Dr. Brown, Karla told him that her therapy sessions were sufficient, especially since the doctor, who was semiretired, sometimes went away for weeks at a time.

Although George cautioned her about opening up to any inmates, he gave her the go-ahead to enter into discussions with the prison psychologist, Jan Heney. Ms. Heney spelled Karla's name Carla, and she, too, had never had a higher-profile "client." By definition, almost all of the women with whom Heney had professional contact had been abused as children or had been in abusive relationships. Abuse and its consequences were Jan Heney's specialty.

For the next few months, Karla and Jan would explore "guided imagery and relaxation techniques," and discuss Karla's fear of the future and all the reasons why "self-care can be difficult." An inmate stabbing had upset Karla. The lockdown that always ensued when there had been violence in the general population barely touched Karla, but certain realities about prison were slowly making themselves apparent.

Late in September, she expressed her fear in a letter to Kristy Maan, who just could not bring herself to completely sever her relationship with Karla: "This place is truly evil. . . . People want me dead in this prison and the one who does it will be a hero. . . . I HATE IT HERE."

But now she had Jan Heney, she duly reported to all her correspondents. Ms. Heney observed that Karla "is dealing better with ambivalent feelings," after an hour and half session in which they discussed "getting in touch with abusive aspects of the relationship—feeling powerless." The relationship they were discussing, at such length and depth, was her erstwhile marriage to Paul Bernardo.

Karla was learning a lot, from the psychologist and from her schoolwork. In her next letter to Dr. Arndt, she wrote: "Women's studies is particularly helpful. It was taught from a feminist perspective . . . it was quite empowering." She was even ready to lament the "death" of her relationship with Paul.

"I almost would rather have him die, because then I'd be able to grieve properly. And visit his grave and say goodbye," she wrote to Kathy Ford. Obviously, there was light at the end of Karla's dark tunnel—in her October datebook she marked in the cancellation of Paul Bernardo's preliminary hearing on the Scarborough rapes in capital letters.

But then Karla had a dream.

6 October, 1993

Dear George,

I'm having a major problem. I've remembered something else that I have to tell Bob Gillies. Paul raped Jane, a friend of mine. I don't remember much of it. I can picture it happening in our living room. She was drunk and had passed out. The next thing I remember is her falling off of the bed upstairs. I've been racking my brain for days now, trying to piece the whole thing together but I just can't. I can't even go to my doctors for help because they'll just report it, what I'm really afraid of is that I was more involved than I can remember. Bob and Ivan showed me a still photograph taken from that videotape and I couldn't identify it. What if it was with Jane? Why didn't I remember all of this when they first questioned me? I have to tell them but what if they nail me for this too? Can you do something to make sure they don't?

I can't talk to you on the phone at all because the conversations are recorded and listened to. They never read mail to and from lawyers—they can't—so this is the only safe way for me to talk to you. Please write back soon with some advice. And also, remember that I want

to tell them. I feel guilty and have to get it off my conscience. Thanks, George. I feel like I'm going crazy."

Karla

Karla's sessions with Jan Heney continued to go very well. Now
that Karla had a recovered memory, she and Heney were away
to the races. They embarked on endless discussions about "how
numbing is used to avoid feelings." Heney explained in some
detail "how this coping strategy developed" in Karla. That gave
Karla something to think about.

Karla was learning lots of new things, and she could hardly
wait to explain it all to Sergeant Gillies. Karla was the highest-
profile prisoner in Canada, in a prison unit that seldom held
more than a hundred women. Given her relationship with the
Crown, she had more nascent power than any other prisoner in
the country.

In the past year, there had been so many people—police
persons, prosecutors, psychiatrists, psychologists, lawyers such as
George Walker—people whom she would otherwise never have
met; smart, intelligent people, paying more attention to Karla
than had ever been given her in the sum total of her days on
earth. Karla absorbed every ounce of it, like an arid desert.

Karla was so eager and self-assured that she tried to call Inspector Bevan directly in mid-October. She became furious
because neither the Niagara Regional Police nor the Green
Ribbon Task Force would accept her collect calls. Undaunted,
Karla wrote another letter to Kristy advising her to save all her
letters for posterity. She concluded, saying, "I won't be mad if
you want to say something about what a nice person I am."

When Sergeant Gillies finally called her on October 19, he
discovered that Karla had been calling Inspector Bevan because
she wanted to know about what effect a broadcast by the U.S.
tabloid TV show "A Current Affair" would have on her position and on Paul's forthcoming trial. The segment contained
banned details from her trial and that greatly concerned Karla.
She had also heard that the British were reading about her and
looking at her wedding pictures in the *Sunday Mirror*. Gillies

assured her that such things were irrelevant and inconsequential. Jan Heney talked about learning to accept things that cannot be changed.

Karla asked Sergeant Gillies for a copy of the *Sunday Mirror* article. A copy of the article was circulating among the prison guards. Someone had an acquaintance in England who had happily faxed a copy. Kristy Maan was keeping her abreast of the coverage.

"Now everyone's got me all curious," Karla wrote to Kristy. "And that's PATHETIC about putting our pictures beside Barbie and Ken's."

Karla's mother had friends who had watched the TV exposé, but, from what Karla heard, it was "mostly a bunch of total crap." The "Current Affair" reporter, Mary Garofalo, had been born and raised in Toronto. She was surprised to discover that the victims' families were more than willing to talk to her. In fact, when Garofalo got to the Mahaffy's house she could not seem to get out. They actually shot six or seven hours of tape.

But it was the fact that Van Smirnis, Paul Bernardo's best friend and erstwhile best man, was willing to talk about things he knew nothing about—for money, and that some unnamed person was willing to share banned details with Ms. Garofalo, that brought the show together. Some details were incorrect, but Garofalo had the gist, which was all that reality-based television required.

Karla's uncle sold "A Current Affair" extensive videotape of Paul and Karla's wedding. Between Mr. Homolka, Mrs. Mahaffy and Van Smirnis, Mary had more footage than she could use.

Wise beyond her years, Karla was unfazed by the media, but she begged Kristy not to talk to them. Although her "deal" specifically denied Karla any right to "give an account, directly or indirectly to the press, media, or for the purpose of any book, movie or like endeavor," five months later Karla told Kristy she was having second thoughts.

"About writing a book . . . believe me, I thought about it.

I really don't know what I'm going to do yet," she told Kristy. "Part of me wants my side of the story to be told, but another part of me feels that the world knows enough about me."

What concerned Karla were the "deep, dark secrets" of abuse that would surface during Paul's trial. "Enough has been said about Kristen and Leslie," she observed. "Anyway, if I do ever decide to 'tell my story' it will definitely be done in a book written by me. . . . And it will be only a story about the abuse I endured."

In closing, she asked for the name of a book Kristy had mentioned in her previous letter about England's infamous Moors Murders and advised Kristy that she was reading a chapter of the Bible every night, starting with the Book of Matthew. Somewhere between the divine and the subhuman, perhaps she could find her literary inspiration. That same day, Karla and her therapist spent another hour discussing the impact of abuse, and they looked at "strategies inherent in surviving abuse."

While psychologist Jan Heney was finding that her sessions with Karla were resulting in "good spirits" and "assertive" behavior," Dr. Brown, the senior psychiatric consultant on Karla's case, was running into a concrete blond wall.

"I absolutely HATE the psychiatrist here now," Karla told Kathy Ford, noting that she now had a helpful therapist and only had to see the shrink every other week.

"He told me the last time I saw him that I would never heal until I told him all the details of what happened. Asshole. He is so mean and cruel. So now I don't really tell him anything."

With Jan, after all, she was able to deflect the past and consider "healing as a process" and ponder the "ways to self-esteem." The delusion must have been a comfort. As she told Kathy: "I can't wait to see what the future holds for me—a new job, a new husband (. . . a loving one this time!) children . . ."

·   ·   ·

When Karla lived in her tidy little house in Port Dalhousie with Paul, there had always been time to decorate the front porch with fake spiderwebs and a toothsome jack-o'-lantern at Halloween. In jail, she found All Saints' Eve "kind of boring."

Karla had talked to her family and watched her beloved cartoon character Bart Simpson star in a "Scare-athon" television special. Being in segregation meant she could not attend the Halloween dance in the prison gymnasium. A considerate guard had brought up some pop and chips, and the girls in seg had their own little Halloween party.

Two days later, on November 2, George Walker gave Sergeant Gillies a copy of Karla's letter about the troublesome memory of the mysterious forgotten victim. Naturally, the police were concerned, so they called to find out how Karla was really doing.

By this time, Karla and her psychologist had moved on to tackle the dynamics of abuse that lead "to immobilization and increased powerlessness of the victim."

When the sergeant and the inspector arrived to interview Karla two days later, Karla had dutifully noted in her datebook "Bob & Vince visiting/hair highlighted."

Inspired, Karla had prepared ten pages of detailed, graphic reminiscences about exactly how Paul had abused her. Her tales of infamy kept getting better and more elaborate, far beyond complaints such as "he spit in my food," which she had benignly noted for Dr. Arndt. And since her well-being was an issue, Karla told Inspector Bevan and Sergeant Gillies that she had lost weight by eating only fruit and vegetables.

The small talk continued the following day. Karla wondered whether or not Paul would be charged in connection with her sister's death. After all, it had been more than three months since they had exhumed Tammy Lyn's body.

She was told the scientists at the forensic center were still working on the samples. That settled, Karla moved on to a more pressing issue—she needed a visitor's pass for Buddy; she wanted her dog to visit. Vince and Bob said they would see what they could do.

The next morning, an obliging Karla offered that she was

helping another inmate with her schoolwork. She wanted to know about the arrangements being made to accommodate her when she had to go to court and testify. Haute couture being what it was in prison, her hair would only remain highlighted for so long. There was also the matter of what she was going to wear.

To further encourage their growing camaraderie, she shared another small insight into her estranged husband. There had been a big fib in the "A Current Affair" television broadcast, Karla said. The guy they interviewed who claimed to have given Paul a haircut and a blow job—they might have traded underwear, but not the blow job. Paul would never let a guy blow him.

Inspector Bevan was way ahead of Karla. Bernardo's willingness to be fellated by a guy was considered by the Green Ribbon Task Force to be of crucial importance. He assigned a constable to rundown the talkative con, a homosexual pimp named Glenn High, who had indeed appeared on "A Current Affair"—disguised with a paste-on mustache and a baseball cap. He had claimed that, among other things, he had had a sexual encounter with Paul.

High, aged twenty-three, had been charged with abduction, sexual assault causing bodily harm, intercourse with a minor and forcible confinement. He had taken the fees paid by "A Current Affair" and run, leaving his lawyer, Loftus Cuddy, with the task of contacting broadcasters, newspaper reporters and book authors with "exclusive" story rights from $5,000 to the $500. One information-challenged newspaper reporter finally broke down and paid. The closest the crack investigators from the Green Ribbon Task Force could get to him was Glenn High's former cellmate, Randy Vandenburg, who was much easier to find since he was still in custody.

The way Vandenburg remembered it, he and High had been in their cell next to Bernardo. Bernardo had been upset over Karla's light sentence and announced that his old lady was "one sick bitch." Randy and Glenn believed him. Vandenburg said that High and Bernardo switched underwear and that the switch had something to do with Bernardo's theory that the authorities were trying to get samples from his underwear for DNA analysis.

Vandenburg also said that High was a homosexual and that Vandenburg "stood 6"—watched out for them—while High gave Bernardo a blow job. Paul Bernardo was obviously more depraved than even Karla knew.

Karla and Jan Heney went back to work, spending a full session working on the psychological mechanism that "triggers self-punishment." Jan noted that "the client" was worried about the future.

A week later, Heney and Homolka talked about the psychologist's consultations with other inmates. Heney suggested to Karla that she might benefit from group-therapy sessions. Karla liked that idea a lot. Of course, Ms. Heney pointed out, it was entirely up to Karla, and if she wanted to participate, Heney would have to get a release.

Heney's suggestion that Karla might want to become involved with other women in the prison was an indication to the authorities that Ms. Heney simply did not "get it." With that suggestion, she had sown the seeds of the end of her therapeutic relationship with Karla. Group therapy was not in Karla Homolka's future.

When Dr. Brown saw Karla next, Karla was remarkably cheerful and spontaneous. Dr. Brown noted: "Although she is feeling stressed about the upcoming trial, her nightmares have all but ceased and her adjustment to the prison environment meant she was not having nearly as much trouble sleeping." His prescription was to reduce her Nozinan by half and send her right back to the psychologist's ministrations.

When it came to her client's well-being, Jan Heney's devotion knew no bounds. It was as if she were caught in Karla's thrall.

"It has come to my attention that there are some anticipated problems with Ms. Teale's dog Buddy," Heney wrote in a memo to the deputy warden, addressing the concern that when Karla's family visited her for a few days in January the dog might not be permitted in. "It is my belief that it would be beneficial for Ms. Teale to visit with her dog. The psychological and therapeutic benefits of pets have been well documented," she noted, adding her professional endorsement and offering to "facilitate this visit taking place."

For this display of loyalty and concern, Karla rewarded Ms. Heney by entering into a discussion, for the first time, that touched briefly on Karla's feelings about Tammy Lyn. Karla had never before broached that topic with anyone affiliated with the prison.

Ken Murray, Paul Bernardo's beleaguered lawyer, continued to hammer away about disclosure—he repeatedly told the media that disclosure from the Crown was like pulling teeth—slow, tedious and painful. On November 22, 1993, Murray and his junior, Carolyn MacDonald, met with prosecutors and police officers at the Green Ribbon Task Force headquarters in Beamsville. They had come to review an odd assortment of exhibits. Among hundreds upon hundreds of exhibits, Murray and MacDonald wanted to see photographs of Norma Tellier and Karla's high-school yearbook. They showed the most interest, however, in a black-and-white, hardcover diary Jane had relinquished and some handwritten notes Tammy Lyn Homolka and Norma Tellier had exchanged in late 1990.

The following day they came back for more, including a "tour" of an elaborate, Plexiglas scale model of the house, which the task force and prosecution had commissioned. With this large, modular, transparent, doll-like house and the extensive videotapes the police had made in the house, Bernardo's judge and jury would see perpetual reality.

But the defense team was far more interested in more pictures of Norma Tellier and Jane and a bunch of "unknown" nudes, various newspaper clippings the police had found in the garage and a November, 1992, issue of *True Love* magazine containing a story entitled, "My Husband Is Attracted to Little Girls."

From the storeroom, identification officers trotted out Exhibit 677, which consisted of twenty-seven books, all true crime and horror, along with four other books—noted as Exhibit 965—that had been personally seized by Inspector Bevan. Perhaps they were looking for clues to their defense in Karla's books: *Understanding Abnormal Behaviour* and *Teenage Sexuality*.

The lawyers started listening to audiotapes Bernardo had made, including one on which the prosecution was clearly focused called "Deadly Innocence," Paul's title for his forthcoming rap album. In the mind of the prosecutors, the lyrics were Paul's theme song.

"I'm young and hype," the rap lyric went. "I get paid to rock the nation. Sometimes I be cool. Sometimes I be chilling. Sometimes I be killing. I'm one in a million. I'll drain your brain. And steal your chain. I got no remorse. I got no shame." Of course the rap ends with the dyslexic white rapper never getting caught, " 'cause I'm a deadly innocent guy." The defense asked for copies.

Before Murray and MacDonald left, the police finally released Exhibit 268—the one-minute, fifty-eight-second videotape known as "Karla's Sex Video." It had been in their possession a full nine months since its discovery on February 21.

The police knew it was an edited version of something, but they had no idea that Ken Murray knew exactly what that something was. The hooker in Atlantic City really meant nothing except that the episode pointed to character and proclivity.

It was the clips with the comatose Jane that meant more to Murray and MacDonald. In those clips, the Crown's star witness—the abused and psychologically damaged, depressed, post-traumatically stressed Karla Homolka—could be seen doing her own despicable thing and obviously enjoying it.

Having seen the entire library of videos from which those clips had been taken, and with Paul Bernardo's help, Ken Murray had been able to figure out that the sequence with Jane Doe happened only six months after Karla had killed her sister with the exact same combination of Halcion and halothane. Ken

Murray also knew that his client had not been at home when Karla put Jane down.

Murray understood two things. Because he had what he felt was a much clearer, truer picture of Karla Homolka than the prosecution had, he knew there was more to the relationship between her, the police and government than his "deal with the devil" hyperbole. Murray had once been a prosecutor. He knew the ropes and he firmly believed he was being railroaded.

It was inconceivable that the police and the prosecution had gone ahead and made the deal, having seen "Karla's Sex Video," which so blatantly portrayed her as other than the battered and abused victim of the sexually psychopathic Rasputin they had so carefully painted. There was much more to their collusion, and he felt that if he could get to the bottom of it he might change the course of his personal history.

Only a week earlier, emissaries from the Green Ribbon Task Force had travelled to Ottawa to have the videotape analyzed by image processing and photogrammetry specialists from the Department of National Defense. Vince Bevan was not satisfied with the results he had received from the police lab in Toronto.

As the meeting came to a close, Constable Michael Kershaw and his colleagues inquired about certain items that had been in the house before Murray and crew did their May, 1993 house clearing: a Giorgio perfume bottle from the upstairs washroom, for instance, and a rubber mallet that was on the workbench in the basement.

Karla had told the police that when she and Kristen French were being "girlfriends" together and trying on perfume, Kristen had chosen the Giorgio. The police wanted the perfume bottle. The rubber mallet was the tool Karla had used to guard Kristen when Paul was out of the house getting Swiss Chalet and renting videos. They wanted that, too.

Murray told the police that when he went into the house in May he had an acquaintance arrange the muscle for the move. He said he deliberately did not know any names. All Murray remembered was this one, big, black guy who had been able to carry the washer and dryer up the basement stairs all by himself.

Murray said he had been much more concerned with

papers than physical objects. They had separated the stuff in garbage bags marked K for "keep" and G for "garbage." Only a few bags, including some foodstuffs, actually made it into his own vehicle. The Bernardos' fridge had been well stocked with fancy condiments, civilized appointments that Murray seized in partial recognition of his services.

Nevertheless, it appeared to Constable Kershaw that certain items had been removed intentionally, while others had been left behind: for instance, the rubber-headed hammer for which they were looking was gone, but a similiar hard-headed mallet was still in the basement.

There had been an antique wood plane that was quite valuable, some Fostner bits and a miter saw. Murray said he did not know anything about those items, or anything else they were looking for.

Kershaw made an off-the-cuff remark about how Murray probably had "the tape," but Murray ignored the reference. He said the garbage bags marked G had been dropped at various dumps around the Toronto area to thwart all the Bernardo souvenir hunters.

Outside of the exhibit room, Murray took aside the smaller and more affable identification officer, Richard Ciszek: "I know what you guys are thinking, another slimeball lawyer, but honestly, I don't know where . . . the items went."

While Canadians scrambled across the border to get copies of the Thursday, November 23, *Washington Post,* which finally provided some accurate details about Karla's trial and described the murderess as a Cinderella, Karla was intently discussing her need to be "nice" with her psychologist.

Karla and Jan Heney talked about what Karla described as her almost pathological need to do what others thought she should do. Karla was continuing to learn her lessons well. She went back to her cell and wrote Kathy Ford: "You know it's not really fair. My trial is over and done with, but none of the pain is. . . ."

Almost wistfully, Karla added that her life with Paul "wasn't supposed to end this way."

At the end of November, Dr. Brown put a note in Karla's file saying that Karla was "gaining in self-esteem and self-confidence noticeably." In her sessions, Heney was hammering on the theme of "niceness" and Karla's "inability to identify an enemy."

The publication ban had become an enemy in the outside world. *Washington Post* reporter Anne Swardson's story was picked up by major newspapers across America, and Canadian Customs was dogged in its determination to confiscate the banned newspapers.

When Canadian universities started shutting down computer bulletin boards, cyberspace cadets went into paroxysms of debate over whether or not the ban was justified, while others sought out or created "gory details."

With her psychologist, Karla discussed her growing paranoia about her lack of control in her current situation. Karla was very concerned about what Heney described in her notes as the "implications of others."

The *New York Times* published an editorial headlined "A Bad Gag Order in Canada." It said that Canada was behaving like a third-world dictatorship, burning magazines and newspapers and stopping people as they tried to cross the border—not searching for drugs or other contraband, but for newspapers and magazines containing banned details of Karla Homolka's trial.

Even CNN talk-show host Larry King blanked out audio portions of his phone-in about the topic. "The ban affects Canada. The ban does not have any effect in the U.S.," typed one American Internet adherent to the website known as *alt.fan.karla-homolka*.

"Obviously false," came the reply. "Since I can't watch Larry King in Washington, tell me in New York what happened. It affects people big time." But at least one Canadian thought things were getting a bit too frenzied. "Honestly," came the reply, "who cares about Larry King?"

·   ·   ·

On Monday, December 6, Karla received a new visitor, Sergeant Gary Beaulieu. Beaulieu had interviewed Karla's estranged husband following his arrest. Karla liked meeting new people. The introductions were handled by her "private" guard, Rick Waller. Waller proved to be the perfect choice for Karla. He had spent years on dog patrol at the men's prison. With guard dogs and sleeping cons, Waller functioned well. Any man who loved dogs was a man Karla could love.

Sergeant Beaulieu spent an hour that morning talking to Karla. From his notes it was apparent that they discussed some issues to do with the Scarborough rapes, which was quite bizarre given what would follow in the afternoon.

Beaulieu asked Karla if she knew when Paul had first committed a rape? The question was loaded, because Beaulieu knew the house search had turned up the chronological list of Scarborough rapes, handwritten and authored by both Paul and Karla. The perennially cooperative Karla's answer was 1983, which was the date of the first charge widely reported in the press. The prosecution knew that Bernardo had not started raping until he met Homolka in 1987. However, they also included an unsubstantiated, unprovable charge they had coerced from Bernardo's unfortunate ex-girlfriend, Jennifer Galligan, thus exonerating Karla as the catalyst and facilitator.

When Beaulieu returned after lunch he brought Sergeant Gillies with him, and they officially screened the one-minute, fifty-eight-second video for Karla. Karla had probably seen this tape before. It was clearly evident she was familiar with its contents. She had been shown stills from the video the previous May, during her "induced" and "cautioned" statements to the police. Knowing what was on the tape, Karla had yet to figure out how it fitted into what she knew the police already knew and where it might fit with her "dream."

The first segment had an orangey tint. In it, a naked Karla, complete with suntan lines, was prone on a beige quilt-covered, king-size bed with another blond. They caressed each other's bodies, then Karla leaned back to allow her nipples to be sucked and she spread her legs to be fondled by the blond hooker she had hired. Karla had already told them what this was all about in an interview before her trial.

"I'm the one on the right," she agreed, but then she said it did not really look like her. She placed the time as August of 1992, when she and Paul had stopped in Atlantic City on their way home from Florida. "He had beat me real badly," she explained, "and he said, 'there's only one thing that's gonna make me love you again and that's if we get a hooker and you do stuff with her,'" so she had said all right.

"He kept asking me, 'What kinda girl do you like? What kinda girl do you want?' and I said I don't care. So he said fine, we'll get a blond." Even so, according to Karla a "pretty" brunette turned them down before Paul convinced this blond to take them on.

Karla and Paul had dined at Ivana's restaurant that evening and dropped a bundle, something Karla seemed to think the entire hotel staff noticed. "People were treating us well and then they saw us walking in with this hooker, I felt so disgusted, so disgusted," she said.

Although she could not remember the hooker's name, she did remember that the woman had said she was four months pregnant. Paul paid her three hundred dollars for one hour and forty-five minutes of her time, and he videotaped the encounter by setting up the camera in a suitcase and triggering the remote to start as soon as they came in the room.

"Paul didn't really like her," Karla explained. "She made him wear a condom and he does not wear condoms, so he never ejaculated." When the hooker left, Karla said she had to "quote, suck him off, unquote."

During the playing of the second segment Karla turned her chair to get a good look, and then she asked for the segment to be replayed. From the carpet, she thought the video must have been shot at 57 Bayview. She suggested that the young woman in the video "had to be" her dead sister, Tammy, but she allowed as how it was hard to tell. When it was replayed from a freeze frame, she identified a quilt as one from Paul's house and said that the segment must have been videotaped shortly after they moved in together, which would obviously rule out her sister as the subject.

In the second section of this short segment, Karla became more certain that what transpired must have occurred in the master bedroom of the house. Her dresser was in the shot. She then speculated that the "unidentified female" could be Kristen French or Leslie Mahaffy, since she had performed with them in that location. Beaulieu noted her comment that the "only person who taped her doing things like that was Paul Bernardo."

There was no noted discussion about the fact that Karla was shown close up in this clip, with her lips on another woman's blond pubic hair, variously blowing on it and burying her face in it, while her right hand lay casually, familiar and unconcerned, on the unidentified female's stomach. There was no discussion about Karla's wagging tongue or her insipid grinning. No question and answer period followed about why Karla had stood up, lifted the unconscious girl's unresponsive arm and inserted the finger into her vagina.

After forty minutes, Beaulieu and Gillies switched off this contentious exhibit. They asked Karla to initial the photographs of her with the hooker and the piece of Trump Tower stationery with the name "Shelly" and a phone number written on it.

Confused, Karla said she thought Gillies and Beaulieu were there to interview her about Jane Doe. She remembered giving Jane booze and pills. She wanted to talk about the fact that she had made an emergency 911 call when Jane Doe stopped breathing while Paul was assaulting her. She had canceled the call when Jane started breathing again. Karla said it must have taken place before the wedding, too. Jane Doe was at the wedding with her mother.

The officers did not want to talk about any of that. They told Karla that any discussion about an alleged rape would be conducted by the Metropolitan Toronto Police. They were handling any and all rape issues. Karla would not be interviewed until long after Christmas—sometime in late January or early February, so Karla should just relax and have a good holiday.

By the middle of December, Karla was feeling much better. Over an hour they spent together then, Karla told Jan Heney that she had been able to use the visualization exercise "to contain and put away feelings."

She was continuing to struggle to put her relationship with Paul into context, but Christmas was coming, and Karla and Heney began to discuss strategies about how Karla could cope with that.

Over the next few days, Karla committed herself to her correspondence. Kristy Maan had a new house and had written to Karla with all kinds of questions. Off the top, Karla advised Kristy that she watched the soap opera "Another World," not "Young and the Restless," although some of the "girls" were trying to move her Y&R-side.

"Ok. The people I'm in with. #1 is Jane. She's 34 and in for smashing a window (???). She's been in & out of jail for 17 years. She's into drugs. Very nice person.

"#2 is Judy. She's in for armed (addendum: She's 33) robbery. She's also into drugs. She's quite a violent and unpredictable person & goes from liking me to hating me. They don't let her & I out together at all. She has lots of tattoos. (So does Jane.)

"#3 is Margaret (addendum: She's 33). She's in for theft over ($1500, I think). She's also into drugs. She's very nice. Also has tattoos. I teach her English and law in the afternoons. (Now I have a full-time job!)

"Those are the only ones up on this side of seg right now. On the other side (the punitive side) there are a couple of murderers, attempted murders, etc.

"I've pretty well made friends with everyone I've met. I guess I'm a naturally friendly person."

Karla assured her old friend that the "little prayer" Kristy had sent had been placed prominently on her cell bulletin board, and although the holidays would be difficult, she had two visits with her family to look forward to. "P.S.," Karla wrote, "What about a title for that book about the Moors Murders?"

From the time she had arrived in prison, Karla had been planning a reunion with all former members of the Exclusive Diamond Club. Early on, she had to except Debbie Purdie, now married, with a child. Karla's erstwhile best friend had seen through her and severed their relationship. Debbie forbade Karla to write her any more letters.

Kathy Ford, however, remained a penpal and encouraged Karla to keep writing.

"Maybe this isn't healthy," Karla wrote to her, "but I don't even think to myself that I'm in Prison for Women. I think I'm away at school. Whether it's healthy or not, it works—I don't feel bad."

Karla took Kathy into her confidence: "I want to work with abused women. I want to help prevent women from being abused and also work with women who have already been abused."

For Christmas, her parents were bringing Sesame Street towels and sheets. "My room is going to be the most juvenile in the whole institution, but, hey—I like it that way," Karla explained.

"I know what you mean about Christmas. It's always been my favorite time of the year. Of course, since Tammy died things haven't been the same. But one thought I've always held is that she wouldn't want us to live in misery over the holidays. . . .

"Whenever I think about it (Paul's preliminary and trial) I get a sick feeling. It's going to be so hard. The cops were here asking more questions last week and it was awful. They were nice! Paul's lawyers are going to try to put the whole thing on me. It will be one of the worst things I'll ever go through. But I keep reminding myself that this is all a million times better than living with him. And it truly is."

. . .

While Karla was contemplating ways to utilize the "coping strategies for Christmas" that psychologist Jan Heney had shared, one of the Scarborough rape victims, Deneen Chenier filed a ten-million-dollar lawsuit against Paul Bernardo [Teale], who, she contended, was "aided and abetted" by his estranged wife, Karla Homolka, during her rape, which had occurred in an underground parking garage on December 22, 1989.

"Wow! I don't know what this woman thinks she's going to get," Karla wrote to Kathy Ford. "Paul and I are broke."

CHAPTER
thirty

There were two sides to the segregation unit in the Kingston Prison for Women: punitive and protective. The punitive side was where they sent prisoners who had broken institutional rules. On the punitive side, the women were locked up twenty-four hours a day. They had no TV and were only allowed three showers a week.

On the protective side, where Karla was, things were different. Every morning Karla got up. She worked. She did her schoolwork. She attended to her vast correspondence. She watched her own TV. She ate her meals.

In the evening it varied. Usually everyone in protective segregation was allowed out together for a half hour. Sometimes, if things were tense in the prison—if someone had been knifed or something—they were only allowed out separately, for a half hour. Whenever Karla was out, she made phone calls and took showers.

Karla had a prison job engraving nametags with a sixty-eight-year-old retired prison guard named Jerry Rembeck, who was a Czechoslovakian immigrant, just like her father. Unlike other prisoners, Karla wore her own clothes.

On Tuesdays, the prison chaplain came up to talk to Karla. He did not talk a lot about God but more about how Karla was doing; how she was feeling about things that were going on in the media, for instance. Karla did not have very Christian feelings about the media.

On January 5, 1994, prison psychologist Jan Heney stopped by, just to wish Karla "Happy New Year!"

Sergeant Bob "Homolka" Gillies was given a short videotape by Constable Mike Kershaw. It showed a teenage girl happily playing with a Rottweiler puppy at 57 Bayview. The dog looked to be four or five months old. Karla Homolka was operating the video camera. In one segment, the camera was focused directly on the girl's crotch—she was wearing cutoff shorts, but the shot was held for so long that it was obviously deliberate—and Karla could be heard to say, "I love videotaping."

The young girl in this video, whom the police knew to be Jane Doe, was wearing a white Oxford Hall sweatshirt that was disarmingly similar to the garment worn by the hitherto unknown female depicted on Exhibit 121212-39, otherwise known as "Karla's Sex Video."

The Metropolitan Toronto Police had recently charged Paul Bernardo with the sexual assault of Jane Doe. The prosecutors had decided that with Jane Doe and Karla's testimony, they had enough evidence.

Fascinated, Sergeant Gillies looked at the tape again the following day. The more he looked at it, the more he saw. For instance, there was some sort of wedding cake off to the side, where Jane and the dog were wrestling. It was not a real wedding cake—it looked to be made from towels.

Ms. Heney received an unwelcome memorandum. Dated January 7, the subject was Karla Teale. The deputy warden reminded Ms. Heney about their earlier discussion and instructed Jan to bring "closure to your treatment sessions with Ms. Teale as of January 31, 1994."

The case was now entirely in Dr. Brown's hands. Heney was to make sure the files were up to date and a final treatment summary was completed. "The file should then be forwarded to Heather McLean as senior psychologist for secure storage. Again, the file storage issue will be revisited if and when the publication ban is lifted.

"Thank you for your cooperation and your attention to this very difficult case."

Sergeant Gillies called Karla and asked her about the wedding cake. He did not mention Jane Doe, nor did he say why he was asking. Karla was accustomed to non sequiturs from the police.

The cake was not real, Karla said. It was made of bath towels and had been a shower gift from a neighbor. She could not remember the exact date Lynn Clark had given the shower for her, but it had definitely been a few weeks before the wedding. To Sergeant Gillies and his superiors, that meant if the girl in "Karla's Sex Video" was one and the same girl as the teenager in the innocuous video with the wedding cake, the incident with the hand and digits had taken place sometime in June, the same month Leslie Mahaffy had been raped and murdered.

Sergeants Gillies and Beaulieu came for another visit on January 11. They spent forty minutes with Karla and got her to sign a couple of Form 14 consents to continue to release medical and psychiatric information; the following day Inspector

Bevan sat in. They talked for an hour and Karla signed two more Form 14s.

In the afternoon, Beaulieu, Gillies and Karla met with Jan Heney. The police needed to get a better feel for the relationship between Karla and the psychologist, and where Karla was at and how she was "coping."

At Karla's request, the deputy warden set up a telephone call for Karla with Sergeant Gillies on January 31. Karla wanted to speak to Sergeant Bob about a pending Metro Toronto Police interview. Gillies reassured her that her old friends Metcalfe and Whitefield would be in on the second and third of February and the interviews would be just like the ones they had conducted at the Journey's End the previous May.

The interview took place in a room in the prison's basement. The prison was under renovation and often Karla's answers or the Detectives' questions would be drowned out by nearby construction. Detective Metcalfe wore a windowpane suit jacket and a big-collared white blouse. With her dark brown hair in a ponytail and her bangs pouffed, she looked more like a 1940s starlet than a hard-nosed detective. The two women sat side by side. Detective Whitefield sat across the table, taking notes.

Karla's face was puffy. Her roots were showing and she had gained considerable weight. Her beige suit was taut. Off the top she told the detectives that the only issue they would be discussing was Jane Doe and that was on the advice of her lawyer, who did not want her mind "confused" while she was busily preparing for Paul Bernardo's preliminary on the murder charges.

"Paul raped Jane Doe," Karla said without hesitation, and then launched into her own peculiar abridged version of the one sexual assault on Jane Doe. It was Paul who made her contact Jane. It was Paul who made her grind up one Halcion pill in the mortar and pestle and mix it in Jane's drink. It was Paul this, and Paul that. When Jane finally fell asleep, Paul had instructed Karla to lie down next to her and face the other way. Then he had intercourse with Jane. Karla did not see it, but she knew it had happened. Suddenly, Paul leaped up and said Jane

was not breathing. Karla ran to the phone and called 911. Then
Jane started breathing again, and Karla canceled 911. She drew
diagrams and carefully initialed everything. That subject out of
the way, Detective Metcalfe and Karla were able to share a joke
or two and have a laugh. Detective Metcalfe gave Karla a list of
topics they would like to discuss, including Norma Tellier; Janine Rothsay, who Paul had allegedly raped in the downstairs
bathroom at 57 Bayview at Christmas, 1991; various writings
that had been seized in the house, the Henley Island rape in
April, 1991, clarification on revelations she had made in her
interviews about Paul being the Scarborough rapist, and any
information Karla might have received about the Scarborough
rapes. They also wanted her to elaborate on her sex life with
Paul Bernardo. After forty-five minutes they took a break. Karla
promised to phone George Walker and get his permission to
cover these topics.

No longer alexithymic, no longer with "no words for mood,"
no longer suffering from "flat affect," Karla was positively
frothy when she returned from phoning Walker. Keeping the
detectives in suspense, she said she had a few things to tell them
first. For instance, did they know that Paul Bernardo had
wanted her to have children—daughters—so he could have sex
with them?

Then Karla popped the good news. The session concerning
Jane had gone so smoothly that her lawyer had given her permission to answer all of their questions, which she proceeded to
do with considerable animated prevarication.

Gillies and Beaulieu carefully monitored Whitefield and
Metcalfe's interviews with Karla. Watching Metcalfe and
Whitefield talk with Karla was too much for the two sergeants
from the Green Ribbon Task Force. After Metcalfe and Whitefield left, Gillies and Beaulieu conducted yet another interview
with Karla in the afternoon.

It proved rewarding. Karla provided them with copies of her
divorce application and her affidavit. She gave them a note,
which she asked them not to review until after she had gone

back to her cell—it was a single sheet of paper with more handwritten reminiscences of the abuse and suffering she had endured at Paul's hand.

Karla's memory for the slightest trespass had become impeccable: she remembered, in great detail, everything about her
sister, even what Paul and her sister had been wearing; the
captivities and deaths of Leslie Mahaffy and Kristen French; but
nothing about the sex acts that had been depicted on the short
segments on "Karla's Sex Video."

The Green Ribbon Task force now knew conclusively that
the unidentified girl in the one-minute, fifty-eight-second
videotape exhibit was the same girl who could be seen in the
innocuous video that had been shot by Karla in the late afternoon and evening of June 6, 1991, in which Jane could be seen
frolicking with Karla's dog and Karla could be heard to say, "I
love videotaping." Karla's discussions about Jane Doe and
Karla's inability to identify her as the unidentified girl in the
video shorts perplexed the police and the Crown—a bit.

Sergeant Gillies kept in touch. On February 8, he called
Karla and said that her recent note had made them want to
speak to her yet again.

The Crown prosecutors Ray Houlahan and Gregg Barnett arrived at the Kingston Prison for Women first thing Tuesday
morning, February 15. Barnett was a soft-spoken gentleman
with a small paunch that was accentuated by his penchant for
ill-fitting vests. The junior of the two, Barnett was well educated and spoke a number of languages, including Punjabi. Unable to hold in his stomach, Barnett held opinions that he
would pop as often as vest buttons. He came off as pompous
and arrogant, but he was simply a fastidious wit with a sharp
tongue. Karla and the two prosecutors would keep each other
company, day in, and day out, every day, all day long, for the
following four weeks.

The process was comparable to that of an actress with her
director and producer. Karla's "induced" and "cautioned"
statements and the videotapes made at the Journey's End and

the transcripts of any other statements or comments that she had ever made to the police would be reviewed and studied, until all the contradictions and inconsistencies were understood and intellectually resolved. Karla must see the clear path. Soon, she would have every line and word she had uttered about this sordid business committed to memory, with all the various contradictions ultimately resolved.

The prosecutors showed Karla how to present her evidence, what they wanted to see and hear in court, how she should hold herself, her demeanor, how she should dress, act and speak. Tireless, Karla was the hardest-working witness they had ever protected.

On Saturday, February 26, Karla decided to sit down and write Dr. Arndt another long letter, starting with a detailed overview of her medications. She had reduced most to minimal amounts and she no longer felt needy in that way.

In another long, chatty letter, Karla told Dr. Arndt that she was presently going over her testimony with the prosecutors and she found that stressful. Since she was not sleeping, Dr. Brown had experimented with some different drugs, such as 500mg of chlorathydrate—"3 days on then 3 days off,"—but that had not worked at all.

"I've adjusted fairly well," she said of prison life. "As soon as people get to know me they seem to immediately realize that I'm not the horrible person the media makes me out to be. And the staff is absolutely fantastic—guards, administration, hospital staff—everybody. They're really making it easy on me here."

Methodically, the prosecutors plodded on—their stamina and determination exceeded only by Karla's—right through the weekend until they finally took a break on Friday, March 10. A long weekend, and then back at it on Tuesday, March 15.

Throughout these marathon sessions, Sergeants Gillies and Beaulieu took rough notes; Karla had never seen this many intense older, well-educated, well-spoken, successfully employed men with steady paychecks in one room in her life. And they were all there for her.

The prosecutors tried to anticipate every possible line of questioning Karla could expect from Paul's defense lawyers.

They discussed her first meeting with George Walker: "I told him basically the gist of it. He told me not to say anything to anybody. I was so upset, I don't recall if he said he was going to talk to the Crown. I think I told him about Tammy as well as Kristen and Leslie. . . . I don't know who mentioned [immunity] first. . . . I put my trust in Mr. Walker."

On March 10, the identification officers joined the session. Constables Ciszek and Kershaw went over exhibits. On March 14, they reviewed Karla's vast correspondence, including well over a thousand missives she had addressed to her estranged husband, between October, 1987 and December, 1992.

Karla's memory about the context for every little love note and card was infallible. She remembered the circumstances under which even the most insignificant "pillow note" had been scribbled. On March 15, Karla was shown a portion of the video she and Paul had made in Hawaii on their honeymoon. They rationalized her "I love you more than the Hawaiian sunset" soliloquy.

The following day, they reviewed portions of what the prosecution had been calling the "suicide tapes," those plaintive audio recordings Paul made after Karla had left him in January.

During the afternoon session on March 17, Karla shared a new memory: on a trip with Paul to Orlando, Florida, during August, 1992, Paul had followed a girl to her country residence. He had parked on a deserted road and the plan was for Karla to flag the girl over for assistance. Then they would rape and murder her right there. It never went beyond the planning stage.

On March 21, the deputy warden, whom Karla had somehow successfully transformed into a personal handmaiden, told Sergeant Gillies that Karla was having trouble sleeping and that she was having dreams again. Arrangements were quickly made for Karla to see Dr. Brown more frequently.

Dr. Brown explained to Karla that her dreams were not reality and that her memories would come back in time. The irony was that her memory was impeccable, except when it came to Jane Doe. Dr. Brown was very kind and understanding, and

Karla was slowly starting to change her opinion about him. She also knew he agreed with Dr. Arndt's diagnoses. She asked. Dr. Brown told her.

Karla met two new men on March 24. Unsolved sex crimes in the hinterland of southwestern Ontario fell in the purview of the Ontario Provincial Police—Karla's favorite force. Two handsome, distinguished-looking detectives named Aspen and Chapman interviewed Karla about the unsolved murder of Lynda Shaw. Lynda, a twenty-one-year-old brunette engineering student, had disappeared over the Easter weekend in 1990. Her body was found in a wooded area of a stretch of highway on Monday, April 16, 1990. She had been stabbed and set on fire.

The fire bit was reminiscent of Martin Thiel's modus operandi in the movie *Criminal Law*. During their search of 57 Bayview, the police had recovered a receipt from the Royal York Hotel dated Tuesday, April 17, 1990. They also knew that Karla had outpatient surgery at Scarborough General Hospital for dysplasia of the cervix on that day.

Karla thought she had seen Paul that day, but she was not positive. She thought she saw him that night. But she might have taken the bus to the hospital; she could not remember. There was also a Cantel record that showed a call to the Homolka residence on April 16. Karla did not remember anything about that.

Karla told the detectives that *Criminal Law* was a movie they both liked and that she had picked out their new name, Teale, based on Thiel; she had just anglicized it to Teale, like the color with a vowel. She and Paul even had a heraldic background for the name, which they had bought in Florida.

"Did he have a fascination with fire?" one of the detectives asked.

"No. But he did like to burn things," Karla replied, not understanding what she was saying.

"Like what?"

"He burned, like, you know, evidence." She told them

about all the things, like leather and nylon jackets and jewelry, that he had burned in their fireplace. Neither of the detectives asked her how he burned material that did not burn easily and would have smelled terrible, permeating the springtime atmosphere in their heavily residential area.

The police proceeded to ask her about Lynda Shaw's possessions. Shaw had a navy purse with a zipper top, a lady's Seiko watch with an expansion band and an expensive, engineer-type calculator. Karla had never seen anything like that.

Dismissing the possibility that Paul had anything to do with Lynda Shaw's death, Karla told these detectives what she had already told the Green Ribbon Task Force and the detectives with the Metropolitan Toronto Police sexual assault squad the previous May: Shaw was highly unlikely. The main thing Karla remembered about Lynda Shaw was that Paul had asked why anybody would want to abduct her?

"She was not his kind of girl." Karla said. "She was too big, wrong hair color. You know, wrong hair type. I'm convinced he was not involved in that."

Prosecutor R.J. Houlahan wanted Karla to be in the St. Catharines jail the day before she had to testify at Bernardo's preliminary hearing. She was to be there a day early. Karla was introduced to the two officers who would be protecting her. Her mother would bring bedding and clothing and her "little house" photos.

Karla called the trailer in the prison yard the "little house." Predominantly used by K4W prisoners for conjugal visits, Karla's little house was known among the prison guards as the "fuck truck." Karla filled out handfuls of PFVUs (Private Family Visiting Unit forms) long in advance, having carefully calculated her eligibility periods, to facilitate long weekend visits with her family every sixth week.

The guards found the Homolkas very strange. They never talked, and the mother and Karla's sister held hands all the time. When they came to live in the little house they never brought any luggage, even though they were invariably holed up in the tiny tin can for three and four days at a time.

The guards did not know about all the mobile homes in the Homolka's background.

On March 25, Karla was told that the Crown was planning to lay manslaughter charges against Paul Bernardo for her sister's murder. At the end of the month, Gillies and Karla talked on the phone again. They had just found out that the Attorney-General was going to "prefer" the charges and send Bernardo directly to trial. The preliminary hearing had been canceled. Karla would not be traveling to St. Catharines after all.

Preferring charges was a controversial move and it was a power that rested solely with the minister. It was seldom invoked. It was viewed as undemocratic and regarded by defense and prosecution attorneys alike as being highly prejudicial to the interests of an accused person. Bernardo was scheduled for a preliminary hearing on the murders on April 15. In Karla's datebook it was marked in block letters, "CANCELLED."

On April 5, it was in the press. The minister said the preferred charges would "speed up the process," and the public would see justice done sooner.

Dorothy Homolka told her faithful co-workers at the Shaver Clinic that it was "a big load off our minds." The Homolkas had been afraid Paul's lawyers would rip Karla apart and they were very glad that the Attorney-General had stepped in and now there would not be any preliminary hearing.

Another visit from Sergeants Gillies and Beaulieu was marked in Karla's datebook on April 6. It was coming up to the second anniversary of Kristen French's death. Karla painstakingly wrote out all the lyrics to the Guns N' Roses song, "Used to Love Her": "Oh, slut, bitchin', fussin', cussin',/I used to love her/But I had to kill her . . ." and gave it to them.

On the fourth of May, Karla turned twenty-four. She was very upset. None of her "friends" had sent her birthday cards.

At the end of the month, Sergeant Bob came down for another visit and brought another new person for Karla to meet, Sergeant Scott Kenney. This was quite exciting for Karla; not only was Sergeant Kenney short enough to allow Karla to look him straight in the eye, but he was also one of the officers who had interviewed her ex-husband on May 12, 1992, a few days after Kristen French's body had been found. Karla assured Sergeant Kenney that Paul could put a "spell" on anybody.

Houlahan and Barnett were back to do last-minute prepping before Paul's lawyers, Ken Murray and Carolyn MacDonald, exercised their right to examine Karla on camera. When the Attorney-General preferred an indictment, the defense attorneys were given the option to do voir dires with the Crown's witnesses.

Barnett and Houlahan explained the rules and procedures in some detail, and Houlahan assured Karla that she did not need George Walker. He, R.J. Houlahan, would be there, looking out for her best interests. Karla was beginning to fully appreciate what it meant to be the Crown's star witness.

Ken Murray and Carolyn MacDonald had set aside five days in late May and early June to examine Karla Homolka. Carolyn MacDonald knew that Ken Murray had some source of information to which she was not privy. She could even imagine what it was, particularly after their law clerk, Kim Doyle, pointed out Murray's unexpensed rental of videotape equipment that would copy 8mm-format videotape onto the more popular VHS format.

MacDonald knew for certain that some of Ken Murray's insights about Karla Homolka were derived from a source other than Paul Bernardo. During their preparation, Murray made it clear he wanted certain questions asked of Karla; unusual questions about the use of underwear—her dead sister's underwear, in particular—as sexual props and aids, and whether or not Karla had used halothane on anyone else other than Tammy Lyn Homolka.

MacDonald and the studious law clerk Ms. Doyle were zealous, to the point of fanaticism, about the fact that Karla Homolka was a killer who was lying through her teeth to save her own skin. They fervently believed that the prosecution's deal with Karla Homolka was a travesty of justice. The women had a picture of Karla blown up to poster size. In the middle of her forehead they had marked in red felt pen the scarlet letter A, a salacious homage to Nathaniel Hawthorne. It was posted prominently on the wall of the office, where they burned the midnight oil, piecing together "the real story." Ken Murray fanned the flames of their fanaticism every chance he got. It meant they did most of the work and he could continue to "dump truck"—dealing out a myriad of lesser, incidental Legal Aid certificates at the Newmarket courthouse.

Karla Homolka and this case would be the pinnacle of Carolyn MacDonald's short legal career—MacDonald would be doing the lion's share of the defense examination of Karla Homolka. She was grateful to Ken Murray for the opportunity, but she did not feel she was on terra firma. Nobody who worked with Ken Murray ever did.

"I have a warning I'm going to read to you," said Karla's keeper, Sergeant Gillies. Then he advised the prisoner Homolka about the repercussions of perjury and her potential liability for prosecution and further punishment. They were in the boardroom at the Kingston Prison for Women.

"I want to determine first of all that you are comfortable," Carolyn MacDonald said.

"As can be expected," Karla replied.

"Are you nervous?" Carolyn asked.

"A little bit, not much," Karla offered, but she was not nervous at all.

"I want you to understand that I'm not here to scare you, intimidate you," MacDonald explained. "I'm not going to yell at you. I'm not going to try and trick you. I'm just trying to get information."

"Well," interjected Karla's prosecutor Houlahan, "I'm here to ensure that you are not going to yell at her or intimidate . . ."

"As long as you're here, I'm sure we'll get the information, Ray," Ken Murray said sarcastically.

MacDonald started off by asking Karla about her aborted efforts to be transferred to a psychiatric facility—efforts thwarted by Dr. Brown—which might have partly explained why Karla expressed such disdain for the kindly, old psychiatrist in her early letters to Dr. Arndt.

MacDonald asked her why she had gone directly into the prison hospital rather than into segregation when she arrived at Kingston.

"They didn't know what to do with me and I was on massive doses of medication—so they wanted me to be in the hospital," Karla icily replied.

Finally she admitted that Dr. Brown had told her on the second or third day that he did not feel Karla met the criteria for committal to St. Thomas.

"How did you feel about that?"

"Um, I was a little bit upset," Karla said. "I didn't feel that this prison could offer me the degree of therapy that was necessary."

MacDonald told Karla that Dr. Brown's memo said Karla had spent most of their early time together talking about her fears of prison life, her drugs and the future after she got out of prison. MacDonald told Karla that Dr. Brown indicated in his notes that she was only interested in pursuing regular therapy sessions with a male—he underlined that. "Is that a request that you made to Dr. Brown?" MacDonald asked.

Karla flatly and emphatically denied that she had ever told Dr. Brown such a thing.

Dr. Brown had done a psychiatric report on Karla on March 23, 1994. It was intended for the psychiatrist who was going to be with her at the preliminary—Dr. Peter Collins, who was known as a consultant to police—particularly the Metropolitan Toronto Police, the OPP and the RCMP.

MacDonald made these observations and then asked a question: "Dr. Brown indicates as of March 23, 1994, 'At the present time she sleeps well considering her situations.' Is that true?" Karla answered in the affirmative.

"Okay, Dr. Brown indicates you showed good insight and you are well motivated with regards to dealing with your sentence. Do you think that is a fair comment?"

"Yes, it is."

"He also shows no evidence of depression. Do you agree with that?"

"He must mean clinical depression, because I am depressed—not all the time, but I don't know what the definition of clinical depression is, either."

MacDonald asked Karla whether she had had anal sex or had penetrated her anus or her vagina with objects between October, 1987 and August, 1988. Karla said she believed the anal sex had started in the summer of 1988, but not the sticking of objects into herself. MacDonald asked her about oral sex and called it "oral sex on him," which somehow confused Karla.

"Why don't you say fellatio or cunnilingus? Use the words," Ray Houlahan said curtly.

"The problem is I can't say them," Ms. MacDonald admitted. "I can't pronounce them. Yes. Okay. Fellation, we'll start with that . . . and I can't say it—cunnilungus. Is that how you say it?"

"Cunnilingus," said Mr. Houlahan.

"Yes, I enjoyed that," said Karla.

CHAPTER

thirty-one

Karla was an enigma to her handlers, more so for the riddle of Jane Doe than for all her other bizarre, criminal, deviant behavior. As far as the police and prosecutors could tell, it was not from Karla's dreams or the depth of her subconscious that Karla "recovered" her memory of the incident with Jane Doe. It was "recovered" by dogged police work and videotapes. The police had finally pieced together the fact that the girl in the innocuous video with the towel cake and the dog was one and the same as the comatose girl in edited clips from "Karla's Sex Video."

Through details garnered from that seemingly innocent video, such as the sight of the Oxford Hall sweatshirt, the presence of a videocassette copy of the movie *Ghost* for which they had found a receipt in the house dated June 6, 1991, the towel cake and the size and age of the dog, they had been able to date the attack on Jane Doe as having occurred late in the evening of June 6 or early on the morning of June 7. This fact they had not yet shared with the defense, partly because they remained confused about Karla's 911 call, which she had linked to Jane Doe. It had been made two months later on August 11.

Paul Bernardo's defense counsel, Ken Murray, was not confused. He had "studied greatly" the aberrant behavior of Inspector Bevan's "compliant victim" on the videotapes. Since he had watched the entire twenty-minute "trophy" videotape of Paul and Karla's attack on Jane Doe and had spoken to his client, he knew that Paul Bernardo did not know Jane Doe and had been out of the house when Karla "put her down" with the same mixture of Halcion and halothane that had killed Tammy Lyn Homolka six months earlier.

Murray also knew, as Karla did, that she had done this to Jane Doe twice. It was on the second occasion, in the wee small hours of August 11, 1991, that Jane had apparently stopped breathing and Karla, in a panic, called 911 only to cancel the call a few minutes later when Jane came around.

Murray was confused about what to do about his knowledge. Everything was infuriatingly gray; there was no clear black or white. Until Murray understood his client's position more clearly, he was not about to tip his hand.

When MacDonald asked Karla about the number of sleeping pills she had given Jane, Karla was definite that she had only given Jane one pill. How could Karla be so definite about something like that, and so vague about everything else?

Karla also categorically denied, time and again, ever administering halothane to anyone but her sister. As the days went by, Ken Murray noticed a remarkable quality in Karla. With each passing hour, with each passing day, like a vampire, Karla seemed to sap energy from her interlocutors. For Karla, her lies were true, and out of her conviction, she took courage and became even more convincing. Carolyn MacDonald was no match for Karla. Then again, neither was Ken Murray.

During the interminable days of questioning, a beleaguered Carolyn MacDonald brought up the fact that Karla had called the Niagara Regional Police at 9:30 on Tuesday morning, February 22, 1993. She had made this call from the Segers' residence. This was significant to Murray and MacDonald because "Karla's Sex Video" had been found and viewed by the police the previous day.

Karla had been sternly warned by George Walker to stay strictly away from the police. The call from the Segers' residence marked the only time Karla disobeyed Walker's explicit instructions. MacDonald suspected Karla's motivation. Somehow, both she and Walker knew that the police had screened the one-minute, fifty-eight-second "sex video," at 5:21 P.M., Sunday evening, February 21.

The defense suspected that Karla was so vexed, she had decided to try and take matters into her own hands and determine exactly what it was the police had found. The defense team had not been able to get any cogent information out of the police or the prosecution about this call, so they decided to pursue it with Karla.

Karla admitted she had made the call, but she said she did not remember why. Shortly after she had made the call, Karla went to Walker's offices with her parents. Karla conveniently had no recollection about the details of that day's discussions. In fact, she testified that she did not even remember meeting with her lawyer on that day.

MacDonald moved on to questions about Karla's contact with Jane Doe. Yes, Karla had contacted her once after Paul's arrest, but she did not remember anything about that either.

MacDonald pursued the short videotape and Karla's selective memory.

"The police officers seized a videotape that I understand you have since viewed," she began. "I believe the videotape is a little bit less than two minutes in length and it has three episodes where you are involved in sexual acts with someone?"

"Yes."

"Were you aware on February 22 that the police had located this video?" MacDonald inquired.

Ray Houlahan interrupted: "If this is something that you became aware of as a result of speaking to your lawyer, it may be privileged."

Karla turned to MacDonald and said, "I can't answer that."

MacDonald pressed on, asking Karla whether she had seen the tape before the police screened it for her and whether or not her lawyer had a copy of it. Karla started to flounder and went into an unconvincing, rhetorical flourish of denial. Houlahan stepped in to save her again.

"If you're asserting privilege," he advised, "say you are, so it shows on the record. If you don't, you are just refusing for no reason that way."

"Okay, I'm asserting privilege," Karla said.

That line of questioning clamped, MacDonald turned to Dr. Arndt's notes from a session in early March, 1993 during which Karla discussed a videotape showing someone else's hand, which she had placed in her vagina. To her psychiatrist, Karla had disclosed the fact that the comatose girl to whom the hand belonged was still alive.

"Do you remember discussing that with Dr. Arndt?" MacDonald demanded.

"I don't remember that," Karla said, gently explaining, as though to a slightly retarded child, that her lack of specific memory was not really surprising since she had been under so much stress and she was still in shock.

"I find your memory selective, because you are able to give . . ." said MacDonald, starting to cite an example.

"It is not—selective," Karla hastily interrupted. "I wouldn't call it selective."

.   .   .

The defense knew about Karla's activities in February from the statements of Kristy Maan. Ms. Maan had visited Karla in Brampton and had been surprised to find her positively ebullient. There were also the statements of Karla's erstwhile Sugar Shack boyfriend, Jim Hutton. MacDonald asked Karla why all the days she had been seeing Jim Hutton were marked with little "x's" in the bottom right-hand corner of her so-called diary.

"Can you tell me what those are for?"

"Yes," said Karla defiantly. "Menstrual cycle."

Then MacDonald asked Karla about her state of mind prior to her hospitalization at Northwestern General—throughout the month of February, while she was staying at the Segers' and after she had returned home toward the end of the month. Everyone was surprised when Karla said: "I felt like killing myself all the time, I was severely depressed."

"What do you mean by depressed?" MacDonald asked solicitously.

"I couldn't eat. I couldn't sleep. I felt like my world was coming to an end. I felt hopeless."

"So before you got admitted to the hospital, describe for me your behavior," MacDonald requested.

"I was just hanging around the house all day, just moping around. I was tired all the time."

"Did you associate with friends?"

"Yes. I was seeing my friends. I was trying to reestablish friendships with my friends. I didn't see them very often."

"Were you drinking alcohol?"

"Not a lot, no."

MacDonald established that Karla had learned a good deal about drugs and their administration during her employment as a veterinarian's assistant. Karla knew how to give injections and had been exposed to narcotics. They had Demerol at the vet clinic and Karla was primarily responsible for the drug register.

MacDonald asked questions about Somnotol. Karla had run afoul of the vets at Martindale when she allegedly poured a bottle of Somnotol—an anesthetic that just happened to be a controlled substance—down the drain. Karla explained, "I was dusting shelves and noticed a lot of drugs out of date, so I decided to throw away the out-of-date drugs. . . ."

Karla should have known that Somnotol was not date-sensitive, nor were veterinary personnel allowed to dispose of it in that manner. The Somnotol incident happened before Karla settled on halothane as her anesthetic of choice.

After considerable obfuscation, Karla admitted she had stolen another bottle of halothane after she and Paul moved to Bayview. She added the caveat that Paul had made her do it.

MacDonald wanted to know if Karla knew what the side effects of Somnotol were; whether or not she had ever looked it up in her pharmaceutical compendium; whether she had ever highlighted it. The answer to all those questions was "yes."

The defense had ascertained, through Dr. Patti Weir, that Karla had attended many autopsies on various animals such as mice, cats and dogs. Karla positioned this as quite a normal practice.

MacDonald asked her if she had ever extended an invitation to Paul to attend a clinical autopsy on an animal.

"I don't recall specifically. I may have," Karla responded quickly, then reconsidered. "Actually, I think I did. For the reason that he was so interested in doing an autopsy on a person. I figured, 'Well, look at an animal,' It was basically the same thing, you know. We have got almost all the same organs."

But Paul never attended an autopsy.

MacDonald asked if Karla brought implements such as scalpels home from the clinic and Karla said "no." MacDonald knew that the police had found a #10 scalpel, which had been taken from the clinic, among Karla's effects at 57 Bayview.

MacDonald wanted to know how much Karla knew about the process of administering anesthetic and if the animals were given some other sort of sedative before the anesthetic was administered.

"Well, not always," Karla explained. "An animal can be what is called 'masked down,' where they are given a high dose of halothane through a face mask and they inhale it and go out that way, or they can be given . . . there's lots of different ways. There are different medications that can be given."

"Is a sedative sometimes given in combination with halothane?" MacDonald asked.

"Yes." Karla replied matter-of-factly. This was Karla's territory—her expertise. Not understanding or taking time to appreciate the relevance of these questions, it was one of the few times Karla let down her guard. "Because first of all when an animal is being 'masked down' they resist, they become almost violent, and when you have a one-hundred-pound dog, you can't mask it down."

Sedating the animal first made the effort "less traumatic and easier."

Karla remembered that Tammy Lyn had called Norma Tellier after she drank the Rusty Nail on December 23, 1990. MacDonald wanted to know how in the world Karla could remember something like that but could not remember what happened to Jane Doe or when? Because she had been talking to her mother a couple of weeks earlier and they had been discussing it, Karla replied dismissively.

Besides, Karla had been in Tammy's room and had overheard her talking to Norma. She also remembered that Paul was wearing his UCLA sweatshirt that night. "Like, he wanted to keep the sweatshirt because it was the last thing he was wearing when he was with Tammy. Just like he had a Captain Crunch cereal box that she was eating out of. . . . Well, Paul kept that box, because it was the last cereal box that she had eaten out of, kind of thing."

MacDonald looked at Karla. "What does the devil represent to you?"

"Well," Karla said as if she were about to tell the teacher what she did on her summer vacation, "the devil is the devil. He is a terribly bad guy. He is the worst guy there is. . . . I don't think the devil has any values. Not values, as values, meaning a normal person has values, you know what I'm saying? Any values he has are bad values, put it that way."

"Does death have anything to do with your conception of the devil?" MacDonald asked.

"Well, only in the way that when you die you go to heaven or hell, or either go to God's kingdom or the devil's kingdom," Karla said ingenuously.

"Is there a difference for you between the concept of the occult and satanism?" MacDonald continued.

"Yes. I believe that the occult is more involved in the spiritual world and doesn't necessarily have to do with the devil," Karla postulated, enjoying her dissertation. "Although some people would say that being involved in the occult is being involved in Satan's world. Some people believe that astrology is the devil's work."

Over the seven days MacDonald and Ken Murray spent asking Karla questions, they covered a great deal of material. They even returned for extra time at the end of July. Because MacDonald was so heavily influenced by Murray, who each night, given Karla's responses, would suggest a new series of enigmatic questions that did not necessarily make any sense to MacDonald, her approach was scattered. MacDonald felt she was vulnerable, at sea, that she was being bested.

MacDonald asked Karla whether battered women were part of her womens' studies program at Queen's? Karla replied, "No, not yet. I believe that's a very small portion of the course, near the end."

They went through a whole discussion about the symptoms of a sadistic sexual psychopath, and MacDonald asked Karla about trophies: "After he was questioned by Metro he threw everything away. Like, he used to keep ID but after, he threw everything away."

This directly contradicted her earlier comments to the police during her "induced" and "cautioned" statements in May, 1993, that she did not know Paul was the Scarborough rapist until he told her on their wedding night. How could Karla know that Paul had thrown all his trophies away after being interviewed by the Toronto police in November, 1990—right after he had come to her window that same Tuesday night—if she did not know he was the Scarborough rapist?

MacDonald asked Karla about underwear, things related to Tammy and sexual props. "Tammy's hair was in a silver-gold box," Karla replied. "Which I have, and I think it is all there." She denied ever using Tammy Lyn's underwear as a prop.

"Is it your evidence that you had no sexual contact with Jane Doe?"

"Yes."

"Is it your evidence that the sexual contact between Jane and Paul when she was unconscious only happened on one occasion?"

"Yes."

"And only one Halcion was used on Jane?"

"Yes."

"Was there an occasion when halothane was used on Jane Doe?"

"No."

"Were there any occasions, other than December 23, when halothane was used?"

"No."

Karla was lying through her teeth, and Ken Murray knew it. The only question now was, how and what was he going to do about it?

Sergeant Bob Gillies and Staff Sergeant Steve MacLeod had talked to Karla on August 8. They were going to provide her psychological and psychiatric records to three new doctors. The examination by Murray and MacDonald had perplexed Ray Houlahan. The tape with Jane Doe and Karla's answers when she was questioned were difficult to reconcile. The prosecution now felt it needed more and better psychology and psychiatry on Karla. Karla was happy to oblige.

The selected team was all male. Dr. Peter Jaffe was a psychologist and a recognized expert in battered spouse syndrome. He was from London, Ontario. Dr. Stephen Hucker, a forensic psychiatrist recently relocated to Kingston, Ontario, from the

Clarke Institute in Toronto, had assumed the position as head of the forensic unit at the Hôtel Dieu in Kingston and Dr. Chris Hatcher, a California psychologist, was allegedly an expert in post-traumatic stress disorder. Karla was very much looking forward to meeting these new doctors.

John Rosen thought it must be something serious because Ken Murray was uncharacteristically early for his appointment at Rosen's offices on Bloor Street in downtown Toronto on August 15. And Rosen was late, so he was even more surprised to find the normally impatient and fidgety lawyer still waiting in the foyer.

Rosen knew who Murray was. At that point, everybody did. Murray was Paul Bernardo's lawyer. But Rosen knew him for other reasons. He had been co-counsel on a case with Murray a couple of years earlier. Also, one of his junior partners, Tim Breen, lived with Carolyn MacDonald. Rosen was not only one of the most respected criminal lawyers in Toronto, but he was also one of the busiest.

A clear-eyed, cherub-faced, well-groomed man in his forty-ninth year, Rosen's nickname was Mr. Murder. Charismatic, he had a deservedly substantial reputation for his eloquent and persuasive jury addresses; his ability for searing, devastating cross-examinations.

During long, often tedious trials, Rosen would slump in his chair at the defense table, and under the pretense of reading transcripts or law do the crossword puzzle from the morning paper. Even on his bad days, he had more law at his fingertips than any ten judges. But it was his ability to translate the law and articulate it that made John Rosen a truly remarkable figure on the judicial landscape.

From behind, slumped down in his chair, Rosen looked almost exactly like Danny DeVito as he had appeared in *Other People's Money*. He had dark hair and a bald spot on top. Visage-wise, he bore a reasonable resemblance to the height-challenged actor as well. But whereas DeVito was short and paunchy, Rosen was tall—almost six feet and in top physical condition.

Clients he could not get off—because they were so evidently guilty that a deaf, dumb and blind jury would find against them—he invariably got convicted on reduced charges and sentenced leniently.

When Murray showed up that day in mid-August, 1994, John Rosen was in the process of defending a Russian emigré. The man had stabbed his wife in the heart with a butcher knife twelve times in front of his two children. The final time he stabbed her, he left the knife in. His youngest daughter pulled it out of her dying mother's chest. Charged with first-degree murder, Rosen's client got eight years for manslaughter. In total, the guy would do a little more time than Karla—but not much. Then he would be deported.

Murray had first called Rosen on July 28. Rosen finally got back to him on the fourteenth. And now here he was, waiting. Rosen was right. It was important. Murray wanted Rosen to take over the Bernardo case.

Murray was pleading with Rosen, saying that he had come to realize that he simply did not have the resources for the Bernardo case. He did not have the staff or the physical plant or the stamina. He simply did not have the wherewithal in any category. Unfortunately, it had taken him a year and a half to realize it. Murray said it was getting worse. New motions every second week and endless court appearances—Murray must have been in court two dozen times, without any end in sight.

The Bernardo case had no appeal for a lawyer of Rosen's status. The best criminal lawyers liked cases they had a chance to win; failing that, some reward—financial or political—commensurate to their efforts. All the major lawyers had been watching Murray's antics with quiet bemusement. Firstly, they wondered how Bernardo had ever found such an obscure lawyer from Aurora, Ontario. One story said his father's lawyer organized it. Another rumor had Murray representing Bernardo's errant brother, David, on some petty charges. However Bernardo got his number, Paul originally called Murray collect from the jail and asked him if he would come and see him. The larger question was, how the hell had Murray managed it this long?

The Bernardo case was sordid, and as far as Rosen could tell, unwinnable. It was wholly funded through Legal Aid. The Green Ribbon Task Force was the largest task force assembled in Canadian history. There were more prosecutors working on the Bernardo case than worked on some major federal-combines cases. And that was only with regard to the murders. The government had gone right off the deep end. There was no up side.

It was the last thing on earth Rosen wanted or needed. But the word "no" was not in John Rosen's vocabulary. He was simply one of those men who had always had great difficulty turning anyone down who got far enough to pose the question. He told Murray he would have to consult with his partner and his family and let Ken know.

His partner, Jim Fleming, who was also his brother-in-law, his wife, his two grown daughters and his teenage son all said no. Rosen called Murray the next day. Typically, he could not get Murray on the phone, so he left a message. "Thanks, but no thanks."

Murray called him back the following day. He implored Rosen to reconsider. Again, Murray pleaded with him. He wanted Rosen to talk to Carolyn MacDonald before he said an unequivocal "no." MacDonald was on holiday in Utah with Tim Breen.

On the telephone MacDonald told Rosen that after completing her examination of Karla Homolka she had told Murray there was no way she would stay on the case if Murray remained as lead counsel. The rift had been serious enough that Murray had canceled the final day scheduled with Karla.

She confirmed what Rosen already suspected—the thing was completely out of control and off the rails. There was something else as well; something less specific, on which MacDonald could not quite put her finger. Whatever it was, it was insidious. Murray had instructed MacDonald to ask Karla questions that seemed to come out of nowhere. Even the prosecution noticed it. MacDonald had an idea where they were coming from, but she did not feel it was her place to speculate. The cross had been ineffective and all over the map.

Still MacDonald found the case and all its machinations enthralling, as any young criminal lawyer might. The way it was when she left on vacation, the whole thing was an unresolved disaster. If Rosen took the case, MacDonald would stay on to provide the continuity. She was sure their law clerk, Kim Doyle, who was just then on maternity leave, would want to return to work on the case as well.

Rosen thought about it. Murray had said to him that the case was "an issues junkie's dream." So that was what Murray thought Rosen was: an issues junkie. There might be some truth in that. It was also very high profile. Not that Rosen needed the profile, but unlike many of his Canadian brothers-at-law, Rosen's appreciation for the media was positively American. He liked the media. He liked the spotlight and he was not the slightest bit timorous in the camera's glare.

Without further consultation with his partner or his family Rosen called Murray and said he would take the case, on three conditions: the client had to agree, Legal Aid had to approve the transfer and the judge had to agree to a lengthy adjournment in order to allow Rosen time to properly prepare.

Murray had already gone ahead and stupidly allowed Bernardo to be formally arraigned. He had entered a plea—not guilty—and had agreed to start the trial in the fall of 1994, which was far too early for Rosen, given the volume of Crown disclosure and his own full calendar. In addition, Rosen was concerned that the prosecution was gearing up for a trial in St. Catharines, without considering the dilemma of jury selection in a traumatized small town or the implicit logic of a change-of-venue application.

On Paul Bernardo's thirtieth birthday, August 27, 1994, Rosen and Murray drove to the Niagara Regional Detention Center in Thorold, Ontario, to talk to the prisoner. Bernardo was housed in a tiny, windowless cell on the ground floor of this bunkerlike, thoroughly unattractive block-and-brick building.

Murray asked to speak to Paul Bernardo alone for fifteen

minutes. Rosen found it a bit odd at the time, but did not give it a great deal of thought. He assumed Murray had been too busy to discuss his wish to get off the record any earlier. As it turned out, Rosen was right. Murray had neglected to mention it. Until that minute, Bernardo had no idea his lawyer was quitting.

Fifteen minutes later Rosen went into the jail. Bernardo looked exactly like his pictures. In turn, Paul said he had heard a great deal about Rosen.

There had been a prison guard, named Johnson, whom Rosen had defended. The guard had murdered an attractive transvestite prostitute and he had been held at the Metro East Detention Center for part of the time Bernardo was there. Nothing but praise from that corner, Paul Bernardo told John Rosen.

Like most criminal-defense lawyers, Rosen was susceptible to praise. Bernardo told Rosen he would be very happy if Rosen took over his defense. Rosen wished him a happy birthday. He explained the other conditions and assured Paul he was considering the case and would let him know, one way or the other, very soon.

The following day, Rosen contacted Legal Aid. They had no problem if he took over the file. Rosen had a well-deserved reputation for integrity. What most appealed to the administrators at Legal Aid, however, was his speed and efficency, particularly with his forte—complex murder trials.

The trial judge was Associate Chief Justice Patrick LeSage, a respected, popular adjudicator. Courthouse scuttlebutt was that LeSage would be promoted within the ranks if the trial went well. LeSage might be a little too quick to compromise for Rosen's liking, but the situation could have been a lot worse. During a meeting in his chambers, Rosen discovered that neither the prosecution nor the judge was particularly happy about this turn of events.

Earlier, Rosen had bumped into a former colleague who was now an assistant deputy minister in the Ministry of the Attorney-General. Michael Code was an ex-rugby-playing, square-jawed man who, along with Murray Segal and Casey Hill, was responsible for the Homolka deal.

Code told Rosen, without knowing where exactly Rosen stood, that the Bernardo case was going off the track and that he was very distressed.

LeSage was troubled because the Bernardo matter had dragged on far too long, as it was. He was determined to get the matter to trial and end it. Rosen made it clear that his participation was contingent on his being properly retained and the trial being adjourned so that he could clear his calendar and prepare properly. Otherwise, there would be a serious miscarriage of justice. Justice LeSage said the matter of Murray's withdrawal and the question of Rosen getting on the record had to be dealt with in open court and he scheduled the matter for September 12, in St. Catharines.

Murray and Rosen went to the Barrister's Dining Room in Osgoode Hall, next to the central courthouse in downtown Toronto where Justice LeSage's chambers were. Rosen told him that it would be necessary for him to prepare a proper, brutally honest affidavit explaining why a senior counsel in the middle of the highest-profile case in Canadian judicial history had to withdraw. If he did not have very good reason, Murray could be sure the Law Society would investigate, and if they found him to be simply incompetent, his professional status would be compromised and his career in jeopardy. Rosen strongly recommended that Murray take his position very seriously and make sure his affidavit was sound and accurate.

It was after 5:00 P.M. the same day when Rosen got a call from the office of another highly respected criminal lawyer, Austin Cooper, Q.C., elder statesman of the criminal bar. Cooper's office called Rosen to say that Murray had retained Cooper to represent him. Why would Murray do that, Rosen wanted to know?

The following day, Cooper himself called Rosen back.

"What ethical problem?" Rosen asked incredulously when Cooper uttered the phrase. Cooper said that he had not explored the exact nature of the problem, only that he was going to accept Murray's word that an ethical issue existed. Rosen suggested to Cooper that Murray's word would not be good enough. There would have to be a definition of exactly what the ethical problem was.

"What would you do?" Cooper asked.

"I'd treat him as a client and read him the riot act," responded Rosen, who felt it would best serve all concerned if truth prevailed.

When Austin Cooper called Ken Murray and told him what Rosen had said, Murray finally came clean and told his counsel that he was in possession of the notorious videotapes.

Perceiving the serious nature of his new client's problem, Cooper went to the Law Society, where an ad hoc committee could render an unbinding opinion. Rosen heard nothing further until the Labor Day weekend was over.

By Wednesday, September 7, sensing something was amiss, John Rosen put in a call to Paul Bernardo. All that had occurred so far was a strange subterfuge. Because of Murray's aberrant, unpredictable behavior and what Carolyn MacDonald had told him, Rosen was highly suspicious. He felt he was being used, that he was dangerously close to the edge of some abyss.

Rosen spoke to the superindendent at the Niagara Regional Detention Center and asked him to have Paul Bernardo call. Preoccupied with other matters, Rosen was shocked to find that by two o'clock he had still not had a call back. He called the jail again and tore a strip off the perplexed warden who said he had dutifully relayed Rosen's earlier message.

A few minutes later, Paul called and apologized. He had been distracted by two visitors—Ken Murray and Ken Murray's lawyer. Apparently, Murray no longer wanted off the record. Bernardo was totally confused and asked Rosen if he would come down and see him. Paul now wanted Rosen, not Murray, to represent him but he did not want to talk in front of the guards on the telephone.

Rosen drove to Thorold again that night with another lawyer from his office. After talking to Bernardo, Rosen quickly realized that Murray was engaged in some elaborate chicanery and the situation was quickly disintegrating. Rosen retained another prominent Canadian criminal lawyer, Clayton Ruby, to assist him in dealing with this festering issue. Ruby agreed, but wanted no part of the trial itself.

On the morning of September 12, a Toronto tabloid newspaper reprinted a bevy of Karla's letters to Kathy Ford. Karla felt as if she was going crazy—again. She called George Walker, furious. What are we going to do about this? she demanded.

John Rosen appeared with Clay Ruby before Justice LeSage. Austin Cooper appeared for Ken Murray. Court was barely in session when Cooper tried to preempt the proceedings and submit a letter from the Law Society and a sealed package to Justice LeSage.

Justice LeSage would not play Judge Ito to Cooper's Robert Shapiro. He refused to accept the package and letter. LeSage instructed the lawyers to sort it out in conference, and then he adjourned the court.

By now, Rosen had a good idea what was in the package. The press was frantic. This was the biggest show since Homolka's trial.

When court reconvened, the lawyers had agreed among themselves that the package would be handed over to Rosen, who would then examine the contents and do whatever was "legally, ethically and professionally" correct. There was a small unpublished caveat: Rosen would undertake not to say anything derogatory about Ken Murray.

Court adjourned and the lawyers went back to the conference room. The package was opened and tipped out to reveal six 8mm videocassette tapes. Rosen, Ruby, Cooper, Peter West, Ken Murray and Carolyn MacDonald were all in the room.

"What about the copies?" Rosen asked.

"There are no copies," Cooper rejoined.

Rosen was about to contradict him, when Murray weakly spoke up from the back of the room. In a weak voice he told them that the copies were at his farm in Newmarket. Cooper, a tall, distinguished, balding man closing in on seventy, held himself in check.

Too much of a gentleman to publicly display his extreme displeasure, Cooper ordered Murray to drive directly to his farm with another lawyer from Cooper's firm and retrieve all copies of the videotapes and deliver them to wherever Rosen stipulated.

They were promptly delivered to Clay Ruby's offices on Prince Arthur Avenue in downtown Toronto. With Carolyn MacDonald, Rosen and Ruby watched the tapes at Ruby's Rosedale home the next day. MacDonald had known there were tapes, but she had never seen them. They were all horrified by what they saw. Rosen got up, went into the washroom and cried.

On Thursday, September 22, 1993, Inspector Vince Bevan was given the perfect excuse for his deal with Karla Homolka—six 8mm-format videotapes. If Ken Murray—who had earlier made a point of telling Bevan's identification officers pointblank that he was not "just another scumbag lawyer"—had given up these videotapes when he found them in May, 1993, as any honorable man would have done, the "deal with the devil," as Murray had so volubly and publicly called it, would never have been done.

God worked in mysterious ways. When the inspector delivered the videotapes to the I-dent officers the following day, Bevan thought Karla Homolka might be assailable after all. Even the compliant victim of a sexual sadist could not be that forgetful.

Each tape had a label that appeared to be in Paul Bernardo's handwriting. One of them even had one of those little heart-shaped cartoonlike stickers that Karla put all over everything. The labels were cryptic descriptions identifying the victims and scenarios depicted in each segment. Constable Kershaw made a number of VHS copies of the videotapes.

On September 24, Inspector Vince Bevan gave I-dent officer Richard Ciszek two sealed boxes containing videotapes. The one box, bearing Center for Forensic Science seal number 1N01142, was opened for examination. The second box remained sealed.

The opened box contained six 8mm tapes. The tapes were photographed and Inspector Bevan requested they all be dusted for fingerprints.

On September 27, Sergeant Gillies had a telephone conversation with Karla. He told her they now had all the videotapes, particularly those relating to her sister, Leslie Mahaffy and Kristen French. Sergeant Gillies and Karla talked for about ten minutes.

The videos were screened for all the members of the Green Ribbon Task Force in the boardroom on the second floor of the Reimer Tower in Burlington on October 11. Afterward, Bevan arranged counseling for the forty odd members of the task force.

The tapes were viewed in sequence. First, the tape labeled "Red Hot Chili Pepper," which depicted an unknown girl being photographed through her bedroom window, followed by footage of murder victims Leslie Mahaffy and Kristen French. The second tape depicted Kristen French, and Tammy Homolka being drugged and raped by Paul and Karla. By far the most distressing sequence—as far as Inspector Bevan's credibility was concerned—was the eighteen-minute segment that showed Karla Homolka doing exactly the same thing she had done to her dead sister to Jane Doe.

Throughout the segment Karla could clearly be seen pouring repeated doses of halothane onto a cloth and holding it over the already comatose Jane Doe's nose and mouth. They saw exactly where the short clips on "Karla's Sex Video" had come from. And just as she had on the short clips, Karla seemed to be having herself one hell of a time. There were approximately three and a half hours of videotape.

It was all there—everything, except for the actual killings.

On the strength of any ten-minute segment from the segments dealing with Leslie Mahaffy and Kristen French, an aurally challenged, one-eyed jury would convict John Rosen's new client, Paul Bernardo, on all nine charges. They would also have convicted Karla Homolka on the same charges, but she was not available for indictment or trial.

CHAPTER
thirty-two

On February 1, Sergeant Bob Gillies went to George Walker's Niagara Falls offices and supplied him with transcripts from all of the police interviews with Karla in which Jane Doe had been mentioned. He also showed Walker selections from the videotapes, including Karla and Paul's attack on the comatose teenager.

There were things Walker had heard and seen over the years that he could have lived without. In the two and a half hours that Gillies was in his office, Walker saw a great deal more of such things. After the sergeant left at 10:00 P.M., Walker seriously wished he was back in Montserrat.

The similarity of the attack on Jane Doe to the one that had killed Karla's sister, and the extent of Karla's participation in the attack on Jane, were two of the things Murray Segal wanted to discuss with Walker when Segal went to Walker's office on February 7. Karla's salacious thirty or forty seconds with what turned out to be Jane's hand in the short tape had not really presented a problem for the Crown or the police. The compliant-victim concept covered a lot of questionable behavior.

But the tapes that Ken Murray had were mind-boggling. Karla had done to Jane exactly what she had done to her sister only six months earlier. This fact brought a lot of second-guessers out of the woodwork around the Crown law office. That Karla could not remember or did not remember or would not remember any details about that assault was difficult for many officials at the ministry to accept. Some individuals simply did not believe Karla's story.

Walker was quick to point out that Karla had mentioned Jane a couple of times during her "induced" and "cautioned" statements. Had he not brought Karla's dream about which she had written Walker on October 6, 1993, to the police and Segal's attention?

Karla had wanted to talk about Jane with Sergeant Beaulieu when Beaulieu showed her the short tape in December, but Beaulieu had told her to wait for the Toronto detectives. Walker would come back to these points and a few others time and again, over the next four months.

Segal left Walker's office around 10:00 P.M. The following day Walker received a formal letter signed by Segal. For such a serious matter, the missive was remarkably chatty and familiar. Segal conceded they had known about the tapes, but had failed to find them.

"Once the police were in possession of them, they had to be authenticated and studied," he advised. "Your client must now be interviewed respecting them, first by the police and then by the Crown Attorney."

Segal then went on to tell Walker just about everything the prosecution was thinking about Karla's situation. With regard to the videotapes and Ms. Homolka there were basically three areas to explore, Segal wrote.

The first areas of exploration were relatively innocuous and basically related to expanding the police and prosecution's understanding about what had happened to whom, when and how. For instance, they needed Karla's observations on conversations and activities depicted on the newly found videotapes.

In the six and a half hours of videotape there was some amateurish voyeurism, including two girls shot undressing at night through their bedroom windows. There were also two surreptitiously taped segments of girls urinating. In one of these segments, there appeared yet another unidentified girl.

There was also the seventy-minute segment featuring Karla and Paul in a variety of sex acts in which Karla impersonated her recently departed sister. Since their star witness had a starring role, the authorities expected that more and better information should be forthcoming.

In light of what the authorities now knew had happened, the Jane Doe issue had become more complicated. Segal acknowledged that Walker had brought a sex attack on Jane Doe to their attention in late 1993, but Karla had said that Paul had raped her friend—she had said nothing about her own considerable involvement. This was problematical.

Karla's statement that Paul had done it appeared to be contradicted by the videotape segment in which Jane is obviously comatose and Karla can be seen, once again, holding a halothane-soaked cloth over the face of a teenage girl. Karla appeared to be anything but unhappy. It did not appear that she was being forced to participate. The Crown knew that this was the tape from which the short clip featuring the hand in Karla's vagina had been taken.

"Your client has been questioned on a number of occasions, sometimes under oath, respecting her recollection of her involvement with Jane Doe," Segal wrote, adding that he understood Karla seemed to be mistaken about her own involvement.

"I understand your client appears to be committing a sexual

assault on Jane Doe and administering what may be a stupefying drug." He noted that Walker had been shown the scenes earlier that month.

Segal fortuitously told Walker exactly what the authorities were going to do next. Segal agreed with the police that any further questioning about Jane should be under caution. Walker knew that meant they were very concerned about the discrepancies between what they had already been told and what, in fact, had actually happened.

To do this, the police were going to go down to Kingston, read Karla her rights and question her about Jane. Given what they now knew, they would question her about what she said she knew or did not know. Once that approach had run its course, they would show her the actual tape and finish questioning her with the tape as a visual aid. They set aside the entire day of February 20 for this undertaking.

Then they would go over the rest of the videotapes. This review would be done under oath, but not under caution. In other words, there was nothing else in these hours of videotape that really concerned or surprised the Crown law office or the police. Segal figured the whole process might take five days.

Segal's letter then became curiously circumspect. He suggested to Walker that they might obtain expert opinion about Karla's avowed memory lapse and the inconsistencies between what she said had happened and what really had happened.

"Might obtain" was an interesting way of putting it, since they had already done so and nobody was more aware of that fact than George Walker. Walker knew that the prosecution had already called in three more doctors to consult and examine Karla with regard to battered woman's syndrome, post-traumatic stress disorder and the Crown's portrayal of Paul Bernardo as a sexual sadist. He knew that the prosecution had retained, at great expense, a psychologist named Dr. Chris Hatcher from California. They had flown Dr. Hatcher in one cold December day and driven him all over God's green acre. Karla did one ten-hour stretch with Dr. Hatcher and she had really liked him. He was relatively young, tanned and handsome, with distinguished silver streaks in his dark hair, very intelligent and soft-spoken. In Karla's words, the California doctor was a "god-send."

On the evening of February 8, George Walker checked into the Kingston Holiday Inn. First thing the next morning he was at the prison. Walker took great pains to explain Karla's tenuous position to her. He did not want her to underestimate the gravity of her situation or have anyone think, in retrospect, that he had not properly advised her.

In Walker's file there was a handwritten note marked 9:00 A.M., February 9. In longhand he noted he had advised Karla that there was a definite possibility the prosecutors could charge her with any number of things in relation to Jane Doe, including sexual assault, unlawful confinement, perjury and administering a noxious substance. These were all serious charges and could quash her deal. If prosecuted and convicted on any of these charges, she could easily get a life sentence.

The meticulously written document stated that there was no inducement for Karla to cooperate with the police or the prosecution. Nothing the police had said in the past—regardless of how she perceived her relationship with them—meant anything now. If the police and the prosecution were not satisfied about her memory loss, they would charge her as soon as look at her.

If Karla was charged, anything she said to them, at any time, would be used against her. She had the right to retain counsel and refuse to cooperate. If she waived that right she did so at her OWN RISK!!! (Walker printed OWN RISK!!! in big letters with three exclamation marks on this sheet.) Then he printed out, READ LETTER ABOVE & FULLY UNDERSTOOD BY CLIENT, dated Feb. 9/95. He signed it and asked Karla to sign it. She did: Karla Teale, which was the name she had decided to use in prison.

In reality, neither Karla nor Walker was terribly concerned. Karla had simply "forgotten" about Jane Doe. The prosecution would not want to renege or recant because it would look bad. Karla had a lot of things going for her.

Karla had told Walker about Jane Doe and her dreams. Karla

said she thought she had told several police officers as well as the prosecutors, Ray Houlahan and Greg Barnett. Karla thought Greg Barnett "typed it with his computer." She had also told Dr. Brown that she had had a dream. In that dream, what had happened to Kristen happened to Jane. That was her new dream.

"I think I began to tell Bob things about Jane Doe," Karla said to Walker, referring to Sergeant Gillies, "but I told him I couldn't remember so he said: 'Don't tell me—only about what you remember.' "

Walker left Karla at noon, quite certain that Karla had a handle on the situation.

John Rosen had his own problems. Carolyn MacDonald did not make the cut. There were noises within and without the Ministry of the Attorney-General about the possibility that Ken Murray might be investigated and charged with obstructing justice for holding onto the videotapes for sixteen months, but there was another possibility—that Murray could be called as a witness for the prosecution against his former client.

The videotapes were the metaphoric equivalent of a "smoking gun." The smoking-gun issue had elicited a number of relatively consistent court rulings in the United States in recent years.

If a lawyer came into possession of physical evidence of a crime, that lawyer was required "professionally, ethically and legally" to immediately surrender such evidence to the authorities. By failing to do so, Ken Murray theoretically became a material witness.

The prosecution could easily call him to the witness stand and ask him exactly where he had got the videotapes. The same possibility claimed Ms. MacDonald. Fortunately, the law clerk, Kim Doyle, escaped unscathed.

Doyle was fanatically dedicated. She had been the defense-team interviewer and client caretaker, a role she retained when she joined Rosen. She was devoted to the idea that they could "get" Karla Homolka. More importantly, because Doyle be-

lieved Karla even less than her former bosses, Doyle's encyclo-
pedic knowledge of the case was already being shaped by one of
the most important questions in this case—the credibility and
culpability of Karla Homolka.

A high-profile case of this size and complexity was enor-
mously time-consuming. An entire room was dedicated to stor-
ing the files and Crown Disclosure, which was contained in
fifty-four Serlox-bound, legal-size, seven-inch-thick volumes.
The Disclosure held all the prosecution's background information on the Bernardos and Homolkas, witness interviews and
statements, exhibit lists, forensic results, and the will-says of
more than 240 police officers. A will-say is a written statement
or report submitted by any officer who had anything whatsoever to do with the case; it reflects what they could say if questioned under oath. The various will-says in this instance ranged
in length from two paragraphs submitted by the cops who had
driven Bernardo from his interview to the jail in Toronto on the
morning of February 18, to hundreds of pages supplied by officers such as Inspector Vince Bevan, Sergeant Larry Maracle
and Detective Steve Irwin.

There was the same volume of material again to do with the
Scarborough rapes and a whole new set of will-says from the
Metropolitan Toronto Police. With the exception of Steve Irwin, there was no one individual officer who had worked on
both investigations.

On top of everything else, Justice LeSage was being prickly
about Rosen's demands for an adjournment. Rosen had been
vociferous about his displeasure, and had told the judge that he
would not go on the record for Bernardo if his schedule could
not be accommodated.

Karla knew that the only way she could garner any credibility
was to confront the doubting policemen about Jane Doe alone.
She waived her right to have George Walker present.

Walker had the Homolkas to his office for three-quarters of
an hour on February 13, to apprise them of the situation and
quell their fears about their daughter's new troubles. He was

also at it again in earnest with Segal. Between February 13 and 17, Walker and Segal spoke on the telephone half a dozen times. Their conversations were lengthy. On February 16, Walker had a half-hour telephone conversation with Inspector Bevan.

On February 20, two members of the Green Ribbon Task Force, Staff Sergeant Steve MacLeod and Constable Scott Kenney, went to the Kingston Prison for Women to question Karla about Jane Doe.

At the beginning of the tape, Inspector Bevan can be seen briefly bringing Sergeant MacLeod a glass of water. The inspector was casually dressed. As if it were a tea party, he politely inquired whether anyone else wanted anything. Karla politely said, "No, thank you." Then Sergeant MacLeod read Karla her rights—he sounded serious. Now she was "under caution" and anything she said could be used against her.

There were a dozen members of the Green Ribbon Task Force in town for these interviews. They set up the audio-visual equipment in the K4W conference room and placed Karla at the end of the table. MacLeod was on her right, Constable Kenney on her left. Inspector Bevan was overseeing the production. He had produced "The Abduction of Kristen French"; now he was going to produce "The Exoneration of Karla Teale." Bevan had a possessive streak; he had referred to the two dead girls as "his ghosts," and now Karla was "his evidence."

These new sessions with Karla were shot in quarter-split screens. One stationary camera remained focused on Karla; another stationary camera shot the three individuals so that their interaction and paper shuffles could be monitored. The bottom-left quadrant recorded the videotape footage Karla was shown with times coded down to the hour, minute and second. The fourth-quarter split screen was blank. That quadrant must represent the unknowable, the unanswerable.

The first day was the hardest. But Karla persevered. During the first half hour, Karla was clearly anxious. This session would have interested Dr. Arndt. Karla actually cried a little—were there really tears? Whining, she effusively protested her innocence. It was not hard for Karla to act that way under the circumstances; her well-being was clearly threatened. She continued to remember nothing of what she saw; she feigned shock. Within fifteen minutes, her composure was back. She was, by turns, surprised, disgusted with herself and candid, taking the police officers into her confidence, explaining why she might not remember.

The sessions usually began in the middle of the afternoon. Karla and the two detectives greeted one another amicably. MacLeod and Kenney asked some generic questions and then they played that day's videotape once through. They would then ask Karla if she had any general comments before they started with their barrage of questions in counterpoint to specific scenes on the videotapes to which they slowly advanced frame by frame or which they reached with fast-forward or reverse searches. Thus, they whiled away the afternoons and evenings with startlingly pornographic questions to which they got frank pornographic answers. Most of these daily sessions were six or seven hours long. As the detectives weakened, Karla got stronger and more relaxed. She checked "background music" titles for them, and she spotted bruises they had never seen. This was Karla's Cannes and she was some kind of star, in all her naked, lurid glory.

The interviews with Karla continued through February 24. They covered every inch of those six and a half hours of videotape, frame by horrific frame. With Jane Doe, Leslie Mahaffy and Kristen French, Karla's affect was anything but flat. But by now her lack of flat affect was beside the point.

One of the first things John Rosen noticed about Karla Homolka was her prodigious medical file. She had told everyone—George Walker, Drs. Arndt, Long and Malcolm, the police, her parents, Drs. Jaffe, Hucker and Hatcher, plus R.J. Houlahan that Paul would never let her go to the doctor. Yet during the three-year period between 1989 and 1992, Karla had been to the doctor twenty-six times, an average of 8.3 visits per year.

None of these doctors had noticed anything unusual about Karla's mental state or her physical condition. According to their records, Karla was a physically fit, well-adjusted, young, white female.

Given the fact that the prosecution expert on battered woman's syndrome, Dr. Peter Jaffe, had said in his report that Karla was abused—emotionally, sexually and physically—from the time she met Paul Bernardo, Rosen found this medical information indicative of the convenient gullibility of the authorities and their experts. Rosen learned that not only had Paul permitted her to see doctors, he had often arranged for her to do so.

In particular, the reports of Karla's general practitioners, Dr. Valerie Jaeger and Dr. Christine Plaskos, held much interest for Rosen. Even though they had seen Karla regularly over the entire period she and Paul had been together, neither of those doctors ever suspected a thing. Both sets of doctors' records contradicted everything Dr. Jaffe and Karla said.

Until Karla was hospitalized in early January, 1993, Dr. Plaskos saw no evidence of abuse. Afterward, when Karla returned time and again to Dr. Plaskos before and after her stay at Northwestern General Hospital, Dr. Plaskos did not find Karla to be depressed, suicidal or with a "flat affect."

Karla complained about aches and pains, so Dr. Plaskos gave her a full physical. Since Karla was going to prison, Dr. Plaskos did her bloodwork, including HIV tests. It was all normal, and Karla was negative. Dr. Plaskos did find Karla to be very upset about her future and petrified about going to prison.

That Karla would lie at the drop of the hat, if she perceived it to be in her own best interest or if her well-being was at stake, was demonstrable. From the experience with her former boyfriend and their Kansas sojourn, as well as the trip she and Paul had taken to Florida in the summer of 1988, she had no hesitation whatsoever about lying to her parents.

Even though she talked to the doctors about how wonderful her parents were, how she would not do this and could not do that to them, her real feelings seemed to be contained in her expletive-filled ten-page missive to Debbie Purdie on February 19, 1991. Her real view of her parents was summed up in one statement: "What assholes."

Neither Dr. Arndt nor Dr. Malcolm thought Karla suicidal. But when Carolyn MacDonald and Ken Murray had examined Karla under oath in the summer of 1994, Karla said she had been heavily depressed and suicidal all the time.

She told the doctors and the police that she was at her worst—black and blue and beaten—when Norma Tellier and her friend Brian had been over to the house on December 27, 1992, but neither Norma, Brian nor Brian's father had noticed anything wrong with Karla on that particular day.

Even the story about how Karla had actually left the matrimonial home had many versions. Her parents claimed they had had to physically drag her out, but to hear Karla tell it, she sat on the white loveseat in the living room and kibbitzed with her mother about Tammy Lyn's relationship with Paul.

In one version, her father, sister and neighbors scurried around the house scooping up Karla's personal effects so that she could survive the escape. In yet another variation, Karla had taken the time to thoroughly search the hiding places for the videotapes—upstairs, downstairs and in the garage—without telling anyone what she was looking for. There was a school of thought that said Karla had her own copy of the videotapes squirreled away somewhere.

Depending on her circumstances, Karla told different people different stories all the time.

Karla had lied in response to a whole series of questions MacDonald had asked Karla during their defense examination in 1994—derived from Ken Murray's review of the videotapes he had hidden away. Karla said she had never administered halothane to anyone except her sister. She said she had never given Halcion to anyone except her sister and Leslie Mahaffy. She qualified that by saying that she vaguely remembered that she had given Jane Doe one Halcion pill. She had completely "forgotten" about Kristen French. Karla said she had never used Tammy Lyn's underwear as a sexual prop.

In February, 1995, under caution, during the review of the video segment that concerned Jane Doe, Karla told the police she had never seen the tape before. That was a lie. But then again, her entire version of her relationship with Jane Doe and what she and Paul had done to the teenager was a lie. Through her intrinsic understanding of the dynamics of "recovered memory" and psychotherapy, lying—or forgetting, as Karla chose to call it—had the opposite effect on Karla than it had on Pinocchio. Karla became less obvious and more beguiling.

On other occasions with other police, she said she had seen the videotapes—but she had not really seen them. In *Michelle Remembers,* a book all about the alleged mechanics of remembering—"seeing" and "not seeing"—the fact that things could be deeply sublimated and then recovered is at the core of Michelle's satanic fairy tale. Michelle tells her therapist, "My inside eyes could sometimes see what my outside was doing. . . ." Karla felt just like Michelle.

When Karla told Detective Mary Lee Metcalfe that she had watched the videotapes but had not really seen them when she watched them, but she had watched herself watching them so she knew she had sort of seen them, Karla asked Detective Metcalfe if she knew what she meant? Detective Metcalfe said "yes."

John Rosen did not know what Karla meant. Particularly since Karla had told both George Walker and Dr. Arndt that she had watched all the videotapes at one time or another, and that they were so horrible she had not enjoyed them at all.

But it was Karla's stories about how the dead girls died that were most important to John Rosen and his client. If Karla lied about anything substantial, her deal was assailable. If Karla "stopped the breath" of any individual, her deal was void. If Rosen could prove that Karla's stories about the death of any one of the three dead teenagers were apocryphal, and break her deal, then he would have performed a service to his client, himself and the community. Even though Rosen's own client was guilty as sin—given the tidbits of forensic evidence and the videotapes, any jury would convict him—Paul Bernardo steadfastly maintained that Karla was as bad as he was. Rosen believed him. As far as Rosen could tell, the matter of Jane Doe had once again tossed Karla's fate to the wind, and theoretically made her extremely vulnerable.

· · ·

Throughout March and April, George Walker kept the lines of communication with the Ministry wide open. There were lots of people to talk to. Segal was no longer alone. There was James Treleavan, Leo McGuigan, Brian Gover and Michael Code. Walker had even been talking to the inspector. On April 11, he had another half-hour telephone conversation with Bevan and was the recipient of a Bevanism: the police "were still reviewing the materials."

By April 24, the Green Ribbon Task Force was ensconced in the Colony Hotel in Toronto, a hop, skip and a jump from the courthouse in which Paul Bernardo's trial would begin on May 1. Bevan had new letterhead printed with the Green Ribbon Task Force's hotel address, phone, fax and 1-800 number.

Inspector Bevan wrote to Dr. Hatcher in San Francisco. He wanted further elaboration on Hatcher's one-hundred-page report; Bevan needed to hear it from the horse's mouth. Allegedly, Bevan was having doubts, wrestling with his conscience, tortured by demons—had he done the right thing when he facilitated the deal in the first place? Now that he suspected Karla was malingering, how could he assuage the nagging uncertainty? She was a black Madonna, but she was the only Madonna he had. He needed the esteemed doctor's counsel and insight.

In Bevan's letter, the inspector gave his own, concise summary of the Jane Doe matter and included the opinions of Dr. Brown, whose written opinions George Walker had provided. Bevan also shared the transcript of another private conversation he had with Dr. Peter Jaffe on the same topic. He wrote out a list of questions such as, "Why is Homolka's recollection of these events blocked? She has some recall of the sexual assault which occurred in August, 1991, but no memory of the incident in June, 1991."

"As you are aware," Inspector Bevan continued, "the Crown is currently arguing a number of legal motions in preparation for jury selection on May 1, 1995. Important decisions regarding the witness Homolka must be made in the very near future."

Bevan's atypical reticence drove Walker to talk to Dr. Brown again on April 26. He wanted yet another letter from the prison doctor.

Dr. Brown responded to Walker's request by reiterating his agreement with all his colleagues' post-traumatic stress disorder assessments. Dr. Brown pointed out that the disorder was apparently more severe and long-lasting when the "stressor" was of human design as opposed to a natural disaster. According to the well-meaning doctor, such things as "bombings, torture and death camps" tended to really disorient people and cause long-term psychological problems.

"Among the typical symptoms are depression, 'psychic numbing,' a loss of feeling and interest in social activities, and impaired memory and difficulty in concentrating," Brown wrote.

Dr. Brown obviously knew nothing about the Sugar Shack and Karla's relationship with Jim Hutton.

Dr. Brown incorrectly stated in this letter that Ms. Homolka had been forced by Paul Bernardo to abuse "mind-altering drugs." The only mind-altering drugs Ms. Homolka had abused had been prescribed. The only other stupefying, state-altering drugs Karla had used, she had given to her sister and her little "friend," Jane Doe. Jane survived, the sister died.

Dr. Brown cheerfully went on: "The apparently systematic forms of abuse that Ms. Teale was subjected to amount, in my opinion, to the form of torture seen commonly in concentration camp reports and in 'brainwashing' techniques used in POW interrogation. . . .

"In my opinion, Ms. Teale has demonstrated a very detailed and consistent recall for most of the circumstances involving her relationship with her ex-husband and the role he played in the commission of the offenses. The gaps in her memory appear related to events in which she participated only under his directions . . ."

Karla had just told Walker and Inspector Bevan otherwise. Gaining confidence in the concept of "recovered memory," now Karla thought she might have enticed Jane Doe solely on her own. Karla was starting to "remember" that Paul was out at the time. Since Paul had been out and had never met Jane, Jane's seduction, stupefaction and rape could hardly have been under his directions. . . .

Dr. Brown concluded his letter by saying, "I trust this will be helpful to you, and hope that Karla's future court appearance will not cause a setback in the progress she has made to date. She will, of course, continue to require long-term therapy for the foreseeable future."

John Rosen had wanted to be a doctor. His first years at university were devoted to the study of science—no time for the arts. Although he had lost his youthful faith in the medical profession, his approach to the law was rigorously scientific. He thought of himself as a logical man. There was nothing interpretative or sentimental or philosophical in the way John Rosen looked at any of his matters before the bar.

Take Karla's story about her sister's death and particularly the phrase "fucking disgusting," upon which she had focused after the videotapes had surfaced and everyone could see that she was uncomfortable in that particular, brief six-minute scene.

The facts were these. Karla was barely out of her teens and living at home with her family when she killed her sister. Her sister had died in the midst of a sexual assault that she had facilitated, and that she and her boyfriend, Paul Bernardo, had perpetrated.

Paul Bernardo knew nothing about drugs; Karla knew a great deal about drugs. When Karla obtained the drugs and organized the plan to drug her sister, Paul was working full-time in Toronto. Karla cheated, lied and stole to get them. In the videotape of the Homolka's happy Christmas that year, Karla Homolka was effervescent, relaxed and playful. There was another explanation for why Karla had said "fucking disgusting," and Rosen would surely get to that.

Then came Jane Doe, about whom Karla was "recovering memory." Otherwise, Karla's memory was impeccable. She re-

membered with disarmingly lucid accuracy everything else, including the day Corrina Jenkins was raped on Henley Island.
Karla remembered that incident, she had said, not because Paul
came home and declared himself, but because it was Karla's cat's
birthday.

Karla's version of how Leslie Mahaffy died was problematic and
did not make sense. Karla said Paul Bernardo beat Leslie. Karla
said she agreed with Paul when he concluded that Leslie Mahaffy had to die. Karla believed Leslie could probably recognize
Paul and they would be caught and go to prison. Karla said Paul
had strangled Leslie with some electrical cord he just happened
to have handy. Once again, even though Karla was there in the
room when Paul allegedly strangled Leslie, she saw, but did not
see. For Karla, it did not matter whether it was live or Memo-
rex, she possessed this remarkable facility where she saw but did
not see.

From the pathology it was impossible to know for sure
whether or not Leslie had been strangled, because her neck had
been decimated by a power saw. However, the postmortem
revealed none of the other nine or ten usual indices of strangulation.

After studying all the pathology and talking to the pathologist, Rosen came to the conclusion that Karla was lying again.
Leslie Mahaffy had not been beaten. There was no evidence
that she had been hit anywhere by anyone. What there was
were two unexplained, equidistant, asymmetrical, subcutaneous
bruises, chest high, on either side of her back. It looked as
though someone had knelt forcefully on Leslie Mahaffy's upper
back. Those marks were the only marks on her body and they
were not visible to the naked eye.

Karla also said that Paul cut up Leslie Mahaffy's body by
himself while Karla was at work. She stated that Paul obtained
all the cement, carried the twenty-two, sixty-pound bags to his
car, then out of the car at 57 Bayview, down the basement
stairs, mixed it and encased Leslie's various body parts in small
cement coffins he shaped, using cardboard boxes he had also

obtained somewhere. Then he returned the twelve unused bags of cement for a cash refund. According to Karla, he did all this while Karla was at work, between Monday morning and Wednesday evening. One other thing, as Karla would say: Paul disposed of most of the cement blocks by himself—Karla only helped with the two-hundred-pound block containing the torso.

What Karla said Paul had done was impossible, unless Paul had, as Sergeant Riddle once suggested, "magical powers." Even for someone with magical powers, dismembering a body would be time-consuming and messy. Dismembering it with a power saw would spew pieces of flesh, skin, bone and blood forty feet in all directions. During the ten weeks the crime-scene analysts were in the house, they did not find any evidence of Leslie Mahaffy in the basement or anywhere else in the house. They picked up blood splatters and ten thousand pieces of hair, but not one speck, not one hair belonging to Leslie Mahaffy.

Paul Bernardo had no history to persuade anyone that he had suddenly decided the best way to hide a body was dismember it, encase the parts in cement and dump it into the lake.

On the other hand, Karla was involved in surgery and autopsies all the time. Animals were just like humans, she kept telling everyone. It only seemed logical that Karla had been instrumental in the dismemberment of Leslie Mahaffy on Sunday evening, after their parents had gone home, the way Paul Bernardo said she was.

With tarps the two had made a tent around the power saw. Karla helped Paul dismember the body, piece by piece, and then she washed each piece, put it in a plastic garbage bag and carried each of the ten body parts to the root cellar, where they were stored overnight.

Paul and Karla took down all the tarps, folded them up and with the other refuse, then threw them in the Dumpster behind the Martindale Animal Clinic. Karla had the necessary keys to the Dumpster.

There was one other thing. Murray Segal had been rightly curious about Karla's insistence that there were ten boxes;

therefore, ten blocks containing the body parts. Karla knew there were ten packages of body parts, because she had handled them. She just assumed that Paul had given each body part its own little box. But he did not. He doubled up a couple of pieces, producing only eight blocks in the end. Karla was undoubtedly involved in the dismemberment, but not in the cement work. If she had been, Rosen assumed, it would have been done properly and the body parts would never have been found.

Karla had been the subject of more scrutiny, more evaluations, had taken more drugs and had more "therapy" than Zelda Fitzgerald and Sylvia Plath put together. Paul Bernardo had been in prison for two years, with nothing more than a cursory new prisoner-suicide evaluation. Karla had had a lot and Paul had none. Rosen thought it was only fair that Paul get some, but he did not want the prosecution to have access to reports—in case he decided to plead insanity. It was no mean feat getting Justice LeSage to remand Bernardo to the Royal Ottawa Hospital for a lengthy psychiatric assessment.

By getting the judge to remand his client to the hospital, rather than grant a motion for a psychiatric assessment, Rosen managed to circumvent any obligation he would have otherwise have had to provide the Crown with psychiatric reports. It was a small but satisfying coup.

Although Bernardo was undoubtedly a sexual psychopath with sadistic tendencies, killing did not appear to be part of his paraphilia.

When Rosen focused on Kristen French, he also found a number of inconsistencies in Karla's version of events and one deeply disturbing, strangely unaddressed fact.

Kristen had been severely beaten around her face and mouth and had aspirated enough blood to kill her. Although the videotapes showed Paul hitting Kristen on the back and even on the back of the head, Karla never said anything about Paul hitting Kristen in the face, let alone hitting her hard enough to beat her to death. Neither could the pathologist conclusively say she had died from strangulation.

While Paul Bernardo underwent a battery of psychiatric tests, John Rosen faced other distractions. The families of the victims sought and were granted intervenor status to argue that the videotapes showing their daughters being assaulted and raped should be suppressed and not shown as evidence in open court. They solicited affidavits from clergy who said that the video camera had captured the souls of their dead daughters. As a consequence, screening the videotapes in open court would be seen as an invasion of privacy to which the dead were allegedly entitled.

The families also flew in an anti-pornography crusader from the United States. Catherine MacKinnon was a questionable resource. In some American feminist circles, she was considered a crackpot. For instance, it was also her published view that consensual sex within a marriage could be viewed as rape.

Ms. MacKinnon viewed the tapes twice: once, early on, at the home of Rosen's colleague Clayton Ruby. MacKinnon and Ruby were acquainted. Without clearing it with Rosen first, Ruby screened the tapes for MacKinnon, hypothetically to solicit her "expert" opinion on behalf of the defense.

The second time MacKinnon screened the videos she was working for the prosecution, which had allied itself on this issue to the victims' families' position. Ms. MacKinnon pronounced the tapes pornography and began proselytizing about the damage these tapes would do to public morals, were they to be played in open court. In fact, the videotapes were the trophies of sexually deviant psychopaths and evidence in a murder trial. John Rosen knew that restricting the presentation of evidence in a murder trial was a dangerous precedent with cavernous pitfalls. It would also further protect Karla Homolka. LeSage reserved judgment.

•   •   •

Jury selection was a psychopath's dream: a hotel ballroom—the same hotel in which Inspector Vince Bevan and his bevy of crack investigators had taken up residence—chockablock with a thousand citizens to whom Paul Bernardo could personally declare his innocence. The prosecution and the defense had finally agreed that it would be very difficult, given the inordinate publicity generated by the case, to select twelve fair-minded, untainted individuals from among the great unwashed. It wasn't.

On the afternoon of May 1, Paul Bernardo was required to stand up and answer all nine charges, which were read out, one by one, like a Satanic liturgy: To each of the nine charges, Paul Bernardo rose and replied in loud, clarion, dulcet tones, "Not Guilty." It was more like what evangelist Jimmy Swaggart called a "camp meeting" than anything judicial. Paul Bernardo was in his glory.

If they had not impaneled a small army, the process would have taken half a day. From the first sixty people, Rosen and Houlahan could have selected two juries. As it was, finding twelve jurors only took three days.

To George Walker, the bureaucrats were anything but "faceless." Legal Aid records showed that Walker spent many hours with four people in particular: Rosen's ex-colleague and an assistant deputy minister, Michael Code; a senior Crown official named Leo McGuigan; James A. Treleaven, the director of the Regional Crown office in Hamilton; and of course, Walker's old acquaintance, Murray Segal.

Were they or were they not going to charge Walker's client? They had had ample time to decide. Walker was convinced that these elaborate discussions were purely theatrical, held for posterity and publicity's sake. This way, no one would be able to say that these "faceless bureaucrats" had not agonized over their decision and considered all the permutations and ramifications.

Walker had yet another intense meeting with all concerned on May 18 in Toronto. By then, the trial was in full swing. The previous time Walker had been with "the boys" in April, the meeting had lasted four hours. This one lasted three. Walker came back again on June 1. They had reached a decision. Rosen was stunned. They gave Karla "blanket immunity" with respect to Jane Doe and anything else she might suddenly remember she had done. The community was outraged.

On June 10, Walker had a chat with Ray Houlahan to try and determine exactly when Houlahan expected to call Karla. She was driving Walker nuts and he would like to be able to give her a definite answer. They talked for an hour and a half.

Walker did not receive formal notification until June 15, 1995:

> After careful consideration we have decided that it would not be in the public interest to prosecute Karla Homolka on a charge of aggravated assault. I am advised that Inspector Bevan has accepted our advice.

On June 20, just before Karla was to take to stand, Walker explained the situation in detail during an hour-long telephone conversation. Karla understood perfectly. It was Paul Bernardo's trial. It had nothing to do with her. Karla was not on trial; she was a Crown witness whom they no longer really needed, given their other evidence, but they were going to put her through it and make her live up to her end of the bargain. She had immunity. It was more for show than anything else. All symbolism aside, Karla was unassailable. Karla was very pleased. She had been waiting to testify against Paul Bernardo for two years. She was very much looking forward to it. She was also looking forward to meeting the famous John Rosen.

When Ray Houlahan rose to make his jury address he told the members of the jury that Karla Homolka, like Paul Bernardo, was guilty of first-degree murder, but that the prosecution had long ago decided to make a deal with Karla in return for her testimony. Karla Homolka was not on trial.

Houlahan looked menacingly at Paul Bernardo and pointed. "But he is."

CHAPTER

thirty-three

Untouchable, Karla finally took the witness stand on June 25, 1995. During those first days, as prosecutor Ray Houlahan took Karla through the videotapes, once again, step by step, frame by frame, there was an interview on the radio with a British psychiatrist serving in Rwanda.

The interviewer wanted the psychiatrist to tell her about the busloads of tourists who had recently been turning up in Rwanda's war-torn landscape in search of mass graves. These tourists not only wanted to see the sites where massacres had occurred but also the hundreds of dead bodies left to rot in the African sun. The interviewer wanted to know who these "tourists" were.

Frankly, the psychiatrist said quietly, these tourists were just like him and the interviewer.

The interviewer was taken aback: "But surely we should revile these people?"

"No," he replied. "We should try to understand them."

To the prosecutors, Karla was a tourist at a massacre. First they wanted the jury to hear what Karla had seen, and then they wanted the jurors to try and understand her.

The prosecution was determined that the jury should see Karla as they did: a hapless, battered woman; the "compliant victim" of a sexual sadist.

This prosecutorial determination to define and explain Karla allowed John Rosen to solicit a different psychological perspective. When Dr. Graham Glancy was approached by Rosen he quickly agreed. An expert in battered woman's syndrome and post-traumatic stress disorder, Dr. Glancy would evaluate the credibility of the prosecution's doctors' overall conclusions that Karla was battered and suffering from the disorder. Confident that he could shed some meaningful light on the woman who had been described by one of the Crown's experts as "something of a diagnostic mystery," Dr. Glancy asked his colleague, psychologist Dr. Nathan Pollock, to critique the three psychologists' reports.

When Lorena Bobbitt bobbed her husband John's penis and threw it out the car window, she was suffering from post-traumatic stress disorder. Virtually every woman accused of a violent crime who had come before the courts since the middle eighties—PTSD was included for the first time in the revised third edition of the *Diagnostic and Statistical Manual of Mental Disorders III (R),* published in 1987—had been diagnosed with post-traumatic stress disorder. PTSD had become the diagnostic fad of the nineties.

Originally derived from the condition called shell shock, first observed in veterans of World War I, post-traumatic stress disorder and its symptoms were fully described in a book by Arthur Kardiner, first published in 1941, called *The Neuroses of War*. The disorder had since been hypothecated and broadly diagnosed in veterans of the Vietnam War. The most poignant and accurate portrayal of a Vietnam veteran suffering from post-traumatic stress disorder was Christopher Walken's Academy Award–winning performance in the 1978 film *The Deer Hunter*.

The disorder was very difficult to treat and had an onerous prognosis: if the conditions were right and the person could be reached at all—Walken's character was locked into a ceaseless, ultimately lethal compulsion to play Russian roulette—the disorder might be managed by sensitive, lifelong therapy.

The idea that the rigors of modern life could produce symptoms in an individual similar to the effects of war proved irresistible to the helping professions.

Looking at Dr. Allan Long's test results, Dr. Pollock saw that they were simply wrong.

Firstly, everything done with Karla at Northwestern General Hospital had been suspect, because Karla had been completely stoned while she was there. Furthermore, Dr. Long had made an error in the computation of the Minnesota Multiphasic Personality Inventory-2 (MMPI-2) subtest scores. Dr. Pollock pointed out that Dr. Long appeared "to have plotted the raw scores from the MMPI-*2* on the profile form designed for the *first* edition of MMPI."

So much for Karla's diagnostic benchmark, which said people like Karla "feel socially inadequate, alienated and lack trust in others. They may be confused and distractable and are frequently diagnosed as schizophrenic."

According to Dr. Pollock's accurately scored MMPI-2 profile, Karla actually was the type of person who would readily report a wide variety of physical symptoms in order to achieve some kind of secondary gain. Karla was among those who frequently saw "themselves as conventional, moralistic": the kind of person "who does what is right."

Karla's corrected MMPI-2 profile indicated that she would categorically deny psychological problems. Karla would crave attention and affection and would be easily slighted when those needs were not met. However, her displeasure would be expressed in indirect ways. Her relationships were typically shallow and exploitive, with little genuine concern for anyone other than herself.

Karla's properly scored MMPI-2 profiled a person who saw herself as confident and socially adept, whereas others often saw her as narcissistic and egocentric. Karla's kind was frequently diagnosed with "histrionic, obsessive-compulsive and/or passive-aggressive features"; traits that defined a classic psychopath.

Dr. Pollock's interpretation of Karla's MMPI-2 scores was certainly more in keeping with the way Karla's parents, sister and friends described Karla, and more in keeping with her behavior while she was in hospital, in court and in prison. She had thrived in a sea of attention bestowed upon her by a plethora of professional handlers and interlocutors.

The notion that Karla had learned early in life to counter her underlying hostility by being passive and submissive was not borne out by Dr. Long's account of his interview with Karla's parents, who consistently described her as "a leader and somewhat bossy." Neither did it jibe with anything Karla's many friends had told the police during their myriad interviews.

It got worse. Not only had Dr. Long scored Karla's MMPI-2 incorrectly, but he had also relied on certain tests—such as TAT and the Rorschach—which were no longer considered useful in forensic assessment because their interpretation was, by definition, very subjective to the individual psychologist.

In his late sixties, Dr. Long could safely be said to be from "the old school." Indeed, he had eschewed more objective options such as the Exner Comprehensive System and had used his best judgment to interpret Karla's responses to the pictures and inkblots. Given the fifty years between them—Karla's psychopathology aside—how much subjective access could Dr. Long have had to Karla's world?

With regard to TAT and Rorschach, Dr. Long's conclusions seemed totally arbitrary. Rather than "depressed, withdrawn and remorseful," Dr. Pollock would have described Karla as "an immature, moody, shallow, rigid, hostile" woman, "preoccupied with themes of violence and victimization."

Karla's anxiety, tension and depression did not represent the lingering effects of battered woman's syndrome, or post-traumatic stress disorder, but were related to her realization that she was "going to be prosecuted and jailed for heinous crimes." At least, that was how Dr. Pollock would have interpreted Karla's test results.

On the morning of July 5, John Rosen was no longer slumped in his chair, looking like a petulant Danny DeVito. There had not been much for Rosen to do over the past two months—except the morning crossword puzzle—while the Crown paraded a phalanx of witnesses through the courtroom. The prosecution called the fishermen who had found Leslie Mahaffy's body parts. They subpoenaed the guy who controlled the water levels in Lake Gibson. They even flew in the world's only power-saw-cuts-made-in-human-bones expert from his obscure lab at the University of Tennessee, in Memphis.

Dr. Steven Symes acquitted himself well by lecturing the jury as he would have done a dozen students. He pointed out that power saws used to dismember human bodies made a remarkable mess.

The next man they called knew more about the mechanics and makes of power saws than Talmudic scholars knew about the Torah. To this man, a power saw was a totem, like Mark DeMarco's Masonic skull. They called the frogmen who had found the cement coffin that had briefly contained Leslie Mahaffy's torso in the murky waters of the reservoir. There was a doctor from Kingston who the Crown presented as an expert on halothane.

From a bottle he had with him on the stand, the doctor dabbed halothane on his face and chin, as if it were Old Spice, to demonstrate how harmless it was. The good doctor was cavalier, but since the potency of halothane was well documented and was irrelevant to the guilt or innocence of Rosen's client, Rosen had few questions.

There were other distracting moments of levity. When they called Dr. Patti Weir, the vet at the Martindale Animal Clinic, where Karla had worked, Paul Bernardo passed Rosen a note marked "Trivia," which read, "Did you know that Patty Weir's husband is the brother of a co-worker of the husband who married Laura Goode, the 2nd girl I ever slept with?"

It also came to Rosen's attention that they had relegated Inspector Tony Warr, who was now the head of the Toronto police sexual-assault squad, to furtively follow certain members of the jury. In particular, he trailed one retired white-haired gentleman whom the press corps had collegially dubbed "drinking man," because he obviously enjoyed the odd pick-me-up.

The memo addressed to Houlahan from Warr read, "On June 26, 1995 Juror #3 . . . went into Mahoney's Bar in Etobicoke with a woman, possibly his wife and was heard to say something about 'giving him (Paul Bernardo) ninety-nine years' . . .

"On June 27 he went for lunch at Hy's, consumed alcohol . . . many people in the establishment seemed to know him."

The day the Maiden met the Raven was the day everyone had been waiting for. John Rosen was absolutely convinced that Karla Homolka could have killed both girls. But he was not naive enough to think that he could get Karla to admit that she "stopped the breath" of Leslie Mahaffy or Kristen French, thereby voiding her deal. The only scenario that would break the deal involved Karla taking the stand under oath and admitting that she had herself killed one or both the girls.

Rosen also knew it was a largely irrelevant point. Even if Karla made that open confession, it would not exonerate his client. As Houlahan had intimated in his opening address, both Paul and Karla were guilty of murder—arguably in the first degree—and his client was demonstrably and by his own admission privately guilty of all the other charges, each of which carried a life sentence, so what was the purpose?

Nevertheless, Rosen was going to give Karla everything he had. The prosecution had put her in front of him, and now he was going to truncate every lie Karla had ever told and at least show her to be the bedeviled witch she was.

"All rise." Justice LeSage greeted the court with a crisp "Good morning," and then instructed the court staff to show the jury in. LeSage knew Rosen was ready, but protocol dictated that he ask if he was. He called for the witness.

Karla came through the back door in the courtroom like a debutante at a ball. The courtroom was hushed. Someone coughed. Just like a schoolgirl, Karla climbed up on the stand and adjusted her microphone. She was blond and petite and dwarfed by the architecture.

Houlahan had kept Karla on the stand for nine days. Once again, the jury had been subjected to a viewing of Paul and Karla's trophies, endless videotaped scenes in slow motion, irrefutably documenting unspeakable degradation. Frequently Houlahan would hold on a particularly grotesque frame so that he could make some irrelevant, pornographic point.

"And what are you doing there, Ms. Homolka?" Houlahan would ask. And Karla would reply with blasé candor: "Well, I'm performing cunnilingus on her, and then I am inserting a wine bottle in her anus."

Houlahan was a very methodical man. He spoke in a monotone. By the time he called Karla Homolka, the press corps had nicknamed him Ray Halothane.

LeSage had finally ruled that the taped sections showing the rapes and abuses of Leslie Mahaffy, Kristen French, Tammy Lyn Homolka and Jane Doe would only be seen by the jury, the lawyers, police, court staff, Paul and Karla. Only the audio portions of the tapes would be played in open court.

At the beginning of the trial, Houlahan had insisted that the jury sit through all the videotapes three times. Once in real time; once with the aid of a transcript of the dialogue, which the prosecutor's office had prepared; and a third excruciatingly long presentation aided by the sworn testimony of Sergeant Gary Beaulieu, whose task it had been to study the videotapes and prepare an affidavit for the court.

With the facility of slow motion and stop action, Sergeant Beaulieu pointed out numerous hermeneutic details in the videotapes. The fact that under normal circumstances ten minutes of either video that portrayed the assaults on Leslie Mahaffy or Kristen French would have been sufficient to elicit the most severe verdict this jury could deliver seemed to have eluded the Crown law office.

Karla had barely settled in the witness box when John Rosen was as dangerously near her as Jim Hutton had been that first night dancing at the Sugar Shack.

"I'm going to show you a picture," he said, holding up a photograph, as though he were a cop showing someone his badge. "Can you tell me who is in the picture?"

"My sister Tammy," Homolka answered.

"Your sister Tammy—alive." Rosen said, matter-of-factly.

Rosen then shoved another photograph under her nose, a photograph taken the night Tammy Lyn had died. Tammy lay white and dead on a gurney with the esophageal tube still protruding from her mouth. The only color in the picture was that huge, bright raspberry mark, mysteriously tattooed on her right cheek and throat.

"Can you tell me who that is?"

"My sister Tammy," Karla said, appropriately taken aback, but not really shaken. A raspy sob, maybe, but no tears.

"Your sister Tammy, in the morgue, with a red stain on her face, dead."

"She wasn't that bad when I saw her," Karla shot back. Rosen did not pause to ponder the oddity of that response.

He went on to Leslie Mahaffy. A photo of Leslie alive, and

then one of Leslie's purplish, headless, limbless torso, washed up on the shore of the reservoir.

Rosen did the same again with Kristen French. First, a photograph of her smiling broadly, very much alive, with her dog Sasha, and then a truly horrific picture of her brush-covered naked corpse, with its crudely shorn hair and grotesque grimace.

By the time Rosen got to Kristen French, Karla was striving to act appropriately because she had figured out exactly what John Rosen was up to. Rosen was trying to appeal to her conscience. He even asked Karla about her conscience.

Karla had a formidable ability to see where others were headed and she was not an inconsequential actress. Kim Doyle, the law clerk, who knew Karla as well as anyone, had not been in favor of this confrontational in-her-face approach.

Doyle had reasoned that this stratagem would not really faze Karla because she believed, along with Dr. Glancy, that Karla was the rarest of all birds, a histrionic, a borderline personality, completely disordered—a female psychopath. As such, just like her estranged husband, Karla had no conscience and no capacity for guilt. Karla actually would have appreciated the theatrical value of Rosen's performance more than anything else, as Paul had appreciated the prop room.

Doyle had favored a more covert approach, one in which Rosen would appear benign and somewhat beguiled, like every other older professional man with whom Karla had had contact.

As it turned out, Doyle's initial instincts had been right. Rosen's performance was startling and theatrical. Everyone was taken aback and enthralled. Except Karla, who, within a few minutes, was settling in, anticipating Rosen's questions.

From where Kim Doyle sat—directly in front of the defense table—she would swear she could hear Karla's mind working. It sounded just like the soft whir of Doyle's laptop computer, searching for some obscure witness's name who supported her version of events, or key words and phrases in the hundreds of hours of conversations with prosecutors and police that Karla had stored in her not inconsequential data bank.

.   .   .

From August through December, 1994, the police and prosecution had supplied Dr. Peter Jaffe, Dr. Chris Hatcher and Dr. Stephen Hucker with all of Drs. Long, Arndt and Malcolm's files and reports on Karla Homolka, as well as those of the prison consultants, Jan Heney and Dr. Roy Brown. They also made available to the doctors the six and a half hours of video-taped evidence, as well as the extensive videotaped statements Karla had given at the Journey's End in May, 1993.

Dr. Peter Jaffe based his conclusions on his review of these materials and ten hours of interviews he conducted with Karla in the fall of 1994 at the Kingston Prison for Women. He also administered a few more psychological tests, including the MMPI-2.

It was Dr. Jaffe's opinion that Paul Bernardo had used emotional, physical and sexual abuse to coerce and manipulate Ms. Homolka into becoming involved in the sexual assaults and murders of her sister, Leslie Mahaffy and Kristen French, as well as any other deviant acts in which she might have participated.

From his test results, Jaffe concluded that Karla had made substantial improvement since Dr. Long's first assessment. He found Karla to be functioning in the superior range of intelligence—the top two percent of the population.

Dr. Jaffe's interpretation of Karla's MMPI-2 scores suggested paranoia, isolation, anxiety and anger that fluctuated between self-blame and hostility, but the doctor attributed this to the traumatic effects of prison life and Karla's involvement with Paul Bernardo.

To conclude that Karla's psychological profile was consistent with the experiences of abused women and a woman suffering from post-traumatic stress disorder, Dr. Jaffe relied, in part, on two computerized interpretations.

Rosen's consultants, Drs. Graham Glancy and Nathan Pollock, found Dr. Jaffe's results to be accurate—but rather than explicative and redemptive, they contradictorily interpreted his results as explicative and damning. It was the way Dr. Jaffe had interpreted those results with which Glancy and Pollock took serious issue.

The results rightly said Karla was chronically maladjusted, suspicious and hostile. If threatened, she would most likely respond with anger and hostility. While Karla could appear naive and trusting, she could also quickly become indignant and hostile. Karla was insecure and needed a great deal of reassurance. She could be petulant and very demanding. In addition, an evaluation on the Overcontrolled-hostility scale suggested that episodes of intense angry outbursts were common.

Contrary to Dr. Jaffe's stated conclusions, none of his test results suggested post-traumatic stress disorder.

Dr. Pollock pointed out that Dr. Jaffe had only examined individual item content on MMPI-2 and rationalized pathognomic indictors to explain away evidence of chronic psychopathology. Even Dr. Jaffe himself, in a remarkably blatant attempt to cover all his bases, pointed out in his report that his method of interpretation was "quite risky" with an instrument such as MMPI-2, because MMPI-2 was meant to rely on verified reference groups and scale elevations, not item content. Nevertheless, he rejected the notion that the MMPI-2 results reflected an ingrained personality disturbance, which would certainly have been Dr. Pollock's conclusion.

The second computer program—the Rainwater Interpretive Report—was consistent with Jaffe's first computer-aided interpretation. Dr. Jaffe had achieved a commendable consistency in his test results; it was his interpretation that was too convenient for the government's position on Karla.

According to Rainwater, Karla was a suspicious, egocentric and rigid person. Antisocial behavior (psychopathic behavior) was common to her type, and was characterized by lying, stealing, substance abuse, aggressive outbursts and sexual acting out.

According to the Rainwater report, people such as Karla tended to be impulsive, irresponsible and rebellious. They frequently demonstrated strong feelings of hostility toward family members and were in conflict, either blatantly or subliminally, with authority. Their relationships were generally superficial and they tended to have marital problems, which in Karla's case was something of an understatement.

Dr. Pollock pointed out that if the details of Dr. Jaffe's interpretation were accepted and his conclusions ignored, Karla would again be diagnosed as a severely disturbed borderline personality, a histrionic, a psychopath.

Chronological order was really the only way to conduct an effective cross-examination on Karla. There are always opportunities for excursions or elaborations, but a good lawyer never strays far from the Book of Days. And Karla had made it relatively easy to stay the course with her voluminous, damning letters and love notes.

According to the details of Dr. Jaffe's interpretations and Dr. Long's revised results, Karla was more than capable of having killed either one or both of the girls herself.

John Rosen was a student of science. In science, problems were approached pragmatically. If it looked like a duck, sounded like duck and acted like a duck, it probably was a duck. Karla had killed her sister. Accidental or not, the circumstances were too diabolical. Given what Karla had seen and done, so was her demeanor.

"Surprise," announced Rosen when he started playing the videotape of Karla and Paul's assault on her sister. "She's wearing some sort of sanitary napkin, isn't she?"

Rosen wanted to take Karla back to that early Christmas Eve morning, scant minutes old, when Karla prodded her inert sister to make sure Tammy Lyn was out and then got the halothane and a white rag to make certain she stayed that way.

"No, I never saw one," said Karla, taken aback, and no doubt rewinding in her mind to the one mention of this cruel exposure of Tammy Lyn. It was on May 17, 1993, during her "cautioned" statements at the Journey's End that Sergeant Bob Gillies had just happened to say: "Okay. What I have here is a copy of the postmortem report concerning your sister Tammy, and in the clothing and effects it mentions a sanitary pad?"

Karla had deflected the issue quite handily by feigning embarrassment in front of the male officers. (Detective Metcalfe had taken sick that morning.) Karla said she had redressed Tammy and had not seen any such thing. "It could have been one of those very thin ones," she offered. She herself always used Always, with wings, and those were "very, very, thin."

Yesterday's news hit home again when Justice Patrick LeSage suggested that Karla might want to take a closer look at what Mr. Rosen was showing her. Moving to within a few feet of the jury, the petite blonde leaned over and watched the scene unfold, frame by frame, frozen in surreal close-ups, on the large monitor in front of the jury box. To keep her hair out of her eyes, Karla pulled it back in much the same way she always had when fellating Paul. The jurors had already seen that move enough times to last a lifetime.

"See, that's the sanitary napkin with belt," Rosen said, as if he were asking her to identify something as undeniable as a cloud in the sky. The male juror closest to the monitor nodded his head quickly in a moment of recognition.

When the tape was forwarded to the next set of coordinates, Rosen pointed out a "white bundle" on the floor near the end of the sofa, which he contended must have been Tammy's personal-hygiene item. One of the older female jurors leaned back and eyed Karla, her lips pursed.

They had not seen that which was now leading them into even darker, more perverse, speculation. Some of the jurors wondered, given the fact that they had been required to review the tapes in such detail by the prosecution, why this detail had never been highlighted for them. For a few minutes, it was just like a virtual-reality pornographic version of "Perry Mason," suffused with meaningful suspense. Just when they thought they had seen everything.

"Advance very slowly," Rosen told his co-counsel. Tony Bryant, manning the 8mm Sony playback machine from the opposite side of the courtroom, was the one who had suggested that they use the original tapes. The finer lines and truer color and clarity of the originals made all the details far easier to see.

"And then just as you bring your finger out . . . right

there. You have red staining on your fingers. It's not a lot of blood. It's just a little blood, right?"

Karla leaned in closer to the monitor's screen. The frames kept churning by in real time as she rubbed her sticky right index finger and thumb together before trying to rid herself of the damn spot. Then she put her forefinger back in, briefly, just a perfunctory poke, because Paul was telling her to put it "inside, deep," and then taste it.

Karla was a fastidious person. She did not like what he wanted her to put in her mouth, so she looked into the camera and told Paul in what was hardly a submissive posture that it was "fucking disgusting," before dabbing her lips with the cuff of her left sleeve and backing away with another toss of her blond hair.

"You take the hand out and you wipe it on the bed, because it has blood on it and he's telling you to lick it and you don't want to lick your sister's menstrual blood, right?" charged Rosen, to Karla's weakened protest. "And that is why you said, 'Fucking disgusting.'"

"That is a lie," Karla said in the firmest, precisest response she had so far given, but it sounded lame against Rosen's visually aided hypothesis.

"Thank you," said Rosen, and turned away with a punctilious flourish of his robes to look at the jurors. "Because you see, Miss Homolka, your whole story, the whole basis of your evidence is based and founded on your assertion that you were forced to commit these perverted acts on your sister . . . that you said 'fucking disgusting' because you did not want to do what he forced you to do to her, that he beat you for saying that and that, therefore, everything that followed had to be looked at with that explanation. . . .

"But if it turns out, as we analyze the video, that the real reason that the kinky sex that you and he were into soured was because your sister had either the beginning or the end of her period and you didn't want to taste her vaginal blood, that's a different complexion, isn't it?"

·   ·   ·

Dr. Chris Hatcher, from California, had submitted his lengthy and discursive report to the prosecution on May 17, 1995. Unfortunately, Dr. Hatcher had relied extensively on Dr. Long's and Dr. Peter Jaffe's conclusions about Karla.

Even though Dr. Hatcher concluded that Karla was suffering from post-traumatic stress disorder, he inexplicably acknowledged that the test results he had derived did not support that diagnosis.

From the lectern, Rosen called Karla's attention to her previous evidence. She had said that she had seen Paul Bernardo beat Leslie Mahaffy while he was "grilling" the captive girl about anything she might remember about things such as the color of his car before she had been blindfolded.

"He beat her; he beat her with his fists, right?" Rosen asked. Karla agreed. That's what Karla had said. Rosen continued describing the closed-fist beating that Karla said she had watched but had been helpless to stop. "This girl must have been black-and-blue all over," he suggested.

Karla had not seen "black-and-blue," but she did agree that there would have been substantial internal bruising.

"Did you know that if you beat somebody on the back with your fists—according to the pathologist—that it's likely to bruise the muscles and cause it to bleed, and force the blood out of the little vessels if you hit them. Did you know that's how a bruise happens?"

"Yes," Karla knew all about bruises. She also knew about the three groups of muscle in the human back. She knew about the levels of bruising through different layers of tissue.

In the first autopsy, Rosen patiently explained, the pathologist had not found any bruising in the superficial layers of Leslie Mahaffy's back; however, when they performed the second autopsy, after they exhumed her body parts, they had seen something more.

"They cut deeper," he told her, and what they found were two bruises on either side of the spinal column. One was 8cm ×

5cm and the other was 1.5cm × 6.5cm. "Two circles, almost side by side."

The pathologist could find no evidence of the beating that Karla alleged had taken place. "Do you understand that, miss?" Rosen asked. Karla said she did.

"But what we do know is that these two little red marks are consistent with a pair of knees about the size of your knees on that back at the deepest layer, pushing the muscle against the ribs while you held her head down on a pillow and suffocated her, isn't that right?"

Karla was taken aback. Jurors' foreheads crinkled quizzically. Ray Houlahan leapt to his feet to object. Justice LeSage, who was as curious about this theory as anyone, allowed as how there was a basis for the question—but not necessarily the editorial comment about knee size. The jury had already seen plenty of videotape showing every aspect of Paul and Karla's anatomy, and his knees were clearly much larger than hers.

Despite the effects of decomposition, Rosen's review of the autopsy suggested that there had been none of the usual indications of strangulation, such as injury to the tongue, lips or teeth.

Rosen suggested to Karla that Paul had wanted to let Leslie go, just as they had the January Girl. Although she had originally told the police that Paul left the room to get an electrical cord to use in the strangulation of the drugged girl, who was sleeping with Bunky in her arms, the videotape clearly showed that there was an electrical cord in the bedroom during the last recorded assault. Karla had no explanation for that. Her timing must have been out of whack.

Rosen offered her another explanation, suggesting that Paul had left the room to put gas in the car, using a small gas tank they kept in the garage.

"He goes out of the room to get ready to take her back to Burlington, and that's when you decided she had to die, isn't it?" he said. All eyes turned to Karla.

"No, that's a lie," Karla said emphatically.

Rosen led her through the "concerns" that she might have had at the time, suggesting that Karla had just as much of a motive for murder as Paul. He cited her knowledge of the samples her husband had given police years earlier when he had been questioned about the Scarborough rapes. He queried her about the possibility that if Leslie lived she might be able to contribute to Paul's ultimate identification.

"He's suggesting to her that she's the killer," Houlahan objected, but Justice LeSage saw nothing inappropriate.

Unrelenting, Rosen continued, suggesting that Karla's attitude toward Leslie Mahaffy had been subhuman and heartless. Rosen quoted from one of her statements to Dr. Hatcher, in which Karla discussed her state of mind before Mahaffy was killed.

"I was very upset because I didn't want him to go to jail, because I didn't hate him quite as much as I do now . . . So I didn't really want him to go to jail and I was afraid of myself going to jail, too."

"She was just a plaything, wasn't she?" Rosen suggested. "She had no personality. You didn't consider her as a real person, did you?" he asked. Then he returned to a statement Karla had made to the police under oath two years earlier.

Karla had said: "I sort of talked to Leslie through Paul. Like, I would whisper questions and, like, I was so stupid, because I never should have gotten to know Kristen, because you get emotionally involved with these people and it really hurts, it hurts a lot more, because I felt like I was friends with both of them, especially Kristen, because we did so much together."

With total disdain, Rosen honed in on the phrase "these people," spitting it out repeatedly while Karla tried to sidestep.

"I don't know what problem you have with those words," she said in a voice so quiet that Justice LeSage asked her to repeat the statement.

"You say you get emotionally . . . involved with 'these people,' " Rosen explained. "i.e., people you bring into the house to sexually play with. That's what you meant?"

Karla's denial led Rosen to read each line and word again, particularly her reference to being "friends" with the dead teenagers.

"I would use the word I was friendly with them," Karla

suggested, leading Rosen to wonder how a friendship could exist, when Leslie presumably knew nothing about Karla, while Karla had gleaned all sorts of information about Leslie and her family and background through the furtive questions she made Paul ask as if he were some sort of giant ventriloquist's dummy.

"You can still be friendly with someone without knowing who they are," explained Karla, haughtily.

"Even though they're captive in your house and forced to participate in degrading sexual activities against their consent?" an astounded Rosen responded.

"Mr. Rosen," Karla patiently said. "You are making something out of this that isn't there."

Dr. Glancy told Rosen that the term battered woman's syndrome referred to a pattern of abuse as well as the psychological consequences suffered by the battered women. As a pattern of abuse battered woman's syndrome was a consequence of a three-phase cycle, which all the experts had accepted as characteristic of all battering relationships.

There was a tension-building phase, with verbal and minor physical abuse and attempts by the woman to prevent more severe abuse by placating the abuser.

Then there was an acute-battering phase characterized by a serious physical assault, followed by the loving-contrition phase, in which the batterer expressed remorse and tried to make amends, much as Paul Bernardo had done so effusively and pathetically on the so-called "suicide tapes."

In abusive relationships, this cycle was then repeated, over and over again. Eventually, the woman developed a sense of helplessness about her situation—hence the term "learned helplessness."

The woman became passive, anxious, depressed, confused, self-effacing and felt trapped in what she perceived to be a hopeless situation.

Increasingly, battered woman's syndrome was being recognized by the courts as a legal defense in cases where a battered woman had been charged with the murder or aggravated assault of her abuser.

There were a lot of women who were battered and abused. Women who actually suffered from battered woman's syndrome were very rare.

There was no doubt Karla Homolka had been physically and emotionally abused by Paul Bernardo at some point. Karla might even have gone through one cycle of the abuse pattern.

Lenore Walker, a world-recognized authority in the field of battered women, had first proposed the three-phase cycle decades earlier. All subsequent clinical experience reinforced the validity of her model.

Ms. Walker insisted that a woman must go through this cycle at least twice and then remain in the abusive relationship before she could possibly be diagnosed with the syndrome. What evidence there was, along with Karla's own statements and the substantial medical records available to the court, said that Karla had gone through the cycle only once and had then left, never to return.

There were other problems with the idea that her behavior with regard to her sister, Jane Doe, Leslie Mahaffy, Kristen French and the prostitute in Atlantic City could be explained away by battered woman's syndrome and post-traumatic stress disorder. Her test results had not been consistent with those reported in research literature as typical of battered women suffering the syndrome.

Battered women occasionally—very occasionally—murder their abusive partners. In Angela Brown's book, *When Battered Women Kill,* the average age of the woman who killed her batterer was thirty-six, she had been married or living common-law for an average of 8.7 years and the vast majority—over seventy percent—had been physically abused in their early family lives.

By the time Dr. Hatcher had arrived in December, 1994, Karla had caught up with much of this information. For the first time in all her prolonged discussions with the police and her myriad doctors and therapists, Karla ironically described her father to Hatcher as "somewhat overly protective," and shared the dark secret that she had been "emotionally abused—daily—while living in her father's home."

When Tammy Lyn was murdered, Karla was twenty years old. Karla was not married nor was she living common-law. She was living at home with her parents. There was no evidence, except in her new malingering fantasy, "recovered" just for Dr. Hatcher, that she had ever been abused—in any way by anyone—as a child.

In all the research, the vast majority of women who committed acts of violence, striking out at their abusers—not at innocent teenage bystanders—were socially isolated and had little or no contact with family and friends. A student of the literature of abuse, Karla had tried to minimize her rather prolific and consistent contact with her family, friends and co-workers, but it ran contrary to her family's, friend's, and co-workers' testimony.

John Rosen simply did not believe that a woman as fastidious and concerned about apprehension as Karla Homolka would leave Kristen French's dead body lying around the master bedroom while she and Paul went over to her parents' house for five or six hours on Easter Sunday.

Rosen contended that Kristen had been killed when Paul Bernardo left the house to get Swiss Chalet and rent a movie on Saturday evening, rather than on Sunday before noon, as Karla had testified. Rosen challenged Karla's contradictory statements to the police, using her May 16 statements as well as the pathologist's report about the condition in which Kristen's body had been found.

Karla Homolka had told John Rosen that the only beating she saw Paul Bernardo administer to Kristen were punches to her back. She had never described any severe injury to Kristen's face and none was evident in the videos.

Rosen pointed out to Karla that she had told the police that Kristen had been tied to the hope chest before she was killed. In cross-examination she could even identify which of the three false handles on the front of the chest Kristen had been tied to—the one closest to the door.

Karla had testified that about an hour after the final video-tape was made, Paul had looped an electrical cord around Kristen's neck and had sex with her again. Then, while he questioned her about death, Karla said Paul cut Kristen off in mid-sentence and strangled her. She had told the prosecution that he held the cord taut for a full seven minutes.

This gave Rosen real pause because the pathologist had duly noted that Kristen French had aspirated blood into her lungs, which meant it had to have been inhaled through her nose or throat before she died.

"Nowhere in your evidence do you ever talk about this girl bleeding from the nose or mouth, do you?" he asked.

"I never saw her bleed from the nose or mouth," said Karla.

"And you don't have any evidence to give that would explain the deep subdural hemorrhages . . . on both sides of the head above the ears that are deep enough and hard enough that it's something more than a fist and more like a mallet. You can't help us with that, can you?"

Karla immediately entered her denial.

"I can't help you with that," she said, parroting Rosen.

Karla's admission that she had guarded Kristen with a hard-headed rubber mallet while Kristen was bound in a closet, when Paul went to get food and rent movies on the Friday night, came back to haunt her.

Rosen had stood beside her earlier in the day, inches from her shiny blond head, and presented the mallet to her for identification. That distressed Karla, because a level of whispering rose in the public gallery as her "audience" speculated on what they would do if they ever got that close to Karla with a mallet.

"And the reason you can't help us with that," Rosen said with full authority, "is because you're the one who did it on Saturday afternoon while he was out and when she tried to escape, isn't that right?"

"I have never hit anybody in my life, Mr. Rosen," Karla responded icily.

"And when he came back from that little trip with food

. . . she's dead on the floor, having strangled herself against the restraint, and that's what you told him happened. That she tried to escape and now she's dead, isn't that right?"

Rosen's theory was that after Paul left the two women alone, Kristen had begged to go to the washroom or offered some pretext to induce Karla to unbind her feet. He suggested that Kristen had seized the opportunity to attempt an escape, and had shoved Karla, who responded by attacking the tethered girl with the mallet. Then a combination of Kristen's frantic straining against the electrical cord binding her neck and the hard blows to her head killed the girl.

No one had ever offered a more cogent explanation for how Kristen came to be so badly beaten about the face. In Rosen's view, and the pathologist had not disagreed, the ligature marks around Kristen's neck were inconsistent with the full-fledged strangulation described by Karla Homolka.

Dr. McAuliffe had found nine indications of probable asphyxia on Kristen's body, including bluish fingernails, but the only thing that pointed to ligature strangulation as the cause of her death were the dark marks on Kristen's neck and McAuliffe could not be conclusive about them. Specific bones that were usually broken when a person was strangled were inexplicably found intact.

Rosen also noted that Dr. McAuliffe had waited fourteen months before signing Kristen's autopsy report. It had not been signed until nine days after Karla pled guilty in July 1993. This was an unusually long time. McAuliffe lamely explained that although he had determined the cause of death almost immediately, he hesitated to sign the report because media reports had suggested that Kristen had been kept alive for almost two weeks and the police did not have a suspect until Paul Bernardo's arrest. It was all too wishy-washy for Rosen. What did the status of a police investigation or the disposition of the media have to do with the coroner's duties and performance?

"I wasn't present for the whole time," Karla offered as a possible explanation for her failure to observe any sign of facial bleeding. According to her story, she had left the room during the proceedings.

Rosen queried her on the reason she had left. In a stunning display of sheer psychopathy, Karla told him that she had taken a shower prior to the strangulation and had left the room to blow-dry her hair.

Karla had celebrated her twenty-second birthday four days after the discovery of Kristen's body and Rosen showed her the hand-printed card she had given her husband on that occasion: "You're the greatest husband in the world," she wrote. "All my love and sweet dreams of you and me together forever. Karly Curls."

"Yes, that's right," said Karla, admitting that she had posed happily with her mother for a photograph on that occasion. She was twenty-two plus four days when she wrote a cheery letter to her old pal Debbie Purdie, indicating that as soon as Paul finished his rap album and had a recording contract, she planned on getting pregnant.

"You could have gotten those tapes and left that marriage, isn't that right?" Rosen asked her in his final minutes.

"First of all, I did not know there were copies of the tapes," Karla began, suggesting that she had indeed found videotapes and taken them out of the house already, but could not be sure they were the originals. It was another bizarre response along the lines of, "She wasn't that bad when I saw her . . ." It, too, went unchallenged.

Karla agreed with Rosen that survival was a "natural human instinct." However, since she had no idea about how many copies of the tapes might have existed, she could not see it that way.

"I felt like I was in a tunnel and I could not see on either side of me," a metaphor reminiscent of the "screaming tunnels" Carolyn MacDonald had asked her about in the summer of 1994. It was almost as evocative as Edvard Munch's painting of the gnomish figure in *The Scream*. "It is so difficult to explain."

"Yes," said Rosen citing her hundreds of lovey-dovey notes and cards, all of her letters and her malingering conduct: "Very difficult to explain, aren't they?"

"They're difficult for me to make people understand," said Karla, positively.

"Yes," agreed Rosen, who had a river of sweat rivulating down his back into pants loosened by the weight he had lost in just these eight days of cross-examination.

"Some people understand," said Karla.

By the end of the day on July 12, Rosen had entered 177 of Karla's love notes and greeting cards as exhibits. He had played the video of Karla's wedding shower, the tape of the wedding rehearsal in which she had looked deeply, longingly into Paul's eyes. Rosen had played the video showing her mother and Paul gyrating to dance music and her Hawaiian honeymoon soliloquy. Karla was intrepid.

"You're pretty smart, aren't you?" Rosen asked. "You are not stupid."

"That's very debatable," Karla replied, pretending she was the sterotypical "dumb blonde," even catching Rosen off guard with her flippant response. A chuckle rippled through the courtroom and Rosen shook his head, mumbling into his white jurist's collar.

Karla had been steadily getting stronger and more self-assured, while Rosen weakened, tiring of the futility of his circumstances. Every morning, Karla looked fresher, almost radiant, as if she were looking forward to whatever arabesques of death and despair Rosen was going to weave. Each day she was more willing than ever to verbally spar with him, a crisis junkie. By the third day, Rosen looked like a man in the midst of a mythic ordeal, one of Odysseus's hapless boatmen as the Siren sang.

Karla Homolka was not the slightest bit afraid. Rosen had realized that early on. What to do? Just the way she behaved on the witness stand proved every point he had tried to make.

There were profound questions about her participation in these crimes but it was her intractability that was most astounding. Karla was smart. Karla had no fear. Karla knew that the real truth was an enigma, never to be resolved in these circumstances.

The cross-examination ended without flourish. Karla was still flicking back her hair. She had good posture. Nothing in Rosen's considerable arsenal had grazed her. He was spent,

Karla was ready to party. With a last toss of her long blond hair, Karla left the witness stand, up on the balls of her feet.

There was another explanation for Karla than the pseudo-psycho-compliant-battered-post-traumatically-stressed-out-otherwise-nice-girl victim the prosecution proffered. Dr. Glancy told Rosen that in his opinion, Karla was a perfect hybristophiliac.

In psychiatric literature hybristophilia describes the phenomenon of a woman who is sexually turned on only by a partner with a history of rape and pillage. The name derives from the Greek *hybridzein* meaning "to commit an outrage." In his book *Lovemaps,* the distinguished Johns Hopkins professor John Money called it "the Bonnie and Clyde syndrome."

The old saying "behind every good man" worked just as well in reverse, in an era dominated by a new kind of "fatal woman." There was nothing to say that a woman could not be the driving force in a hybristophilic relationship. In another variant of the syndrome, the female hybristophile taunts and provokes her lover or spouse to commit criminal acts in order to fulfil the requirements of her paraphilia.

Significantly, the hybristophilic's "lovemap" excludes the possibility of oneself as a victim. So long as the two partners remain bonded in their paraphilia, then each victim would always be someone else. If the ties that bound somehow unraveled—if one partner became unstable, as Paul Bernardo had— the hybristophilic partner could well become the victim. As Paul began disassembling, Karla willfully reassembled as a battered woman. In fact, Karla was a histrionic, psychopathic hybristophile.

Karla felt as though she was going home as the authorities quickly returned her to her tiny cell in the segregation unit at Kingston's Prison for Women. Karla would soon be eligible to apply for unescorted day passes. She would be able to go shopping in downtown Kingston or get her hair streaked, buy a pair of glasses, get new shoes, meet new friends.

• • •

Paul Bernardo did not look like the devil incarnate when he took the stand in his own defense. Neatly dressed in a dark suit, white shirt and a floral-patterned tie, he looked like the boy next door. John Rosen's examination-in-chief had been brisk and to the point. It lasted less than three hours. In his introduction, he acknowledged that there were few mysteries to the case. At least the jurors recognized, at that moment, that they were not the only ones who realized that salient fact.

"You just have to push play on that video machine and you have the whole case before you," Rosen told the jury. "There is no doubt in the world both of them—Karla Homolka and Paul Bernardo—sexually assaulted and unlawfully confined . . . The real question is who caused the victims' deaths?"

During his exam-in-chief, Bernardo often regarded Rosen quizically, as though he was wondering where Rosen was taking him. Early on, Paul took an opportunity to make his own opening statement to the jury, stretching both arms toward them in a gesture that was part Praise-the-Lord evangelism, part soap salesman and part doofus.

"People," he said, as sonorously as possible, "I know that I've done some really terrible things, I know that. And I've caused a lot of sadness and sorrow to a lot of people, and I really feel sorry for that and I know I deserve to be punished, but I didn't kill these girls."

With minimal questioning, Rosen led Paul through each incident. With morbid attention to detail, Paul described the dismemberment of Leslie Mahaffy. He told the jury the saw had repeatedly jammed in the flesh.

"Every time I had a piece done I would hand it out and Karla would reach under the tarp and take it to the bucket and take it over to the sink and lay it down," he explained, as if he were describing a dockside fish cleaning.

Rosen had argued that both Karla and Paul had dismembered Leslie Mahaffy after their parents left that Father's Day dinner in 1991. There was no way, Rosen told the jury, that Bernardo could have dismembered, cemented and disposed of

Leslie's body parts by himself. It was not physically possible within the two-day time frame Karla had given for those activities.

Even less plausible—unless there had been far more preparation than Karla had ever described—was the fact that there was no trace of Leslie Mahaffy in the Bernardos' basement. Bernardo concluded, "And she [Karla] would put each one in a garbage bag and those pieces were eventually placed in the root cellar" and left over night.

When it came to the deaths of Leslie Mahaffy and Kristen French, Paul insisted that on each occasion he had left Karla alone with each girl, and when he returned, they were dead. He said he kept the videotapes because he could not bring himself to throw them out. "It was the last memory of these girls' life and I just couldn't do it," he said.

When his turn came to cross-examine Paul Bernardo, prosecutor Ray Houlahan was up immediately, trying to tear a righteous strip off the man he dubbed Captain Video. His opening salvo mimicked John Rosen's assault on Karla Homolka.

"I realize I am going to need some psychiatric help at some point," Paul said, in all seriousness. The courtroom was suddenly alive with noisy incredulity.

"That is a face of a killer," Houlahan declared, freezing on a video frame of Bernardo just after he had punched Kristen French.

"No, it's not," said Paul.

Disclaiming Karla as victim at every turn, Paul referred to a fantasy life of three-way sex in which everyone was happy.

"What's this fantasy garbage? This is real, this is happening, isn't it?" Houlahan snorted after Paul explained that drinking champagne out of special glasses with Leslie Mahaffy was part of his fantasy.

"Yes, sir. This fantasy had now been carried out," Bernardo replied, cooly. Had Houlahan been paying attention, he might have caught the cliché. It harkened back to something Gordon

Gekko, one of Paul's heroes, had said in *Wall Street:* "The illusion has become real. . . ."

Every once in a while Paul stymied the prosecutor by astutely citing inconsistencies in statements that his ex-wife had given the police and those that she finally testified to.

"You think you're smarter than the lawyers here?" Houlahan asked incredulously, his face flushed with anger.

"Don't answer that," Justice LeSage advised, and again a flutter of tittering rippled over the courtroom.

Houlahan got totally lost in what seemed an infinite galaxy of irrelevant trivia. Paul Bernardo was enjoying his time in the spotlight; once again he got to review his trophies in minute detail. His testimony was awash with inanities.

"You're right-handed, aren't you?" Houlahan asked, showing Paul one of the sixteen pornographic Polaroids he had taken in the summer of 1988, this one where he was entering Karla from behind, holding a cord around her neck and a knife to her throat with his right hand.

"I'm ambidextrous," Paul replied.

"Which hand do you write with?" Houlahan asked.

"My right hand," Paul replied, "but I throw with my left."

Although he had only recently learned to pronounce the word *anal* correctly—throughout the trial Houlahan said "annal"—the prosecutor dwelt on the topic exhaustively. After reviewing the video involving Jane Doe, Paul rejected Houlahan's accusations.

"Here we see that part of your . . . cleanup of Jane Doe in the area of her anus, right?"

"Yes sir, I was wiping blood from her hymen that was in that area," Paul said, describing the graphic trophy, which Houlahan had now replayed another four or five times.

"You appear to be wiping blood from her anus, according to this," Houlahan observed.

"The anus and the vagina, sir, are closely situated," came the reply.

Then Houlahan replayed the videotape again.

"You want to see it again?" he asked.

"Sure," Paul responded.

As the cross-examination plodded along, Houlahan grew increasingly impatient with his implacable witness. He called the answers he was getting "blarney," and wearied of the accused calling him "sir."

"What's this 'yes sir,' 'no sir,' three bags full, sir? That's not the real you, is it?" Houlahan demanded. It almost seemed like a spontaneous outburst, a break from the litany of prepared questions Houlahan kept before him. Nothing, however, was too far off the cuff with Houlahan. He had borrowed the observation from one of the media with whom he had spoken earlier in the day and worked it in to his barrage.

Houlahan was unflappable, in spite of the fact that almost nothing he asked was relevant to the object of his prosecution.

The washing of Kristen French's body in the Jacuzzi following her death had always posed unsavory questions. Houlahan used this incident, which Paul and Karla both agreed had taken place, to try and show that Paul—and Karla—had committed premeditated murder, because Karla had testified they purchased a commercial douche solution in advance, anticipating their need to destroy any forensic evidence in the anal and vaginal cavities of their victim.

Paul countered with the bizarre image of them using a plastic beer-drinking funnel he had purchased during one of his innumerable trips to Florida to celebrate spring.

"That holds about twenty-four ounces," Paul explained. "And it was done at least twice per cavity."

Houlahan's cross of Paul Bernardo lasted an interminable six days. During the confrontation, many admissions were made, including Paul's own assessment of himself as a "jerk." The only possible explanation for Houlahan's inane persistence would be the prosecutor's fantasy that he could elicit a confession from the accused. But Paul Bernardo was so obviously guilty of all the charges that it had made the past three months and three weeks of trial a farce. The irrelevant confession—that is, that he, Paul Bernardo, had actually strangled both girls with a black electrical cord—was not forthcoming. Paul Bernardo admitted his guilt. He did everything else they had said he did. But according to him, the two girls had not died the way Karla

Homolka said they did, and there was no evidence to show that they had.

Thus Canadians wiled away the Summer of 1995, watching the O.J. Simpson trial on television and reading, riveted, the garrulous daily reports served up by a self-censoring media about the seemingly endless pornographic revelations at Paul Bernardo's trial.

Celebrity trials about domestic abuse and passion-driven spousal murders were hardly comparable to trials that dealt with the serial crimes of sexual sadists and psychopaths.

There were two similarities: in both cases only a dog and the killers knew the real truth about who had actually murdered the victims. In Simpson's case, it was his dead wife's white Akita, Kato; in Bernardo's, Buddy the Rottweiler.

The other similarity was an irrefutable sense that police bungling and incompetence had set two murderers free.

Ray Houlahan instructed the jury to forget about Karla Homolka—they did not need Karla to find Paul Bernardo guilty on all counts.

The jurors looked bewildered. What had the last four months been all about? If they did not need her, why did they have her?

Rosen made an impassioned plea to the jury, full of reason and rhetorical flourishes, but his passion was misspent and imprecations futile. His client was what his client was. Seeing was believing. Ultimately, no one has any sympathy for the devil— or for his advocate.

Juries in Canada are seldom, if ever, sequestered—except when they deliberate. Since it was late in the day, the jurors decided to partake of the free hotel dinner and accommodation that had been prearranged. But that was it.

It was the Thursday evening before the long Labor Day

weekend—traditionally the last holiday weekend of the summer—and enough time had been vaporized by this sonorous,
lugubrious, pornographic prosecution.

The eight men and four women who had served as a jury of
Bernardo's peers had been forced to sit through four months,
when a week would have sufficed. At around noon on Friday
they found Paul Bernardo guilty as charged on all nine counts.

The jury might have wanted to give Rosen the concession
he had asked for—say second degree on Mahaffy—something
for his commendable efforts, but there was no room for senti-
mentality. Anyone who saw those videotapes lost whatever capacity they might otherwise have had for pathos.

Even though the nine-charges of which Bernardo was found
guilty all carried life sentences, in Canada an accused person can
only be sentenced to one lifetime in jail. There is no death
penalty. Paul Bernardo got life with no possibility for parole in
less than twenty-five years—the maximum sentence allowable.

Later, the Crown insisted Bernardo be declared a "dangerous
offender," an esoteric designation that did not mean what it
said, at least not within the bureaucracies of the judicial and
penal systems. A man such as Bernardo would never get out of
jail; in fact, had he not been declared a "dangerous offender,"
life in jail would have been much harder on him. This way his
status would be reviewed more often, and more people would
talk to him.

The Kingston Penitentiary for Men built a new holding cell in
Paul Bernardo's honor. He would have to remain in total isolation for the rest of his natural life; because the prisons in
Kingston were federal institutions, they ran like government
bureaucracies. Prison guards were civil servants. When they
were charged with keeping a man separate and alive, they did
so. No "skin beefers"—a con's term for child molesters and
rapists such as Paul Bernardo—had been murdered in a federal
Canadian penitentiary since the riots at Kingston in 1972.

Where Bernardo's cell faced the corridor, the bars were covered with bulletproof Plexiglas through which small holes had

been punched for air circulation. Reminiscent of the cell inhabited by Dr. Hannibal Lector in *The Silence of the Lambs,* Bernardo's cell was a third that size.

Only four feet by eight feet, it was barely large enough for the six-footer to move between his cot, combination stainless steel sink and toilet, writing desk and television stand. There was a twenty-four-hour video surveillance camera that recorded his every waking move and sleepless twitch.

Eventually, a cassette of Bernardo in prison showed up on television, with an accompanying story and picture in a Toronto tabloid. It was a postcard from hell. Even though he was still alive, Paul Bernardo had been "disposed of."

Sister Josephine was doing quite well. Dr. Arndt's "buzzing" had worked. She was back in the world, trying to fulfil her mission, challenging the daily travail. Sister Josephine remained in a quandary about her spiritual colleague's remonstrance that there was "no such thing as a disposable human being."

The more she heard about Karla Homolka and Paul Bernardo, the more she wondered about whether or not the preferable God was the vengeful, wrathful Old Testament God in the Book of Job. After all, what was hell for, except eternal damnation. She remained afflicted with the ambivalence she felt about Karla Homolka.

In Niagara Falls, the undisputed tabloid capital of the World, not everything was turning out the way the residents might have hoped. The Houdini Museum had burned down in 1994. The casino went ahead as planned, but apparently there was some problem with the Maharishi Mahesh Yogi's $879 million transcendental meditation theme park, Veda Land. One out of two ain't bad, said the mayor, who had once posed as a beefcake Sunshine Boy for a Toronto tabloid newspaper.

In the Criminals Hall of Fame, which sits atop Clifton Hill overlooking the "frightful Abyss,"—as Father Hennepin had called Niagara Falls when he first laid eyes on them in 1683—

there are no immediate plans to install a Paul and Karla Bernardo exhibit.

The Criminals Hall of Fame is a strange place. It used to be a restaurant, until the owners died and left it to their sons. Restaurants were too much work, so the Lombardi boys turned it into the Criminals Hall of Fame. Like most things in Niagara Falls, it's tacky and a bit of a sham. The bevy of exhibits are not built around real wax figures like those in Madame Toussaud's. Al Capone, Joe Valachi, the Boston Strangler—Albert DeSalvo—and the Moors Murderers, Myra Hindley and Ian Brady are all stick figures, like scarecrows.

Their wax faces appear to have been cast in a single mold, the differences between them articulated only by wigs, facial hair and dress. The curators of the Criminals Hall of Fame do not distinguish between real and fictional crime figures. Right next to Charlie Manson's exhibit, wherein the word "PIG" is scrawled on the back wall in Day-Glo red, is Freddy Kruger's stall. But Paul and Karla are so far verboten—the brothers do not want to outrage the community.

Nonetheless, business has been brisk. The Lombardis have just given The Criminals Hall of Fame a neon-inspired, hundred-thousand-dollar face-lift and today, it may just be the finest facade on the hill in the city of Niagara Falls.

In the meantime, Casey Hill's ship came in. The senior official in the Crown law office got several millions of dollars from the Church of Scientology. He had sued for slander a decade earlier, and the courts had finally found in his favor. Shortly after he started work on the search warrants with Detective Steve Irwin, Hill was appointed to the bench.

Two years later, Marion Boyd, the attorney-general who sanctioned Karla's deal, was voted out of office. The assistant deputy minister, Michael Code, who had been instrumental in getting Karla her deal, quit. Murray Segal left his wife and three children, and moved in with Michal Fairburn. Some faceless bureaucrat inexplicably fired the Scarborough prosecutor Mary Hall.

All the ground-breaking profilers from the FBI have since retired, including John Douglas, Roy Hazelwood and Gregg

McCrary. Hazelwood tersely observed that now he could "make some real money" on the lecture circuit.

John Rosen has left the criminal bar. Francis "Doc" Kovacs is retired. The media's appeal of the publication ban he levied during Karla's so-called "trial" in July, 1993, is still pending. Ken Murray tried to explain himself in a Toronto tabloid newspaper. He is still under investigation. Iguanas are still eating George Walker's hibiscus on Montserrat. Mark DeMarco's Masonic skull still sits in its bulletproof glass case at the center of his store, surrounded by a bevy of tiny, erotic, ivory netsukes.

Inspector Vince Bevan has become Superintendent Vince Bevan and has been kept busy chasing motorcycle gangs. He is very worried about the Hell's Angels. The Parkway Hotel and Bowling Lanes has become a Ramada Inn. Buddy's Bar is gone.

Even though Karla's cell is just a stone's throw from her ex-husband's, they live in two different worlds. The compound in which Paul Bernardo resides is half a block south of the Kingston Prison for Women, at the base of Sir John A. Macdonald Parkway on the river bank. A thirty-foot-high limestone wall inhibits the prisoners' view of the scenic St. Lawrence River and the United States.

Kingston, Ontario, is known for three things—Queen's University, the prisons and ex–Lovin' Spoonful Zal Yablonsky's restaurant, Chez Piggy's. Paul Bernardo is as gone as the dead girls. Karla has finally learned to accentuate the positive and let "the trouble"—as prison psychologist Jan Heney called it—go.

At six-by-nine feet, Karla's cell is about the same size as her ex-husband's, but unlike his specially configured closet Karla's is just a normal cell—one of ten in segregation. Karla calls it "her room" and tells everyone that segregation is really just like a university dorm.

Toward the front of the cell is her single bed. At arm's length directly across from the bed is a dresser, and beside the dresser is Karla's desk, where she writes and studies.

In her letters to Dr. Arndt, Karla tells him she is reading classics such as *Crime and Punishment*. She has already successfully completed a series of correspondence courses offered by the university, including the Principles of Psychology, Sociology of Deviance and introductory courses in women's studies. To anyone who wants to understand her, Karla recommends Lenore Walker's *The Battered Woman* and the gruesome *Perfect Victim*. After her "godsend," Dr. Hatcher, visited Karla, she took to mailing out highlighted copies of the definitive "Compliant Victims of the Sexual Sadist."

To one such lucky recipient Karla wrote, "I've highlighted the parts that are directly applicable to me. It's frightening to know that there are so many of these men out there. But it's also a relief to know that I'm not the only woman who has ever gone through this. . . . Please note that the woman referred to in the last highlighted paragraph is not me. It's so eerily similar that I thought I better make that clear."

At the end opposite the bars, her toilet and sink are separated by what Karla calls a tallboy. Karla is allowed to put up drapes— called "shams"—on the outside of her bars. She has specific guards assigned to her, such as Rick Waller. It is part of the guards' routine that they visually observe her every fifteen or twenty minutes.

Karla reclines on her bed and flips absentmindedly through the pages of a fashion magazine. She fingers the crucifix Sister Josephine gave her. She is thinking about her life. After all this, what sort of woman could she become? What will the future bring? She would like to work with battered women. She would like to find a good man and get serious, this time, about starting a family.

She has plastered her walls with Mickey Mouse posters, dog pictures and photographs of her family and friends. The "friends" part of the wall display is getting thinner. Fully aware that the facets of friendship in the Exclusive Diamond Club were really only Zircons, Karla relished the collapse of Debbie Purdie's marriage. And she is sure Kathy Ford will rot in hell. Karla is glad that she and Paul "ruined" the Fords' wedding video—like Kathy said when she was testifying at Paul's trial— just by being in it. Imagine selling out their friendship and Karla's letters to a tabloid for a few thousand dollars.

Karla is trying to determine what she is going to look like when she is paroled next summer. Perhaps she will dye her hair black—Paul always liked black-haired girls—and buy a pair of Gaultier glasses. They are so expensive. What will she do for money? She thinks she will start horseback riding again and take jumping lessons. One thing is for certain, she will never take anything for granted in her life again.

Karla usually gets out every day for a walk in the prison yard. At night she does stomach crunches and spot training, and then every other day she rides the stationary bike. Since she is only out of her cell for an hour each day, she does not want to ride the bike for forty-five minutes like she used to. But Karla is in good shape. On the weekends she plays badminton in the gym.

Every sixth weekend she is allowed a "little house" visit with her mother and sister. Her father often stays home and looks after Buddy. Karla is even permitted to stay in the "little house" alone sometimes, three-day stints that she cherishes. It is almost like vacationing at a trailer park.

Karla bides her time, sitting in her cell, reading about the Moors Murders, studying women's issues, painting her nails, planning her new look.

Karla's sister Lori sent her a letter in which she observed how easily people were conned and how great it was that Karla could apply for unescorted day passes already, and somehow that letter turned up on the front page of a tabloid paper in Toronto. People were outraged and everybody made a big deal out of it.

It did not matter. Karla knew, when all was said and done, the new Karla Homolka would be out next year, and nobody could steal letters from a woman they could not see.

acknowledgments

I want to thank my companion, Marsha Boulton. Without her strength of character, and her skills as a researcher, reader and writer, this book would never have been written. Neither would the book ever have been finished without her survival skills and humor.

I want to particularly thank my publisher Kim McArthur and everyone at Little, Brown Canada for their unflagging enthusiasm and support for this book from the beginning. I am also grateful that Allan Samson of Little, Brown U.K. shared his Canadian counterparts' sentiments as did my American agent, Sterling Lord, and Elisa Petrini at Bantam Books, New York. Special thanks go to my Canadian agent, Bruce Westwood, for his unwavering and fervent support over the last three years.

There are a number of other people I must thank and it is ironic that Justice Francis "Doc" Kovacs is among them. Prior to Karla Homolka's trial in July, 1993, Justice Kovacs decided that books are not media, and put me out of his St. Catharines courtroom along with the American press and the Canadian public.

His order drew the attention of *The New York Times,* the *Washington Post* and the world to a situation that would have otherwise gone relatively unnoticed internationally. I am more in his debt than anyone could ever imagine.

Secondly, I must thank CKNX 102FM, easy-listening radio out of Wingham, Ontario, and Gord Dugan for allowing me the distinction of being their first ever "stringer-for-a-day." Having been removed as a book author, I was able to return to Justice Kovacs' courtroom as a member of the Canadian media and witness the "trial" of Karla Homolka.

I want to thank Associate Chief Justice Patrick LeSage, who officially recognized that people who write books, such as myself, are working for as important a medium of communication as the daily press and tabloids and broadcast media.

My editor and friend Tom Hedley added his style, skill and compassion during the difficult times. Comrade-at-arms Barry Callaghan offered astute perceptions of the world-at-large and the language of stories. I was grateful for their unflagging companionship and encouragement as we all descended to the Seventh Circle.

A special thanks goes to Patrick Watson for his graceful example and understanding of the pressures that both plague and inspire all forms of serious inquiry. Another friend, David Roffey, offered support and counsel without which this book would have never been completed.

I want to break with tradition and thank a number of lawyers. Firstly, John Rosen and his defense team, Tony Bryant and Kim Doyle. Mr. Rosen and Ms. Doyle did much to help me navigate the turbulent waters of law and rancor that swirled around this case. Also, George Walker and his wife, Lori. When I most needed to win a bet, Lori obliged.

I also want to thank two defenders whose services were invaluable—Toronto criminal lawyer, Paul Tomlinson and St. Catharines lawyer, John Lefurgey. Mr. Lefurgey's able representations to Justice Patrick LeSage helped to clear muddied waters and dignify difficult issues with learned and humane argument. I am also indebted to Doug Elliott, who has also spent a difficult and trying three years, for other, even more tragic reasons.

I am indebted to many psychiatrists and psychologists, including Dr. Graham Glancy and Dr. Hans Arndt, for their patience with my interminable questions.

Among the legion of police involved in this case many thanks to a few good men: Chief Grant Waddell, Inspector K.R. Davidson, Sergeant Bob Ciupa, Staff Superintendent (retired) Jim Moody and his sons, particularly Sergeant Dan "the Man" Moody, Inspector (retired) William Bowie—all of the Niagara Regional Police force—as well as retired Chief William McCormack, Staff Superintendent (retired) Joe Wolfe, Detective Steve Irwin, and Acting Inspector Mike Sale from the Metropolitan Toronto Police force.

I want to thank Doug Lucas, the now retired Director of the Center for Forensic Sciences of Ontario for his forthrightness.

I am privileged to have many friends in the media: men and women who care deeply about what they do and do it with pure heart and a sense of public responsibility, including Geoff Ellwand, Kirk Makin, the stogie-chompin' Bennie Chin, Peter Murphy, Gay Abate, Joy Malbon, Barb Brown and expatriate tabloid television sleuth Mary Garofalo, whose hospitality and openness made one of my New York trips not only delightful, but informative. Thanks also to Anne Swardson and Charlie Trueheart of the *Washington Post,* who have since been "banished" to Paris, probably as a consequence of their excellent reportage on the Homolka fiasco.

There are also a number of private citizens who offered their support and hospitality over the past three years, including Jackie Bomber, Bruce Ricker, Investigator King, David Harrison, Alfred Caron, Bill Marshall, William McLaughlin, Clair

Weismann Wilks, Cathy Clyke, Ross Cronk, and Ron Moor. Nigel Dickson graciously provided the great photo of John Rosen. I am particularly indebted to my old friend, photographer John Reeves, whose studio became my second home during the long hot summer of 1995.

There are a great number of Niagara Region residents who were both hospitable and helpful. These include the former proprietor of the Parkway Hotel, Convention Center and Bowling Lanes, Archie Katzman, and Mark DeMarco and his friend, retired radio reporter *par excellence* Gerry McAuliffe, whose initial overview of the internecine and diabolical machinations of politicians and police in the Niagara Region stood me in good stead. Tim Rigby's able explanations of the esoterica of skulling and the Henley Regatta were a delightful sidebar. T.K. and all the staff of Bistro 990 were pillars of strength, and I also thank Blue Mermaid stalwarts Nick, Karen and Tammy for offering a haven in a heartless world. And of course Nikki, wherever you are—thank you for your second sight.